urban
political
movements

THE SEARCH FOR POWER BY
MINORITY GROUPS
IN AMERICAN CITIES

Norman I. Fainstein
Department of Sociology
Columbia University

Susan S. Fainstein
Department of Urban Planning and
Policy Development
Livingston College
Rutgers University

Prentice-Hall, Inc.
Englewood Cliffs, New Jersey

Library of Congress Cataloging in Publication Data

FAINSTEIN, NORMAN I
  Urban political movements.

  Includes bibliographical references.
    1. Community power. 2. Municipal government—
United States. 3. Minorities—United States.
4. Political participation—United States. I. Fain-
stein, Susan S., joint author. II. Title.
HN90.C6F27   301.36   73-21876
ISBN 0-13-939330-7
ISBN 0-13-939322-6 (pbk.)

TO ERIC AND PAUL

PRINTED IN THE UNITED STATES OF AMERICA

10 9 8 7 6 5 4 3 2 1

PRENTICE-HALL INTERNATIONAL, INC., London
PRENTICE-HALL OF AUSTRALIA, PTY. LTD., Sydney
PRENTICE-HALL OF CANADA, LTD., Toronto
PRENTICE-HALL OF INDIA PRIVATE LIMITED, New Delhi
PRENTICE-HALL OF JAPAN, INC., Tokyo

table
of contents

iii

8

A FUNCTIONAL ASSESSMENT 215

appendix

SOCIAL AND POLITICAL MOVEMENTS 237

acknowledgments

Without the gracious assistance provided by community activists and professionals, this study could not have been conducted. We wish to extend special thanks to Barbara Rosen, Billie Dolin, Hannah Hess, Shelley Alpert, Terry Berl, Ann Braver, Lillian Weber, Sidney Morison, Leroy McRae, Donald Merit, and Betty Barnett in New York; and to the leaders of North Side Forces in Paterson, New Jersey.

Alan Altshuler, who supervised the dissertations from which Chapters Three and Four have been drawn, provided scholarly advice, practical guidance, and personal support, which we cannot repay. Frederick Frey and Leonard Fein also assisted our work while we were graduate students at M.I.T.

Marilyn Gittell helped us contact parents and school officials in New York City, as well as giving us many useful insights into local politics.

Our writing has benefited from the many suggestions—some of which we followed—provided by colleagues who read the manuscript in earlier versions: Anthony Oberschall, Dorothy and Judson James, George Sternlieb, Herbert Gans, and Angela Aidala.

Cynthia Lewis did an endless amount of typing with great care.

Able research assistance was provided by Angela Aidala, Lilly Hoffman, and Gary Redish.

The research upon which this study is based was facilitated by grants from the Columbia University Council for Research in the Social Sciences, the M.I.T.-Harvard Joint Center for Urban Studies, and the M.I.T. Urban Systems Laboratory.

Part of Chapter Seven derives from our article, "Innovation in Urban Bureaucracies: Clients and Change," *American Behavioral Scientist*, 15 (March/ April 1972), 511–31.

introduction

The rediscovery of the urban poor by the larger society, which took place in the 1960s, was partly precipitated by, and itself reinforced, a rediscovery of the political process by urban minority groups. While this renewed interest in politics was reflected in an increase in the number of black officeholders in major cities, its most notable manifestation was in the development of noninstitutionalized attempts by inner-city residents to gain power over public service bureaucracies on a neighborhood basis. The decline, and in many places virtual disappearance, of a local political infrastructure meant that these activities required the development of new organizations, the use of nonroutine channels of communication, and heavy reliance on mobilization and protest as a means of articulating demands and source of bargaining strength.

We call these organizing efforts *urban political movements,* even though we are aware that the phrase might also cover efforts with different or broader aims. Within the course of this book, however, we consistently restrict the usage of the term *urban political movements* to movements acting on behalf of blacks, Latins (and other "nonwhites"), and consisting in large part, although not wholly, of individuals drawn from these collectivities. We do so for reasons of convenience and analysis. In terms of convenience, there seems to be no better, easily substitutable phrase. While often called poor people's movements, nonwhite movements, or protest movements, participation in them is not restricted to the poor or nonwhites, and their activities go beyond protest.

The analytic reason for calling them movements is that a conceptual framework deriving from the study of social movements is the one most useful for understanding these efforts by urban minority groups. A social movement is an emergent group that proposes to innovate and depends for its success upon the conversion of a social collectivity into an action group.[1] Because social movements are emergent phenomena they never assume a permanent form. Throughout their lifespan movements are likely to change in size and structure. Each external success or failure affects aspects of internal structure, and vice versa. Urban political movements share these defining characteristics; they differ from more stable, routinized organizations—such as interest groups—in existing almost entirely through their activity rather than through a defined organizational structure, which can be maintained by resources that do not derive directly from short-term achievements in obtaining programmatic goals. While the size and extent of mobilization represented by urban movements is minute compared to some movements of the past, many others were similar in scale, and probably all, at some stage in their life cycle, consisted mainly of unrelated congeries of small organizations with a larger body of sometimes active participants and a much larger group of sympathizers.[2]

The boundaries of this study are limited by practical considerations and by theoretical and empirical decisions as to which phenomena are representative of the basic type of urban political movement and which are marginal or unrelated to it. Thus, we exclude distinctly professional movements such as advocacy planning or the open classroom except as they involve participation by lower-class or nonwhite individuals. The movements under consideration encompass a continuum ranging from reformist to radical in their professed ideology; none has so far engaged in revolutionary action. Our study is biased toward the more moderate organizations to which we have readier access; the main thrust of efforts to improve the condition of the nonwhite urban poor, however, has been under the auspices of the kinds of groups discussed here.

In addition, we have deliberately refrained from analyzing locally-based movements with other aims such as excluding blacks from white neighborhoods or opposing sex education. Such groups may use tactics similar to those employed by movements advancing the interests of nonwhites. But their social basis, ideology, and relationship to the influence structure is so dissimilar, as to constitute a wholly different object of research. Although comparisons between markedly different types of social movements are certainly of interest, they do not address themselves to our principal concern.

Finally, the activities of national organizations acting on behalf of minority groups are not examined at length, even though the most important source of benefits for the inner city is the federal government. Groups

[1] We have chosen to present a general overview of the literature on social and political movements in an appendix rather than interrupting the flow of the analysis here or in the following chapters. The reader is referred to the appendix for elaboration of our definition of social movements, and for a justification of our basically rationalistic approach to the subject.

[2] Even the contemporary women's movement, despite its seeming widespread impact and the interest it has evoked among millions of women, has only 3,000 members in its largest national organization, the National Organization for Women (NOW). See Betty Friedan, "Up from the Kitchen Floor," *The New York Times Magazine*, March 4, 1973, p. 34.

representing the interests of urban minorities at the national level are mainly established organizations—the National Association for the Advancement of Colored People (NAACP); some labor unions; and a portion of the Democratic Party. The National Welfare Rights Organization is almost the only exception. The significant impact of the urban, nonwhite lower classes is felt at the local level and is transformed into national demands through the activities of individuals within the regular political structure. To the extent that there is a national movement of poor blacks and Latins, it exists in the combined activities of a multitude of local efforts.

There are several reasons for wishing to explore the behavior of urban political movements. First, they represent a new kind of political institution. Since the collapse of machine politics there has been an absence of structures enabling poor people to take part in politics. The recent heightening of political activity in urban neighborhoods, channeled not through traditional party mechanisms, but through a baffling variety of temporary and permanent groups often focussed on single issues, signals a change in the modes of representing local interests within the American political system. A desire to understand the workings of political institutions alone justifies exploration into the structures, causes, membership, and operations of urban movements.

Second, inquiry into the experience of these organizations is necessary if we are to address one of the several most significant questions in the analysis of American politics. Is it possible for citizens with little power, money, or status to use the political system as leverage to increase their relative share of these goods? Or is inequality of condition destined to perpetuate itself indefinitely, even in a pluralistic, democratic political system? One of America's most eminent political scientists argues that most citizens use their political resources hardly at all, that everyone has the possibility of mobilizing additional political resources and converting them into power.[3] Is he correct?

Urban political movements are of additional scholarly interest because they represent a type of political phenomenon that usually goes unrecorded. History is most often written by and about the winners of various historical struggles. Although opposition from below may not always be ignored, its origins are often lost, and it is seldom presented from the perspective of ordinary participants. E. P. Thompson, in a comment on the paucity of reliable materials concerning the Luddites and the largely unsympathetic treatment which they have received from historians, notes:

And here we may make several obvious points, as to the study of Luddism in particular. If there had been an underground in these years, by its very nature it would not have left written evidence. It would have had no periodicals, no Minute Books, and, since the authorities watched the post, very little correspondence. One might, perhaps, have expected some members to have left personal reminiscences; and

[3] Robert Dahl, *Who Governs?* (New Haven: Yale University Press, 1961), p. 305.

yet, to this day, no authenticated first-hand accounts by Luddites have come to light.
. . . Many active Luddites, while literate, were not readers and writers.[4]

Even in the case of groups which are not conspiratorial, if their composition is largely lower- or working-class and nonintellectual, there will probably be few written accounts by participants. And while contemporary grass-roots citizens groups do keep records, there are few archives where such material is stored. Were urban political movements to succeed to their fullest potential, their effect would be the decentralization of power and greater responsiveness of government to deprived sectors of the society. They would not capture the central social positions which determine the content of official history. Thus, whether successful or not, they are in danger of being lost to those future scholars who might wish to determine the way in which out-groups have attempted to advance their causes and modify the American political structure.

We are, in fact, inhibited from comparing urban political movements to other, similar phenomena by the scarcity of relevant studies, both of urban movements in particular and of grass-roots political movements in general. Etzioni, for instance, when examining the bases of loyalty in social movements, remarks:

Little is known about the nature of compliance of other core [movement] organizations [besides political parties or labor unions], especially with respect to the relative weight of remunerative and normative powers. Even a tentative placement of these organizations according to the relative importance of normative controls must be delayed until more information is available.[5]

Very little more information is available today.

The heavy reliance on case study and participant-observation materials to develop the themes presented in this book derives from the belief that they offer the most fruitful data for answering the kinds of questions we raise. We desire to study intensively the dynamics of political organization at the urban grass-roots level. This is largely not a quantifiable subject, since our principal concern is with interactive processes rather than the presence or absence of particular attributes in various movements. We are, accordingly, more interested in why such strategies as the provision of services by movement organizations lead to certain consequences in terms of organizational structure and functioning, than in whether or not most movement organizations provide services, or whether there is a correlation between organizational size and service provision. Being able to count the number of times certain factors are present or absent in the etiology of urban political movements is not necessarily enlightening in terms of understanding essential

---

[4] E. P. Thompson, *The Making of the English Working Class* (New York: Random House, 1963), pp. 494–95.

[5] Amitai Etzioni, *A Comparative Analysis of Complex Organizations* (New York: Free Press, 1961), p. 54.

causes, both because their existence does not prove their importance and also because their meaning varies according to context and sequence. We do wish to know certain quantifiable facts—who participated? how many? how much did they share beliefs?—and we present such evidence as is available on these points.

It is difficult to demonstrate conclusively that the various cases presented in Chapters Two through Five are representative of the full range of urban political movements. We do believe, however, that the forces at work in these movements, their internal dynamics, and their interaction with potential constituencies and enemies, are characteristic of urban movements. Moreover, if we assume that protest emanates from a movement substructure, then there is some quantitative evidence to indicate that our case studies of small, single-issue-oriented groups are representative of a larger universe in both social composition of participants and the character of movement targets. Peter Eisenger surveyed newspapers from a random sample of 43 cities with populations between 100,000 and 1,000,000 (N = 141) during a six-month period in 1968.[6] He found 120 cases of reported protest (which he distinguishes from riots). In the 96 for which there was an estimate of the number of people involved, 200 or fewer individuals were said to have participated in 69 incidents, and only five involved the participation of more than 1,000 people. Blacks participated in the great majority of cases (73 percent). By far the largest number of protests were directed against school systems (39 percent), with police and welfare bureaucracies next in order. Two of our major studies focus on movements directed at educational change; the remainder are concerned with other efforts at bureaucratic reform.

This study is aimed at addressing the following questions: What are the social and political conditions that have given rise to urban political movements? What do they tell us about American parties and political ideology? What are the characteristics of urban political movements, how do they create a following, and what are the dynamics of developing consciousness, mobilization, and action? Finally, what is the likely potential impact of these movements, both locally and nationally?

The question of the ultimate effect of urban political movements is still open, and we feel that positivistic statements about the success or failure of particular movement strategies should be avoided. The success of movements depends partly on their own ability to mobilize resources and partly on the national political context in which they are located. They create some portion of this national context through their own activities, but much of it is caused by extraneous factors. Thus, the probability of success for urban movements depends on who is in power nationally, and while the present ascendancy of conservative Republicanism can be partially attributed to a reaction to black militance, it is also a result of numerous other causes. Since

---

[6] Peter K. Eisenger, "The Conditions of Protest Behavior in American Cities," *American Political Science Review*, LXVII, March, 1973, 11–17.

what may be wise strategies at certain historical junctures can be counterproductive at others, universalistic generalizations concerning the impact of political movements are inappropriate. It is more worthwhile to try to spell out the dilemmas they face, the processes they set in motion, and the logic which causes them to take on particular forms.

The overarching issues for us are whether or not the capacity to mobilize political resources genuinely exists for urban minority groups or whether mobilization itself depends on the presence of a critical mass of resources which they do not have, the manner in which urban movements function as mobilizing vehicles, and their effectiveness in doing so. Although, as has been previously indicated, these issues are germane to theoretical questions in political sociology, they also arise from our personal values and priorities. We wish to describe the means available for lower- and working-class minority groups to ameliorate their social situation. Moreover, we are sympathetic to the professed aims of urban political movements. We have tried, nonetheless, to weigh the evidence objectively, and to separate that which we would like to conclude, from the actual conclusions of our research.

the social
and political
setting

1

An adequate introduction to urban political movements must examine both how nonwhite[1] residents subjectively interpret their social problems and the actual social and political situation in American cities which has formed their ideas and shaped their political activities. The consciousness of the urban lower strata, as of other collectivities, stands in a complex and interactive relationship with their objective conditions, the ideas which command public attention, and the behavior of other groups. One need not study the extensive literature on relative deprivation to see that the meaning of a given social situation must be understood contextually. The feeling of being poor, for example, depends on the prevalent definition of a decent standard of living as well as on absolute measures of wealth. The same holds for the sense of political oppression or injustice. It is the strain between the consciousness of *what should be* and the perception of *what is* that produces analyses leading to collective action.[2] In examining the tensions which have caused the emergence of urban movements, however, we must be careful not to view disadvantaged minority groups as lumps of clay being pulled apart here, pushed there, molded by social forces. They are, and have been, producers of the forces of which they are a product. Their own political action has increased the hostility of other groups and undermined the legitimacy of official institutions (e.g., the schools, police), in short, contributed to the situations and analyses which then shape their collective activity.

[1] This term will be used to include blacks, Puerto Ricans, Mexican-Americans, and other minority groups. When a discussion applies primarily to a single group, that group will be identified. In cases where the circumstances of different nonwhite groups are dissimilar, our analysis will usually be limited to blacks.

[2] Such strain is usually labeled *relative deprivation*.

The context within which urban minority groups have sought to better their own position through political action has been shaped by two historical forces: the political machine and the Progressive reform movement. The institutional dominance of the political machine contributed to the present difficulties of the ghetto in several ways. It socialized conservatively a generation of the American working class, it inhibited the growth of a socialist party which would now benefit the poor, and it helped shape the upper class reform movements which sought to save the immigrant poor both from the machine and their poverty. The political machine constituted a first stage in urban political development significantly affecting the present; the Progressive movement comprised the second.

"Progressive" institutions supplanted those of the party machines and remain dominant in the city today. Similarly, the ideology of Progressivism has been the basis for the political ethos of contemporary urban elites, and to some extent, of all classes within the city. The Progressive approach to the social problem of the poor has been the characteristic mode of reform for liberal political activists. The present allies of the poor are not, as in Europe, socialist parties centered in the working class, but Progressive reformers with middle and upper class origins. Progressivism has thus not only produced a historical legacy germane to explaining contemporary urban political conflicts, but has continued to be a political force upon the urban poor. The machine and Progressivism have helped define the political situation of inner-city residents and channeled the direction of grass roots political action. As we shall argue, contemporary urban political movements represent a potential "synthesis" in a dialectical process in which the machine was "thesis" and Progressivism "antithesis."

The following sections will develop in detail the themes we have touched upon so far: the basis for political conflict within the city, the urban traditions of machine and Progressive reform, and the manner in which urban political movements represent a synthesizing response. Together, these themes delineate the social and political setting within which movements have appeared.

BASES OF URBAN POLITICAL CONFLICT

In recent years our cities have become the center of intense political conflict. Most of the conflict has been associated with issues arising from the demands of some groups—especially blacks and Latins—for change, and from the resistance of other groups and institutions to these pressures. Racism, fear, and objective conflicts of interest have resulted in a threat to many urban whites, a threat arising from the culture and social behavior of blacks and Latins as well as from their collective political activity. These whites have worked for the containment of their "enemies," often in the quite literal geographic sense of the ghetto, and for more effective control of lower class behavior through the coercive instruments of local governments. Their activities have, in turn, exacerbated black and Latin resentment and political efforts, including urban political movements.

the situation for blacks:
poverty, racism, segregation

Blacks are at the center of the basic conflicts in most northern cities. They constitute the social group whose interests and activities have been most antagonistic to established institutions and better-off strata. Underlying the collective political behavior of blacks are three interrelated factors: poverty, racism, and segregation.

The distribution of income among blacks has produced a truncated class structure. The black middle class is small in comparison to the white. In 1969 approximately 62 percent of white families residing in metropolitan areas had incomes in excess of $9,000, a reasonable minimum for supporting a lower middle class life-style. The corresponding figure for black families was 32 percent.[3] Most urban blacks can be divided into two strata; on the one hand, those with some skill and steady employment who comprise a large proletariat and small bourgeoisie; on the other, a poverty stratum, partly employed, often at very low wages, and dependent upon transfer payments for subsistence. The latter may be identified as families receiving less than one half of the median income of white families living in metropolitan areas, i.e., less than $5,000 per annum.[4] According to this criterion of poverty, almost 34 percent of metropolitan black families are poor.[5]

Many observers believe that there is a growing gap between the economic position of the black poor and other blacks. Most of the improvement in the overall median income of blacks vis-à-vis whites is accounted for by younger, male-headed families. There has been, as Moynihan puts it, a "schism in black America" between the underclass of the continuing poor, and the (slowly) rising, "solid" working class and small bourgeoisie.[6]

The underclass.   The black underclass no longer expects to take the Horatio Alger route of individual upward mobility and has come increasingly to adopt an analysis which explains its economic position in terms of social and political phenomena (especially racism) rather than in terms of personal failure or bad luck. For lower class blacks the lack of improvement in economic position and the infusion of black power ideas have combined to reduce the legitimacy of white power and of the urban institutions which

[3] U.S. Bureau of the Census, *Statistical Abstract of the United States: 1971* (Washington, D.C.: U.S. Government Printing Office, 1971), table 506, p. 318.

[4] The median income of white families living in metropolitan areas in 1969 was $10,694. *Statistical Abstract of the United States: 1971*, table 506, p. 318.

[5] Calculations based on *Statistical Abstract of the United States: 1971*, table 506, p. 318.

[6] Daniel P. Moynihan, "The Schism in Black America," *The Public Interest*, No. 27, Spring, 1972, 3–24.

structure it. The poor, however, require the services of these institutions, whether the welfare office or the baby clinic, to a much greater degree than those above them in the economic structure. The urban poor thus live under a kind of impoverished socialism, since their lives depend so much upon the governmental sector. These factors in combination encourage antagonism against urban governments and their agencies.

Even if the black underclass acted only through legitimate political channels, it would threaten other groups within the city in several ways. First, the racism of many whites, especially of lower strata whites who must compete with the black poor, results in a constant pressure to keep blacks geographically confined; to prevent them from gaining scarce jobs; and, in general, to minimize governmental welfare payments, which are often viewed as taxation of the industrious to support the undeserving. This feeling that blacks are undeserving is illustrated by data from a 1968 survey of more than 2,500 whites in fifteen cities. Fifty-six percent of those interviewed thought that the inferior economic condition of blacks was "mainly due to something about Negroes themselves rather than to discrimination." [7]

Second, the black underclass is the source of much of the most visible and threatening urban crime. Blacks have been disproportionately represented among those arrested, especially for crimes of violence. In fact, the number of blacks arrested for robbery (43,000) and for aggravated assault (49,600) in 1969 exceeded the number of whites arrested for the same crimes (21,100 and 49,400, respectively) despite the great difference in the proportion of the general population represented by the two races.[8] Although these arrest data may be inflated and most black crimes are directed against blacks, there exists some objective basis for the perception among whites that inner-city blacks pose a threat to their physical security. This perception has led whites (and blacks as well) to identify crime as the most significant urban problem, and to call for tighter police control.[9] Increased policing of blacks has, however, heightened black resentment, triggered civil disturbances, and exacerbated conflicts over black community control of the police. Whether increased policing has also reduced the crime rate is unclear.

The black underclass presents whites with another threat in the schools. Black children enter school behind whites in terms of all achievement indicators, and fall even further behind with each additional year of

[7] The item read: "On the average, Negroes in (Central City) have worse jobs, education and housing than white people. Do you think this is due mainly to Negroes having been discriminated against, or mainly due to something about Negroes themselves?" Nineteen percent said it was mainly discrimination, and 19 percent a mixture of both factors; 6 percent did not know. Had there been specific reference to the black poor a higher percentage would undoubtedly have placed the blame for poverty on the poor themselves. Had respondents been limited to less educated, working class whites there would also have been a higher percentage blaming blacks. Angus Campbell and Howard Schuman, "Racial Attitudes in Fifteen American Cities," in *Supplemental Studies for the National Advisory Commission on Civil Disorders* (New York: Praeger, 1968), p. 30.

[8] U.S. Bureau of the Census, *Statistical Abstract: 1971*, table 230, p. 145.

[9] Peter H. Rossi *et al.*, "Between White and Black: The Faces of American Institutions in the Ghetto," in *Supplemental Studies*, table 2.6, p. 84.

schooling.[10] For blacks the failure lies in the inability of the schools to provide "equal educational opportunity." To many whites, however, the disadvantaged situation of black children—whatever the cause—means that blacks, especially those of the underclass, reduce the educational quality of schools in which they are significantly represented. In addition, the problems of violence and drugs in the schools are directly associated with the presence of lower-class black students. The perceived deterioration of urban schools has been one of the most significant reasons for white exodus from central cities; while for those who remain behind the schools are a major center of political controversy.

The "solid" strata.   The black proletariat, unlike the underclass, has realized economic improvement in recent years despite the racism of dominant groups. But in a fundamental sense, racism has triumphed in denying these working-class blacks the fruits of increasing affluence. White racism forces working-class (and to a lesser extent, middle-class) blacks like their poor brethren to remain in the central city and older suburban ghettoes. In spite of the prevalent notion that segregation is a product of black poverty, i.e., of the inability to purchase better housing, the weight of evidence points to racism as a primary factor in explaining racial segregation.[11] This means, in effect, that most upwardly mobile blacks cannot depart from the ghettoes in the manner of earlier immigrants who followed the "tenement trail."

The extreme political decentralization of the United States, as well as its tradition of local initiative, has fostered a structure of geographically-based class divisions. The system permits most white citizens to purchase political protection for certain valued "commodities": social homogeneity, neighborhoods with particular architectural qualities and densities, schools which reflect communal values, etc. Political protection takes the form of zoning ordinances, building codes, responsive police forces, and control of property taxes. This system is characteristic of suburbia in particular and American local government in general. It has functioned to permit Americans to choose their neighbors and to avoid the necessity of paying for the needs of excluded social groups. While the system has come under attack—especially the practice of supporting public education primarily from local property taxes[12]—it is still fully in operation. It has been very effective in

---

[10] See James S. Coleman, *Equality of Educational Opportunity* (Washington, D.C.: U.S. Government Printing Office, 1966), pp. 272–77.

[11] A study of urban residential segregation by Karl and Alma Taeuber, *Negroes in Cities* (Chicago: Aldine, 1965), pp. 94–95, provides support here. The Taeubers developed and then empirically tested alternative models for explaining segregation patterns. After a statistical analysis of census data from about 200 cities they concluded that segregation is primarily a product of race and racism, rather than of poverty and income stratification. See also Karl Taeuber, "The Effects of Income Redistribution on Racial Residential Segregation," *Urban Affairs Quarterly*, IV, September, 1968, 5–14.

[12] In *Serrano vs. Priest* (1971) the California Supreme Court ruled that differences in local property tax bases could not determine the quality of public school systems because education is a "fundamental interest" which must provide students with "equal protection" as guaranteed by the Fourteenth Amendment to the U.S. Constitution. See "Serrano v. Priest: Implications for

keeping out blacks, even those who could afford to pay. Most suburban communities are not Scarsdales or Beverly Hills; rather they are the ordinary working-class municipalities whose names are forgotten at the county line.

While racism has denied geographic mobility to the black proletariat, it has also had the unintended consequence of preventing the individual "exits" which maintain the overall stratification system and inhibit the growth of group solidarity and collective political action. Unable to exit, the black proletariat and some part of the middle class find themselves forced to respond to the institutions of the city through "voice" [13]—through protest, demand, and organized political efforts. The substance of that voice has, in recent years, built upon the ghettoization which has precipitated it; political demands recognize territoriality and ask for local autonomy, community control, an end to the colonial [14] rule of white institutions in black territory. This kind of voice directly threatens the interests of other groups which have a stake in the "colonial" institutions (as we shall consider below). Many urban political conflicts are over the ownership of the institutions which rule and service the ghetto.

urban bureaucracies and clients

There is nothing new in the resentment which inner-city residents feel toward the bureaucracies whose ostensible mission is to serve them. Herbert Gans, describing a working and lower-class Boston Italian community in the 1950s, noted that "the West Enders became most suspicious of, and hostile toward the outside world when they [had to] deal with government and the law." [15] Twenty years earlier William F. Whyte observed a similar situation in another Italian neighborhood.[16] In recent years, however, clients[17] have

---

Educational Equality," *Harvard Educational Review,* XLI, November, 1971, 501–34. This interpretation, however, has not been accepted by the U.S. Supreme Court.

[13] Albert Hirschman describes two typical responses among customers and members of deteriorating organizations, both of which serve to alert "management" to dissatisfactions. The first response is commonly associated with economic markets, while the second is usually thought to operate within the political system:

1. Some customers stop buying the firm's products or some members leave the organization: this is the *exit option.*
2. The firm's customers or the organization's members express their dissatisfaction directly to management or to some other authority to which management is subordinate or through general protest addressed to anyone who cares to listen: this is the *voice option.*

Hirschman shows that the choice of exit or voice (or some combination) will have different consequences for management—in our case, local jurisdictions—and for those dissatisfied; whether one or the other is more effective in bringing change depends on the context. Albert O. Hirschman, *Exit, Voice, and Loyalty* (Cambridge: Harvard University Press, 1970), p. 4. Italics in original.

[14] Cf. Robert Blauner, "Internal Colonialism and Ghetto Revolt," *Social Problems,* XVI, Spring, 1969, 393–408; Stokely Carmichael and Charles V. Hamilton, *Black Power* (New York: Random House, 1967), pp. 2–34.

[15] Herbert J. Gans, *The Urban Villagers* (New York: Free Press, 1962), p. 163.

[16] William F. Whyte, *Street Corner Society* (Chicago: University of Chicago Press, 1955), *passim.*

[17] We will use the terms *clients* and *bureaucrats* in a general sense to designate, respectively, citizens

sometimes been able to articulate their alienation, and to marshall the power necessary to translate feelings into action. While blacks and Latins have not been the only groups advocating bureaucratic reform, they have felt most abused by the urban bureaucracies. Since they have the least opportunity for exit, they have been the core of client-based protests.

Urban minorities, influenced first by the Southern Civil Rights Movement, then by governmental reform efforts and the militant ideologies associated with Black Power, have attacked the legitimacy of the urban bureaucracies, their right to command deference and subordination. The attackers have alleged that public service institutions are not doing their job—the schools are bad because they are run badly; hospital clinics have three hour waiting times as a result of administrative incompetence; junkies make connections on the street because the police are corrupt.

Whether the actual performance of urban institutions has declined in the last decade is not clear. Expenditures, number of personnel, training, and similar indicators point toward improvement. Greater dissatisfaction with performance may, in fact, be the product of the declining legitimacy of urban institutions—a result of a complex interaction among several historical factors, among which a heightened sensitivity to racism is most significant. The actual direction of causality is less discernible than are the interacting variables involved in the tension between bureaucrats and clients.

The perception of racism.   Increased racial sensitivity has led blacks and Latins to believe that the institutional structure of urban governmental agencies is biased so as to discriminate categorically against them.[18] For example, tracking in the elementary school creates a situation in which nonwhite children are sorted out of high success paths early in their educational careers; heavy police surveillance of ghettoes raises the likelihood of black–white police clashes; planning decisions in renewal agencies frequently result in nonwhite removal. The perception that decisions made by urban bureaucrats according to supposedly professional criteria regularly deprive them *as a group* of important benefits has encouraged minorities to deny the professional designation of the decisions. Rather, they are identified as primarily political.

This *naming*[19] of agency decisions as political, rather than professional or

---

who deal with or depend upon urban public service institutions and those who are employed by such institutions (whether in strictly bureaucratic roles or not). Clients are schoolchildren, their parents, welfare recipients, hospital patients, and individuals arrested by the police; bureaucrats are school teachers and administrators, welfare case workers, doctors and other medical personnel, and policemen.

18 "Racism is both overt and covert. It takes two closely related forms: . . . individual racism and institutional racism. . . . Black people in the United States have a colonial relationship to the larger society, a relationship characterized by institutional racism." Carmichael and Hamilton, *Black Power*, pp. 4–6.

19 By this we mean the application to a phenomenon of a symbolic term which evokes a response set from onlookers. Naming provides a definition of a situation; it informs the onlooker of what frame of reference to perceive and evaluate the "thing" in. Some often used names are:

technical, undermines the legitimacy of urban bureaucratic structures and procedures. The traditional definition of schools, welfare offices, police, and hospitals as nonpolitical has provided the rationale for the insulation of agency personnel from external pressure and the appointment and promotion of cadres according to universalistic criteria. The renaming of these institutions means that they must be evaluated according to political criteria. Thus, community groups have asserted that key positions should be filled through election; that the ultimate source of agency sovereignty rests in its clients and should be expressed through "community control"; [20] that racial group representation in the civil service is as American as the balanced ticket.

A related aspect of heightened racial sensitivity has been the identification of personal racism. The belief that many whites are prejudiced against nonwhite clients, insensitive at best and brutal at worst, has reinforced the push for changes in agency practices. Efforts have been directed at permitting client participation and veto power in personnel selection so as to screen out "racist" white candidates. Where groups have been successful in attaining a degree of community control, the burden of proof has shifted to white job applicants. Community screening has facilitated the recruitment of nonwhite personnel, a factor which produces a conflict of interest between whites and nonwhites.

Unionization.   The superimposition of racial divisions on client-bureaucrat cleavages has been heightened by the growth of municipal unionism. During the last decade the most rapid expansion of unionization has been among employees in the public sector, and particularly among whites occupying previously unorganized professional or semiprofessional jobs: teachers, social workers, firemen, and police. Resistance to public service unionization based on either professional norms or public law has mainly disappeared. In many instances municipal unions have successfully carried out illegal strikes with relatively minor penalties afterward. [21]

The effect of public unionization has been twofold. First, a major goal of municipal unions has been to determine working conditions, administrative practices, hiring and promotional criteria and, in some instances, substantive agency policies. As a result, more and more aspects of agency

---

professional, loyalty, educational, extremist, the Free World. In many political disputes contending parties struggle over how an event should be named ("Our goals are *educational,* not *political*") or who has the right to appropriate complimentary names to their own action ("I am saying that the war is immoral because of my *loyalty* to the *nation*"). For a general discussion of symbols in politics, which does not, however, use the term "naming," see Murray Edelman, *The Symbolic Uses of Politics* (Urbana: University of Illinois Press, 1964).

[20] For a general discussion of how this term has been used and what it implies, see Alan A. Altshuler, *Community Control* (New York: Bobbs-Merrill, 1970).

[21] The number of man-days idle as a result of strikes by employees of local governments increased from 57,000 in 1960 to 1.3 million in 1970; comparable figures for teachers show an increase from 5,500 to 936,000. *Unions and Government Employment* (New York: Tax Foundation, Inc., 1972), pp. 29–32. Cf. Everett M. Kasalow, "Trade Unionism Goes Public," *The Public Interest*, No. 14, Winter, 1969, 118–30; and Sam Zagoria, ed., *Public Workers and Public Unions* (Englewood Cliffs, N.J.: Prentice-Hall, 1972).

policy have become specified in contract, and removed from the discretion of policymaking officials. Even where political elites and top administrative officials have been responsive to client demands, they find their activities limited by the detailed contractural terms which have been added to the old civil service regulations. Unionization has raised another barrier to protect the mostly middle class, white group inside from the nonwhites and poor outside.

The second effect of union growth has been to increase the stakes in the competition between whites and nonwhites for jobs in the urban bureaucracies. Minority groups are pressing for positions which have become unionized and consequently better paid. A basic interest for whites lies in the control of these municipal jobs; an interest both for the groups that have already used them as a vehicle for upward mobility, and for those only now doing so.[22] Minority groups, however, forced by ghettoization to remain in the older cities while private employers discriminate against them or exit to the suburbs, find the control of municipal jobs of compelling importance. The stakes are high in the struggle to control the municipal administration, for it is the only game in town.[23]

Counterattack.   White groups with an economic interest in urban governmental institutions have acted to defend themselves and the structural arrangements which benefit them. One means of doing so has been to split the liberal-black coalition which pressed for organizational reform during the sixties. Thus, prejudicial statements against white ethnic groups by some black activists have been propagandized to give the impression that the community control movement is inherently racist and, especially, anti-Semitic.[24] Defenders of the status quo have also attempted to show that the goals and tactics of client groups oppose certain values and beliefs widely held by liberals who might otherwise intervene in their behalf. The legitimizing slogans of professionalism and the nonpolitical nature of public service bureaucracies have been invoked to portray blacks as violators of the universalistic norms which middle-class reformers long struggled to effect in city government. Minority leaders have been accused of being unrepresentative of the will or interest of their constituencies; of being concerned entirely with advancing their own political power rather than with institutional performance ("taking over the schools, not improving education"); and, in general, of trying to reintroduce the political machine with its venal byproducts of patronage and corruption.

The flavor of the white counterattack is captured in the weekly (paid) *New York Times* column by Albert Shanker, President of the New York City

---

[22] Formerly, the low pay of civil service jobs meant that upwardly mobile groups passed through them quickly, except, perhaps, for the Depression cohort.

[23] See George Sternlieb, "The City as Sandbox," *The Public Interest*, No. 25, Fall, 1971, 14–21.

[24] See, for example, documents in the section on "Anti-Semitism and Racism," in Maurice R. Berube and Marilyn Gittell, eds., *Confrontation at Ocean Hill-Brownsville* (New York: Praeger, 1969), pp. 163–214.

United Federation of Teachers (UFT). The following editorial is representative.

In the controversy over school decentralization [in New York City], those who expressed fear that decentralization could lead to the capture of school districts by unrepresentative extremist groups and to the employment of racial bigots were bitterly assailed. . . . Yet, the outrageous has happened.

Shanker asserts that "militants" have, with the cooperation of city officials, managed to gain control of a school board in Manhattan, then continues:

One of the first acts of the new board was to announce an ethnic quota system in hiring professionals—a policy it later rescinded under pressure of widespread protest. Last week it appointed Luis Fuentes to a $37,000-a-year position as community superintendent. [There follow a number of allegations concerning Fuentes' honesty.] Mr. Fuentes' character . . . is merely incidental to the basic charges against him—that of outright bigotry. . . . [But] thus far, except for protests by five Jewish organizations, the appointment of Luis Fuentes . . . has been greeted by silence. The Fuentes matter is no more a Jewish issue than the Carswell and Haynsworth appointments [to the U.S. Supreme Court] were black issues. . . . Now is the time for all those who oppose bigotry and racism to speak up. There should be no place in our school system for Fuentes or for the community school board which finds in him the embodiment of its ideals.[25]

As this example indicates, public servants feel that minority client groups threaten the foundation of decent and rational public administration. They view themselves as the primary defenders of the interests of the entire community, white and nonwhite alike. Client groups, however, believe the bureaucrats to be privileged and powerful, not innocent and beleaguered.

institutional deficiencies

City governments find themselves in a fiscal crisis which interrelates with the other political problems we have outlined. The crisis is a product of the American Constitutional structure, of the policy position of the central government, and, significantly, of the institutional mechanisms for pressing demands at the governmental level where resources are most available.

The fiscal crises of local governments.   The threat presented by the urban poor has led local governments to increase significantly their social service expenditures, as well as to expand police forces and programs designed to contain and control ghetto populations. Concurrently, the unionization of urban agencies, and the combat conditions under which public servants have often been forced to work, have combined to raise salaries in many categories of municipal employment. Thus, for example, during the period 1950–1969, federal civilian employment increased from 2.1 million to nearly 3 million, while local employment went from 3.2 million to 7.1 million.[26] Between 1965

---

[25] Albert Shanker, "Where We Stand," *The New York Times,* July 30, 1972, Sec. 4.

[26] The latter data underemphasize the even more rapid expansion in big cities. U.S. Bureau of

and 1969 the average annual salary scales for policemen and firemen in cities with more than 100,000 population increased by more than 30 percent.[27] And the per capita law enforcement expenditures for all governments (to which localities contribute about 80 percent of the total) nearly doubled in the 1960s, going from $11.28 (1960) to $21.01 (1969).[28] In cities with more than 500,000 population, the local per capita cost of the police department alone exceeded $44 by 1969.[29]

While municipal budgets were rapidly expanding, the urban tax base grew slowly at best. New office and industrial development has taken place in the suburbs. Whites have moved out, and their replacement by poor black and Latin groups has contributed to a relative decline in the value of inner-city real estate. Since the structure of public finance within the federal system forces municipalities to rely primarily upon property taxation, city governments have responded to the financial squeeze by raising tax rates. Such policies, however, have further contributed to the suburban exodus, while increasing the tax burden on a poorer city population. Jurisdictional boundaries have released the suburbs from financial responsibility, while the state and federal contribution remains limited. These factors constitute the fiscal crisis of the city, a crisis which increasingly limits the ability of urban governments to deal with political unrest in other than a symbolic manner.

Federalism and national social policy.   American cities are the locus of political conflicts which have been mitigated in other capitalist nations through the mechanisms of the welfare state. The federal government has a revenue base sufficiently large and flexible to address the social problems of the cities. It has, however, traditionally played a limited role as a provider of social welfare services, refusing to assume the burden from local governments which lack sufficient resources to meet the need. One explanation for the current situation points to our areal division of power[30] as an obstacle to effective action by the central government.

Our Constitutional arrangements derive from the conditions and social values of a rural society, one in which local governments provided few services and in which the overall homogeneity of the population meant that local jurisdictional boundaries did not sharply demarcate economic groups in a system of geographic stratification. The police and welfare powers were explicitly reserved for the states and their legal creations, the cities. Education, for example, has traditionally been supplied and controlled at the local level, with strong traditions resisting the intrusion of the central government. As cities have come to assume welfare burdens of immense proportions compared to those of only a few decades ago, jurisdictional lines

the Census, *Pocket Data Book, USA 1971* (Washington, D.C.: U.S. Government Printing Office, 1971), p. 95.

[27] Ibid.

[28] Ibid.

[29] U.S. Bureau of the Census, *Statistical Abstract*, p. 148.

[30] See Arthur Maas, *Area and Power* (New York: Free Press, 1959).

have become a shelter for groups which do not wish to be taxed for the benefit of the ghettoes.

National programs aimed at benefiting the poor have never been intended to do more than maintain a bare level of subsistence. Thus, the average monthly payment per family under Aid to Dependent Children (ADC), the largest welfare category, was only $187 in 1970 ($46 per recipient).[31] The Nixon Administration's proposal to place a floor under family assistance payments would still, in 1970, have provided a minimum payment of only $133 per month for a family of four. Neither the Economic Opportunity Act nor the Model Cities program were funded at anything like the levels envisioned by their framers. These programs were sold primarily as vehicles for "eliminating the paradox of poverty in the midst of plenty"; no program has ever been adopted with the ostensible goal of income redistribution.

The reluctance of the national government to assume primary responsibility for the urban poor is not, however, explained by the constraints of the federal system. The central government has entered many policy areas in spite of jurisdictional obstacles. The most significant example is provided by agriculture. Here the national government first contributed to the increased capitalization and concentration of farm production, then acted to assure the economic position of the remaining farmers as a class through programs of market planning and subsidization. This transpired in an area where the barriers to intervention existed not only in political structure, but in the traditional separation of the governmental and economic spheres. Impediments were overcome, however, when those assisted by federal policy were farmers. In order to explain the national government's role in urban social policy one must look beyond federalism to the political situation of the group which would benefit directly from federal intervention—the poor.

Federal programs have been inadequate in dealing with the existence of poverty in large part because government officials have always viewed the poor as alien, not as constituents but as a foreign group requiring attention. Policy toward the poor has been shaped by dominant American attitudes of ethnic and racial hostility, and by beliefs which advance individualistic and moralistic explanations of poverty. These attitudes, combined with the relative powerlessness of the poor as a collectivity, have contributed to their exclusion from the national policymaking process. Policy has been made for them, not by them, and it has tended to be underfunded, with the implication that the poor were fortunate to be supported at all.

Since the solution to the problem of poverty has always been seen as the assimilation of the poor into the "normal" occupational structure, welfare has been regarded as a temporary measure to assist the needy until the foreseen absorption should take place. People capable of regular employment are considered to be malingering if they receive governmental assistance, and elaborate eligibility checks have almost always been part of public assistance

[31] U.S. Bureau of the Census, *Pocket Data Book*, p. 190.

procedure. The Nixon welfare proposals, for example, cut off benefits to any family member with children above five years of age who turned down "suitable employment."

Because the poor are viewed as alien and their poverty is attributed to personal deficiencies, even if their failings are ultimately traced to environmental causes, the poor suffer moral stigmatization. They are categorized as "deserving" or "undeserving," and only the former are deemed worthy of governmental assistance. That such assistance is a privilege rather than a right was reaffirmed in 1971 by the Supreme Court, which ruled that state and local welfare officials could insist on inspecting the homes of welfare recipients and could cut off benefits from those who refused to admit them. In his decision, Justice Blackmun explicitly equated public welfare with private charity:

One who dispenses purely private charity naturally has an interest in and expects to know how his charitable funds are utilized and put to work. The public, when it is the provider, rightly expects the same.[32]

The inadequacy of political mechanisms.   Urban minority groups have not been able to marshall sufficient political power to overcome the jurisdictional and ideological barriers to federal action on their behalf. While the political interests of these groups have been articulated to a national audience, they have not been mobilized into an effective national political force. In the European liberal-capitalist states the mechanism for mobilization has been the political party of the left, advancing some form of socialist or communist program. No analogous party organization exists in the United States for aggregating the interests of poor and nonwhite city populations or for providing an institutional link between the central cities and the central government.

Many explanations have been offered for the uniqueness of the American party system: these include the dominance of liberal ideology, the extension of the suffrage prior to industrialization, the divisions produced by immigration and racism, the developmental path of the trade unions, and the tactical errors committed by fledgling working-class parties.[33] We will omit a detailed recapitulation of factors which others have extensively discussed. Rather, we will consider a characteristic specific to the history of American cities—the political machine and the Progressive movement which largely supplanted it. The resulting structural and ideological framework has created the institutional setting within which urban political movements have arisen.

[32] *The New York Times*, January 13, 1971, p. 1.

[33] Cf. David Shannon, "Socialism and Labor," in *The Comparative Approach to American History*, ed. C. Vann Woodward (New York: Basic Books, 1968), pp. 238–52; Seymour Martin Lipset, *The First New Nation* (New York: Basic Books, 1963), pp. 170–204; Daniel Bell, *The End of Ideology* (New York: Crowell Collier and Macmillan, 1962), pp. 275–99; James Weinstein, *The Decline of Socialism in America* (New York: Random House, 1967); Louis Hartz, *The Liberal Tradition in America* (New York: Harcourt, Brace & World, 1955).

THE POLITICAL TRADITIONS
OF THE CITY:
MACHINE AND REFORM

Past events affect contemporary situations through a legacy of institutions and ideologies. All previous phenomena, or all those equally distant in time, do not have the same effect on the present. Only those forms which survive continue to be of importance. Historical forces act through a cone or pyramid of causality upon which the present social system rests. At some past point—lower down in the cone—more factors were operative and more options were available. The victory of certain structural or cultural forms, however, biases the likelihood of future events further "up" toward our own time.

Thus, the same historical forces which produced the political machine may also have deterred the development of a major socialist party. From our historical perspective, however, the triumph of the machine, the *fact* of machine dominance, is more important than its cause. The machine monopolized the political representation of the urban proletariat in a conservative manner, thereby further inhibiting the growth of a socialist movement and establishing an institutional and ideological tradition which continues to be a force in the present. Similarly, we need not establish whether Progressive reform destroyed the machine, or whether the decline of the machine and the victory of Progressivism both resulted from antecedent factors, in order to describe the contemporary significance of the Progressive movement. Progressivism, shaped by its antagonism to the machine, created the programs and institutions to which urban movements are now opposed. Today, the legacies of machines and reform channel conflict in American cities.

machines

A political machine is a hierarchical form of party organization functioning within a situation where mass suffrage exists. It "depends upon inducements that are both specific [i.e., particularistic] and material" in order to control elections and government.[34] Machines are run by "bosses" and depend upon the allegiance of lower- and working-class voters; their upper echelons usually contain individuals with such backgrounds. Voters are manipulated primarily through patronage, and are reached by workers at the block level. These workers interact in a quasi-feudal manner with their "lieges" at the neighborhood level, who in turn share mutual obligations with precinct captains, and so on up the formal structure to the ward, city, or county level.[35] High officials in the machine control party nomina-

[34] Edward C. Banfield and James Q. Wilson, *City Politics* (Cambridge: Harvard University Press and M.I.T. Press, 1963), pp. 115–16.

[35] At the peak of machine dominance around the turn of the century, machine organizations reached the state and congressional levels.

tions, influence the conduct of elected officials beholden to them, and, in exchange for money, they direct governmental policies (especially contract and franchise decisions) to the benefit of particular businessmen. Indeed, the machine itself may be viewed "as a business organization in a particular field of business—getting votes and winning elections." [36] The machine does not advance programs; "it is interested only in making and distributing income—mainly money—to those who run it and work for it." [37]

This description most accurately applies to political organizations which were dominant at the turn of the century. There are differences among cities, however, both as to the extent to which local machines became fully developed, and as to their duration. In a few places machines are still flourishing, though there is a general consensus among observers that the era of machine politics has long been over.[38] While most analysts would agree with our description of the machine, they have come to divergent evaluations of its performance.

three analyses of the machine

There are three views of the machine which more or less follow one another historically. The first is that of the Progressive reformers, who condemned the machine as a perversion of the democratic process, acting in the interest of no one but its own members. The second, functionalist analysis, becomes fully developed after the machine has passed its peak.[39] This view is more evenhanded and sociological; it explores the unintended consequences of the machine, and the ways these function to fulfill the needs of various groups in the city. There is also a third interpretation which modifies and builds upon the functionalist position, suggesting the dysfunctions of the machine to the class interests of the urban proletariat, and the historical consequences of machine dominance. This is our own argument, which we will outline after discussing the other two.

The Progressive view. Associated with Progressivism as a political movement was a stream of intellectual analysis. We shall describe the political implications of Progressivism later. Here we are concerned only with the critique of the machine expounded by these reformers, who looked at the city through the prism of Protestant morality, middle class sensibility, and the tenets of schoolbook democracy. They found that "with very few exceptions

[36] Banfield and Wilson, *City Politics*, pp. 115–16.

[37] Ibid.

[38] A somewhat different position has been taken by Raymond Wolfinger, who asks if the machine is really dead. However, his argument really concerns personal-influence or leader-follower politics rather than the coherent organizational structures which constituted the machines. Raymond Wolfinger, "Why Political Machines Have Not Withered Away and Other Revisionist Thoughts," *The Journal of Politics*, XXXIV, May, 1972, 365–98.

[39] Jane Addams and Lincoln Steffens were, however, early proponents of this view.

the city governments of the United States . . . [were] the worst in Christendom—the most expensive, the most inefficient, and the most corrupt." [40] They believed that machine politicians used for their own gain "the suffrage of a host of ignorant and pliable voters." [41] The machine destroyed democratic institutions which should have worked in the interest of all citizens: "Where the machine is supreme, republican institutions are in truth but an idle form, a plaything wherewith to beguile children." [42] The machine stood in the way of "a government of the people, by the people, for the people." [43] Its political mechanisms fostered a narrow partisanship which permitted "a crowd of illiterate peasants, freshly raked in from Irish bogs, or Bohemian mines, or Italian robber nests . . . [to] exercise virtual control. How such men govern cities, we know too well; as a rule they are not alive even to their own most direct interests." [44] Oblivious to their own biases, the reformers condemned the machine as morally pernicious and as empirically incompatible with urban governance "in the public interest." This view of the machine interacted with their more general political ideology; both led them to work actively for the machine's destruction and replacement with new institutional forms.

Functionalist analysis.   Since the decline of the machine a new and more sympathetic understanding replaced the established interpretation of reformist moralism. It was inspired by functionalist theory in American sociology, particularly by the idea of latent functions as developed by Robert Merton. This concept suggested that structural forms like the machine functioned to fulfill social needs, even if those needs were not openly recognized. Merton argued that

the key structural function of the Boss is to organize, centralize and maintain . . . 'the scattered fragments of power' which are at present dispersed through our political organization. By this centralized organization of political power, the boss and his apparatus can satisfy the needs of diverse subgroups in the larger community which are not adequately satisfied by legally devised and culturally approved social structures. [45]

He then outlined the needs which the machine satisfied for three major groups in the city: the "deprived classes," racketeers, and business groups. First the machine provided the urban proletariat with certain benefits. These

[40] Andrew D. White, "Municipal Affairs Are Not Political," in *Urban Government*, rev. ed., ed. Edward C. Banfield (New York: Free Press, 1969), p. 271; reprinted from *Forum*, 1890, where it appeared under the title, "The Government of American Cities." White was the president of Cornell University at that time.

[41] James Bryce, *The American Commonwealth* (New York: Putnam's, 1959), p. 198.

[42] M. Ostragorski, *Democracy and the Organization of Political Parties*, II (New York: Doubleday, 1964), p. 300.

[43] Ibid.

[44] White, "Municipal Affairs Are Not Political," p. 271.

[45] Robert K. Merton, *Social Theory and Social Structure*, rev. ed. (New York: Free Press, 1957), p. 72.

included jobs in both the public and private sectors—policeman, gar-bageman, longshoreman, construction worker—remuneration for services rendered at election time; emergency aid to the needy; gifts such as the Christmas turkey; and the intangible commodity of personal loyalty. The hierarchy of the machine, like that of organized crime, constituted an alternative channel of social mobility through which some members of immigrant groups, lacking the socially sanctioned means (Protestant lineage, education, and middle-class backgrounds) could nonetheless attain the socially prescribed ends of higher income, power, and prestige within their communities.[46] Machine cadres, in addition, served as intermediaries be-tween the immigrants with their *Gemeinschaft* orientation and American institutions organized along impersonal, *Gesellschaft* principles. The machine humanized the process of interaction between the immigrant community and city officials, providing just outcomes rather than due process. Merton cited Lomasny's quip to Lincoln Steffens: "I think . . . that there's got to be in every ward somebody that any bloke can come to—no matter what he's done—and get help. Help, you understand; none of your law and your justice, but help." [47]

Second, the machine served organized crime. Although various activi-ties such as gambling, bootlegging and prostitution were legally proscribed, they were supplied by economic structures similar to legitimate businesses. Success in commodity sales indicated large market demand, regardless of the official normative system. Through an intricate system of payoffs, the machine permitted illegal operations to function "without due interference by the government." [48]

Third, the machine served business groups. The institutional structure of the city in the era of laissez faire capitalism did not provide a mechanism for coordination between business and government. Government depended upon the private sector to capitalize the urban physical plant, to build bridges, sewers, subways, water systems, streets. Private enterprise in turn needed government contracts and franchises. The absence of legal procedures and the different social backgrounds of businessmen and city officials made efficient interaction difficult. The boss and the machine "rationalized the relations between public and private business." [49] In doing so, however, the machine distributed benefits unequally, providing immediate economic gains only to those willing and able to pay for their privileged political connections. The interests of a sector of the bourgeoisie and the political machine were thus tied together in a symbiotic relationship.

Merton's formulation has in general been accepted by scholars who discussed machines after him.[50] The list of functions he enumerated is not,

---

[46] Ibid., p. 76.

[47] Ibid., p. 75. Lomasny was a boss in Boston prior to World War I.

[48] Ibid., p. 76.

[49] Ibid.

[50] Cf. Oscar Handlin, *The Uprooted* (New York: Grosset & Dunlap, 1951); Martin Meyerson and Edward C. Banfield, *Politics, Planning, and the Public Interest* (New York: Free Press, 1955);

however, entirely adequate. Merton himself notes that he is not considering possible dysfunctions of the machine for various social groups.[51] Such analysis becomes necessary, though, when one desires to assess the historical meaning of machine preeminence among the political organizations of the urban masses. By building upon the functionalist discussion we can show the impact of the machine in inhibiting the growth of organizations which might have threatened the status quo, and its significance in contributing to the Progressive reforms which did occur.

A radical critique of the machine.   The machine was tied to the urban business class through more than the exchange of favors for money. It was a prime vehicle for supplying and controlling labor employed in construction, private maintenance, longshoreman's work, and transportation. It differentiated within the pool of available labor, providing a privileged position to some workers in exchange for political work, loyalty, and the vote. It was, in fact, itself a business organization, a kind of subcontractor.

The function of controlling the labor force is now fulfilled by trade unions. Unlike unions, however, the machine had no direct interest in increasing wages, or in opposing employers.[52] In its operation the machine undoubtedly provided services to many proletarians, but always as individuals, never as a collectivity. It did not use its organizational power to foster even trade union consciousness. Whereas the unions depended for their success upon the creation of labor solidarity, the interests of machine cadres depended upon upholding the position of the capitalists who financed them.[53]

The interests of the machine were therefore antagonistic to the growth of trade unions and of radical, class conscious organization of the urban proletariat. The precise role of the machine in directly repressing such activities is, however, not entirely clear. Certainly, the machines at the least acquiesced to systematic police efforts against trade unions and "reds." The

---

Banfield and Wilson, *City Politics;* and, for an application to third-world politics, see Myron Weiner, *The Politics of Scarcity* (Chicago: University of Chicago Press, 1962).

[51] Nor should Merton be criticized for the limitations in his analysis, as his primary concern was in exemplifying the concept of latent function, not in thoroughly considering all aspects of the political machine.

[52] The machine probably did benefit the proletariat in the ways the functionalists have described. The question, however, is one of quantity and comparison. The most significant, tangible return which the largest number of immigrants received from the machine was a job. Most of these were unskilled governmental or private-sector positions which the machine did not create, but only distributed. In other words, in terms of these jobs the machine was primarily an allocative mechanism within the working class; it did not increase the sum of jobs, or their pay. It did create some new jobs and a channel for upward mobility through its own organizational structure; but here we are talking about a relative handful of beneficiaries.

[53] Wolfinger comes to a similar conclusion. He says that the real constituency for the machine is a sector of the middle class: "Certain kinds of business and professional men are *more* likely to have interests requiring repeated and complicated relations with public agencies, and thus are potentially a *stronger* constituency for machine politics than the working classes." (Wolfinger, "Why Political Machines Have Not Withered Away," p. 390.)

When one considers that only businessmen can supply the machine with the income which is its life blood, it becomes apparent that they are its prime constituency.

boss stood for free enterprise and Americanism; he was as willing as any businessman to denounce socialist ideas as foreign and dangerous. Cochran and Miller argue that he

was the man who made it possible to conduct government in the interest of the upper middle class in spite of a great lower-class electorate. . . . In English and German cities as well as American, he helped to preserve the established structure of society. . . . Against the bosses such radicals [as Henry George and Eugene Debs] could get nowhere, and the bosses, for their success in reconciling equality at the polls with inequality in property, were allowed their price in graft.[54]

A full assessment of the contribution of the machine to the failure of leftist working-class organization in America is difficult to make, and depends upon evidence which we do not have. But we can argue that even had the machine taken no part in directly repressing radical groups, it still had a conservative impact on the immigrant working class through its effect on their political attitudes.

In order for the machine to fulfill its functions for business groups, it required a working-class constituency which did not seek to use party organization as a means for advancing class demands. The southern and eastern European immigrants (except for some Jews) came to America with little class consciousness or experience of political activity. The machine functioned to socialize these potential constituents into orientations which meshed with its interests. If it depended upon recruits with conservative predispositions, it also helped inculcate and support a political consciousness compatible with extant social arrangements.

The strength of the machine meant that the immigrant was presented with a single model of political activity in which working-class individuals might engage. This model was one of self-interested and materially oriented political behavior, of practical politics as antiprogrammatic—a business tied to the business world. The machine, instead of presenting the alternative analyses characteristic of European working class party organizations, helped to socialize conservatively a generation of the working class.[55] The hegemony of the machine as the organization of the working class was reinforced by the reformers.[56] The conflict between machine and reform which extended over several decades defined for the urban proletariat the range of possibilities. The machine was on its side; reform was for the well off. Missing in the conflict, and thereby in the communications which helped socialize the working class, was the third alternative of class conscious ideology which might have threatened the liberal-capitalist political formula.

[54] Thomas C. Cochran and William Miller, *The Age of Enterprise: A Social History of Industrial America*, rev. ed. (New York: Harper & Row, 1961), p. 267.

[55] In an analysis of the meaning of machine politics for political development which is along lines similar to our own, James C. Scott concludes that: "Machines, by the nature of the rewards they offer and personal ties they build into their organization, may well impede the growth of the class and occupational bonds implied by economic change and thus prolong the period during which family and/or ethnic ties are decisive." James C. Scott, "Corruption, Machine Politics, and Political Change," *American Political Science Review*, LXIII, December, 1969, 1156.

[56] Richard Hofstadter, *The Age of Reform* (New York: Random House, 1955), p. 185.

The machine monopolized not only the channels of communication but the most effective basis for power available to the immigrants: control of the urban party apparatus. Party organization, prior to the Progressive reforms, provided an institutional link between the working-class neighborhood, the state capitals, and even the Congress. But machine leaders never sought to mobilize the masses except to keep themselves in office. No programs were advanced in the economic interest of the urban proletariat as a class.

The machine gave the great mass of immigrants mostly symbolic rewards—the opportunity to take ethnic pride in the presence of a few countrymen in high political or economic positions. The latent function of fostering ethnic pride was to increase ethnic group solidarity and identifications which cut across and undermined class consciousness. In this way the machine functioned to prevent the use of either of the major party organizations to advance the class interest of the immigrants.

The conservative working-class tradition associated with machine hegemony has contributed to the disadvantaged position of ghetto groups, who have not benefited from reforms that were won in other countries by a mobilized proletariat. Were there a working-class party advancing demands for welfare measures and more egalitarian income distribution, we could expect a number of basic changes in the provision of public services, in the incidence of taxation, and in the government's role as a guarantor of social security. Such reforms, while not the product of the political mobilization of urban minority groups, would assist them. But as the situation now stands, there is no socialist movement with which the poor (whether white, black or Latin) can become allied.

The machine and Progressive reform.   One chain of causality links the machine to the present urban situation through the mechanism of party development; the second proceeds through the intervening phenomenon of Progressive reform. The argument here is not that Progressivism was only a response to the machine; the movement addressed many other aspects of social and political life, and its program transcended the merely negative goal of destroying boss-dominated government. Nonetheless, the specific institutional changes which the urban Progressives sought were directly influenced by the practices of the machine.

For the urban Progressives the machine constituted an institutional *thesis.* The *antithesis* which they provided was shaped by their general political ideology, by class interests, and by the intention to create mechanisms which would counter specific evils of machine politics. The machine in its day channeled the power of the urban mass in a conservative direction. The Progressives redesigned urban institutions, diminishing the political mechanisms through which the interests of the present urban mass may be advanced.[57] While the activities of the urban Progressives did not alone

---

[57] Greenstone and Peterson come to a similar conclusion:

> Both the machine and the reform movement had conservative consequences. For businessmen 'on the make,' machine politics provided franchises and special privileges.

account for the decline of the machine,[58] Progressive institutions and ideology did supplant those of the machine, and constitute the historical legacy against which urban political movements are today reacting.

the characteristics
of urban progressivism

The term "Progressive" applies to a number of reform movements based in the Protestant middle and upper classes and operating most forcefully in the first decades of the twentieth century. Progressive reform included efforts against monopoly and dishonest business practices, the muckraking critiques associated with *McClure's* and *The Nation*, the restructuring of Congress, the settlement house movement, progressive education, the city planning movement, and drives to provide recreational facilities. The urban Progressives particularly focused on the problem of the immigrant poor.[59]

The Progressive concern with social welfare led to the development of many institutional forms aimed at bettering the lot of the poor. Settlement houses, parks, playgrounds, vocational education, and new tenement codes

---

For their better established successors good government seemed both efficient and morally praiseworthy. The machine *controlled* the lower class vote, while somewhat later the reformers' structures *reduced* it. By drastically reducing party competition each protected vital business interests from significant political interference. Their consequences were similar to those of the one party system of 1896 [to 1932] which, as Burnham shows, dramatically reduced and disoriented the [working class] electorate in national and state party politics.

J. David Greenstone and Paul E. Peterson, "Reformers, Machines, and the War on Poverty," in *City Politics and Public Policy*, ed. James Q. Wilson (New York: John Wiley, 1968), pp. 270–71. Ital. in orig.; internal citation to Walter Dean Burnham, "The Changing Shape of the American Political Universe," *American Political Science Review*, LIX, March, 1965, 7–28.

[58] Banfield and Wilson, in *City Politics*, suggest that the disintegration of the urban machines resulted primarily from the increasing affluence of their constituencies and the diffusion of Protestant, middle-class political values, rather than from the efforts of the Progressives. They nonetheless accept that the political institutions of the city today are very much a product of the changes which the Progressives wanted (p. 148). The "WASP" political ethos which they see as becoming predominant is essentially that of the Progressives.

[59] The generalizations in this section are based, in part, upon a number of works. Hofstadter, *The Age of Reform*, and Hartz, *The Liberal Tradition in America*, provide helpful interpretations of the Progressive movement as a whole, but devote little attention to urban Progressivism. Data and analyses germane to specifically urban reform efforts are provided by: Samuel P. Hays, "The Politics of Reform in Municipal Government in the Progressive Era," *Pacific Northwest Quarterly*, 55 (1964), 157–69; Banfield and Wilson, *City Politics*; Allen F. Davis, *Spearheads of Reform: The Social Settlements and the Progressive Movement, 1890–1914* (New York: Oxford University Press, 1967); Clarke Chambers, *Seedtime of Reform: American Social Service and Social Action* (Minneapolis: University of Minnesota Press, 1963); Harold A. Stone, Don K. Price, and Kathryn H. Stone, *City Manager Government in the United States* (Chicago: Public Administration Service, 1940); Roy Lubove, *The Urban Community* (Englewood Cliffs, N.J.: Prentice-Hall, 1967) and *The Professional Altruist* (New York: Atheneum, 1972); and, especially, Sol Cohen, *Progressives and Urban School Reform* (New York: Bureau of Publications, Teachers College, Columbia University, 1964).

In the following pages, analysis will be limited to the urban Progressives, though, for the sake of style, the adjective urban may be omitted.

were all part of the Progressive program. Underlying these attempts to assist poor people was an optimistic belief that, through rational policymaking under the direction of persons concerned only with "the public interest," human misery could be sharply mitigated, if not eliminated altogether.

The bourgeois social basis of the Progressive movement and the tying of all reform to an overarching concept of the public interest meant that particular measures had to be justified not in terms of their benefits to a single group—the immigrant poor—but in terms of their value to the entire society. Thus, improving the lot of the poor was not interpreted to mean increasing their power or wealth at the expense of other social strata. The idea that advancements in social welfare might require measures antagonistic to the interests of the bourgeoisie was either inconceivable to or not countenanced by the Progressives. Programs which exclusively benefited the poor were ipso facto contrary to the public interest and unacceptable.

The Progressives defined the public interest in terms of assimilation, individual mobility, and equal opportunity. They did not consider equality of condition to be part of that public interest, nor did they question the possibility of achieving genuine equality of opportunity given an initial condition of social inequality. The association of social policy with class interests, which dominated European thought within the corresponding period, could be evaded in the United States by the liberal formula of procedural freedom—the focus upon fair market practices rather than on fair outcomes, on opportunity rather than result.

Reliance on the standard of the public interest as the measure of social welfare programs led to a great stress on education as the instrument for ameliorating poverty. Educating the poor could not hurt those better off; it would increase the sum of social opportunity while simultaneously assimilating the immigrant children into the American culture. The schools could provide the multiple functions of acculturation and political socialization, constituting a path of upward mobility for the deserving while teaching practical skills to prepare the majority for their social station. Progressive schools, directed by professional educators who were in turn accountable to public-spirited citizens, would allow the poor to realize the value of equal opportunity.

Similarly, the social service agencies and settlement houses aimed at providing slum dwellers with models of appropriate life-styles. Community workers acted as socializing agents on behalf of middle-class society, offering opportunities for mobility to those able to take advantage of them. Genteel, educated young people would live among the poor, thereby showing their own faith in the innate humanity of the slum dweller, while permitting these deprived groups to emulate their culturally superior habits. Although social workers were personally active in pressing for governmental reforms such as improved housing and public services, they never conceived of themselves as political organizers of the poor. Rather, their function as political missionaries was to break the lower classes of their dependence on the party machines, and to disseminate the middle-class, "good government" political ethos. The urban Progressives were, to be sure, the left wing of the bourgeoisie, but they were nonetheless respectful of bourgeois modes. While they rebelled against the selfishness and shortsightedness of their class, they did not have a political consciousness which might have led them to incite the poor to direct action.

Progressivism as a political philosophy emphasized increased democratization of political policymaking, and the improvement of governmental performance through application of the norms of economy and efficiency. While the growth in professionalism and the increased power of the expert implied by the second objective seem to contradict the first, the two aims nevertheless fit together. In the light of the doctrine of the public interest, they explain how Progressivism could avoid the question of giving political power to the poor, yet advocate greater democratization.

Progressive thought assumed a sharp separation between *political* and *administrative* functions and decision making:

> A city is a corporation. . . . As a city it has nothing to do with general political interests . . . party names and duties are utterly out of place there. The questions in a city are not political questions. They have reference to the laying out of streets; to the erection of buildings . . . to the provisions for the public health and comfort. . . . The work of a city . . . should logically be managed as a piece of property.[60]

The frequent proposals for the council-manager form of government, for example, assumed that political and administrative functions could be easily dissociated, and the city could be spared having untrained citizens making administrative decisions and unaccountable officials devising political policy.[61] *Political* policy should be under the direct control of the electorate, with no organized interests or intermediate structures separating citizens from elected officials; the Progressives specifically rejected party organization as a mechanism for democratic government.[62] Government would be both democratic and free from the influence of particular interests—the neutral arbiter settling political questions in the public interest.[63] *Administrative*

---

[60] White, "Municipal Affairs Are Not Political," p. 271.

[61] Three principal ideas characterized the city manager movement:

> First, there was the idea that the most capable and public-spirited citizens should serve on the governing body as representatives of the city at large, to determine policies for the benefit of the community as a whole, rather than for any party, faction, or neighborhood. . . . Second, there was the idea that municipal administration should be delegated to a thoroughly competent, trained executive. . . . Third, there was the idea that the voters should hold only the councilmen politically responsible and should give the city manager a status of permanence and neutrality in political controversy.

Stone, Price, and Stone, *City Manager Government,* p. 236.

[62] Judson L. James, *American Political Parties* (New York: Bobbs-Merrill, 1969), p. 34.

[63] Government "must be severely neutral among all the special interests in society, subordinating each to the common interest and dealing out even-handed justice to all. It would be for neither the rich man nor the poor man, for labor nor capital, but for the just and honest and law-abiding man of whatever class. It would stand, in fact, where the middle class felt itself to be standing—in the middle, on neutral ground among self-seeking interests of all kinds." Richard Hofstadter, *The Age of Reform,* p. 234.

decisions, on the other hand, would best reflect the will of the enlightened public and most efficiently serve all groups if made by trained professionals. Together, greater political democratization and administrative professionalization would guarantee good government.

Mobilization of the lower classes would be dysfunctional to these objectives because, prior to their socialization into middle-class behavior patterns, the political activities of the poor would tend to be selfish and irrational. The proper way to bring the lower classes into the political system was through education. Once the schools and social agencies had achieved their objectives, poor people would naturally participate in political life. Their politicization, however, should occur only after adequate preparation.

the legacy of progressivism

The political philosophy of the Progressives, reacting against the urban institutions presented by machine organization, produced a number of specific reforms. Perhaps the most obvious of these institutional legacies of the Progressive movement is the civil service system. In their endeavor to protect the poor from being "manipulated" before they "matured" politically and to provide them with better services, the Progressives worked to improve the honesty, economy, and efficiency of municipal government. A prime means of doing so was to eliminate the patronage system associated with machine dominance. In its place civil service regulations were devised which would assure meritocratic recruitment through qualifying exams and credentials requirements, and protect jobholders from political pressure by guaranteeing them tenure.

The elaborate structure of the civil service system is but one of the products of the Progressive era. Others—often equally significant—include:

INSTITUTIONAL DISSOCIATION of "nonpolitical" local government from state and national politics by means of (1) home rule; (2) electoral systems designed to make impossible *any* party designation or other collective labels for candidates; (3) staggered local and state/federal elections to prevent "contamination."

ELIMINATION OF POPULAR ELECTION of most city officials in order to permit reasoned choices by the citizenry through voting the "short ballot."

ATTENUATION OF THE MECHANISMS for representing the "partial" or "particular" interests of subgroups by (1) eliminating ward and precinct representation in the city council; (2) greatly reducing council size (in some cases from several hundred to eight or ten members); (3) electing council members at-large.

MINIMIZATION OF POPULAR CONTROL of bureaucratic administration by (1) establishing many agencies and boards completely independent of the political executive (boards of health, some park boards, trusts, etc.); (2) staggering terms of office on boards under popular control so as to maximize policy continuity; (3) limiting political control over education to executive or (in some places) electoral veto over school budgets, but with no "item analysis" permitted.

PROFESSIONALIZATION of service and control agencies, with (1) protection of agency personnel from direct client influence; (2) professional control over recruitment criteria demands; (3) self-policing and performance evaluation—all of which add a layer of professional insulation on top of that provided by civil service regulations.

The social concern of the Progressives resulted in a great expansion of the services provided to the lower classes, and, through the professionalization of many agencies, an improvement in quality as well. But Progressive innovations also insulated public agencies from clients who were becoming ever more dependent on them. Moreover, Progressivism weakened mechanisms for aggregating and channeling the political demands of geographically concentrated minority populations. While the machine prevented the political party from being employed to advance class interests, the Progressives inhibited the very use of the party to organize government at the local level.

Progressivism has also left an ideological legacy. The political analysis first advanced by the Progressives is still employed by governmental officials and bureaucrats to justify their independence from political controls. Clients demanding structural changes are accused of bringing political criteria to bear upon the schools, the police, or medical facilities, as the case may be. Middle-class groups and the media tend to view bureaucracy-client conflict through Progressive assumptions. Clients come in this way to be identified with machine and power politics while their adversaries are presumed to be upholding the public interest. The dominance of Progressive ideology constrains urban movements to profess their disinterest in power or political goals because they are unable to change the terms of discussion so as to show that agencies are *already* politicized. Political action by minority groups is interpreted primarily in one of two ways: by unsympathetic observers according to conservative criteria; by sympathetic—liberal—observers according to the criteria of Progressive ideology. Urban movements are accordingly faced with the problem of creating new analyses which can counteract the present bias of political debate against their position.

Continuity of the Progressive approach in recent efforts to benefit the poor. The Progressive movement is important not only because of its direct effect on contemporary city politics, but also because it represents the characteristic American approach to "the social question." The absence of a socialist movement, combined with the overall ideological hegemony of liberalism, means that Progressive ideas are the typical ideas of American social reformers. Progressive reformers with middle-class roots are the chief patrons and allies of the urban lower classes, just as they were two generations ago. For this reason Progressivism is of signal importance in its continuing effect on the process by which domestic social policy is formulated.

The Progressive movement arose out of a heightened sensitivity among a segment of the privileged classes to the distress of the poor, and from an awareness that poverty threatened social stability. Likewise, the reform program of the 1960s can be traced both to a growing consciousness among members of the upper strata of the extent of poverty and their perception of the danger to social stability presented by the civil rights movement and black nationalist groups. While the impetus to recent policy can be attributed partly to pressures exerted by black leaders, its content was framed by college professors, foundation officials, and occupants of positions in the federal government. We see, for example, the paradigm for the War on Poverty and Model Cities in the programs of the President's Committee on Juvenile Delinquency and the Ford Foundation's Gray Areas Program.[64] Similarly Title 1 of the Elementary and Secondary Education Act (ESEA) derived from certain emphases in these programs, and found its support among advisers to President Johnson who viewed improved education as essential to bettering the lot of the poor:

It is important to understand that the reform [Title 1 of ESEA] was not a response to public pressure. Unlike the great national programs passed during the New Deal, Title 1 did not arise from public demand. The poor were unorganized and had made no demands for such legislation.[65]

As in the earlier period, reform has been *brought to* "the people" rather than arising in response to their demands. The preface to a recent book on the settlement house movement, itself reflecting the general Progressive ethos, manifests the extent to which noblesse oblige still dominates, even among the more radical reformers:

Despite differences between the two generations of reformers [Progressive and modern], they have much in common in spirit and tactics. The settlement worker who went to live in a working-class neighborhood in the 1890s, the peace corpsman who settled in an African village, the SNCC member who moved into a Mississippi hamlet, the Southern Christian Leadership Conference worker who lived in a slum tenement in Chicago in the 1960s all began their reform efforts from the inside: *they went to the people,* to the neighborhood, and started there.[66]

Because the program of reform has originated not among the poor or their direct representatives but among well-meaning middle- and upper-class leaders, it continues to reflect the same biases as did the program of the

---

[64] See Peter Marris and Martin Rein, *The Dilemmas of Social Reform*, rev. ed. (Chicago: Aldine, 1973); Daniel P. Moynihan, *Maximum Feasible Misunderstanding* (New York: Free Press, 1969); James L. Sundquist, "Origins of the War on Poverty," in *On Fighting Poverty*, ed. James L. Sundquist (New York: Basic Books, 1969), pp. 6–33.

[65] Jerome T. Murphy, "Title 1 of ESEA: The Politics of Implementing Federal Education Reform," *Harvard Educational Review*, XLI, February, 1971, 37. Moynihan makes the same argument about the Economic Opportunity Act: "The war on poverty was not declared at the behest of the poor: it was declared in their interest by persons confident of their own judgment in such matters." Moynihan, *Maximum Feasible Misunderstanding*, p. 25.

[66] Davis, *Spearheads of Reform,* p. xiv; ital. added.

Progressive era. Liberal policy toward the poor remains defined by the values of assimilation, individual mobility, and equal opportunity. The policy goal of the modern reformers, like that of the Progressives, is an increase in the sum of social opportunity, achieved through the provision of education and services, rather than a redistribution of income and power.[67]

the dialectic of the
urban tradition

Contemporary urban political movements represent an alternative to the contest between the machine and Progressive reform. Urban history may be interpreted as displaying a dialectical development of institutions and ideologies. The thesis is the political machine. The antithesis is Progressivism. Urban movements constitute a potential synthesis. Minority group leaders find it necessary, in order to advance the collective interests of their constituencies, to reject some of the basic tenets of institutionalized Progressivism. While they work for institutional forms resembling those of the machine era, the substance of policy demands, calling for the redistribution of benefits to whole categories of previously disadvantaged citizens, reflects a new group consciousness and solidarity. These movements are not, then, as some observers have charged, a return to machine politics. Rather, they are an emergent form, a vehicle for change which is partly the product of the machine, of Progressivism, and of concomitant political developments, but which reintegrates these past elements in a new way.

Urban political movements may be compared with Progressivism and machine organization in terms of three major characteristics: social basis, goals, and means or tactics. The social composition of movements working for change in urban institutions is reflective of their clientele. Contemporary movements have their roots in lower- and working-class minority groups; and even their leaders usually have origins beneath the middle-class level. Urban movements in this respect resemble the machine in social composition rather than the Progressives, with whom the contrast is sharp indeed.

Urban movements are also similar to the machine in lacking influential defenders within the intellectual stratum. Every reform effort is significantly influenced by the position of the intelligentsia, those who create and disseminate ideas, explanations, and moral evaluations. Sometimes these

---

[67] The federal program of Aid to Families with Dependent Children (AFDC) is an apparent exception. AFDC was created during the Depression and viewed by its proponents as a temporary measure, designed to help families who tried, but could not support themselves. There was no recognition at the time that AFDC would become the largest component of welfare and would turn into a costly program of direct transfer payments to the poor. Subsequent reform efforts have all been addressed to ultimately "getting people off the rolls." The program has never been justified as a redistributive measure, but only as a means necessary to prevent starvation. Present attention is directed primarily to eliminating "cheating" by clients, to reducing payments, and to increasing incentives for clients to enter the labor market regardless of low wages. See Gilbert Y. Steiner, *Social Insecurity* (Skokie, Ill.: Rand McNally, 1966) and *The State of Welfare* (Washington, D.C.: Brookings Institution, 1971).

individuals are allies or members of the effort, sometimes they ignore or oppose it. During the period of active Progressive reform there were virtually no members of the intelligentsia allied with the machine. Many professors, novelists and journalists were indifferent to urban reform. But those who cared were, to varying degrees, Progressive. In fact, the major vehicle by which the Progressives elicited support from the middle-class public and from legislators was the printed media. Progressivism was a movement of individuals who were in positions of social prestige, economic power, and considerable intellectual influence.

A small number of intellectuals have supported urban political movements. In general, however, the intelligentsia has been indifferent or hostile. The basic problem these movements have faced in this regard is that they counter both the universalistic values of the liberal left and the pro-labor, pro-centralization position of American socialists. The liberal left, as reflected in the editorial page of *The New York Times*, is still Progressive. Since the ideas of urban movements oppose some of those of Progressivism, these movements tend to be labeled as atavistic, "a return to the machine." Moreover, the nonwhite and poor social composition of urban movements, their use of unusual or militant tactics, and their attack on agencies whose mission is the advancement of social welfare goals all combine to threaten potential intellectual sympathizers. Like the machine, urban movements find it difficult to propagate an effective ideological counterattack against Progressivism. But whereas the machine did not depend for its success upon ideology and symbolic appeals to third parties, urban movements do, and the Progressive hegemony over the intelligentsia represents a serious obstacle to their survival and effectiveness.

Goals.   While urban movements do not have the service of a vanguard of intellectuals, they do aim at conscious goals; they have programs and policies they seek to implement. First, they are working for improvement in the quantity and quality of the governmental social services provided inner city residents and for the expenditure of governmental funds to their benefit. Second, they are attempting to force governmental institutions to recognize the legitimacy of social group differences. They demand that institutions demonstrate sensitivity to the cultural forms and values of their clients, usually by recruiting individuals with specific racial or ethnic backgrounds to official positions. Machine politicians also were attuned to the principles of "specificity," and used ethnic group symbols in building and maintaining their power. They did not, however, develop a program for group advancement. The Progressives had a program which, like that of urban movements, aimed at improving social services and ameliorating the condition of the poor. But the Progressives recognized only universalistic principles of organization and denied the legitimacy of any collective goal except cultural assimilation.

A final goal of urban movements is that governmental institutions be politically accountable to their clients and to the communities in which they are located. Increased politicization, however, does not represent a complete rejection of the professionalization of urban agencies effected by Progressivism. Urban movements want both political accountability and professionalism. The "synthetic" nature of the goals of urban movements is, in fact, manifested by a degree of acceptance of Progressive ideology. Activist groups often deny that they wish to intrude politics into professional or technical matters. While these movements work for goals which frequently counter the political analysis of the Progressives, they use some of the symbols and language of Progressivism.

Means.   There are two aspects of the "means" or tactics employed by a political reform effort. The first includes the intermediate or instrumental goals which are seen as necessary to the attainment of desirable ends. For urban movements these means are administrative decentralization and community control. Decentralization permits the representation of relatively homogeneous client groups in bodies which can exercise oversight of institutional policy and administration. Without external political direction (in the form of governing boards, local councils, etc.) administrative decentralization by itself does not restructure the reference groups and interests which strongly influence bureaucratic behavior. Efforts toward community control encompass both decentralization and changes in governance. As such, they seek to reinstitute the structural situation which prevailed prior to Progressive reform. Here again, however, they accept some of the basic products of Progressivism. Perhaps the most important of these is the civil service system. What urban political movements are attempting to do is to modify the structural arrangements which supplanted the machine so as to change the distribution of benefits in their favor. Thus, in the case of civil service, the goal is not to eliminate credentials and review committees, but rather to change the cultural biases of the former, and to gain minority group representation on the latter.

The second aspect of "means" involves the political mechanism by which change is to be effected. Like the Progressives, contemporary urban groups have attempted to mobilize citizens to direct political action. Yet the differences between the Progressive movement and contemporary urban political movements are very significant. Because urban movements are composed of people at the bottom they usually lack the power resources to effect change through normal political channels. They must use numbers and protest in the streets where the Progressives could use personal influence and control over political office. Moreover, the groups which urban movements threaten and from whom they seek concessions represent much higher social strata than did the machine at the time of the Progressive onslaught. Finally, the triumph of Progressive forms and ideology makes the demands for community control appear to be irrational or venal to many groups outside the ghetto. For these reasons, ghetto reformers have been forced to adopt a conflict approach to political change. They feel they must mobilize collective power through movements that are ready to engage in open and occasionally violent conflict in order to bring about concessions from entrenched groups. The appearance and behavior of contemporary urban movements is thus different from the genteel movement of the Progressives and from the individualist and materialist politics of the machine, even while they have been molded by the structural and ideological legacies of both.

the character
of urban movements

2

A wide variety of grass-roots organizations fall within the category urban political movements. While they are sufficiently similar to constitute a distinct type of political phenomenon, they differ from one another in significant and interesting ways. Some have been stable; many more have been ephemeral. Some have broad-range programs; others have objectives limited to specific functional areas, such as housing or education. A number of them trace their origins to federal programs such as the War on Poverty, Model Cities, or the Community Mental Health Program, while others have arisen independently of government stimulus.

In this chapter we provide brief descriptions of various urban movements. The organizations portrayed here have been chosen because of their seeming representativeness of the great array of such groups—because they indicate the range of differences within the basic type. Our purpose is to present the phenomena we have labeled urban political movements in concrete terms, to describe their distinctive elements. Later, we shall provide lengthier, more detailed case studies of a few groups in order to show the dynamics of organization; here we limit ourselves to quick sketches.

FEDERAL PROGRAMS
FOR THE POOR

The Economic Opportunity Act of 1964 authorized the establishment of Community Action Programs (CAP's) in inner-city areas across the country. The CAP's, which were to incorporate maximum feasible participation of neighborhood residents in policymaking, aimed at broad scale community development. While most of the approximately 1,000 CAP's in the country limited themselves to service-providing and coordinating functions, a small percentage interpreted their role, at least for a period of time, as community mobilization.[1] A 1965 study based on a 51-city sample indicates that 5 percent of CAP's emphasized institutional change;[2] a three-year study of a 20-city sample covering the 1964–66 period presents a figure of 3 percent.[3] A 100-community study performed in 1969 found that 5 percent of CAP executive directors considered that organizing the poor so as to increase their political power was their agency's best developed goal.[4]

These activist CAP's can be considered a part of a political movement of urban minorities, but their relationship to the movement is complex. The CAP itself may play only a precipitating role in social action—through the recruitment and training of leaders, who may then act under the auspices of other organizations; through the provision of specialized resources such as legal aid; or merely through making available a forum for the presentation and discussion of demands. Thus, Vanecko, in a discussion of findings based on the 100-city sample cited above, concludes that militant Community Action Agencies (CAA's) are effective

not because of the generation of direct pressures on these [public] institutions but because of general organizational involvement. Schools and social service agencies do change in such cities. Why they change is less clear. They may change in anticipation of demands or pressures being directed at them, because the organizational density of such neighborhoods creates a culture defining such changes as desirable, or simply because organizational activity makes change a viable alternative to the status quo. . . .[5]

In other words a CAP by itself would probably not constitute a militant political movement, but in conjunction with general community activism it becomes an important contributory element.

A report on a rent strike in an unidentified city, apparently in California, illustrates the way militant action organizations can link up with the Poverty Program. The rent strike organization, named the Neighborhood Action Club (NAC), was set up independently of the Poverty Program; its

[1] A number of critics of the War on Poverty have seen it as a thinly disguised attempt to divert the efforts of militant leaders of the poor into harmless channels. Saul Alinsky makes a forceful statement of this point of view in "The War on Poverty—Political Pornography," *Journal of Social Issues*, XXI, January, 1965, 42.

[2] Kenneth Clark and Jeanette Hopkins, *A Relevant War Against Poverty* (New York: Harper & Row, 1969), p. 65.

[3] Stephen M. Rose, *The Betrayal of the Poor* (Cambridge, Mass.: Schenkman, 1972), p. 142.

[4] Bruce Jacobs, *Community Action and Urban Institutional Change; A National Evaluation of the Community Action Program* prepared for the Office of Economic Opportunity by Barss, Reitzel and Associates, Inc., Cambridge, Mass., August, 1970 (Springfield, Virginia: National Technical Information Service, PB193967), p. 17.

[5] James J. Vanecko, "Community Mobilization and Institutional Change: The Influence of the Community Action Program in Large Cities," in *Planned Social Intervention*, ed. Louis A. Zurcher, Jr., and Charles M. Bonjean (New York: Chandler, 1970), p. 270.

chairman, however, was a staff organizer for the CAA. He worked out of the Poverty Program district office and conducted NAC business on agency time. But when he and other agency staff personnel were criticized for the way they were conducting the strike by the CAP director, they argued that theirs was an independent organization not subject to CAP supervision.[6]

The relationship between CAP militancy and general community politicization is brought out again in Kramer's case studies of poverty agencies in the San Francisco Bay area.[7] The San Francisco Economic Opportunity Council (the CAA) was originally appointed by the mayor in 1964; it was selected so as to provide for strong representation from business, industry, and labor. A group, representing a coalition of 25 civil rights, ethnic minority, and neighborhood groups, calling itself Citizens United Against Poverty (CUAP), demanded a greater voice for the poor in developing community programs. The mayor at first rejected these demands, but eventually, "with the reverberations of the Watts riots still in the air," [8] he capitulated. The resulting reorganization of the EOC led to the devolution of program authority to the Target Area Organizations (TAO's) in the four affected areas.

The governing ideology of the four TAO's, which had earlier been articulated by CUAP, was one of community power—"organizing the poor to exert leverage on existing community institutions as the best use of the limited funds and time available." [9] The most extensive program of community organization took place in the Western Addition, which had historically been the base of black activism in San Francisco. The Western Addition in 1960 had a population of 62,000, 43 percent of whom were black, representing one-third of San Francisco's black residents. Two-thirds of its families had incomes of less than $6,000 per year; unemployment was twice the city average; and there was extensive dependence on public assistance.

Out of this community emerged a group of young, militant civil rights activists who had fought discrimination and redevelopment and taken the initiative in forming CUAP, and who were subsequently involved in the organization of the Western Addition interim [poverty] board.[10]

Under its "Area Development Plan" the Western Addition organizing staff set up 28 neighborhood councils, although only six of them were believed to be actively functioning. Controversies over the allocation of organizer jobs and the extent to which the organization should provide neighborhood services led to a great deal of internal dissension, causing Kramer to

[6] Harry Brill, *Why Organizers Fail* (Berkeley: University of California Press, 1971), pp. 39–42.

[7] The following summary of the development of the San Francisco Poverty Program is drawn from Ralph M. Kramer, *Participation of the Poor* (Englewood Cliffs, N.J.: Prentice-Hall, © 1969), pp. 25–67. See Clark and Hopkins, *A Relevant War Against Poverty*, for a description of the community organization-oriented CAP in Syracuse, New York.

[8] Kramer, *Participation of the Poor*, p. 33.

[9] Ibid., p. 35.

[10] Ibid., p. 37.

conclude: "Although a shaky organizational structure emerged after a year, its composition, representative quality, and capabilities fell far short of the intent of the architects of the Area Development Plan." [11]

We see, then, that even as militant a poverty board as the Western Addition TAO did not constitute an effective political movement. Nonetheless, the creation of the San Francisco EOC contributed to the general political potency of black and poor people in the area. Most important, perhaps, was its effect on the continued development of indigenous leadership.

The war on poverty provided an opportunity for this younger leadership to consolidate its influence further, because the same set of coalition skills that had been developed in previous controversies over civil rights and redevelopment were called for.[12]

The community mobilization achieved by the San Francisco EOC was used largely for the employment of conventional methods of bringing pressure on public officials. Despite the furor that these efforts sometimes provoked, they were, Kramer argues

distinctly middle class in their emphasis on self-help, local initiative, and democratic cooperative action. . . . *What was different was that these milder forms of citizen action had never been developed in most low-income areas and were stimulated and sustained by the war against poverty.*[13]

The CAP, then, may represent an element in the various movements of urban minority groups. Even when the CAP itself does not succeed in generating widespread involvement, it may serve as a vehicle for the development of public awareness and the formation of communication linkages among potential activists. Membership on a CAP board or a staff job may result in the recruitment of individuals into general community leadership roles. The CAP becomes part of the political infrastructure of the ghetto, serving as a base of operations, a possible source of support, and a prize to be captured.

model cities

The federal Model Cities program was established under the Demonstration Cities Act of 1966. It required coordinated planning of social services, intensive redevelopment of selected model neighborhoods, and participation of target area residents in policymaking. As was the case in the Poverty Program, most of the Model Cities agencies did not pursue militant strategies and made little attempt to mobilize their communities. Many became involved in jurisdictional conflicts with poverty agencies. Again, however,

[11] Ibid., p. 41.
[12] Ibid., p. 180.
[13] Ibid., p. 235, ital. added.

there were exceptions, one of which, West Oakland, represented a significant example of the use of federal programs to increase the political power of lower-class black and Spanish-speaking groups.

In response to the federal mandate for participation of residents in the Model Cities effort, a group of community leaders formed the West Oakland Planning Committee (WOPC).[14] WOPC was set up as a delegate assembly with an unusually broad basis of representation—any organization of at least ten members operating within West Oakland could become a member and send two delegates. By the middle of 1968, 165 organizations, including political, religious, social, economic, and professional groups, had joined.

WOPC subsequently also became the target area organization for West Oakland of the Oakland Economic Development Council, Inc. (OEDCI), which was the city's community action agency (CAA) under the Poverty Program. In an earlier struggle, neighborhood representatives had won majority control in the Council for target area delegates and had achieved substantial devolution of program power to the target area level.

West Oakland leaders were among the indigenous representatives who fought for control over the poverty program. Many of the attitudes and strategies which they brought to the Model Cities fight were formed in the evolving relationships between indigenous and at-large members of the Oakland Economic Development Council and between the Oakland Economic Development Council and the city.[15]

Moreover, in the initial stages of the Model Cities negotiations the OEDCI staff gave important assistance to WOPC; the OEDCI executive director openly endorsed the goal of community control for West Oakland residents through the Model Cities vehicle; and the West Oakland office provided extensive staff support. The director of this office became the key political adviser and staff man for the WOPC.

The goal for WOPC from the start was to insure that control over all programs in the Model Cities area, regardless of their source, would rest ultimately with the representatives of its inhabitants. Oakland's regular municipal government was chosen on an at-large basis in nonpartisan citywide elections. Since West Oakland had no independent existence and did not contain an electoral majority, it had no way of exerting significant influence through the regular political process. City councilmen "pride[d] themselves on representing 'the community as a whole' rather than special interests, and [were] notably conservative in ideology." [16]

In pursuit of their objective of neighborhood control, WOPC attempted to limit the role of technical and administrative personnel in policymaking. It strongly resisted a dominant position for professional planners, even those

---

[14] This case is drawn from Judith May, "Two Model Cities: Political Development on the Local Level," paper presented to the American Political Science Association, New York, September, 1969. A revised version of this paper has been published in *Politics and Society*, II, Fall, 1971, . 57–88.

[15] Ibid., p. 14.

[16] Ibid., p. 8.

acting ostensibly as advocates for West Oakland, in the Model Cities planning process. It also sought to prevent the Oakland city manager from acting as an independent review authority mediating between WOPC and the City Council:

The City Manager remarked after one frustrating negotiating session: "What they can't understand is that my function is purely one of coordination." . . . By coordination, the City Manager implied the application of technical skills, whereas West Oakland residents anticipated conflict. . . . They felt that their knowledge—the knowledge of experience—was equal in quality, if not superior, to that of the formally trained expert. . . . From the point of view of West Oakland residents, if the experts worked for someone else, the goal achieved efficiently might not be their own.[17]

Negotiations over the authority of the Model Cities agency and the boundaries of the Model Cities district continued for a protracted period. Simultaneously, tension was increasing in the black community. Leaders mounted a boycott of a local shopping district, and a Black Strike for Justice Committee listed ten demands concerned primarily with recruitment and behavior of the Police Department. Three of the five negotiators for the Black Strike Committee were members or staff of the WOPC Executive Committee. Eventually, WOPC compromised on some of its Model Cities demands, and the major differences between it and the city were resolved. It succeeded in its overriding goal of obtaining what was essentially a second government for West Oakland, controlled by the residents of the community.

The West Oakland experience demonstrates the way in which federal programs may provide leadership and resources for political activity within poverty areas. In addition, it shows the interrelationship between traditional and militant forms of political activity, as individual leaders shifted between official and unofficial roles. The West Oakland leaders were participants in an urban political movement directed at black power and community control. They can be classified as participants not because they occupied positions in the Poverty Program or Model Cities, but because they seized on these governmental programs as devices for obtaining their political goals. Whether these federal programs spawned radical movements, as many of their white critics complained, or co-opted community leaders, as radical detractors in many cities argued, depended greatly on individual characteristics of the community leaders involved and on the more general character of political life in the municipality.

COMMUNITY CONTROL
OF SCHOOLS
IN NEW YORK CITY

Another example of the capture of a government-sponsored organization is provided by the movement for community control of schools in New York

[17] Ibid., p. 41.

City. Here the vehicle for community mobilization and the pressing of militant demands against the school system was a demonstration project, a device frequently used by governments to symbolize their innovative intentions without going through the process of thoroughgoing change.[18]

The demonstration project was an attempt by the school system in New York to deal with growing activism among parents. During the first half of the 1960s the efforts of activist black parents to improve their children's schools had been directed not at an overhaul of the system but rather at obtaining racial integration. Their frustration in failing to achieve this objective and their belief that the school system was continuing to deteriorate led them to seek power for themselves within the system. The most significant single incident that precipitated this change in direction was the opening of Intermediate School (IS) 201 (grades six–eight) in the autumn of 1966.

IS 201, an entirely segregated institution in East Harlem, signified to the residents of the area the hypocrisy of the Board of Education in claiming integration as a goal, and consequently the hopelessness of making integration their own objective.[19] When they discovered that 201, although established as an intermediate school ostensibly to further integration, would be entirely nonwhite, parents demanded that they then be allowed to control the school themselves.

The IS 201 parents interested the Ford Foundation, which had sponsored other programs for increasing community participation in the planning of neighborhood services, in funding an experimental small school

[18] Frances Piven comments in relation to Mobilization for Youth, originally a Ford Foundation demonstration project, that "strategies like the demonstration may be used to 'cool out' . . . agitation [among the poor], . . . but they may also provide a form guiding agitation into coherent pressure for reform." Frances Piven, "The Demonstration Project: A Federal Strategy for Local Change," in *Community Action Against Poverty: Notes from the Mobilization Experience,* eds. George Brager and Francis Purcell (New Haven: College and University Press, 1967), p. 103.

[19] The story of IS 201, the moves and counter-moves of the principal actors in the community control-decentralization controversy, the events in Ocean Hill-Brownsville, the causes and repercussions of the 1968 school strike, and the passage of the 1968 and 1969 decentralization laws have been chronicled and debated by many. The account here is as abbreviated as possible and is intended only to give the reader unfamiliar with the circumstances a bare outline of what happened. More detailed accounts are in the following sources: Thomas K. Minter, "Intermediate School 201, Manhattan: Center of Controversy" (Cambridge: By the author, 1967); Maurice R. Berube and Marilyn Gittell, *Confrontation at Ocean Hill-Brownsville* (New York: Praeger, 1969)—this work contains a number of documents and articles, pro and con, relative to the whole dispute; Naomi Levine with Richard Cohen, *Schools in Crisis* (New York: Popular Library, 1969); Jason Epstein, "The Politics of School Decentralization," *New York Review of Books* (*NYR*), June 6, 1968, pp. 26–32; "The Brooklyn Dodgers," *NYR*, Oct. 10, 1968, pp. 37–41; "The Issue at Ocean Hill," *NYR*, Nov. 21, 1968, pp. 3–4, 44; "The Real McCoy," *NYR*, March 13, 1969, pp. 31–40; Martin Mayer, "The Full and Sometimes Very Surprising Story of Ocean Hill, the Teachers Union and the Teacher Strikes of 1968," *The New York Times Magazine*, Feb. 2, 1969, pp. 18–23, 42–71. The Epstein articles favor the community control people; the Levine book and Mayer article the Teachers Union. Marilyn Gittell *et al., Demonstration for Social Change* (New York: Institute for Community Studies, Queens College, 1971) is an evaluation of the performance of the districts as well as a history of the events.

district around IS 201 and its feeder elementary schools. At the same time the Foundation offered similar planning grants to parent organizations in Brooklyn (Ocean Hill-Brownsville); on the lower East Side of Manhattan (Two Bridges); and on the upper West Side (Joan of Arc). The upper West Side group asked that the award of the grant be postponed until the community had been made aware of the new district.[20] The Board of Education accepted the money on behalf of IS 201, Ocean Hill-Brownsville, and Two Bridges and established them as "demonstration districts" in July 1967. Their declared purpose was to test the effects of decentralization of educational policymaking and citizen involvement in the schools.

The three demonstration districts quickly elected governing boards, which interpreted their mandate as going well beyond the planning function visualized by the Board of Education. Their view that decentralization involved a transfer of control to the local community led to continual bickering with the Board of Education. There was also hostility between the governing boards and school employees within the districts who opposed community control.[21] The culmination of these tensions was the prolonged school strike in the fall of 1968, when the United Federation of Teachers (UFT) called its members out in response to the attempt by the Ocean Hill Governing Board to transfer a group of teachers and supervisors out of the district.

The chronology of the citywide strike was as follows. On September 9, 1968, the UFT struck all city schools, demanding that the Board of Education reinstate the ten transferred teachers whom it claimed the Ocean Hill-Brownsville Governing Board had illegally "fired" during the spring of that year. The next day the Board of Education acquiesced, and the Ocean Hill Board, not a party to the agreement, stated that it would not prevent the return of the teachers. However, when the previously suspended UFT teachers were faced with running a gauntlet of several hundred community residents, the Board of Education asked State Education Commissioner Allen to intervene and the union threatened to walk out once more. It did so on September 13 and did not return until September 30, when the central Board agreed to guarantee that the ten teachers be assigned to regular teaching duty. Again, the agreement was made without the participation of the Governing Board. This was followed by two weeks of turmoil in the district schools (particularly JHS 271), with community activists accusing the union teachers of sabotage, and the UFT countering with the charge that its members were being harassed and physically threatened, in several instances with death. The union escalated its demands to include the closing of JHS 271, the removal of the Governing Board and Rhody McCoy, the unit

---

[20] This group is the subject of the case study presented in Chapter Three.

[21] Circumstances in the Two Bridges District, where the majority of the population was Chinese, differed from those in the other districts. The concept of community control won little favor there, and residents made no attempt to sustain the district after the passage of the 1969 Decentralization Law. Our discussion here will be limited henceforth to the IS 201 and Ocean Hill districts; when the term demonstration districts is used, it will refer only to these two unless otherwise indicated.

administrator, and the termination of the Ocean Hill-Brownsville "experiment." When these demands were not met, the union began the third, and lengthiest strike of the year, lasting from October 14 until November 17.

The period of the strike was characterized by a very high level of activism in connection with the schools. Parents opposed to the UFT's anticommunity control position broke into a number of schools and proceeded to run them, using teachers who split from the union and volunteers to man the classrooms. Frequent stormy meetings took place throughout the city, and some in Ocean Hill-Brownsville included the presence of armed men. Officials of the UFT widely publicized the anti-Semitic statements of a few people connected with the Ocean Hill-Brownsville district, and succeeded in equating the Governing Board's dismissal action with anti-Semitism in the minds of many. Community control of schools became perhaps the most controversial issue to affect New York in the decade.

The crises that surrounded the districts mobilized many people who might not have been interested in the routine deliberations of an institutionalized school board. The Governing Board members at IS 201 and Ocean Hill became identified not just as educational activists but as community leaders; Rhody McCoy, the black unit administrator in Ocean Hill-Brownsville, acquired national renown. While the Governing Board members and district staffs initially had hoped to concern themselves with the implementation of educational programs, they came to see themselves primarily as insurgents whose role it was to make changes in the organization of the schools rather than to act as governors of an established institution. Despite their positions as elected officials within the school system, the situation of confrontation caused them to define themselves as opponents of the system rather than participants in it. The Board of Education had attempted to contain and channel protest by creating decentralized vehicles for community participation; instead Governing Board members sponsored protest activities, including mass meetings, harassment of dissidents, propaganda pieces, and community organization efforts.

The demonstration districts came to an end with the passage of the 1969 School Decentralization Act,[22] which set up a system of large "community school districts" designed in such a way as to inhibit their domination by pro-community control forces. The IS 201 and Ocean Hill-Brownsville boards had both used foundation funds to pay professional organizers. When the board members lost their official status, they maintained their insurgent role, but they no longer had the resources of official legitimacy or governmental and foundation financing. The demise of the districts caused the movement for community control to cease as a significant force in New York City as a whole, although it continued on the district level in some parts of the city.

Ocean Hill-Brownsville and IS 201 had been named "demonstration

---

[22] State of New York, Senate-Assembly, 1969/1970 Regular Sessions, An Act to Amend the Education Law (S.5690/A. 7175).

districts" because they were supposed to show the value or lack of it in organizing an urban school system on a neighborhood basis. In practice, however, the experience of the districts offered little data concerning the effects of neighborhood control in a routinized situation. The districts were in a continuous state of flux, and their backers were almost totally involved in the process of gaining power rather than consolidating or exercising it. Thus, although the districts enjoyed a measure of delegated authority, members of the governing boards should be viewed as participants in a movement to gain power rather than as members of an established board of education. The authority they possessed was primarily used as a resource in the struggle to achieve more power.

The case of community control of schools is not one where the birth of the movement can be entirely attributed to the formation of a group under official auspices. But the impact of the movement—both its ability to mobilize for a period large numbers of people and its effect on the school system—resulted largely from governmental sponsorship. As in those cases where the CAP's or Model Cities agencies produced widespread political ferment, the combination here of official sanction with outside bases of militance resulted in the growth of a movement rather than the co-optation of community leaders.

COMMUNITY CONTROL OF
HEALTH

Federally sponsored activities, under the auspices of both the Office of Economic Opportunity (OEO) and the Community Mental Health Program of the Department of Health, Education, and Welfare, have provided the framework for movements aiming at community control of local health facilities. The establishment of community boards under these programs, which usually operate in conjunction with municipal or teaching hospitals, has precipitated a number of clashes between professional medical personnel and local residents. In many cases locally trained paraprofessional employees have also participated in these disputes.

A typical community movement aiming at control of a local clinic in Denver has been described by Elinor Langer.[23] At the time of her study the Neighborhood Health Center, serving an area of 40,000 people with a staff of 130, constituted the most important OEO project in the city and became a central political issue. The most militant local group consisted of Mexican-Americans, who used the Health Center Board as a vehicle for mounting their demands. One of the major points at issue, as it has been in virtually every community control dispute, was the personnel selection process.

[23] This section is a summary of the case study presented in Elinor Langer, "Medicine for the Poor: A New Deal in Denver," *Science*, CLIII, July, 1966, 508–12. Copyright 1966 by the American Association for the Advancement of Science.

Community representatives on the Board wanted aides chosen on the basis of personal need rather than credentials, given a higher civil service ranking, and provided professional recognition for participation in their as yet experimental training program. They also feared that the Health Center was using the 58 paraprofessional jobs at its disposal to buy off potential neighborhood dissidents. Their specific demands were, however, less significant than their general goal:

> The unrest in the relations between the health center staff and its neighborhood advisory board is focused not so much on the content of particular decisions but on who makes them. It appears that the staff of the center honestly wanted advice; they wanted to know what hours would be convenient, how people felt about paying, what facilities were most needed. They wanted assistance in spreading word of the center around the neighborhood and in running a ceremonial open house. They did not want to share their authority or to include the poor in substantive policymaking decisions.[24]

As in so many other controversies over control of public service institutions, the opposition to community demands came from individuals of nominally liberal persuasion who believed themselves to be acting in the best interests of their clients:

> To a certain extent, the doctors who have started them [neighborhood health centers] are reformers—even radicals—within their profession. They are fighting decades-old battles—for comprehensive, family-centered, preventive medical care; for group practice; for the development of new kinds of health manpower that cuts across lines made fast by the domination of professional associations and certification and licensing boards. But they are doing all this through the War on Poverty and—at least in Denver—have found themselves confronting radicals with a very different set of priorities, militant leaders (particularly Spanish-American) seeking to use the centers not only to improve the health of their people but to advance their political power as well.[25]

A similar confrontation between liberal professionals and militant community groups occurred at Lincoln Hospital in New York City.[26] Here the community program had been established under the auspices of the National Institute of Mental Health. Again the central issue was the selection and use of paraprofessional personnel. The climax of the lengthy battle for administrative power over the facility, which served more than a third of a million people in the South Bronx, was reached in 1969 when nonprofessional health workers seized control of the center. During the two weeks in which they maintained control, the professional staff split between acceptance of and opposition to the insurgent administrators. The most significant demands of the health care insurgents were the removal of the Mental Health Center's

[24] Ibid., pp. 511–12.
[25] Ibid., p. 508.
[26] *The New York Times*, March 6, 1969. Information on Lincoln Hospital is derived from newspaper reports and various issues of the *Health/PAC Bulletin*.

director and associate directors, the establishment of a policy planning and review board, and the development of "a meaningful community board with significant decision-making power and responsibilities over the administration and policies of Lincoln Hospital and L.H.M.H.S. [Lincoln Hospital Mental Health Service]." [27]

The movement at Lincoln Hospital to achieve community and worker control of the facility spread from the mental health center to encompass many of the hospital's services.[28] Since 1969 leadership of the movement has rested largely with the Health Revolutionary Unity Movement (HRUM), a citywide organization of black and Latin health workers, and the Think Lincoln Committee, a coalition of white, nonwhite, professional and nonprofessional Lincoln Hospital workers in alliance with community activists, including some South Bronx street gangs. The Young Lords, a professed revolutionary organization of Puerto Ricans, was also active in the Lincoln controversies. The official Community Advisory Board to the hospital, established in 1967, has had only momentary flurries of activity. In 1970, however, it was successful in forcing the city's Hospital Department to select its own candidate, a Puerto Rican gynecologist, as administrator of the hospital.

The Think Lincoln Committee, formed in 1970, initiated a complaint table in the emergency room where patients and workers registered grievances about hospital conditions.[29] During 1970 two sit-ins in administrative offices led to the granting of additional services demanded by community members—a diagnostic clinic and a methadone treatment center. The latter has been entirely run and staffed by community residents. Pressure from radical interns and residents, who formed the Pediatrics Collective, resulted in the replacement of the chief of pediatrics by a Puerto Rican. The chief of the obstetrics-gynecology department was also forced to resign following a furor over the death of a patient during a therapeutic abortion.

The experience of the Pediatrics Collective reveals some of the problems of a commitment by middle-class whites to serve the poor. The nature of these problems is reflected in the following comment from the *Health/PAC Bulletin*, the newsletter of a group aiming at health care reform. Although the report is not written by a detached observer, the underlying bases for conflict are clearly shown:

The Collective has had to face the crucial issue of the role of white professionals in a third world community. An HRUM member has said, "Their role is to serve the

---

[27] Quoted in Barbara and John Ehrenreich, *The American Health Empire*, Report from the Health Policy Advisory Center (Health-PAC) (New York: Random House, 1970), p. 260.

[28] *The New York Times*, December 21, 1970.

[29] *The New York Times*, July 29, 1970; July 30, 1970. Such complaint tables have often been used as a mobilizing device in controversies over institutional control. Thus, the establishment of a complaint table manned by parents in George Washington High School in Manhattan precipitated a sometimes violent clash over rights of parents and teachers. (See New York Civil Liberties Union, "A Report on the Tensions at George Washington High School," mimeo, April, 1970). In New Brunswick, New Jersey, the legitimization of a complaint table was part of a formal settlement between community groups and the school system.

people with their technical skills in a human way. We know what class they're coming from. They must understand that they are the weakest link." The response from the Collective, not unlike other white movement groups, has been the politics of guilt and the politics of adventurism. Both arise out of the Collective's inability to work out a self-conscious definition of their role. A guilt response has often resulted in the group's virtually unquestioning support of HRUM. The Collective has not acted as an autonomous unit, with a unified political perspective, that should be dealt with on its own terms. The other response is to "organize the community," which arises out of a romantic notion about the medical savior who leads other people's struggles; or the voyeuristic tendency that defines a "total politic" as "rapping with the Lords." [30]

In health as in education, professional efforts to improve services to the poor precipitated community-based movements to take over the administration of such services. Health care has traditionally been the public service most insulated from popular control. The expertise associated with the medical profession is particularly inaccessible to the layman; while many might doubt a strong correlation between good teaching and credentials in education, few would claim that amateurs should perform surgery. The efforts of community groups to oversee medical practices have thus forced a redefinition of certain aspects of medical services as requiring different kinds of competence from that learned in medical or nursing school. Similar efforts at redefinition have been central to all the movements aimed at changing control of public service bureaucracies.

OPPOSITIONIST GROUPS

The seemingly most common and most successful form of urban political movement has involved primarily negative objectives. Virtually every city has seen the development of groups responding to the threat of residential demolition presented by urban renewal, highway building, or institutional expansion. The effectiveness of these groups was such that urban renewal projects involving the razing of large tracts have virtually ceased, and plans to build the remaining links of the interstate highway system through urban areas were halted in many places. Where urban renewal programs did continue, they had to take into account the potential mobilization of neighborhood residents. [31]

Although single-issue organizations lose their reason for existence when the issue is settled, some of the urban renewal groups had considerable longevity as negotiations over renewal programs continued for a period of years. The Cooper Square Development Committee (CSDC) in New York

---

[30] Susan Reverby and Marsha Handelman, "Emancipation of Lincoln," *Health/PAC Bulletin*, XXXVII, January, 1972, 15–16.

[31] See James Q. Wilson, "Planning and Politics: Citizen Participation in Urban Renewal," in *Urban Renewal*, ed. James Q. Wilson (Cambridge: M.I.T. Press, 1966), pp. 407–21; James C. Davies, III, *Neighborhood Groups and Urban Renewal* (New York: Columbia University Press, 1966), Chap. 9.

City, which functioned for more than eleven years, is an example.[32]

The Cooper Square area, located on Manhattan's lower East Side, houses a heterogeneous population including European ethnic groups, blacks, Puerto Ricans, aged derelicts, and bohemians. In 1961 the average income per household was $4,000, and 93 percent of the families in the area were eligible for public housing.[33] Controversy over the fate of this neighborhood began in 1956 when the New York City Ad Hoc Slum Clearance Committee drew up a plan that would clear a twelve-block area for the purpose of constructing 2,900 units of middle-income housing. The implementation of these proposals would have displaced 2,400 tenants, 450 furnished room occupants, 4,000 beds used by homeless men, and over 500 businesses. The CSDC was formed in order to protest the proposal.

Early in 1960 the CSDC met with an assistant to the Mayor, who declared that if the area's residents disliked the city's proposals, they should formulate their own renewal plan. The CSDC accepted the challenge, and with the assistance of some foundation grants hired a professional planner, Walter Thabit. Many community meetings and discussions were held, and subcommittes consisting of artists, businessmen, and tenants were formed to evaluate different proposals and renewal alternatives. Eventually an alternate plan for physical renewal of the area with minimum displacement of residents was produced and endorsed by the head of the City Planning Commission.

Despite promises from the city to adhere to the alternate plan, the CSDC received little cooperation from the government. In 1963 New York revealed a new renewal plan for the Saint Mark's-Cooper Square area. Linking the two areas made impossible the CSDC strategy for staged relocation. It was not until 1966, after a sit-in in the office of the Housing and Redevelopment Board, that the Committee managed to get the two districts separated. This success was, however, followed by a series of new setbacks.

Although he supported CSDC when he was campaigning for mayor in 1966, after the election John Lindsay announced the indefinite delay of projects outside of the three core areas of the South Bronx, East Harlem, and Central Brooklyn. In 1968 the Committee finally received a commitment from the city that renewal activity would begin in the Cooper Square area, but a variety of obstacles delayed actual implementation. In the meanwhile the Committee led battles against the rezoning of Third Avenue for luxury housing and staged rallies and protests to gain for itself the planning funds to which it was entitled as the official neighborhood renewal organization. It was not until 1970, however, that there were even the beginnings of progress in renewing the area.

[32] The material on Cooper Square presented here is drawn from David Listokin, "Community Organization: An Evaluation of a Strategy for Social Change," unpublished seminar paper, Rutgers University, Department of Urban Planning and Policy Development, January, 1971. Other cases of groups spawned by urban renewal are described in Davies, *Neighborhood Groups and Urban Renewal*; and Peter H. Rossi and Robert A. Dentler, *The Politics of Urban Renewal* (New York: Free Press, 1961).

[33] Nathan Leventhal, "Citizen Participation in Urban Renewal," *Columbia Law Review*, March, 1966, p. 512.

While the Cooper Square Committee could claim only a modest achievement in the execution of the alternate plan, it did attain almost total victory in blocking area redevelopment opposed by residents. Several factors account for its gains and losses. First, the CSDC followed a coalition strategy and obtained the support of the diverse groups inhabiting the area. It avoided identification with any single element in the community. The Committee was also successful in gaining the support of groups outside the immediate community. It received financial assistance from foundations and sympathy from key members of the city bureaucracy.

Second, the Committee capitalized on unrelated issues in order to maintain its constituency and insure neighborhood loyalty. It served as a local source of information concerning tenants' rights and eligibility requirements for welfare and medical benefits. It became involved in rent strikes and demonstrations for park and recreational facilities. Like other neighborhood organizations the Committee performed many of the functions of the traditional political machine—it assisted residents in dealing with the city bureaucracy in exchange for their support. In return community members responded positively to calls for "bodies" to participate in the various demonstrations, protests, and sit-ins sponsored by the Committee.

Third, the Committee had resources of expertise. Some of its members were experienced in community organization and in dealing with the city bureaucracy. The services of the professional planner, Walter Thabit, were especially important. The city could not easily dismiss the alternate plan as utopian or technically imcompetent.

Yet, despite these assets, the victory of the Cooper Square Committee was limited and primarily negative. For this reason Frances Piven saw Cooper Square as an object lesson in the futility of advocacy planning:

After ten years of arduous effort on the part of an extraordinary neighborhood group, a small portion of the Alternate Plan had been given formal sanction even though that portion was still far from implementation. The chief accomplishment was that the neighborhood had stopped the early threat of renewal. As Walter Thabit said sourly when it was all over, "protest without planning could have done as much." [34]

Ironically, although the alternate plan provided a positive program around which residents could mobilize, its principal function was the solidification of protest rather than the attainment of its stated ends. Whether "protest without planning" would have worked is, however, an open question. The plan was of strategic importance, both for mobilizing the neighborhood and for impressing city hall. It lent legitimacy to the effort, giving the Cooper Square spokesmen a positive image both for their constituency and outside it.

The greater power of poor people's groups—or for that matter, of higher status groups—to block action than to initiate it has roots in both the character of specifically American political structures and in general aspects

[34] Frances Fox Piven, "Whom Does the Advocate Planner Serve?" in *The View from Below: Urban Politics and Social Policy,* eds. Susan S. Fainstein and Norman I. Fainstein (Boston: Little, Brown, 1972), pp. 231–32.

of institutional behavior. The checks and balances which operate at every level of American government mean that there are usually a number of structural points where the intervention of veto groups can effectively halt policy. Qualities of inertia typical of all bureaucratic bodies create a force conserving the status quo, which favors those groups attempting to impede action. Moreover, it is usually easier to mobilize a following against a particular policy whose negative impacts are clear and immediate than for a policy the effects of which cannot be confidently predicted.

These factors which favor groups seeking to protect the status quo also militate against organizations desiring change. Checks and balances create endless obstacles to implementation of programs, result in the inability of governmental officials to make meaningful commitments, and permit them to excuse their unwillingness to act. Bureaucratic inertia results in lengthy delay and the dissipation of energies. The lack of immediate benefits makes their value appear low relative to the costs of attempting to achieve them.

In the case of urban renewal, as in health, opposition to programs arose in reaction to policies being followed by public institutions. In both cases the devices provided under various federal programs for insuring at least minimal citizen participation created pressure points for local organizations. The neighborhood councils established according to federal urban renewal legislation encompassed community elements opposed to large-scale renewal and, like the poverty councils, often became the basis for general community activism. They also—and one can see this ambiguity everywhere—siphoned off tension, co-opted leaders, and used up energies. For this reason Piven has argued that "involving local groups in elaborate planning procedures is to guide them into a narrowly circumscribed form of political action, and precisely that form for which they are least equipped." [35] Even movements which began entirely in conflict with local governments were, when they incorporated positive goals, susceptible to the same temptations as movements which arose directly out of an official mandate.

TENANTS MOVEMENTS

Opposition to landlords has proved to be a frequent basis for the development of poor people's organizations. The most common form of action against landlords, either public housing authorities or private firms, has been the rent strike directed at obtaining improvements in maintenance or lower rents. While most rent strikes have been short-lived, they have provided a basis for solidarity among their participants and their possibility constitutes a new parameter of the real estate market of the ghetto.[36]

[35] Ibid., p. 232.
[36] For case studies of rent strikes see Michael Lipsky, *Protest in City Politics* (Skokie: Rand McNally, 1970); Harry Brill, *Why Organizers Fail*; The Black Research and Development Foundation, Inc.—MBA Research Team, "The South End Tenants Council" (Boston: Intercollegiate Case Clearing House, 1969). See also Alan S. Oser, "Rent Strikes Grow Widespread in the South Bronx," *The New York Times*, March 19, 1972, Real Estate, Sec. 8.

Squatters movements occur when vacant or partially vacant apartment buildings are taken over by non-rent-paying tenants. Their continuation seemingly depends on the fear by civil authorities that large-scale eviction proceedings will provoke direct reprisals, adverse publicity, or civil disturbances. The effort of maintaining the building requires a high degree of organization among the squatters. Thus, individuals who have no general political program but are only concerned with keeping a roof over their heads become involved in illegal organizational activities, thereby growing increasingly politicized and militant.

The history of a successful squatters group in the Morningside Heights section of Manhattan presents an example of a movement with no official ties.[37] Even this organization, however, did have access to skilled staff workers and some outside funding. The Morningside Squatters (or "Keep the Faith Tenants Organization") were organized by five Columbia University students working for the Columbia Community Service Council as urban summer interns under a federally funded program. The ostensible mission of the Council, which occupied a University-owned office rent-free, was to provide services such as tutoring, prison work, legal help, etc. The five students became involved with the squatters movement when a hold-out tenant of a building slated for demolition appealed to the Columbia group for help. The students, who included two Cubans in their number, made up a list of families desiring to move into vacant buildings as well as the names of skilled workers willing to assist in making the buildings habitable. They acquired most of the names in both categories from other squatters groups.

The building in question and a neighboring one were part of a group of six structures which Morningside House, Inc., an Episcopal institution, wished to demolish so as to build a home for the aged. These were sound, low-rent structures; by the time of the move-in, however, all but three tenants had been relocated, and demolition had begun. The projected occupants of the old age home were to be, with a few exceptions, white Episcopalians; the original occupants of the buildings were also white. None of the squatters was among the original tenants of the buildings. The squatters were entirely impoverished nonwhites, with the largest proportion Spanish-speaking black Dominicans and the remainder chiefly Puerto Rican. Half were on welfare.

With the assistance of the Columbia students, who rented moving vans on their behalf, the squatters moved into the two, tinned-up buildings.[38] Later a third building was also taken over. Although the organizers were threatened with long jail terms under "breaking and entering" (rather than "trespassing") charges, no effort was made to remove the squatters from the buildings nor to indict any of the leaders. Many local community associations, leading Democratic Party figures, and the borough president expressed verbal support for the squatters.

The move-in was followed by daily meetings on the steps of the Episcopal Cathedral of Saint John the Divine. These meetings, conducted in

---

[37] This case is developed from interviews with participants and newspaper articles.

[38] See *The New York Times*, July 27, 1970.

Spanish, were attended by a large proportion of the 83 squatter families; many of the meetings, which made decisions concerning maintenance, trash collection, and other building management questions, were led by the two Spanish-speaking Columbia students. Eventually the squatters established a delegate organization, although major decisions continued to be made in well-attended mass meetings.

More than two years after the squatters moved in, the buildings remained fully occupied. Half of the 1972 tenants had been there since the beginning. An article in the Columbia University newspaper stated:

The area in and around the building was cleaned, and the residents now live under fairly normal conditions. . . . The squatters claim excellent security for the buildings, and a spokesman for the 26th Precinct of the New York City Police Department said there are 'no drugs, no crime, and no problems of cooperation with us.' [39]

The most serious problems faced by the squatters, beyond that of poverty of resources, were factionalism and mutual distrust. These were exacerbated temporarily during the summer of 1971 when some white, middle-class Latin students, who had not been part of the original Columbia group, participated in the endeavor. By 1972, however, problems of internal solidarity seemed to have been settled. Leadership of the squatters devolved from the Columbia students to lower-class residents of the buildings, who occasionally continued to call on the Columbia Community Service Council for such support functions as mimeographing press releases. Except for an initial contribution of $2,000 for food from the West Side Community Corporation and the eventual provision by the Episcopal Church of $30,000 to replace the boilers destroyed by wreckers, the squatters financed building maintenance themselves through fund-raising activities and payments in lieu of rent.

The success of the squatters in maintaining their hold on the buildings resulted only partly from their own internal cohesiveness and determination. They benefited also from splits within their opposition. A group called Episcopalians for the Poor was instrumental in their obtaining heat for the buildings. A new Episcopal bishop was also sympathetic. The president of Morningside House, Inc. backed down from an initially intransigent position to a seemingly passive one. In 1971 he was quoted as saying that while he opposed the use of police force to vacate the buildings, "I won't say I won't do it if it becomes necessary." [40] Later that year he stated that he would not call in the police, although he would seek a civil court order to remove the squatters.[41] By late 1972 Morningside House had apparently dropped all plans for construction on the site and was intending no legal action against the squatters.[42] Unquestionably the socially liberal Episcopal Church was an easier target than a private owner or even the city.

[39] *Columbia Daily Spectator*, September 14, 1972.

[40] *Columbia Daily Spectator*, February 11, 1971.

[41] *New York Post*, July 24, 1971.

[42] *Columbia Daily Spectator*, September 14, 1972.

The effort to maintain control of the buildings led to an increased politicization of the squatters. The original group contained a number of people with some political experience and a relatively militant consciousness developed through political battles in the Dominican Republic. According to the Columbia organizers, militance became more widespread during the months following the move-in as many of the squatters began to attribute their personal indigence to general political causes. The students felt that they were able to withdraw from an active role in the organization because of the increased political sophistication of the lower-class members. While the Morningside Squatters as a group mainly focused on activities within the buildings, some individuals among them have taken increasingly large roles in the general political scene of the area.

The Morningside Squatters represent the most homogeneously poor grass-roots organization we have examined. Even they, however, had access to some outside resources. While the amount of aid they received was not large, it was crucial both in timing and quality. Without the initial staff work of the Columbia student organizers, who in turn were available because of federal funding, there would have been no squatters movement at all. Contributions of labor from plumbers and electricians were essential for making the buildings usable, and without the provision of a heating plant by the Church, it is unlikely that the residents could have withstood two winters. By 1972 the organization had become largely self-sufficient and self-perpetuating; without outside organizing skill at the beginning, however, there would have been no basis from which it could have developed.

SERVICE-ORIENTED ORGANIZATIONS

A great variety of service-providing organizations have developed in urban ghettoes in the last decade. Many of these are direct offsprings of federal programs.[43] In addition, a number of unofficial groups have attempted to politicize their publics through the provision of services. These groups have sought to use benefits to individuals as vehicles for enticing people to listen to their message, attempting to weld a coherent group out of those who initially came for help or companionship. Even groups which had primarily an action orientation like the Cooper Square Association or the various community control organizations devoted considerable time and effort to assisting individuals with housing or welfare problems and to providing a meeting place for social activities.

The obvious drawback to using services as the principal device for mobilizing and maintaining a constituency is that the organization will end up entirely as a social service agency rather than a force for social change.

---

[43] As we noted earlier, most of the federally sponsored organizations have restricted themselves to service functions.

Harold Weissman's observations on the Mobilization for Youth (MFY)[44] experience have proved generally true:

Low-income organizations, like organizations of any other group of people, can be stabilized by social activities or by providing social services to members and others, but such stability will not necessarily lead to social action. . . . The provision of individual services to members of an organization by the staff is extremely time-consuming. . . .[45]

There is a plethora of inner-city organizations exemplifying the characteristics described by Weissman. They extend from groups which are almost purely social or service-providing to others which profess a radical ideology and sporadically involve themselves in political issues. In this section we will look briefly at several such groups.

the community
protection organization

The Community Protection Organization (CPO), located in the Bedford-Stuyvesant section of Brooklyn, was established in 1970 primarily to rid the neighborhood of drug traffic.[46] Its director cited police negligence as the reason for the establishment of the CPO, which operated three-man patrols of volunteers. Both foot and car patrols were used, and some men carried walkie-talkies. About fifty men served on patrols during an average day and 150 at night. The director was ambivalent as to whether the organization represented an attempt to establish a community-controlled police force:

We aren't hung up on usurping police power. The community belongs to us and we're tired of the drug problem and are dealing with it. They [the police] have been derelict in their duty, especially since they don't live in this area. I don't think they would tolerate the drug problem in their own areas. I don't think the policeman who lives in this area could turn his head when there's a danger of his own kids becoming narcotized.

The CPO is an example of a proliferating type of self-help, service-providing organization. Organizations offering protection to community residents (sometimes called vigilante groups) have sprung up in many big cities in response to street crime and drugs. As was the case of the CPO, many have aroused a high level of membership activism and commitment. Mainly, activity has been directed specifically at the policing function. The highly

---

[44] MFY was a program in New York's Lower East Side which was one of the experimental precursors of the War on Poverty.

[45] Harold H. Weissman, "Problems in Maintaining Stability in Low-Income Social Action Organizations," in *Community Development in the Mobilization for Youth Experience*, ed. Harold H. Weissman (New York: Association Press, 1969), pp. 174–75.

[46] Information on the CPO was provided by Gary Redish and is based mainly on interviews with the executive director of the organization.

visible political use made of a white group headed by Assemblyman Anthony Imperiale in the North Ward of Newark and the election of the CPO's executive director to the New York State Senate, however, demonstrate the political potential of such organizations.

escuela

This Puerto Rican group in New Brunswick, New Jersey, illustrates the difficulty of maintaining a social action orientation in a service organization.[47] Escuela had the dual objective of acting as a social work agency on behalf of the Spanish-speaking community and working as a catalyst for Puerto Rican consciousness and representation. It was provided with free quarters by a church; the New Brunswick Community Development Corporation, a poverty agency, donated office equipment. The core of Escuela was a volunteer staff which varied at times from one to six.

Among Escuela's activities were the development of a Spanish language high school equivalency program, support of a nonwhite boycott of the high school through the provision of a meeting place and counselling for striking students, and the establishment of a forum where Puerto Rican community leaders could meet with each other. Although Escuela became known to some community members who took advantage of its services or who participated in the sewing group it sponsored, it had relatively little impact upon the political awareness of the Puerto Rican community as a whole.

The provision of services to individuals took up most of the staff's time. Because the organization had few resources, even in this capacity its effectiveness was limited. The desire of the staff to maintain the organization's independence from official sponsorship meant that its chief asset was the time and energy of volunteers. The following excerpt from the report of a Puerto Rican student volunteer gives a picture of Escuela's operations:

My first impression of the charitable agency occurred when I knocked on the door of Escuela and was led through a dusty room towards the back of the basement. . . . A young Spanish male [Ramon] around the age of 20 was trying to introduce me to this gentleman sitting on the desk talking to someone on the phone and at the same time trying to listen to two middle-age Spanish ladies.

Ramon introduced me to the gentleman who was the head of the agency, a college instructor named José Lopez. He asked me to wait for a few minutes while he talked with the two ladies. I sat down on a sofa and listened to the two Spanish ladies tell of their misfortune with the New Jersey Welfare Department. One of the ladies had recently moved to New Jersey from New York State where she was receiving welfare assistance. She had moved to New Jersey without notifying the Welfare Department that she had moved. When she arrived in New Jersey she applied for welfare assistance for herself and her three sons. Her application was accepted, and she was to receive $340. Because she had not notified the Welfare Department in New York that she had moved, they had continued to send a check to her apartment in New York.

[47] Information on Escuela is drawn from conversations with and unpublished term papers by Urbano Venero and José Colon (Livingston College, Rutgers University, May, 1972). Mr. Venero and Mr. Colon both worked as volunteers at Escuela.

The landlord of the building her apartment was in was confiscating the checks and cashing them. The New York Welfare Department notified the New Jersey Welfare Department of the incident occurring with one of their welfare recipients. The New Jersey Welfare Department cancelled the assistance given to the lady; the reason they gave for the cancellation was that the lady had failed to notify the New York Welfare Department that she had moved. The lady came to Escuela to find if something could be done to get the assistance of welfare renewed.

Mr. Lopez, the head of Escuela, suggested to the lady that he would call the Welfare Department and talk to someone that he knew and the problem would be solved. He called the Welfare Department and talked with one of the caseworkers for two minutes, hung up the phone and said to the lady that she was to go down to the welfare office and she would be taken care of. The two ladies left the building with a smile and expecting cooperation from the Welfare Department. As soon as the two ladies had left, we began to talk and during the conversation he told me that the lady would be back tomorrow because she would not get any cooperation.[48]

Escuela represented the attempt of an independent organization to use a service approach in order to create community consciousness. The need of the Spanish-speaking community in New Brunswick for an intermediary seemed apparent, since many of its members were unable even to communicate with public officials. The effort of providing services, however, proved distracting for the staff. While middle-class Puerto Ricans who served Escuela as voluntary personnel became more militant politically as a result of participation in the organization, its effect as an agent of political socialization on the larger community was minimal.

youth organizations
in elizabeth

Two youth organizations with somewhat overlapping membership in Elizabeth, New Jersey, illustrate again the tension between services and activism.[49] Representative Youth of Elizabeth (RYE) consisted of politically conscious high school juniors and seniors who had been influenced by doctrines of black power but were uncertain of their specific social and political goals. Initiated during the school year 1966–67, it had a membership of between thirty and forty. RYE conducted a number of workshops on subjects such as black power, political goals, and the black community of Elizabeth. It became actively involved with school politics when it confronted the Board of Education over its decision to fire a teacher of Afro-American studies. While the group failed in its objective, this incident constituted the first confrontation between black students and school officials in Elizabeth, setting a frequently repeated pattern of interaction.

Although for a brief period RYE achieved a high level of mobilization around racial issues, interest in it quickly dissipated. Many active students

[48] Report of José Colon.

[49] Information on the Elizabeth organizations is taken from Allen Pernell, "The Success and Failure of Three Black Organizations in Elizabeth," unpublished term paper (Livingston College, Rutgers University, May, 1972). Mr. Pernell had participated in the organizations.

graduated; some took up other interests; and no new mobilizing issue arose. In contrast, another youth group, the Youth Leadership Club (YLC), founded simultaneously by black boys in Elizabeth, remained in existence. YLC unlike RYE was not geared to open conflict. It assisted members with college applications, performed the functions of traditional boys' clubs in neighborhood improvement, brought in public speakers, and provided a meeting place. All members were given organizational responsibilities, and devices were established for rapidly integrating new members into the organization so that the departure of a graduating class did not affect its stability.

The club's disavowal of overt political activity contributed to its longevity while detracting from its ability to attain collective social goals:

Probably most important the organization didn't tackle community problems such as school tensions in a leadership capacity as RYE did. For many people outside the organization this is a major fault. The Youth Leadership Club hasn't taken sole leadership of community issues. They have united with other black organizations and leaders over the last school issue. I believe it should be realized that YLC wasn't a trouble-seeking organization. By this I mean that YLC didn't attempt to solve all the community's problems or bring them to light at the expense of their organization becoming divided. This is the major reason why the club has continued to exist. Though the members were politically aware, they were not conscious enough to alleviate the problems of the community.[50]

Service organizations in their manifold activities of advocacy on behalf of individuals against bureaucratic offices, assistance with landlords or college admissions, and provision of a friendly local meeting place resemble the old-time ward organizations. They are not wholly movement organizations, but they sometimes perform functions of political socialization and provide a ready made communications network within the ghetto. Frequently individuals who have learned organizational skills in such a setting will become politically active under the auspices of other groups. Occasionally when a community issue arises, the service organization will become actively involved. Such organizations, when they declare aims of group power, represent the outmost limits of the phenomena we have classified as urban political movements.

ATTRIBUTES OF URBAN POLITICAL MOVEMENTS

The kinds of urban political movements we have described apparently exist in most major American cities. Many have brief lives and pass unrecorded; others function as movements only while in a transitional state and end up becoming established organizations. Their only lasting impact may have been their effect on the consciousness of a few members or on the attitudes of

[50] Ibid.

ublic decision makers. Even in cities like New York where there have been a great number of such organizations, the total number of participants in them has been small.

While only the haziest guesses can be made concerning the absolute strength of urban political movements, one can still assert that their appearance demonstrates a qualitative change in the nature of urban politics. For they represent the first grass-roots political organizations in lower-class areas since the political machine. Thus, the 1960s saw the growth of a political infrastructure in the ghetto where none existed before. Unlike the machine these movements have an ideological basis; they thus represent the first important effort by poor communities to organize on the basis of class or race solidarity.

Urban political movements have originated in both public programs and private ambitions. Even, however, where the movement was not organized as part of an official program such as the War on Poverty, it often derived from governmental activities. The example of the Morningside Squatters, who received staff assistance from students on a federal payroll and legal aid from Poverty Program lawyers, is a case in point. There seems little question but that governmental initiatives toward remedying the condition of the poor have contributed directly to the growth of militant organization among them.

While the organizations discussed here have had as their principal constituency disadvantaged minorities, they have not necessarily restricted their membership to this group. Most of the movements had only a small active membership, consisting of staff plus occupants of positions on governing councils. In many cases these activists were middle class, and some were white. In addition to the activists, there was usually an inactive group of adherents who could be called upon when there was a need for "bodies" to picket city hall or pack a meeting. These were organizations of the masses, but they were not mass organizations.

Urban political movements gain their significance primarily through their multiplicity. Although no organization is very big, the existence of a multitude of groups demanding power for the residents of inner-city areas adds up to a general pressure for decentralization of power. The prevalence of community groups calling on ghetto residents to unite has both raised the group consciousness of their publics and made officials and local corporations aware that they are being monitored by volatile community elements. The increase in the number of groups with similar goals, however, has not resulted in local or nationwide coalitions of poor people's groups. While representatives of such groups occasionally convene, and activists in a single city come to know each other and often move from one group to another, there are few formal links and a low level of communication among the various urban political movements. The impetus to action seems to spread more by contagion arising from an awareness of the efforts of others than by design.

Because urban movements are concerned with power and the distribution of benefits, they should be classified as political. Nonetheless, they operate largely outside the party, which has been the traditional locus of political competition. While there are close links between the Democratic Party and a number of Model Cities or OEO sponsored organizations, neither the more militant groups springing from these programs nor the various community control, housing, or oppositionist groups have operated as party branches. Participants in elective politics have rarely taken an active role in these organizations, although individual congressmen or representatives may have endorsed their positions, spoken at movement-initiated rallies, or, as in the case of the movement for community control of education in New York City, sponsored legislation on their behalf.[51]

Movement organizations range from being programmatically specific, i.e., being concerned with one issue area such as education or housing, to being generally concerned with all community issues. Participants in specialized organizations report a tendency toward a broadening of scope, so that housing organizations, for example, inevitably become involved in welfare and school matters. Paradoxically, organizations which establish overall involvement as their initial goal seem to founder; a number of writers have commented on the difficulty of establishing block or neighborhood organizations with the general goal of community power.[52] The report of a community organizer quoted by Ralph Kramer sums up the problems:

Only a few people need jobs, not everyone has personal complaints about the school or trouble with his landlord. In the search for an issue on which everyone can agree and take action they end up with the lowest common denominator. Street cleaning or the need for a stop light are not the most pressing problems poor people face but they are the problems that face everyone in the neighborhood: poor and non-poor alike. That is why the group turns to them as issues. It is at this point that the poor start dropping out.[53]

The nature of the organization's objectives affects the method by which it seeks to attract a following. Organizations which aim at stopping governmental activity like urban renewal spring up in response to the official initiative and devote themselves to protest activities such as marches, rallies, picketing, or sit-ins. Other groups which are seeking to initiate positive programs themselves do not have highly focused community anger from which to build and must either capitalize on an issue or offer some form of activity in addition to protest. The possibilities are several: they may provide services to needy individuals; they may seek outside sources of funding so as

[51] The leader of the drive in the New York State Legislature for a strong bill on community control of schools was State Legislator Jerome Kretchmer, who later became head of the Environmental Protection Agency in the Lindsay administration and a Democratic aspirant for mayor.

[52] See Ralph M. Kramer, *Participation of the Poor* (Englewood Cliffs, N.J.: Prentice-Hall, © 1969), pp. 226–31; Walter Gove and Herbert Costner, "Organizing the Poor: An Evaluation of a Strategy," in *Planned Social Intervention*, ed. Zurcher and Bonjean, pp. 275–88; Peter Marris and Martin Rein, *The Dilemmas of Social Reform*, 2d ed. (Chicago: Aldine, 1973), p. 186.

[53] "Report on Component 12 Neighborhood Organization to Oakland Economic Development Council," Council of Social Planning, Oakland Area, Report No. 88, December, 1966, quoted in Kramer, *Participation of the Poor*, p. 228.

to support a salaried staff, using it to establish a stable base and make a sustained effort at ideological conversion; and they may act as advocates in negotiations with public officials in the hopes of achieving group gains which will insure constituency loyalty.

The character of urban movements is also affected by the nature of their targets. These may be bureaucratic, as in the cases of the movements for community control of health and education; overtly political, as in West Oakland Model Cities; or private, as in the cases of some rent strikes and squatters movements. The most vulnerable targets—the example of the squatters and the Episcopal Church is notable—are those most sympathetic to the objectives of the movements. This produces the ironical result of making enemies of potential allies:

The primary urban activity since late 1967 has been a struggle for the division and control of what already exists. Although one may argue that this is a rational response if one believes there is no hope for new social legislation, it has the notable drawback of creating political divisions which even further diminish the likelihood of such legislation. The greatest division of this kind has occurred between Negroes and white liberals. . . . In a sense, the social welfare bureaucracies—schools, welfare, antipoverty programs—were the least strategic places to attack. They have, after all, been among the most liberal institutions, they have a common interest with blacks in the expansion of social-welfare legislation, and they are typically populated by whites who are noticeably more liberal than the average.[54]

While the costs of attacking "liberal" institutions may be high, their salience to the lives of ghetto inhabitants is great; Congress or big business might be more important causative factors in the situation of the poor, but they are much less visible and much less the immediate creators of people's misery than the schools, hospitals, and welfare offices. The latter, therefore, become the foci of attack, and the movements develop an ideology to counter the Progressive ideology which supports these institutions. This is apparent in both the general black power or community power cast of movement programs and in their more specific aims. The concepts of community control and group identity fly directly in the face of the universalistic norms of Progressivism.[55] The opposition by the West Oakland Model Cities Council to selection of political representatives on an at-large basis and its unwillingness to accept the neutrality of the city manager; the attack by proponents of community control of education on civil service procedures for the selection of teachers and principals; the demands by nonprofessional hospital personnel for an authoritative voice in the administration of health services; all were programs which evolved out of opposition to the liberal (Progressive) institutions which provide public services.

The posture of opposition to Progressivism has shaped the ideology of

---

[54] David K. Cohen, "The Price of Community Control," *Commentary*, XLVIII, July, 1969, 29–30.

[55] See Leonard J. Fein, "Community Schools and Social Theory: The Limits of Universalism," in *Community Control of Schools*, ed. Henry M. Levin (Washington, D.C.: Brookings Institution, 1970), pp. 76–99.

urban political movements just as opposition to the machine affected the Progressive ideology. While urban political movements have largely not possessed a well-developed, coherent political analysis, they have all tended to act from a common premise and to share certain goals. Underlying their programs is the premise that the process of representation in American cities is biased in a way that prevents the poor and the nonwhite from acquiring their proportionate share of power and benefits. The acquisition of benefits ranging from good education or health care to jobs and contracts is seen as dependent upon the occupation of positions of power by representatives of these groups. Present lack of power is attributable to a variety of sources: racism; lack of wealth and education—themselves a product as well as a source of powerlessness; and a political system which inhibits minorities from obtaining political or bureaucratic office. The overall common goals of the movements thus become the acquisition of institutional power so as to stymie the operation of racism, improve the delivery of services, and directly provide benefits such as jobs and contracts. Achieving these objectives requires changing the processes of selection for official positions so that other criteria are employed besides majority support within a large geographic area or credentials based on educational achievement and seniority. These criteria are the legacy of Progressivism, and thus the ideology of urban political movements involves an attack on the still widely held values underlying the Progressive movement.

The emphasis on seeking institutional power forces the movements to center their attacks on "liberal" institutions because it is only here that the possibility of power is realistic. The poor and the black can never hope to control Congress or the economy; they can succeed in controlling municipal governments or, where they are a citywide minority, particular social welfare institutions or geographic areas within the city. Both the social base of the movements in individual communities and the local nature of their adversaries combine to make the attempts at gaining power small-scale and piecemeal.

The general political importance of urban political movements therefore depends on the accumulation of numerous small successes. The constituency that any particular movement can mobilize is small and its effectiveness limited. Nevertheless the awareness of government and business that they are being monitored and the increasing influence of the previously excluded within the structure of municipal government can lead to a change in the overall distribution of power and benefits.

the joan of arc planning/governing board: a case of organizational disintegration

3

Urban political movements attempt to use the resources of numbers and organization in order to realize the goals of their participants. These resources are, however, necessarily unstable. They are swelled by success, diminished by failure. Movements are always in process of becoming either more or less powerful. In this and the next two chapters we examine the interaction between particular movements and the forces impinging on them so as to discover the factors shaping their development. We shall later generalize from these case studies in order to identify what seem to be typical dilemmas and strategies. We also realize, however, that in each of these cases a number of determining events are idiosyncratic or fortuitous. This fact limits the extent to which one can make general inferences from the cases. On the other hand, the key role of historical accident is in itself significant. We continue to be impressed by the importance of particular individuals occupying crucial positions and the way in which extraneous forces may have a significant, uncalculated impact in local arenas.

The history of the Joan of Arc (JOA) Planning/Governing Board illustrates the many difficulties which beset grass-roots organizations in their attempts to form viable political movements. The Joan of Arc Board consisted of a group of residents of Manhattan's West Side who felt that their neighborhood schools would improve in quality only if "the community" could control educational governance. Despite the willingness of members to devote much time and effort to their cause and the existence of general community support for educational change and "community control" of schools, the Board was never able to activate an effective constituency behind its demands. During the period 1968–69 the Board, first on its own then with the assistance of a paid staff, tried to back its demands on the school system with the threat of an activated community pressing for drastic action. But it could not produce a convincing display of mass mobilization. Rather, it was subject to a declining degree of community interest, dissension among the small number of community members who remained concerned with school issues, and tension between itself and its staff.

While we have no hard data to support this assertion, our feeling is that the JOA Board was quite typical of efforts at urban political mobilization in its small size and short life. Joan of Arc achieved few of its long-range goals, but it did leave some mark on the educational institutions of its locale. In narrating its history we shall emphasize the kinds of people who became involved with the organization; the structural and personal limitations on action; the strategic problems facing the Board; and the political conscious-ness of the Board, its supporters, and its detractors. Our purpose is to uncover the dynamics of a locally based political movement by examining the sources of its support, the causes of its failures, and the perceptions which led different individuals to join a movement directed at institutional change.

FORMATION OF THE
GOVERNING BOARD

The Joan of Arc Board was one of a number of organizations involved in the movement for community control of schools in New York City during the end of the 1960s. As such it was a constituent element in what proved to be one of the most politically divisive and consequential episodes to affect the city's governmental structure during the decade (see Chapter Two for a description of the citywide movement). Its birth out of a citywide experiment initiated by the central Board of Education and its participation in the general movement, did not, however, mean that it operated largely in concert with other groups. Rather, it was an independent entity whose potential achieve-ments depended primarily on its ability to mobilize followers in a confined geographic area with minor outside assistance. For most of its activities it took little cognizance of what was happening elsewhere in the city. The intersection between the Board's narrow perspective and larger events and concerns illustrates the relationship between idiosyncratic and general factors in determining the outcomes of movement efforts.

The history of the Joan of Arc Board began in April 1967, when the New York City Board of Education, as part of its experiment with school decentralization, proposed a demonstration educational project on the Upper West Side of Manhattan under the supervision of a locally elected board. Its purpose was to "bring the parents and community into a more meaningful participation with the schools." [1] Four elementary schools and one junior high school (Joan of Arc) were to take part in the project, which would affect approximately 5,000 school children. [2] The Governing Board's origins thus

[1] New York City Board of Education, *Staff Bulletin*, May 15, 1967, p. 3.

[2] In 1956, 91 percent of the school districts in the country had enrollments of fewer than 1,200 pupils. An additional 7 percent of school districts had enrollments of between 1,200 and 6,000

derived from governmental action rather than local pressure, and the governmental action itself was in response to the political situation in other parts of the city. The choice of the Joan of Arc district as a focus for school decentralization activities was mainly accidental, but it acted as a catalytic event in the development of a movement on the upper West Side.

In response to the mandate from the Board of Education, a few members of the Strycker's Bay Neighborhood Council (SBNC), the official local housing council for the West Side Urban Renewal Area,[3] joined with other individuals from the school Parent Associations (PA's) and various community organizations to form the West Side Committee for Decentralization (WSCD). The aim of this group was to prepare for decentralization by involving the community in planning the new decentralized school district. It attempted to do this through holding public meetings, sending out informational bulletins, and acting as the nominal representative of the area to the central Board of Education until an official planning body should be elected. The membership of the WSCD was predominantly black and Puerto Rican.

The WSCD postponed holding elections for the proposed community school board until it was satisfied that the public was well informed. In contrast, governing board elections were held in the IS 201, Ocean Hill-Brownsville, and Two Bridges districts during the summer of 1967, and these boards were functioning by the following school year. By December 1967 the Board of Education, reacting to the political conflict in those three districts, rescinded its promise of a community school district on the Upper West Side.

The West Side activists nonetheless pressed on for the establishment of a community school district, and when they continued to meet rejection, decided to hold a governing board election on their own. They argued that if the Board of Education was acting out of political expediency, the only logical counter-strategy was to make the political costs of withholding district status even greater than those of granting it. Accordingly, the WSCD sought the endorsement of various notables[4] for its program and went ahead with the election. It obtained a grant of $5,000 from the Institute for Community

---

pupils. Alpheus L. White, *Local School Boards: Organization and Practices*, Office of Education Bulletin No. 8 (Washington, D.C.: United States Government Printing Office, 1962), pp. 1, 5. Thus, a Joan of Arc school district would have been larger than the great majority of districts in the country.

[3] See James Clarence Davies III, *Neighborhood Groups and Urban Renewal* (New York: Columbia University Press, 1966), pp. 120–46; and Joseph P. Lyford, *The Airtight Cage* (New York: Harper & Row, 1968), pp. 121–34, for descriptions of the organizational effects of the urban renewal program on the West Side.

[4] A flyer issued by the WSCD before the June 15, 1968, governing board election listed the following individuals, *inter alia*, as supporters of the election and of a community school district for the Joan of Arc complex: Percy Sutton, Manhattan Borough President; Herman Badillo, Bronx Borough President; Albert Blumenthal, N.Y. State Assemblyman; Basil Patterson, N.Y. State Senator; Kenneth Clark, educator and member of the N.Y. State Board of Regents; Evelina Antonetty, Executive Director, United Bronx Parents; Paul O'Dwyer, Democratic candidate for the U.S. Senate; Preston Wilcox, Columbia University professor; Robert Sarnoff, Chairman, Citizens Committee for Decentralization.

Studies of Queens College, which was administering the Ford Foundation support to the three existing districts, for the purpose of publicizing and administering an election on June 15, 1968.

A flyer put out by the WSCD stated the purposes of the elected board as follows:

1. To inform itself and the community on conditions in the schools as they really are.
2. To act as a grievance committee for parents who need help in dealing with school officials and staff.
3. To lead a day-to-day fight for the general improvement of school conditions now.
4. To consult with professional advisors on developing plans to transform our schools radically, so as to rid them of their most basic and long-standing weaknesses.

At the same time as our elected Board leads in the fight to improve our schools, it shall also participate in our general fight to win for it official Board of Education sanction as the Planning-Governing Board of the West Side Decentralization Demonstration Project No. 1.

The Board will also participate in the legislative fight to win for itself and for the other decentralization demonstration projects the kind of powers that are needed for them to govern, not, as now, in name only, but in fact. Then they will be doing the job we are really electing them to do.[5]

The American Arbitration Association was hired to supervise and certify the election. Its report showed that twenty-five candidates ran from the five schools, of whom fifteen were elected. Of a possible 5,000 ballots, 1,048 were cast.[6] The 523 individuals voting represented somewhere between 20 and 35 percent of the eligible voters, and probably reflected the extent of active support for community control of schools in the area.

There was some local opposition to the election, and a group calling itself Parents for New Alternatives in Education (PNAE) issued a leaflet urging parents to boycott the election. This statement, which did not identify any of its sponsors by name, noted that the election had no official authorization and concluded:

THE PURPOSE OF THIS ELECTION IS *NOT* TO ELECT A GOVERNING BOARD, BUT TO GIVE POWER TO A PRESSURE GROUP—A PRESSURE GROUP WHICH WILL NOT BE ACCOUNTABLE TO YOU OR YOUR CHILDREN. SUCH PRESSURE GROUPS HAVE CREATED HAVOC IN OCEAN HILL-BROWNSVILLE, TWO BRIDGES AND THE I.S. 201 COM-PLEX.[7]

[5] Mimeo, March 6, 1968.

[6] American Arbitration Association, Election Department, "In the Matter of West Side Committee for Decentralization. Certification of Results," August 20, 1968. Notarized copy in the files of the Joan of Arc Planning/Governing Board. A parent received one vote for each child, and only one parent could vote.

[7] Mimeo, n.d.; capitals and italics in the original.

It is difficult to estimate the extent of community agreement with PNAE, as voting turnouts are normally low in local elections. Given that this was a special election for an unauthorized school board, the extent of citizen interest and implicit endorsement of the Board, as evidenced by the number of voters, seemed relatively high.[8]

At the time of its election, therefore, the Board had reason to feel that many people in the community wished it to play an active role in school affairs. It was faced, however, with the dual task of maintaining its support and acting as an effective articulator of community aims and grievances. The difficulty of carrying out this task was partly a function of the leadership qualities of the Board members and partly of the situation in which it found itself.

the new board

Board members shared a common interest in forcing change in the schools and felt that their position would enable them to make the school administration respond to parents' demands for innovation. Each of the schools in the complex had its special problems, but members felt that these problems all derived from a larger pattern of inflexibility, ritualism, and racism on the part of school personnel. There appeared to be widespread dissatisfaction with the schools within the neighborhood; there was a very vocal constituency in opposition to the status quo; and the Board assumed that it had a genuine popular mandate for change.[9] Among some of the community activists, both on and off the Board, the desire to make the schools more responsive was almost an obsession. A number of the mothers devoted forty-hour weeks to school affairs, attending meetings and hearings, working as school volunteers, walking the halls of the schools to see what was going on. Some of them considered that their children were physically and psychologically endangered by the operation of the public school system, and they infused the situation with an element of hysteria.

All the Board members were parents, and their interest in education arose almost wholly out of this status. Three had been elected from each school in the complex, primarily from among those who had been active in their school Parent Associations. Most were newcomers to school politics—or politics of any sort; a few had been WSCD activists. Eleven of the original fifteen

---

[8] The median national figure for percent of adults voting in nonpartisan municipal elections held independently of any other election is 27 percent; the figure for cities over 500,000 (partisan and nonpartisan) is 20 percent. G. Theodore Mitau, *State and Local Government* (New York: Scribner's, 1966), p. 424. Voting turnout in the Joan of Arc election probably exceeded that in the officially sanctioned elections of the Governing Boards of IS 201 and Two Bridges.

[9] There are no reliable measures to evaluate the extent of popular dissatisfaction with the schools. But one good indication of the sentiments of parents in the complex was their activity during the long school strike of 1968. Parents opened all five schools in the complex, and attendance during the strike averaged 40 percent of normal. The figure for the adjacent IS 44 complex was 30 percent. Most areas without a majority black population kept their schools closed. Opposition to the strike was generally interpreted as a protest against the centralized school system.

remained active after the initial few months following the election, and our discussion of the Board will refer only to these eleven who stayed on to form the core of the West Side community control movement.[10]

Table 3-1

Background Characteristics of JOA Board Members

RACE/ETHNICITY	N
Black	4
Puerto Rican	2
White	5

SEX	
Male	4
Female	7

EDUCATION	
Some high school	2
Completed high school	1
Some college	4[a]
Completed college	1
Graduate school	3

OCCUPATION	
Welfare or educational services (paraprofessional)	5
Clerical	1
Skilled worker	1
Teacher	1
Housewife	1
Psychiatrist	1
Plant supervisor	1

CLASS AFFILIATION OF JOA GOVERNING BOARD MEMBERS[b]	
Lower/working[c]	5
Lower middle	2
Middle	2
Upper middle	2

[a] Three of those with some college were still going to night school and included poor people in paraprofessional programs.

[b] This classification is based on rough estimates by the authors. Four of the five individuals in the first category live in low-income housing; the two in the final category have medical specialist's incomes; the distinctions between "lower middle" and "middle" are the result of a subjective judgment.

[c] At least two of these had been on welfare during the previous two years.

[10] Information on the participants was gathered in a series of interviews by the authors in the spring of 1969. Additional data on the characteristics of Board members appears in Chapter Six.

A comparison of the ethnic composition of the Governing Board (Table 3-1) with that of the schools in the complex (Table 3-2) shows that both blacks and whites were disproportionately represented on the Board. Puerto Ricans, who comprised more than a third of the school population, were underrepresented among the active members. This fact reflects the generally low participation of Puerto Ricans in community activities, a situation that had changed little since Davies described it in the early sixties:

The Puerto Ricans [in the West Side Urban Renewal Area] showed little interest in joining any of the existing organizations, and they did not organize themselves on a neighborhood basis. The organizations that they did form tended to fall into two categories. A number of "home-town clubs" were formed whose membership consisted of those who had come from the same town or city in Puerto Rico. These groups limited themselves to purely social functions. In the second category were a number of citywide organizations. These groups tended to shy away from political activity except insofar as such activity furthered the careers of their leaders. None of the citywide Puerto Rican organizations had a high degree of grassroots support.[11]

Although a slim majority of the Board's membership was middle class,[12] and none of the members came from the most deprived segment of the population, the members felt their constituency to be in the black and Latin poor[13] and considered it their duty to represent the interests of this group. In this respect they resembled the poverty boards in San Francisco described by Kramer:

Most of the representatives of the poor were not impoverished themselves, but instead were working- or middle-class persons. The conditions under which area elections were conducted and the small number of voters resulted in a process of self-selection favoring the more ambitious, upwardly striving, affiliated members of ethnic groups, who perceived themselves as spokesmen for the poor. . . .[14]

The question of whether the Board represented its neighborhood was

[11] Davies, *Neighborhood Groups and Urban Renewal*, p. 115.

[12] Governing Board members were of much lower status than the members of the District 5 Local School Board (LSB). Seventy-five percent of the LSB were professionals (lawyers, directors of public agencies), as compared with 9 percent of the JOA Board (or 18 percent if the teacher member is included). Commensurate with their high level of occupational achievement, members of the District 5 Board also had a much higher level of educational attainment—all eight members had attended college, and five had gone to graduate school.

[13] The best indicator of the extent of deprivation in the Joan of Arc complex is the number of children entitled to receive free school lunches. In order to participate in the free-lunch program a child must come from a family classified as poor according to Board of Education standards (income below $4,500 a year for a family of four). The figures for children receiving free lunches in the four Joan of Arc complex elementary schools in spring 1970, stated as a percentage of school enrollment, were as follows: PS 75: 30 percent; PS 84: 58 percent; PS 163: 63 percent; and PS 179: 60 percent. (Information supplied by the New York Board of Education School Lunch Service.)

[14] Ralph M. Kramer, *Participation of the Poor* (Englewood Cliffs, N.J.: Prentice-Hall, © 1969), p. 66.

made especially complicated by the nature of its locale. An examination of the setting in which the Board found itself reveals some of the most idiosyncratic features of this case. For the Upper West Side of New York was an extremely unusual area. The neighborhood did, however, have a considerable degree of poverty, and if the Board faced the difficulty of dealing with an atypically variegated population, it also had the advantage of containing middle-class, educated people within its constituency. The failures of the Board demonstrate the obstacles to mobilization which exist even for collectivities in possession of middle-class skills.

the setting

The area defined by Joan of Arc (JHS 118) and its four feeder schools was one of the most varied and changing neighborhoods in Manhattan. It originally housed members of the Jewish bourgeoisie along three of its major avenues while taking in mainly Irish, working-class families on the side streets and other avenues. During the period of major Puerto Rican immigration, this section of the Upper West Side was a principal recipient of the new arrivals. Puerto Ricans and a smaller group of blacks moving south from Harlem took over the converted brownstones and tenements that had been occupied by older immigrant groups. Their arrival led to a sharply increasing crime rate and set off an exodus of Jews from the area, who sought sanctuary in the suburbs and on the East Side.

In 1962 the New York City Board of Estimate approved the final plans for the West Side Urban Renewal Area (WSURA). Within the boundaries of WSURA was the entire eastern half of the section served by Joan of Arc Junior High School and its feeder schools. Thus, this neighborhood was in the midst of extremely rapid change. Columbus Avenue, once lined with small stores forming the ground floors of tenement structures, by 1968 boasted a row of new middle- and upper-income buildings that attracted families from throughout the metropolitan area. The occupants of these new highrise apartments constituted an ethnically mixed group, including a number of middle-class blacks. Amsterdam Avenue remained partly unreconstructed, but it also had several finished new buildings and others in process of being built. In addition, there were two large public housing projects plus several smaller low-income buildings in the area. The residents of the low-income buildings were almost entirely black and Puerto Rican.

The large old buildings facing the park, West End Avenue, and the river had mainly become cooperatives and, along with the reconverted brownstones on the side streets, housed many of New York's intellectual elite. The area had a high density of actors, writers, doctors, professors, and other cosmopolitans who wished to stay in Manhattan and could not afford sufficiently spacious quarters on the East Side or in Greenwich Village.

The schools in the area serviced an extraordinarily mixed group of children. A large proportion of upper-middle-class families, both white and black, sent their children to private schools. But many whites kept their children in the public schools either out of principle or because, unlike blacks of similar income status, they did not qualify for scholarships to private schools. In October 1967 the ethnic breakdown of the five schools in the Joan of Arc complex was as follows:

Table 3-2

SCHOOL	PUERTO RICAN		BLACK		OTHER		TOTAL NO. CHILDREN
	N	Percent	N	Percent	N	Percent	
PS 75	255	25	185	19	557	56	997
PS 84	277	31	191	21	436	48	904
PS 163	346	44	243	31	193	25	782
PS 179	484	45	458	43	127	12	1069
JHS 118	468	35	324	24	548	41	1340
Total	1830	36	1401	27	1861	36	5092

Source: Joan of Arc Governing Board leaflet, mimeo, n.d.

The variation in ethnic composition among the schools created different types of tensions within them. The extent of parent dissatisfaction and the reasons for it were rather different in each school, although none of them was without serious problems. The most troubled, and probably also the most vexing in terms of finding any solution for its ills, was the junior high school.

Joan of Arc Junior High School (JHS 118). Until the 1968 school year the principal of JHS 118 had been the only black junior high school principal in the city holding a permanent supervisor's license. She had attempted a number of changes in Joan of Arc, including the use of module-type scheduling. Just as her programs were reaching the implementation stage, however, she was promoted and left the school. Her replacement was another black woman, but of conservative orientation. The new principal halted the earlier innovations, restoring older types of methods and curricula. Not only did the administration of the school return to traditional ways, but discipline became lax, and a large group of teachers resigned. The morale of the remaining teachers was very low, and a number of white parents who had supported the earlier reforms withdrew their children from the school.

Dissatisfied parents perceived the school not only as failing in its educational mission but also as downright dangerous. Rumors circulated concerning drug addiction and cases of assault against students and teachers. Pupils roamed the halls. Most of the classrooms were half empty, confirming rates of absenteeism of up to 40 percent. Several of the lavatories were locked, and the others were completely without supplies of towels, toilet paper, or soap. Children had to carry their overcoats with them from class to class as there was no safe place to deposit them. While some teachers seemed to be conducting lessons, there were a number of classrooms in which there appeared to be no planned activity.

Further evidence of deterioration of the school existed in the steadily declining performance of Joan of Arc students on the citywide Metropolitan Achievement Test, which showed that students could expect to be further below grade level when they left the school than when they entered it.[15] More important, the scores corroborated the precipitous descent in quality sensed by parents—average reading scores for each grade dropped a full grade level between 1967 and 1969. The junior high school thus presented the full range of problems which could afflict an urban school. It was characterized by a growing majority of nonwhite children with low achievement; a high level of internal disorder and resulting fear; and a hesitant administration.

While none of the elementary schools in the complex had comparable problems of low attendance and breakdown of discipline, all except PS 163 had troubles which called for remedy.

PS 179.   One parent referred to PS 179 as "the plantation." It was the most segregated school in the complex with an 88 percent nonwhite population. It was also the oldest and most dilapidated, had the lowest reading scores, and served an almost entirely lower-class population that lived in the adjacent Frederick Douglass Houses. Only a few parents took an active interest in the school, although almost all were extremely displeased with the school building.

PS 179 was housed in a seventy-year-old, five-story building without elevators. It was filthy, smelly, inconvenient, and ugly. Some students had to climb four flights of stairs to reach their classrooms; the two wings were not accessible to each other above the third floor. Classrooms were old-fashioned, poorly lighted, and had inadequate sound insulation. Because the school had been scheduled for replacement for years, it was not eligible for renovation money and thus had not been painted in as long as anyone could remember. Since funds for its replacement were never placed in the capital budget, pupils continued to attend it in its unrenovated state.

The school's Parent Association devoted most of its effort to campaigning for a new building and finally won approval of two small schools to replace the existing one. The future of the new school remained in doubt, however. The Strycker's Bay Neighborhood Council, in its drive for more

---

[15] **Scores of JHS 118 Students on the Metropolitan Achievement Test**

DATE OF TEST:	APRIL 1967	APRIL 1968	APRIL 1969
Grade 7	7.3[a]	6.8	6.5
Grade 8	7.8	7.6	not given
Grade 9	9.1	8.7	8.1

[a] Each figure following the grade heading denotes the average score in years and months of attainment. Nationwide norms in 1969 were 7.7, 8.5, and 9.5 for the seventh, eighth, and ninth grades respectively.

Sources: Scores for 1967 and 1968 were taken from Gertrude Miller, Language Arts Coordinator, District 5 Manhattan, "Survey of Metropolitan Reading Test Scores, April, 1967, and April, 1968, District 5, N.Y.C." issued by Local School Board, District 5, n.d. Scores for 1969 appeared in *The New York Times*, February 15, 1970, p. 64.

public housing, succeeded in persuading the city to grant an additional low-income site, which turned out to be the location on which one of the new schools was to be built. The city's action put the parents seeking a new school, who themselves lived in low-income housing, in the position of opposing the construction of a new public-housing project.

The remaining schools.   PS 84, which is the subject of Chapter Four of this book, had a mobilized group of parents who were seeking to change the pedagogical methods and governance of the school. PS 75 was the only predominantly white school in the complex, and the reading test scores of its students were among the best in the city. Here the pressure was principally for a stable administration, an enriched curriculum, and greater pedagogical freedom. PS 163, while mainly nonwhite and containing some parents who were generally discontented with the New York City school system as a whole, apparently did not have any specific acute conflict.

THE PROBLEM OF FORMULATING A STRATEGY

The problem for the JOA Governing Board upon its election was to fuse the various components of its public into a single constituency. Members of the Governing Board argued that, despite divergences in goals among parent bodies at the various schools, in all cases the attainment of community control was a prerequisite to success. It set up an open-membership organization, the West Side Parents Union (WSPU), which it envisioned as providing an institutional basis for parent participation in the schools. The purpose of the WSPU was to act as a constituency to which the Joan of Arc Board would be accountable, provide a vehicle for active parent involvement in the schools, and offer services to parents with school-related grievances:

The West Side Parents Union is made up of a group of parents in the district. Our history has been one of serving parents who have problems with school, such as

1. Suspension
2. Harassment
3. Transfers etc.

We recognized as we began to service and help individual parents, there was a need for a new form of organization which would allow for involvement and full participation in the public school system.[16]

The executive director of the Parents Union was also a member of the Governing Board.

The WSPU tried to provide both organization and services, but it was

[16] Leaflet distributed by the West Side Parents Union, mimeo, n.d.

more successful at the latter. Mary Scott,[17] its black executive director, while a good public speaker, seemed more comfortable and adept in her service function. She was always willing to accompany a parent to school to discuss the treatment of a child or call the welfare office on someone's behalf. But while parents would seek out the WSPU for help, it was difficult for them to see advantages in ongoing participation in it as against their own school Parent Associations.

Thus, the Parents Union, which was to have acted as the link between the Governing Board and its constituency, evolved into a separate, service-giving arm of the movement. It was the only organization which could have integrated parents from the various schools in the complex, but parents focused on the particular conflicts within their own schools rather than on the overarching issue of gaining power for the Governing Board. Even though a legitimized Joan of Arc Governing Board could have had more impact than any of the school parent groups individually, parents lacked the high degree of involvement in the fate of the Governing Board which they felt toward issues that affected their children directly.

During its first months of existence the Board tended to be immobilized by its desire to serve all the elements in its constituency. It still had hopes that it would be recognized by the city as the official school board of the complex, and refrained from taking strong stands on issues in individual schools for fear of losing its status as spokesman for the whole community. The school strike of 1968, in which the United Federation of Teachers closed the schools for two months over the issue of community control, proved to be a catalytic event converting the Board into an action group. It also brought into focus the major tactical problems confronting it in pursuit of an active political role.

A report by an observer from the Institute for Community Studies at Queens College indicated the impact of the strike and the dimensions of the Board's problem:

The Joan of Arc Complex kept these five schools opened and manned with regular teachers, substitutes, paraprofessionals and parents. When the custodial staff went out, the parents of three schools in the complex took over and slept in. One thing came across very clearly during the strike. The Board did not function as a group, but rather as individual parents working in their own schools. The Governing Board showed no leadership as a group. This was also obvious to parents and community, who became frustrated during the strike. The Board recognizes their own incompetence and lack of leadership—they began to fight with each other as a result of this. . . . The Governing Board on the whole seems to be in need of help in how to set some goals and priorities. . . . With all this in mind, Mr. M. [a consultant to the Board, on the staff of and paid by the Field Foundation] along with the Board made a proposal [for funding of a community organization staff] to be distributed to all foundations.[18]

---

[17] All the names used in this chapter, except for those of well-known political figures, are pseudonyms.

[18] Report in the files of the Institute for Community Studies, n.d.

After the strike the Governing Board was successful in receiving $30,000 from the Field Foundation and $10,000 from the New York Foundation. The grants were intended to support a staff consisting of five community organizers, a staff writer, and a staff coordinator for a period of thirty weeks. An earlier grant of $10,000 from the Institute for Community Studies was already being used to pay a secretary and rent an office located on the ground floor of a low-rent apartment building.

The principal effect of the strike on the members of the Governing Board was a sharp change in their consciousness. Where they had previously conceived of their role as limited to the educational sphere, they now felt that improvements in education required substantial political change. Earlier they had hoped to hire an educational consultant, with whom they would work out new educational programs for the district. Now they decided that they had to have power before they could present an educational agenda.[19] The decision to hire a staff of community organizers reflected this new consciousness. The Board considered its primary resource in the struggle to gain power to be an active, vocal constituency. The high level of community participation during the strike indicated that the basis for such a constituency existed. But the Board, made up mainly of people with fulltime jobs, lacked the time and ability to do the kind of organizing necessary to mobilize it.

constraints on action

Three events transpired while the Board was searching for a staff that illustrated the problems of developing organizational momentum.

The capital budget hearings.   In late February 1969 the New York Board of Estimate, which decides on the city's capital expenses, was holding hearings on the capital budget for education. The Governing Board member from PS 179 requested that the Board provide funds to transport a busload of parents from that school to the hearings to lend force to their demand for money for a new school. She soon reduced her request to cab fare, as it became apparent that few people were interested in making the trip to the Municipal Building. In the end only three women showed up for the hearings: the Governing Board representative, the 179 PA president, and a member of the school's supervisory staff. The three women were very disappointed by the low turnout and agreed that the show of enthusiasm in the school during the autumn strike had turned out to be temporary. They noted that while it was possible to mobilize parents sporadically, it was extremely difficult to maintain any enduring level of activism except among very few. Yet, effective opposition to the school administration was a full-time job, requiring

---

[19] Sympathetic critics of the Governing Board argued that it would have been more successful had it first provided a program for educational improvement which could then, like the open classroom program at PS 84, have become a rallying point for community sentiment.

continual vigilance and never-ending readiness to appear at the seemingly endless stream of protests, hearings, and meetings.[20]

The Joan of Arc rally.   Also during February the Board attempted to act on parent discontent with Joan of Arc Junior High School. Mary Scott, the executive director of the Parents Union, reported to the Board on her experience at a meeting between community representatives and the supervisory staff of the junior high school. She said that the principal assured them that she was attending to their complaints concerning dope addiction, disorder in the halls, the filling of teacher positions, the running of the lunchroom, and the lack of books and supplies. Mrs. Scott concluded: "The parents felt they were being given a snow job, but they could not think of an effective answer. They could not prove that what they said was still true, and nothing was really being taken care of."

The Board decided that it would have to take more militant action in order to make changes in the school. Members thought that the issue of the junior high was one about which all parents in the complex were concerned, and thus would provide a means for mobilizing more people. Accordingly, the Board scheduled a community rally around the problem of reforming Joan of Arc. The Governing Board chairman, David Good, persuaded the rest of the Board that the rally should be directed not at removing the principal but rather at what was wrong with the school. He hoped that the meeting would galvanize people into a takeover of the school, in which parents would sit in on the principal's office. He thought that such a move would result in increased support and publicity for the Governing Board. Several Board members however, felt that occupying the principal's office would be unwise. After considerable discussion the Board finally agreed that it should leave the decision concerning militant action to the people attending the rally. If the rally so decided, those present would stay in the school overnight.

Despite widespread circulation of a rather inflammatory flyer and several preliminary small meetings for parents in the complex, attendance at the rally, held in the junior high school auditorium, was disappointingly low. Of those (approximately 90 people) present, at least half were either Governing Board members, officials from the two reform Democratic clubs in the neighborhood, PA officers, or specially invited guests who were not community residents. After several very long speeches, discussion was opened to the floor. A number of people explained why conditions in JHS 118 were unacceptable: "Nobody relates to kids." "Kids know what's good, not the administration." "Mrs. B. [the principal] is impossible to communicate with." Many speakers said that something had to be done, that parents had to organize. But no one made any specific proposals.

Nearly three hours after the meeting had begun, in an atmosphere of almost total ennui, and with at least one-third of the original audience departed, the Governing Board chairman proposed the following resolution:

---

[20] Unless otherwise indicated, accounts of incidents and meetings, as well as quotations of the participants, were originally transcribed by the authors.

We have lost confidence in the administration. . . . Therefore, we have decided to take control of the school. A committee of two Governing Board members and three parent representatives will take control of the administration, and the school administration will either abide with it or get out.

The proposal evoked almost no response in the audience. Without a vote being taken, the meeting was closed and everyone left.

The decentralization bill.   At a meeting with community figures including the Democratic district leaders and Father White, who was president of Strycker's Bay Neighborhood Council, the Board discussed its role in influencing the New York State Legislature to pass a strong decentralization bill. The district leaders noted that none of the West Side representatives was working within the Legislature for a Joan of Arc complex. Mr. Good explained that the representatives from the area had refused explicit support for recognition, although they were not in opposition. The following interchange took place:

Father White: Why are the West Side legislators not supporting their own district when they are supporting the other three? Why is no pressure being put on them?

Rev. Washington (local black activist and well-known folksinger):   I'm willing to go to Albany. All the legislators and community leaders should be contacted.

Mrs. Mendoza (Governing Board member):   All this talk is useless.

Mr. Good: This notion of rushing to do something tomorrow in Albany rubs me the wrong way. Don't the rest of you find it distasteful?

Ultimately the Board was persuaded by the politicians present to compose a letter calling on the West Side's representatives to support legislation that would enable the Board of Education to authorize the JOA Board as an official demonstration governing board. The letter was signed by the presidents of the two reform Democratic clubs, the district leaders, and the Democratic state committeeman and was distributed in Albany the next day, to no apparent effect.

Significance of the three incidents.   The three events described here in one sense showed the ineptitude of the Board: its inability to capitalize on situations, its failure to develop community loyalties, and its reluctance to do the kind of lobbying that might persuade legislators to support it. They reveal that the most obvious deficiency of the Board members was their lack of political, not educational, expertise. Despite accusations that the supporters of community control were seeking power rather than improvement of the educational system, many of them, like the chairman of the JOA Governing Board, had a positive distaste for political manipulation.

The apparent ineptitude of the Board resulted as much, however, from structural factors as from a failure of political leadership; it was an open question whether, given the situation, anyone would have been more successful. Board members had only the time left after work and child care—a number of the members were working mothers—to devote to

Governing Board matters. If, for example, they had decided to do an impressive job of lobbying in Albany, several of them would have had to make the trip numerous times. They had little to promise the legislators in return for responsiveness, and they foresaw minimal attention and much frustration in return for their efforts.

In addition, they had few ways to publicize their aims and point out injustices committed by the school administration. Except on the day of their election they received no notice from *The New York Times*. The local West Side newspaper, the *Manhattan Tribune*, was published by William Haddad, a member of the Board of Education. Haddad, while claiming to sympathize with the Governing Board's objectives, rarely covered its activities.[21]

Difficulty of communication was superimposed on the problem of attempting to mobilize a highly pluralistic community. Differences of race and class made alliances difficult and meant that the only possible basis for unity had to be ideological. But the creation of a common consciousness among disparate groups required, even if one assumed a common interest in school reform, energetic and constant efforts at building bonds and an efficient and widespread communications network. The Governing Board had neither the time nor the talent for such feats of organization, and there was no ready-made communications network available. Certainly word of mouth alone could not suffice to carry messages in a neighborhood made up of large apartment buildings with most of the inhabitants unknown to each other.

IDEOLOGY AND ACTION

Once the Board members had decided that educational change required political action, they attempted to gain community support for this undertaking through holding community meetings and seizing upon particular issues. But the questionable legitimacy of entangling the education of children with the acquisition of power never ceased to bedevil the Board in its attempts to promote community action.[22] The suspicions evoked by the Board were summed up by the president of one of the school Parent Associations:

To me community control is only a tool to get a good education. . . . You are the Planning/Governing Board. Has educational planning been done? Have you planned for the future? People seem to be losing sight of the fact that education is what this is all about.

Distrust of the Board's ideology led to a reduction in support among

[21] The *Manhattan Tribune* in general gave little coverage to events on the West Side. Unlike its defunct predecessor, the *West Side News*, it consisted mostly of feature articles, reviews, and editorials.

[22] Keith Thompson cites a number of instances where similar accusations about the illegitimate intrusion of politics into "educational" matters were made in England against school reformers. See his article "A Critique of the Distinction between 'Social' and 'Educational' Issues as a Basis for Judgements Concerning Secondary School Reorganization," *British Journal of Educational Studies*, XVIII, February, 1970, 20.

some of its original allies. Many parents began to regard the Board as too radical, as willing to sacrifice the interests of children for the abstract principle of community power. Along with every effort the Board made to capitalize on an issue came a negative reaction from at least some community members. Thus, an attempt by the Board to exert leadership in the struggle to gain a new principal for PS 84 and its expressed willingness to use its own funds to pay such a person provoked the following discussion at an open meeting:

Mrs. Glick (Local School Board member):   I came to question the expenditure of money by the Joan of Arc Board. I am a member of the [official] Local School Board, which has no [discretionary] money. I resent the idea of money going into paying a principal for PS 84 when PS 179 needs a reading program.

Mrs. White (Governing Board member, PS 179):   New educational programs are mainly gimmicks. They haven't worked; they haven't been set up to work.

A parent: The principal has not been functioning for years in PS 179. If we can choose a principal for 84 with our own money, it will prove something.

Mrs. Washington (GB member, PS 75):   There should be a halt in the filling of personnel vacancies until Spanish and blacks are represented proportional to their numbers in the community. At PS 75 the office staff is lily white.

Mr. Keen (Black Panther Party):[23]   Children get a complex in school from being taught by whites.

Mr. Adams (GB member, PS 84):   We should discuss what we want the Joan of Arc complex to spend its money on. The Governing Board should hire an educational consultant to suggest programs.

Mrs. Reed (parent; GB staff writer):   We can't say: "There's a system here; let's make it work." The system must be changed fundamentally.

Mr. Jenkins (GB staff coordinator):   The only way to get change is through organizing parents. So-called "innovative programs" don't involve parents. Community control means parent participation in all aspects of running the schools. It doesn't mean negotiations with the Board of Ed. to get any little thing. The conflict over 84 sharpened parents' consciousness.

A parent: We must educate parents also. Why have an educational consultant? Why waste funds paying salaries to high-paid consultants?

Mr. Good (GB chairman):   Local school board meetings are only an illusion. They are used to shut parents out. The Joan of Arc Board's underlying idea is that the community should tell it what to do.[24]

the developed consciousness
of board members

The Governing Board professed that "its underlying idea is that the community should tell it what to do." But the raised consciousness of its

[23] As far as is known, this was the only Joan of Arc meeting attended by members of the Black Panthers. The young man and woman who came to this meeting were conservatively attired and subdued in manner.

[24] Meeting of April 29, 1969. Governing Board is abbreviated as GB.

members meant that the Board had a clearer conception of what needed to be done than did the community at large. Active participation in the conflict over community control had forced the Governing Board's members to develop a more explicit formulation than most people of what was wrong with the school system, the causes of malfunction, and the remedies for it.

Board members had a strong ideological commitment to educational change, although the exact nature of that change was unclear to most of them. They felt that present failures of the educational system were the result of mismanagement and were correctable through changes in educational procedures. The Board, as a result of restrictions on nominations, consisted entirely of parents of children in the public schools. This characteristic created an acute awareness of the problems of parents and a lack of sympathy with teachers and administrators. The status of parent was surrounded with special dignity, and it was seen as defining a group with shared interests and shared antagonisms.

Many of the JOA Board members called themselves militants or radicals. All of them believed that school personnel should be accountable to parents in the community and that there should be institutionalized channels for parent participation in operating the schools. Only one condoned the use of violent measures to bring about change, although several felt that violence was inevitable if nonviolent forces failed to achieve change. Many of the members feared the effects on children of using schools as a battleground in the fight to reform the system. All the Governing Board members had worked out fairly sophisticated diagnoses of what was wrong with the present system of education and had reached a variety of conclusions about the possibility of changing it. The following quotations are excerpts from open-ended interviews with each of the active Board members; they were selected so as to give a reasonably accurate summary of the general attitudes of each respondent (respondents are identified by race, class, and sex).

Donald Adams (white, middle class, male):   For many parents at PS 84 the crucial issue was merely getting a competent principal. But I feel that changing the principal is not enough. It is necessary to change the system. I have attempted to focus on who has the right to select the principal, and who the principal is accountable to. Serving on the personnel hiring committee has made me start to think realistically about what kind of people I really want. You can't ask for supermen. I have come to realize that the main thing to look for in the candidates for principal was whether the person understood the concept of community control and was willing to be accountable. There can be no change without the accountability of professionals. The power struggle over this basic issue must be decided before anything else can be.

I have come to realize that it [gaining community control] will be a lengthy process, that the problems will not be solved in Albany but within the community, and that their solution requires rallying support.

There must be revolutionary tactics—not necessarily guns and bombs, but a complete breaking down of centralized systems in all aspects of society—labor, hospitals, etc. But if there were armed confrontation, my side would lose. Violence, however, is inevitable if no one really deals with the problems. I don't condone riots but I do not blame the rioters. Personally I will support any form of action short of violence.

Viola Lincoln (black, working class, female):   The worst problem in Joan of Arc [Junior High School] is that students are not working up to their potential because teachers cannot teach them and teachers feel that they are unteachable. Administrators are not doing their duty. School is not doing what it is supposed to. Black children don't believe in white teachers. This must be brought out. The white man is not the black man's educator.

The Governing Board must become more militant. It must do irrational things. . . . I feel myself to be the suppressed militant member of the Governing Board. The Board restricts me from doing my thing. It brushes over opportunities. If community control is to happen, there has to be a real bloody muddy. There is no other way out.

I have not become more radical, only more frustrated. There must be communication between parents and administrators.

Michael Shapiro (white, upper middle class, male):   I have learned more and more that groups of people getting organized actually does work [to force action by the political structure of the city].

I have become more radical. The basic problem is organization. Political consciousness must be sharpened through struggle. There is a need for large-scale political organization. I am opposed to violence; I do not see it as inevitable. People must have the wisdom to meet demands, adjust themselves to shifts in political power not to save the system but to save society. Violence is a deterrence to social change.

The greatest obstacle to education is racial prejudice.

Ann Washington (black, upper middle class, female):   People want something done for their children now, and they haven't gotten anything concrete. This is especially true for black parents.

I have become more realistic about what can be accomplished. I see how difficult it is to make the smallest change—I had not realized this before. The greatest obstacle to change is power.

I have always felt the need to force change. I am, however, beginning to see that community control is not the panacea that I once thought it was. But it would be a beginning.

The Governing Board has tried everything. I don't know what else there is to do short of violence that would make a difference. I would not participate in violence myself though.

Helen White (white, lower class, female):   The Board of Education does not really care about what is going on in the schools. It allows the system to exist the way it is. Local personnel would produce if they were pushed. I want the big dream where you can hire and fire, just like any other employee.

I have always been a radical. But I am now more pessimistic that things can be done in an orderly way. Still, if more parents can be involved and made to feel they can bite and nag and aggravate, so that changes are made, this would be a great deal accomplished.

Marie Lincoln (black, lower class, female):   Parent involvement is the main force for change. But community control is one thing; progress is another. Children have to have security, strict supervision. Teachers should have a responsible role. Parents should not be after them all the time.

If the Governing Board had done its thing in our own community it would have been better off than spending its time supporting Ocean Hill-Brownsville. It didn't succeed in pulling parents and principals closer together. It only provided opposition to the principals. This was no good. You have to negotiate with them, not scare them. You have to leave a person with respect.

Anna Mendoza (Puerto Rican, lower middle class, female):   The greatest problem with the schools is the system itself. It is too big. Things are not getting better. We have reached almost to the bottom. There will be a revolution soon.

People think community control means getting rid of principals. But it really means holding them responsible. People don't realize how community control will help their kid. Especially decentralization of budgeting, planning, and so forth. People don't realize how much inefficiency is due to the centralized system.

The effects of the confrontation [during the 1968 school strike] are still evident among the kids. This is unfortunate. It has broken down authority. The city government and the central Board are the real ones to blame, because they did not specify the powers of the demonstration districts. This is an adult fight and the kids are suffering from it.

Maria Lopez (Puerto Rican, working class, female):   Teachers believe in jobs, not kids. They are afraid. Parents are not well informed. People who really need to know what is happening with their kids—poor people—are lied to.

Principals go by the rule books—they prevent change. They are too insecure. They fear a threat to the credentials system. They are afraid of minority group people. We need non-status quo people.

I am the same way I was [i.e., just as radical]. But I have become more diplomatic.

David Good (white, middle class, male):   Being on the Governing Board has made me somewhat more cynical. I feel that I understand the meaning of power better for viewing it in actual rather than abstract terms. It has made me see that a righteous cause is inadequate for reaching one's objectives.

I see ongoing participation [by parents] as necessary both to get schools that operate in the interests of those they serve and as a goal in itself.

I have become more radical. I feel that grassroots organization and militant confrontation are a necessity. I have become aware of the feelinglessness of the establishment, of those in positions of power. The establishment is the principal obstacle to change. Confrontation is a necessary organizing tactic, but it is only useful in conjunction with other methods of organizing people, like meetings, coffee-clatches, newsletters, educational programs and so forth.

James Richards (white, lower middle class, male):   The greatest problems [in the schools] all evolve from poor administration and incompetence. Teachers are not equipped to handle the problems of the children in the system, especially of the black and Puerto Rican children. The schools did not help my own children to learn, but they could learn despite the defects of the system. They did it on their own; they were lucky. I had fears for their safety at Joan of Arc [Junior High], however, and my fourth kid is going out of the district because of this.

I'm a union man, but I was not bothered by crossing a picket line [during the school strike]. I was proud to. I know there are good unions and bad unions.

I have become more radical. I do not believe that the existing system can be improved to solve educational problems. It must be destroyed. It is not possible at this time to bring about needed changes through legislation. But whites can't work out the strategy for change—it must be evolved by trained black people.

Mary Scott (black, working class, female):   The two worst problems in the schools are suspensions and that report cards don't tell the truth. The confidential reports on children say something else, and parents don't know what it is.

We need masses of parents demanding change. At present, the people making demands are isolated. If the community really wanted to run the schools, it could. Apathy is the greatest problem.

I don't go for violence. At least, not yet.

The essence of the Board's ideology was a view of parents as a cohesive social interest group, and of an enemy embodied in the school administration. Change in the nature of that administration constituted the principal goal of the movement, and this goal would be achieved through raising the consciousness of other parents. Board members tended to express their ideology in specific terms. While they identified the school system as an intrinsic part of the entire process of racial and class discrimination in the United States, their consciousness was mainly of educational matters. Their general political analysis tended to be vague. Most members assumed the existence of a "power structure" and took a casually cynical attitude toward national and metropolitan politics. Within the realm of education they were alert to subtleties and had become experts on the formal and informal procedures governing the school system. They were quick to seize on particular incidents as symbolic of patterns of domination which they sought to destroy.

The incident of the suspension of a student to be described in the next section is illustrative of this process of symbolic interpretation. The facts of the case were unclear, and the Board found itself supporting the suspended student on general principles rather than a clear belief in his innocence. Nonetheless, it participated in a sit-in at the District Superintendent's office which ended with the arrest of a group of twelve. Later, Governing Board members disrupted a meeting of the Local School Board, precipitating the following exchange between a Joan of Arc Board member and a member of the Local School Board:

Mrs. Mendoza (Governing Board member):   We wanted to fight the way in which suspensions are handled, not this particular suspension itself. It is very unclear why the child was suspended. It is wrong that the child should be kept out of school on the basis of such confusing evidence. Suspensions are a symptom of the school system.

Mrs. Glick (Local School Board member):   The disruption of the school board meeting forced a kangaroo court kind of atmosphere.[25]

The clash over the suspension was symptomatic of the deepest issues underlying the community control controversy and indicated why many liberals supported the United Federation of Teachers (UFT) in its opposition to the drive for parent power. School personnel argued that the intrusion of parents into the question of discipline would result in an atmosphere of intimidation precluding the possibility of impartial judgments; the result would inevitably be, as Mrs. Glick described it, a "kangaroo court."

Moreover, teachers regarded control over classroom discipline as essential to the maintenance of order. In 1967 UFT efforts to establish in its contract the right of teachers to expel "disruptive pupils" precipitated the teachers' strike of that year. The UFT contended that disciplinary procedures should remain a matter of professional discretion. Thus, at an informal

[25] Meeting of April 29, 1969.

hearing held by the District 5 Superintendent on an accusation by a child that a teacher had kicked him, the UFT representative argued: "This is not an adversary situation. The Superintendent is making a professional decision concerning what is involved, and the parent has no right to bring an attorney." [26] Similarly after parents set up a complaint table at George Washington High School the UFT's vice president was quoted as saying that parents had "taken over professional functions of guidance, consultation and complaints." [27]

Parents, however, reacted strongly when their children were suspended or severely rebuked. Because most suspended children were black or Puerto Rican, the outputs of the school, in this respect as in the more conventional ones measured by achievement tests, favored white middle-class children. Black and Puerto Rican parents felt that teachers overreacted to minor offenses committed by their children, which would have been disregarded when performed by whites. Several parents in District 5 accused school personnel of using disciplinary measures to harass mothers who had challenged school authorities. In general, advocates of community control argued that only locally elected school boards with power over disciplinary procedures could protect the interests of parents and children against abuses of administrative authority.[28]

THE STRATEGY OF THE PAID ORGANIZER

The Joan of Arc Board's ideology caused it to visualize itself as an educator and organizer of the community. But Board members early recognized their own limitations and sought a paid staff which would have greater time and talent for these roles. They wished particularly to arouse the occupants of the public housing projects, and thus they sought a staff coordinator with previous experience in mobilizing ghetto residents. So as to avoid projecting an image of white paternalism, they looked for a nonwhite. Eventually they hired a black man who had been a leader in the Harlem rent strikes of the mid-sixties. The new coordinator, George Jenkins, set as his principal goal the organization of the black and Puerto Rican elements in the community, arguing that the whites were already relatively well organized and, furthermore, required the least effort to activate. He felt an effective strategy required that blacks and Puerto Ricans form their own groups, as they would be either intimidated by organizations with a white membership or consider that such organizations did not represent their interests and be unwilling to participate in them.

No matter what sort of person the Board had chosen to head its

[26] October 29, 1969.

[27] *The New York Times*, April 17, 1970, p. 47.

[28] As well as demanding review procedures over disciplinary actions, parents were insisting on their rights to see and protest inscriptions on students' record cards.

organizing staff, it would have confronted problems. Hiring a white would have made it susceptible to accusations of white domination and probably would have rendered it ineffective among blacks and Puerto Ricans. Perhaps it would have been best off finding an integrationist black, but among experienced community organizers in 1969, integrationist blacks were hard to find, and none presented himself for the Board's consideration. George Jenkins was a forceful, dynamic individual, well-equipped with ideas. He was not a strident separatist, did not refuse to associate with whites, and, in public at least, favored concentrating on nonwhites for tactical rather than ideological reasons. Nonetheless, his appointment upset many of the active whites, who were participating in the school struggle primarily out of integrationist conviction. Many of these whites understood Jenkins' point that lower-class blacks could not be organized into integrated groups. But his strategy did not give them a direction and essentially offered them no place in the movement to reform the schools on the West Side.

One woman, who worked as an administrative assistant for the Governing Board as well as being a parent activist herself, summed up the strategic dilemma of the organizing staff very perceptively:

Jenkins may have been right about the need to organize blacks and Puerto Ricans separately, but in this community, with the goal of integration, it was very divisive. Also, he presumed a kind of developed lower-class consciousness in the black and Puerto Rican community that did not exist. The people in the Douglass Houses are mostly intact families with ambitions. They are upwardly mobile. They don't identify themselves as lower class.

Although it may indeed have been impossible to organize blacks and Puerto Ricans into integrated groups, it was also very difficult to organize them separately. Moreover, choosing the path of separatism meant sacrificing the enthusiasm of the whites who had until then provided a major, although by no means the only, impetus for reform.[29]

At any rate the Board accepted Jenkins and his strategy without dissent. It also hired one black and two Puerto Rican women as organizers to work with him and a white woman to compose the weekly newsletter. The administrative assistant and the bilingual secretary, who had previously constituted the entirety of the Board's staff, were white.

functions of the staff

The existence of a paid staff made the Joan of Arc Board into a community reality. Until the Board hired its staff, it was unable to print a newsletter, send a representative to a daytime meeting, or arouse people sufficiently to provoke a sit-in or a demonstration. The organizers succeeded

[29] As was noted in Chapter Two, the movement for community control of schools represented a turning point in New York City as black groups seemed to repudiate integrationist goals. Nonetheless, all the groups pressing for community control had some degree of white involvement.

in doing all these things. Previously the Governing Board's office had been the domain of one part-time secretary who could not even fill up her time with the work generated by the Board. The arrival of the staff transformed the office into a center of activity. Two secretaries were kept busy typing and mimeographing newsletters, notices of meetings, informational bulletins and manifestos. Neighborhood people would drop into the office with complaints and communications, or just to talk.

The two Puerto Rican organizers assisted the newly formed Spanish-speaking parent group at one of the elementary schools in gaining control of the Parent Association there. A women's black caucus, with a membership of about twenty, was organized and met every other week to discuss school problems. Jenkins tried to form a similar group for men—the Organization of Concerned Black Male Adults—with limited success. The organization had a brief existence, highlighted by an unannounced tour of the junior high school by eight black fathers. They visited all the classrooms while school was in session and publicly questioned teachers and administrative staff concerning the abuses which they claimed to have found. One of Jenkins' purposes in leading this tour was to demonstrate to the children in the school that black men as well as women cared about their welfare. He had difficulty, however, in knitting the men into a permanent group, and after the flurry created by the tour of the junior high school, the organization faded away.

The organizing staff assisted in the publication of an "underground" student newspaper in JHS 118. Board members probably expected the students to produce an exposé of the school; instead, in the first issue they got the conventional wisdom:

Should students have student power? . . . I don't think students should have power (a say in what should go on in the schools). I say that because students don't know an intelligent way of going about getting what they want.[30]

The attitudes displayed in "To Tell It Like It Is" revealed the way in which student consciousness remained determined by the adult models available. While Joan of Arc students were not satisfied with their school, they could not, even when given free scope and encouragement, think of alternative modes of organization and discipline to displace those which were then operating unsuccessfully. Rather, they could only recommend more of the same, applied more rigorously. Jenkins spent considerable time holding conferences with the predominantly black group of students who put out the newspaper. At the end of the school year the students spent a weekend at a conference center in the country with Governing Board members and staff for the purpose of discussing school problems. The result of Jenkins' efforts was the development of a well-defined and verbalized demand for changes in the school among the students.

the organizer's legitimacy

In addition to organizing groups on behalf of the Governing Board and directing the Board's office and communications, Jenkins frequently acted as

[30] "To Tell It Like It Is: A Publication of Joan of Arc Students," mimeo, n.d.

the public spokesman of the Governing Board. This role on several occasions led to fundamental challenges to his legitimacy. Immediately after he was hired, he collected the names of blacks and Puerto Ricans on a petition which stated that the signers were boycotting a meeting on educational issues with West Side legislators sponsored by the Strycker's Bay Neighborhood Council. Although no one really imagined that the signers would have attended the meeting, regardless of the sentiments behind the petition, the effect of its presentation was to create a small furor. As the "official" history of the Joan of Arc Board described it:

In keeping with this policy [of separate organizations for blacks and Puerto Ricans] George Jenkins organized a black and Puerto Rican boycott of a meeting with West Side politicians called by Strycker's Bay Neighborhood Council. The boycotting parents and community people stated that they would not sit down with politicians who had consistently refused to act for community control of schools. Strycker's Bay Neighborhood Council took this boycott as a personal affront, instead of an attack on the politicians, and a community-wide explosion occurred. When the dust had settled, the Governing Board and Strycker's Bay were no longer close allies in the fight against bureaucracy, and cries of "divisiveness" were heard from many white middle-class community people.

The reaction to Jenkins' move by those who disapproved of the boycott was to inquire what right he had to claim to be representing blacks and Puerto Ricans in the area:

"Jenkins is a militant, trying to be tough," [Assemblyman Jerome] Kretchmer went on. "I don't believe him. And just which section of the community is he supposed to represent? I've never laid eyes on him in my life!"
[Assemblyman Albert] Blumenthal described Jenkins as "an outraged, inflamed man." "He was trying to make a racist issue out of the Joan of Arc complex," he went on. "He said he represented black and Puerto Rican parents. Well, I represent black, Puerto Rican and white parents." [31]

The shaky basis of Jenkins' authority as a spokesman also came out sharply following another of the confrontations between the PS 84 Parent Association (PA) and the District Superintendent, Dr. Rosen. In the middle of April some of the parents from PS 84 picketed Rosen's office, calling on him to hire a new principal to replace the acting principal. They were joined by Jenkins and two other members of the Governing Board staff, as well as a few members of the Governing Board. The group of about fifteen proceeded to occupy the Superintendent's office, and Jenkins took over his desk. The group refused to leave until they got an immediate meeting with the District 5 Local School Board (LSB). The chairman of the LSB first refused and then granted the meeting. At the meeting the District 5 Board agreed to let a committee of parents select the principal and pay him from the JOA Governing Board's own money. [32] Throughout the day Jenkins acted as spokesman and negotiator for the group.

[31] *Manhattan Tribune*, April 19, 1969.

[32] This event never actually came to pass, and the LSB soon changed its mind concerning the

The role that Jenkins played that day caused several of the parents on the PS 84 PA executive board to question his right to act as the leader of their group. In response the Governing Board held a special meeting with the PS 84 executive board. The following excerpts from the minutes of the meeting indicate the nature of both the attacks on Jenkins and the way in which he was defended. In general, the meeting showed the anomalous position of the paid organizer who, while a salaried employee of a group, was expected to exert leadership and take initiatives.

Mrs. Graff (PA president) called the meeting to order. She described the reasons for the meeting as a concern on the part of the parents about their relationship with the Planning/Governing Board and the role of Mr. Jenkins (he is essentially unknown to many 84 parents). She hoped we could discuss the meaning of community control to the parents and the Board and the directions both should take from here.

E.C. (white parent): I would like to know how the Board sees the community. What was their purpose in hiring Jenkins? Is he to work with the total community? . . . Do you feel that Jenkins can organize all segments of this integrated community?

J.B. (black parent): We are not an integrated community.

David Good (GB chairman): Our decision was whether to hire an educational administrator to work out a plan or an organizer to get the power to implement a plan. We decided we needed an organizer. . . . We thought we needed a trade union organizer type. He was hired to organize parents.

S.R. (parent): Didn't you want a community meeting to introduce him?

Donald Adams (PS 84 GB representative): We have been lax in holding public meetings.

Good: He has been on the staff for three weeks and knows many parents.

J.P. (parent): I don't think the Governing Board should have consulted [the community]. I first met Mr. Jenkins at the Strycker's Bay meeting. We all felt the same way at Rosen's office: outside to demonstrate; inside to disrupt. But no one took leadership. Those who wanted to take the moment stayed; those who didn't want to take a chance left. . . . I think he has been good for us and the kids.

E.R. (PS 84 parent; GB staff writer): We are nitpicking. . . . We must cut off talk and act. It is quite obvious to everyone that Jenkins stayed back until no one knew what to do. No one knew how, but he did. The only way you can organize is around an action.

J.B.: The demonstration was meaningless; it was saved by Jenkins.

Good: It has been said that George Jenkins will divide the community along racial lines. . . . Jenkins is a professional organizer. These people work for themselves as a political commitment. We will part ways when we disagree. What are his beliefs? In order to do an effective job on the West Side, black and Puerto Rican parents must be organized because their kids are being hurt. The black caucus is necessary. He asked the Governing Board to legitimize this method. It does not mean he is organizing along racial lines. He has come upon hypocrisy. I hope he doesn't fail.

---

propriety of permitting the Joan of Arc Board to pay a principal. The parents' committee did select a principal, but the candidate backed out at the last minute. The following year the new district superintendent managed to appoint an acting principal supported by the parents' group.

J.M. (former PS 84 PA president):   It is going to be divisive if he is coming in to organize 84 parents. I am not pleased with the results of the demonstration. The Planning/Governing Board could use its money better. What if at the end of four months there is no more money [to pay the principal].

S.T. (PS 84 parent):   The basic issue is that we are a non-integrated community. We constantly make believe. We have a working relationship with black and Puerto Rican parents. They hang on because the whites have the power. We want change. . . . Jenkins is the best kind of organizer. He listens to people. He attacked an SBNC vice president—me. [But] he handled that situation. . . . He hasn't worked here [in this community], but he lives here. . . . Because of the complexity of the neighborhood, we have unusual problems. We should get a white organizer too maybe. . . . Jenkins was giving the word at the demonstration. . . . None of us did so.[33]

The organizing staff provided considerable resources to the Governing Board. Its presence, however, had unexpected costs. Jenkins and his subordinates gave the Governing Board the advantages of skill in communication, initiative and leadership in situations requiring action, and full-time application to the job of organization. But their activities also led to distrust of the Governing Board's motives, reluctance to volunteer, envy of those being paid for their services, and a dependence of the Board on its staff.

The Governing Board's decision to hire a paid organizing staff and to concentrate on building a power base was regarded by some people in the community as an abuse of its mandate. Critics of the Board did not see a necessary connection between community organization and educational reform; they feared that the Governing Board was seeking power for the purposes of self-aggrandizement.

The control of a $40,000 treasury and the power of patronage enabled the Board to be of material benefit to individuals, but this was not an unmixed blessing. Money and jobs meant that staff members were now being paid to do work that was once done by volunteers. As a result, people became reluctant to offer their services for free. The job of organizer for the Board was an attractive one for neighborhood women. The Board chose Jenkins' subordinates from among people known in the community, thereby avoiding the "outside agitator" charges that were leveled at him. But the female staff evoked envy from similarly situated residents. Community reactions to the female staff exactly paralleled those of poverty organization staffs in the San Francisco area:

Because they [the staff members] were the lucky ones to be selected from a large number of equally qualified applicants, envy, distrust, and resentment were aroused in the population they hoped to organize.[34]

The Governing Board members themselves, in comparison with the staff, were amateurs and were often left without a role. Jenkins devised the

[33] Minutes of the Special Meeting of the PS 84 Parents Association Executive Board and Representatives of the Planning/Governing Board, April 20, 1969 (in the files of the PS 84 PA). Governing Board is abbreviated as GB.

[34] Kramer, *Participation of the Poor*, p. 230.

slogan "Every parent an organizer" and urged the Board members to work as parent organizers, involving the community in school affairs. But, as organizers, the Board members had to depend on their employees for guidance; and as supervisors of the staff they were forced, like the executive boards of most bureaucracies, to rely on their employees for information and program ideas. Although, with the addition of a staff, the activities sponsored by the Board increased greatly in number and scope, the real participation of Board members in the day-to-day events carried on in their name diminished. Most programs ostensibly under the auspices of the Joan of Arc Governing Board were experienced by that entity only secondhand. Whereas the Board members themselves formerly were at the head of the community control movement on the West Side, they now became a board of directors for a staff which to a significant extent supplanted them.

THE COLLAPSE OF THE
GOVERNING BOARD

By the autumn of 1969 it became clear even to the diehard members of the Governing Board that they were never going to gain official power. By then the New York Legislature had passed its Decentralization Law establishing 20,000 pupils as the minimum size of a decentralized school district in New York City. While the continuation of the Governing Board as a pressure group and community organizing agent remained possible, few Board members enjoyed this kind of activity. Their funds were running out, and they did not even trouble to write a funding proposal that would permit them to perpetuate themselves. Eventually the JOA Governing Board consisted only of the staff of six plus two or three still active members, including the chairman. Public interest in the Board never extended much beyond the original core of supporters. Having an active paid staff lent the Board the appearance of life. But when Jenkins quit in September 1969, to take another job, the Board essentially folded, and continued in name only until the following January.

At the final and (ironically) well-attended open meeting of the Joan of Arc Board in January 1970, community members accused the Board of failing its mandate for leadership. David Good defended the Board's performance, arguing that, given the external situation, it had accomplished as much as could reasonably be expected. Some parents wanted to see the Board continue in existence, but Board members refused to consider the request.

The tone of this concluding meeting was dolorous, for it seemed to mark the end of a movement that had, for a while, promised change on the West Side. The community-control activists among the parents felt betrayed, in part by the Joan of Arc Board, but mainly by the New York political structure. No one among the activists believed that the Decentralization Law offered genuine power to neighborhoods in the administration of the schools.

Without such power they thought that the bureaucracy and the teachers union would successfully stifle any efforts toward fundamental reform of the system. They felt that if they had not been misled by the false promises of the Board of Education into organizing around planning for the Joan of Arc complex, they would still have a viable movement. The unkept promise of a demonstration district, then the eventual withdrawal in Albany of the legal basis for genuine community control, and the concomitant reluctance of foundations to support community education groups,[35] resulted in a paralysis of the reform groups. Their strategy had been based on the premise that legal decentralization of power to community representatives would take place in the near future. When this event did not occur, they were without direction.

legacies of the board

The JOA Board did leave some positive outcomes. Most important, perhaps, was its effect on the administration of District 5. While the Governing Board looked somewhat like a paper tiger to those most knowledgeable, it operated as an effective public in holding the District 5 Local School Board and Superintendent accountable. Dr. Rosen resigned his superintendency, apparently because he found dealing with community groups and their demands frustrating and unprofessional. His replacement, Dr. Hammer, had been a popular principal in Harlem, was a self-proclaimed reformer, and was held in exceptionally high esteem by blacks and Puerto Ricans on the West Side. Subsequently a Puerto Rican Governing Board member commented about him:

I think he's very groovy, very flexible. He's a political-minded man. Rosen was a good human being, but he was very naive. Hammer just appointed a new principal at 84 on his own. Everybody is scared of what he is going to do next.

Hammer's appointment assured the initiation and continuation of policies which the JOA Board had supported. He discontinued disciplinary suspensions. He permitted parent participation in the selection of principals and managed to cut through red tape sufficiently to appoint acting principals satisfactory to parents in the four Joan of Arc elementary schools; by the end of the next school year, he had even succeeded in transferring the junior high school principal to the district office.

These changes could be attributed only in part to the existence of the Joan of Arc Board. But it would be an error to explain them as the result of unilateral action by a reformist administration in District 5. The District 5

---

[35] The Ford Foundation, after the passage of the 1969 Decentralization Law which required that all foundation grants to community school districts pass through the central Board of Education, decided that it would cease funding community education groups in New York City. Since Ford had been by far the largest means of support for these groups, its withdrawal was shattering. Ford had its fingers badly burned by its association with Ocean Hill-Brownsville. Moreover, at the time of passage of the Decentralization Law, a Congressional committee was investigating the role of foundations in financing community action groups. The 1969 federal tax law effectively eliminated such grants.

Local School Board never instituted reforms until pushed by parents groups; Hammer was appointed Superintendent because parents were demanding an activist in that position. The JOA Board for a year and a half was the neighborhood articulator of the demand for school reform. It was not alone in expressing the sentiments of reform-minded parents in the complex. But during the period of its existence, it and the PS 84 Parents Association were the most highly organized neighborhood groups calling for change in the schools.

The great failure of the Joan of Arc Board, a failure that was beyond its capacity to avoid, was in not achieving any form of institutionalized community power. The District 5 administration could choose to involve parents in school decisions, but it did not have to do so. With the disappearance of an organizational infrastructure and without de jure power, the de facto power of the parents might also wither away.

THE SIGNIFICANCE OF AN ABORTIVE POLITICAL MOVEMENT

The lessons of Joan of Arc are largely lessons in the dynamics of failure. One might, in fact, question whether the study of the Joan of Arc Planning/Governing Board is an appropriate contribution to a book on political movements. The Governing Board was a small body of individuals with some claim to community support. It did not, however, succeed in translating that support into very much power. In some sense Joan of Arc was a movement which never happened.

The importance of Joan of Arc is twofold. First, the case study clarifies some of the issues raised by the pluralist defense of American politics. The pluralists argue that the existence of slack political resources permits potential groups to organize and demand changes in governmental policy when collectivities feel strongly aggrieved. Robert Dahl, for example, asserts:

Most of the time . . . most citizens use their resources for purposes other than gaining influence over government decisions. There is a great gap between their actual influence and their potential influence. Their political resources are, so to speak, slack in the system. In some circumstances these resources might be converted from nonpolitical to political purposes; if so, the gap between the actual influence of the average citizen and his potential influence would narrow.[36]

Implicit in Dahl's argument is the assumption that if citizens really desire to bring pressure on government, they can do so. He fails, however, to specify the way in which the "average citizen" can narrow the gap between his actual and potential influence when the demands he is pressing require significant concessions by present power holders; nor does he estimate the degree of effort required.

[36] Robert A. Dahl, *Who Governs?* (New Haven: Yale University Press, 1961), p. 305.

The Joan of Arc experience indicates how difficult it is for citizens to utilize their political resources.[37] Polsby notes that one of the preconditions for success of groups in a pluralist system is their "ability to choose goals that do not strain the compliance of others in the system." [38] But this limitation, which Polsby does not recognize as detracting from the merits of pluralism, points to the narrow parameters within which groups must operate in order to realize gains through the political process. For people such as those who wished to change the distribution of benefits in New York City schools, the only possibility of obtaining their goal lay in organizing a political movement which would challenge the limits of the system. This movement, however, both at the citywide and neighborhood levels, was not able to sustain itself. At Ocean Hill-Brownsville, as well as at Joan of Arc, it proved impossible to maintain the involvement of sympathizers once the immediate goals of the movement seemed out of reach.

The second reason justifying the study of Joan of Arc is its usefulness in revealing the factors which cause a movement to falter or never gain momentum—factors which are potentially operable in the cases of all neighborhood-based, grass-roots movements among normally inactive people. One of the most interesting aspects of the Joan of Arc Board's failure to excite its community arises from the rationality of its appeal. The Board never promised a utopia; it never claimed that there were easy solutions to the problems of New York schools. Community control was pictured only as a first step, necessary but not sufficient for school reform. The result was that few benefits were proffered to overcome the opportunity costs of action. Although the opponents of community control attempted to discredit its adherents as irrational militants, the very reasonableness of the movement's leadership diminished its inspirational possibilities. Irving Horowitz comments that:

It is no accident that nonrational rhetoric is used with equal facility by the Right and by the Left. The only political sectors who are unable to use it are the liberals. . . . But liberalism could not be accepted by . . . [those] in search of transformation.[39]

The Joan of Arc Board was seeking transformation, but it never promised that such would arrive as the result of any particular action. The consequence was that no action ever seemed quite "worth it" to very many people.

The Joan of Arc case also exemplifies certain structural factors which affect all urban movements and which are serious obstacles even to leadership with greater charisma. Joan of Arc was crucially affected by events over which it had no control, such as the initial decision of the Board of Education

[37] See Michael Parenti, "Power and Pluralism: A View from the Bottom," *Journal of Politics*, XXXII, August, 1970, 501–30, for a discussion of the failure of local groups in Newark to realize their "pluralist" potential.

[38] Nelson W. Polsby, *Community Power and Political Theory* (New Haven: Yale University Press, 1963), p. 137.

[39] Irving Louis Horowitz, *Foundations of Political Sociology* (New York: Harper & Row, 1972), p. 89.

to experiment with decentralization and the later one of the Legislature to terminate the experiments. The West Side, like most populous urban communities, had no important political institutions operating at the neighborhood level. The few existing official organizations, like the Local School Board or the Community Planning Board, had differing geographical and functional jurisdictions and were at best intermediaries between local citizens and central authorities. Thus, the links between local groups and decisionmaking bodies were highly attenuated. The problems created by lack of linkages to authority were aggravated by the paucity of media concerned with the local situation. The Joan of Arc group had considerable difficulty sending messages to its supporters; attracting the interest of the noninvolved was beyond its means. The best it could usually hope for in the way of media coverage was attention in the little-read neighborhood weekly newspaper.

The dearth of individuals with political skills willing to assume leadership positions in the movement was also partly associated with the attenuated political infrastructure of the area. Few people had much experience with political organization; those who did were already working at a higher level of government. In turn, the inability of inexperienced people to create a viable infrastructure of neighborhood groups perpetuated the absence of political skills. Recognizing its political ineptitude, the Joan of Arc group resorted to the strategy of the paid organizer. Ocean Hill-Brownsville and IS 201 similarly employed a salaried organizing staff in their attempts to gain widespread popular support. But the use of professional staff led on the West Side as elsewhere to oligarchical tendencies and a diminution of legitimacy.

Perhaps the most obvious conclusion one can draw from Joan of Arc is that its failures were self-reinforcing. Few people want to waste their time in a hopeless effort. Most groups with limited resources start out looking like losers and are thus always at a serious disadvantage. The most important correlate of success or failure in any particular incident may well be the outcome of the incident which preceded it. Joan of Arc demonstrates the snowballing effect of defeat; the case of PS 84, which we shall consider in the next chapter, is one where a movement was able to develop sufficient momentum to experience the snowballing effect of success and to see the realization of its goals.

the movement at
ps 84: a
case of success

4

At the same time as the Joan of Arc Planning/Governing Board attempted to achieve community control and failed, a group of parents and some teachers at Public School (PS) 84 (Manhattan) mounted a political movement which effected major innovations in school policies and socio-political relationships. The movement introduced "informal" or "open classroom" pedagogical methods, with the aim of providing a higher quality of education in a racially integrated setting.[1] Interrelated with this educational innovation, and essential to it, was a fundamental change in the governance of the school. The movement succeeded in removing two principals hostile to its goals. Procedures were established whereby parents played a significant part in the selection of a new principal, one with a role conception differing from the usual professional orientation.

The political movement at PS 84 established community control of a single school in one of America's most bureaucraticized and insulated educational systems. The movement grew in bits and pieces in direct relation to changes in consciousness of the parents about schools and client-bureaucrat relationships. The revolution at PS 84, like revolution in general, depended upon the loss of legitimacy of the governing elite, its inability to suppress or co-opt dissenters, and significantly, upon a number of discrete occurrences—catalytic events—which altered the consciousness of participants, pushing the elite into defensiveness and the moderate reformers into a more radical stance. Analysis of how this movement developed, what it

[1] The terms "informal methods," "open classroom," and "infant school" will be used interchangeably. The designation "infant school" was frequently used by PS 84 parents and teachers since informal methods were most widespread in the English infant schools (which taught children age four through six or seven).

demanded, how it acted and was resisted, provides insights into client-bureaucracy relations in the domain of education, and into the dynamics of an urban political movement centered about the statuses of parent and teacher.

The movement at PS 84 had its base in a group of white and black parents on the Upper West Side of Manhattan who felt decent education could be provided on a socially integrated basis. PS 84 already seemed to be doing this. It was housed in a modern building, with adequate space and facilities. Its student body appeared to be integrated in terms of both race and social class. In 1967 it was 48 percent white, 21 percent black and 31 percent Puerto Rican; with about 40 percent of the children coming from middle or upper-middle income homes, and the others from working-class or poor homes (though, as might be expected, most of the white children were in the former category, and most of the blacks and Puerto Ricans in the latter).[2] Moreover, the overall level of educational achievement seemed respectable, if not outstanding. Average reading levels in the second and fourth grades, for example, were somewhat above the national norms during the years 1967 and 1969.[3]

Many of the parents who would later become activists believed, however, that the aggregate situation masked the reality of the school. PS 84, they asserted, was internally segregated. The system of tracking children by ability created mostly white classes with high achievement and few disciplinary problems and mostly black and Puerto Rican classes where children performed poorly and received inferior educations. In this sense, the parents believed, PS 84 was like the neighborhood which it served—integrated in appearance, but functionally segregated; racist less in terms of overt expressions of bigotry than in the covert outcomes of extant policies and procedures.

Actors in the political conflict at PS 84.   A minority of the parents at PS 84 comprised the core of the movement which engaged the educational bureaucracy. They used the Parent Association (PA) as the organizational structure through which activity was planned and conducted. Both before and after the period described in this case study, the Parent Association functioned as a social organization and/or as a routinized interest group. For more than two years, however, it constituted the core of an urban political movement directed at thoroughgoing change of the local educational system.

A plurality of activists in the movement was white. Most of the goals of these whites were similar to those of their black allies. The white parents were committed not only to racial integration, but to the elimination of practices they believed affected blacks and Puerto Ricans adversely. They were, in this regard, atypical of whites in the United States, but not necessarily of the

[2] Ethnic composition data drawn from files of Local School District 5, Manhattan (now designated as District 3). During 1969–70 the ethnic composition of the school was 41 percent white, 24 percent black and 35 percent Puerto Rican and other Latin nationalities. The estimate of 60 percent of the children as working class or poor is based on interviews with school personnel and on the percentage qualifying for the school lunch program.

[3] Source: District 5 records.

white liberals who kept their children in the West Side's public schools. The fact that there were few divisions within the group of white activists, and almost no opposition from other parents to their demands, supports the inference that they were fairly representative of the white clientele of the school. These white parents were always conscious of racial differences and sought to introduce changes acceptable to all groups within the movement and parent body.

Black parents, perhaps two-thirds of whom were below the poverty line, constituted a large minority of movement participants. Blacks were in leadership roles at all points in the movement's development, especially, however, during the period of peak mobilization in the fall of 1968. While blacks were proportionately represented in the movement, Puerto Ricans were not. At a time when more than a third of the school's 900 children were Puerto Rican, hardly a single Puerto Rican parent had any involvement in the PA. The Puerto Ricans had no effect one way or the other upon the course of events at PS 84.

The greatest number of parents mobilized at any time was on the order of 200, this during the crisis period associated with the 1968 teachers' strike when (as we will describe) the PA governed the school.[4] During the year of greatest activity, 1968–69, sixty parents attended two or more meetings. These parents comprised the core of the movement; twenty-two of them were black, and the remainder white. The leadership of the movement was centered in the PA Executive Board, which prior to October 1968 had eight white and four black members, then expanded to thirty-three members, half of whom were black. Most of the people on the Executive Board were women. With the exception of the Puerto Ricans, then, the parent movement at PS 84 was integrated in terms of race and class.

Associated with the efforts of the parents were those of a number of teachers at the school. These teachers were part of the overall movement, though they stood outside of the PA. They initiated many of the events which were catalytic to the parent mobilization, provided their parent allies with "inside" information, and themselves acted to attack the movement's targets. Of the forty or so teachers on the staff of PS 84 in 1968, about ten were active in the movement, and an equal number sympathetic to it. Three or four teachers played significant leadership roles.

The Joan of Arc Planning/Governing Board was the only neighborhood organization which became involved in the reform efforts at 84. During the spring of 1968 the Governing Board staged a joint sit-in with the PA at the office of the District Superintendent. For some time thereafter it appeared that it would finance an illegal acting principal at PS 84. The attitude of the Board toward the 84 movement was, however, somewhat ambivalent, and its resources proved to be relatively insignificant in directly affecting developments at the school.

A "third party" to the conflict at PS 84, sometimes aiding the

---

[4] These data and those which follow pertaining to the movement are derived from the files of the PS 84 Parent Association and from interviews by the authors.

movement, sometimes itself a target, was the Local School Board (LSB) of District 5.[5] Before 1968 the LSB functioned primarily as a sounding-board for parent grievances in the district, although it did have some influence over the District Superintendent of Schools, Dr. Rosen.[6] The LSB was committed to decentralization and to expanding its own powers, but it eschewed all forms of activity which violated normal procedures. When its authority was increased in 1969, it provided some assistance to the movement, particularly in its appointment of a new and radical superintendent, Dr. Hammer.

The main target of the movement's activities was the principal of PS 84, Mrs. Wertzel. She was a professional of long tenure in the city schools, somewhat past middle age, who held a traditional conception of the principal's role. Early in 1969 Wertzel was replaced by Mrs. Rubin, a protagonist of similar background and behavior. The second prime target of the movement was Dr. Rosen, whom the movement felt had the authority to effect the changes it demanded, yet who actively defended the system from innovation.

The final major actor during the period of intense conflict was Professor Lillian Samson. Professor Samson was one of America's leading experts on British methods of primary education. A coalition of parents and teachers arranged her hiring as a teacher-trainer in PS 84, where she brought about significant changes in classroom techniques and school policies. While never actively allied with the parent movement, her efforts were supported by it, and, as we shall argue, her educational innovations depended upon its presence.

THE FREEDOM SCHOOL:
A CATALYTIC EVENT

A crucial determinant of a political movement is the existence of a group with shared consciousness of deprivation. One of the most important empirical questions raised by the theory of movements then becomes how such a group consciousness comes about. What is the process by which a collectivity perceives itself as sharing common goals and a common basis for action? Usually there can be identified in the formation of political movements a point when consciousness seems suddenly to crystallize, when some event or individual precipitates a realization of group identity and interests such that the collectivity becomes transformed into a movement. The Freedom School at PS 84 was such a catalytic event.[7] It is of interest less

---

[5] At this time New York City had thirty local school boards appointed by the central Board of Education in addition to the three experimental governing boards. Local boards had advisory powers and in 1968 acquired the power to hire, but not fire, the district superintendent. They were given additional authority under the 1969 School Decentralization Act.

[6] Pseudonyms are used for all persons in this case except for members of the New York City Board of Education and a few widely known political figures. Wherever possible the pseudonym chosen reflects the original name in ethnic quality.

[7] Some historically significant catalytic events are the calling of the Estates General by Louis

for its particular content than as an example of the way in which disparate dissatisfactions can suddenly become sharply focused; the way in which the multiplicity of factors producing a particular situation seem in the minds of individuals to reduce themselves to a few causal variables. The result of the Freedom School was the creation of a movement which identified the PS 84 administration as the source of difficulties in the school and which had a vision of a specific educational alternative involving changes in classroom methods and administrative procedures.

When the United Federation of Teachers (UFT) struck the New York City schools for almost two weeks in 1967 over the issue of wages and the power of professionals vis-à-vis disruptive children, parents and teachers at PS 84 were divided in their allegiances. After two conflict-ridden meetings a few parents suggested the possibility of running a "Freedom School" [8] during the strike, thereby honoring the picket lines while providing education for children whom the UFT was "using as hostages." Space was found at the nearby Goddard-Riverside Community Center. Once word spread about the Freedom School's existence, it acquired a faculty of eight and had more than 100 children in attendance.

The makeshift arrangements at Goddard encouraged innovative approaches on the part of the self-selected group of teachers. Classes tended to be heterogeneous in age and to make use of the neighborhood as an educational resource. About a dozen parents provided logistical support to the professionals and themselves helped teach. The atmosphere at Goddard was one of excitement over parents and teachers working together, and over newly unfolding educational possibilities.

The Freedom School experience stood in sharp contrast to the way in which parent-teacher relations were structured in the public school. Everything about PS 84 discouraged communication between parents and teachers, and maintained social distance between the two groups. Parents were not permitted to accompany their children into the building. Rather, pupils had to be dropped off in the school yard, where they lined up and were marched into their classrooms by school aides. Teachers were wholly engaged during the day by the necessity of filling up class time and maintaining order; they had little time to spare for parents. A parent coming into the classroom felt like someone trying to talk to an air-traffic controller on duty. Even gaining physical access to teachers was difficult, as one of the striking teachers noted:

In PS 84 there are signs all over the doorways saying that you need a pass to walk in. And all the doors but one are kept locked, though there is nothing to indicate to the parent which of the eight doors is open. If he does persist long enough to find the open door, the parent is confronted by an aide who asks him what he wants and sends him

---

XVI, the British Stamp Act, and the refusal of Rosa Parks to sit in the back of a Montgomery bus. See Appendix.

[8] This term was generally used by groups in various parts of the city which conducted classes outside of school buildings during the strike. It was coined by the Reverend Milton Galamison (who later became a member of the Board of Education) during a black boycott of New York Schools in 1964.

to the office for a pass. . . . So usually the only reason parents see the teacher is because they have been called in because the child has done something awful.[9]

In the Freedom School there was no established structure which defined parents as outsiders, nor was there an isolated building to protect teachers from intrusion. Parents supplied materials, helped arrange schedules, and worked to recruit new children. For the teachers who had previously felt that professionalism demanded protection from parental intrusion, the Freedom School produced a jolting change in consciousness. One teacher commented:

I was an untouchable for two years teaching second grade in Queens and then music at 84. I was the teacher. My professionalism kept me well insulated from parents. But here the parents were in the room. The Freedom School depended on the parents. For the first time it dawned on me that one could be a professional yet have parents in the classroom working with children. . . . You see, I had always believed that parent involvement was an attack on professionalism.

Similarly, the Freedom School awakened parents to the practical possibility of a school in which they were not outsiders, whose interaction could only be negative. According to a parent who worked in the Freedom School:

What I see in the Freedom School—and it's beautiful to watch—there's no question about whether or not to request the help of parents. . . . There's no reason for the teacher to doubt what the parent will do when she's in there . . . because the teachers here have nothing to hide. So the parent comes in without trying to find out what's wrong with the school—comes in to work with the teachers and does. When the teacher sees this she begins to trust the parent, and the two begin to trust one another more and more.

The Freedom School not only contributed, as this parent put it, to the "trust" between parents and teachers, but also facilitated solidaristic ties within each group. This was particularly the case for the teachers, who for the first time in their experience had the opportunity to teach together and see how each related to children. The informality of the physical arrangement at Goddard-Riverside and the high teacher-to-pupil ratio made possible a degree of mutual interaction and assistance among the teachers rarely found in the public school. Teachers with a potential community of interest came into contact, and the situation was structured by circumstances so as to facilitate the development of a common consciousness.[10]

[9] Thomas Hogan, an interviewer for the Oral History Project at Columbia University, conducted tape-recorded interviews with participants in the Freedom School. The interviews were conducted unofficially, and no use has been made of them except for a few excerpts which appeared in *The Center Forum*, II, October 5, 1967, 5–7. Except where noted, this and other quotations from Freedom School participants are drawn from the Hogan transcripts.

[10] There are three aspects or dimensions of commonality which we have in mind here: first, commonality or similarity in ideas and values among members of a collectivity; second, the recognition of these shared ideas, i.e., the recognition by each member that others think like him or her; and third, the growth of a collective identity partly as a product of aspects one and two.

A teacher made this point clearly in describing her feelings about the school:

One of the thrilling things about this was to find that these other teachers whom I had known somewhat, but always within the formal circumstances of the school where we worked—to find that they really felt very much the way I felt; to find that they really worked the way I had wanted to work; that this was their natural way too, as well as mine. It was an eye-opener, because we'd never really—we suspected it, I suppose. Certainly we never knew that we were all ready to do these kind of things, to teach in this way. And for me, I can't talk for them, I don't think I would ever have taught like this in the public school; I would never have taken the chance. Here, there was nothing to fear. We helped each other. We all experimented at once and together.

Another teacher commented:

Different people tried out things more or less spontaneously. Then we would talk about what we saw happening in the classroom, you know, about what things were reaching the children. . . . I just never had that feeling of being alone that you get in the public school. It's more than being alone, it's that you have no support to try something new—at least I didn't at PS 84. But your supervisors are always ready to come in and tell you you failed with whatever you are trying. So you play it safe, by the book.

The informality of the neighborhood-house setting, the small rooms, the missing pupils' desks and "front of the room" (defined by blackboard and teacher's desk), all helped create a definition which discouraged hierarchy and student passivity.[11] Thus, a teacher described her recognition that the order expected in the public school classroom, while rationalized in terms of its instrumentality in facilitating learning, had become a ritualistic end in itself:[12]

You know, there's a lot more disorder here than I would ever have tolerated in 84. Certainly more than our principal would have taken. But what did all the order get

[11] Discussions of the social structure of traditional classrooms may be found, inter alia, in Eleanor B. Leacock, *Teaching and Learning in City Schools* (New York: Basic Books, 1969), pp. 86–115; Philip W. Jackson, *Life in Classrooms* (New York: Holt, Rinehart & Winston, 1968), esp. pp. 39–112; and Willard W. Waller, *The Sociology of Teaching* (New York: John Wiley, 1965; orig. pub. 1932). Waller's analysis remains incisive today, perhaps because its conflict approach fits well with the reality of urban schools where much of the legitimacy suburban teachers enjoy has been lost. In many ways the changes brought about in the Freedom School represented a reversal of the structural differentiation, role specificity, professionalization and the like associated by some functionalist sociologists with the modern school. See, for example, Robert Dreeben, *On What Is Learned in School* (Reading, Mass.: Addison-Wesley, 1968) and Harold W. Pfautz, "The Black Community, the Community School, and the Socialization Process: Some Caveats," in *Community Control of Schools*, ed. Henry M. Levin (Washington: Brookings Institution, 1970), pp. 13–39, both of which provide functionalist analyses.

[12] Merton presented the concept of ritualism in his ends-means typology: ritualism being the maintenance of means (or rules) which have become dissociated from goals (or the original purpose of the rules). Robert K. Merton, *Social Theory and Social Structure* (New York: Free Press, 1957), pp. 131–60. Merton saw ritualism as endemic to bureaucracies and as dysfunctional for their overall rationality; but, as Michel Crozier shows more elaborately, ritualistic behavior is rational for individuals in bureaucratic situations. Michel Crozier, *The Bureaucratic Phenomenon* (Chicago: University of Chicago Press, 1964), pp. 175–208.

us? So much time was spent making children do this and do that. All because these things were supposed to be essential if learning was to take place. . . . But they became ends in themselves. Nobody really cared whether the kids were getting anything out of my room. I kept control and so it looked like they were learning. . . . That's why Mrs. Wertzel [the principal] thought I was doing a good job.

The teachers, responding to the demands of the situation and their own predispositions, experimented a little, were reinforced by success and supported by one another, and went on to create an educational environment and educational theory radically different from that of PS 84. On their own they moved in the direction of the child-centered, open structure of education just beginning to be advocated in America by men like Herbert Kohl, John Holt and Joseph Featherstone, and in England by the Plowden Commission.[13] In discussing their feelings about the Freedom School the participants referred continually to the "atmosphere," and to how different it was from the public school. Here there was "real communication," "openness," "responsiveness." The school was part "*of* the community" rather than an institution situated *in* the community. Parents were able to "go in there and do something," to see what was happening to their children and affect the process. Teachers began with "the needs of the children" not with those of the organization. Perhaps most important of all the atmosphere in the Freedom School was defined by "how alive the children were . . . how much happier they were than at 84."

We see, then, that the Freedom School experience provided its participants not merely with a sense of relative deprivation when comparing the possibilities demonstrated at Goddard-Riverside with the realities at PS 84, but with new criteria for defining that deprivation. The terms participants used in making comparisons involved a different set of categories from the strictly educational criteria usually considered in discussions of how to measure school quality. The aspects of school which they now emphasized were no longer limited to academic achievement. They had come to include:

1. The structure of command and control employed by teachers within the classroom, i.e., the power structure of the classroom.

2. The nature of the parent-teacher role interface and the extent to which the school responded to parental input.

3. The relationship between curriculum goals and the motivation of pupils, i.e., the extent to which pedagogical methods began with and encouraged student initiative and freedom.

[13] Cf. Herbert Kohl, *36 Children* (New York: New American Library, 1968) and *The Open Classroom* (New York: Random House, 1969); John Holt, *How Children Fail* (New York: Pitman, 1964); *How Children Learn* (New York: Pitman, 1967); and "Children in Prison," *New York Review of Books*, IX, December 21, 1967, 5–10; Joseph Featherstone, "Schools for Children"; *The New Republic*, August 19, 1967, pp. 17–21; "How Children Learn," *idem*, September 2, 1967, pp. 17–21; and "Teaching Children to Think," *idem*, September 9, 1967, pp. 15–19; United Kingdom, Central Advisory Council for Education (England), *Children and Their Primary Schools (The Plowden Report)*, 2 vols. (London: H.M.S.O., 1967).

Together these criteria comprised a radically different analysis of how to describe and evaluate schools.[14]

Having become aware of new evaluative criteria, the Freedom School participants felt increasingly dissatisfied with PS 84. Their new consciousness encouraged them to view the practitioners of traditional educational methods as comprising an opposition group. In this way the Freedom School experience both facilitated the formation of a set of new goals and a strategy to fulfill them through the identification of an enemy who had to be displaced. The labeling of school professionals adhering to traditional teaching practices as "them" represented a major step in the transformation of the collectivity of parents and teachers into an "us."

ORGANIZATIONAL DECAY
AND THE
RADICALIZATION OF CONSCIOUSNESS

The Freedom School provided a significant push for the would-be reformers. But the growth in political activity which followed during the 1967–68 school year also depended upon the decay of the "existing" authority structure at PS 84. Morale on the faculty had been deteriorating since Mrs. Wertzel came on as principal during February of 1967. Several teachers remembered incidents transpiring "right from the start." Many of these seemed to be associated with Wertzel's demand for strict adherence to official school rules, and her insistence that she approve any pedagogical innovations teachers might want to adopt. Staff relations took a sharp turn for the worse, however, immediately following the 1967 UFT strike, which Wertzel strongly opposed. The principal formally reprimanded the returning teachers (who comprised 60 percent of the staff), and wrote to the District Superintendent asking that two union officers be charged with insubordination. They countered that her letter ". . . is a current example of the pattern of intimidation to which we and others have been subjected." [15]

A majority of teachers broke from the usual professional solidarity and, under the leadership of Freedom School participants, organized a series of meetings with parents to discuss "problems at our school." The teachers who

[14] By using these broader criteria the Freedom School participants emphasized the importance of evaluating schools in terms of the quality of life within them. From the perspective of teachers, parents, and certainly children, schools have many of the aspects which Goffmann has associated with "total institutions." Erving Goffmann, "The Characteristics of Total Institutions," in *A Sociological Reader on Complex Organizations* (2nd ed.), ed. Amitai Etzioni (New York: Holt, Rinehart & Winston, 1969), pp. 312–38. Issues of who has power, who has liberty, who is confined, and how students are motivated, are thus all very significant in their own right. Professionals, however, have been highly successful in obfuscating the positions of people criticizing the way public schools are run, by claiming that their own evaluative criteria are "educational," while alternative criteria are "partisan" or "political."

[15] Letter to Dr. Nathan Rosen, September 21, 1967.

attended felt that only parent intervention could improve conditions, and twenty-two of them signed a letter to the president of the PA asking that parents act to ameliorate their "very unhappy situation." [16]

Throughout the year Wertzel was in serious conflict with some of the teachers who had been at the Freedom School, most notably with Mrs. Davis and Mrs. Silver. They refused to accept school regulations, reformed their pedagogical methods without her permission, and more or less openly fomented rebellion among their colleagues. Mrs. Wertzel, for her part, increased her direct supervision and accused Mrs. Davis of introducing religious music (Bach) into the curriculum, finally bringing Silver and Davis up on charges for not leading their classes in the flag salute. These teachers, however, received the backing of the PA Executive Board, retained an American Civil Liberties Union attorney, and eventually not only won their point but successfully labeled the principal as opposed to civil liberties, a real epithet to many of the liberal parents. In addition, Wertzel involved herself in the larger conflict over community control in New York City by sending a telegram to the Governor supporting a conservative law in the name of "the staff at PS 84." The result was public condemnation of her action by twenty-four teachers. The culmination of these and other incidents came at the end of the year when sixteen teachers left PS 84, several voluntarily and the others on Wertzel's orders. At this time the PA picketed the school, and a local newspaper wrote two uncomplimentary articles about Wertzel's principalship, so that issues associated with staff relations had moved from inside the professional organization to the public arena. Political cleavages sharply cut across the professional-client boundary.

the parent response
to organizational decay

The parents' attitudes toward Wertzel were, by the spring of 1968, negative, though in varying degrees. Some parents felt they had made limited gains in working with her. Others believed that nothing had been achieved and that she was incapable of becoming the type of principal they desired. But nearly everyone agreed (in March, 1968) that trying to "get rid of Wertzel" was tactically unwise. In the first place, although the principal was untenured, there was no assurance that a concerted parent drive against her would be successful. If the parents failed, they felt they would certainly eliminate the possibility of having any communication with her from then on, and there was no way to prevent her from retaliating against their children.

In the second place, the parents were not at all confident that Wertzel would be replaced by someone better. Authority to appoint principals resided with District Superintendent Rosen, who could only choose among the top three names on a ranked list of eligibles for the city as a whole.[17] Most of the parents believed that as bad as Wertzel might be, she represented the type of

---

[16] Letter to the president of the PA, December 1, 1967.

[17] He could go lower on the list provided that bypassed individuals waived their rights.

principal to be found on "the list"—though the more disaffected teachers and several parents thought her to be worse than average.

At its meeting on March 21, 1968, the PA Executive Board resolved (by a vote of eleven to one) "to retain Mrs. Wertzel and direct our energies in a more positive direction." [18] But a minority of the Executive Board stated their intention to create a "Profile" of PS 84, i.e., to investigate conditions within the school, collect evidence, and then suggest ways to improve things. This "Profile group" was comprised largely of the parents who had been associated with the Freedom School and several new parents who had just moved into the district; it represented about half the active PA members.

The Profile of PS 84.   The Profile was a lengthy document of more than 150 pages.[19] It recounted the low morale and dissension on the teaching staff, and included signed statements from a half-dozen teachers. It emphasized that the principal had failed to comply with the District 5 Balanced Class Program, which involved the elimination of classes for the intellectually gifted (IGC) and tracking in the lower grades—and thereby of the means to maintain de facto segregation within integrated schools like PS 84. Many statements charged racial bias on the part of the administration and some teachers. The Profile concluded with a request for an "official study," which would suggest "new methods and new ideas in the educational process" in order to find effective ways "to educate economically, ethnically and racially varied school populations."

The Profile was submitted to the principal, District Superintendent, and Local School Board. Of these, only the LSB replied, with a general affirmation of its interest in maintaining "professional standards" and in facilitating parent-principal communications. From the point of view of the Profile group, its efforts had come to naught, save perhaps to publicize the tensions in the school.

The reformers offer a program for radical change.   Shortly after the reformers used the Profile to wage a critical attack on practices and administrative personnel at 84, they created a proposal for change. They outlined the ways in which PS 84 would be reorganized into a "child-centered" school.[20] The school would be racially integrated, open to the community, and managed by a democratic process involving parents and teachers in policymaking. Moreover, a method of transition was proposed which gave lay people a legitimate role in both evaluating the feasibility of various parts of the rather complex plan and in deciding what administrative changes were necessary to implement it.[21] The proposal for a child-centered school represented a major threat to local school officials, especially the principal of 84, since it demanded radical changes in methods and role conceptions, changes which would necessarily require the recruitment of a new *type* of supervisor.

[18] Minutes of the PS 84 PA, hereafter cited as "minutes."

[19] "A Profile of PS 84," May, 1968, xeroxed. Following quotations from this source.

[20] "Plan for a Child-Centered School," May, 1968, mimeo.

[21] Ibid.

The crystalization of discontent into a concrete alternative formulation —in effect, a "utopia"[22]—was in part a product of the inability of Freedom School participants to make piecemeal changes within the old regime. Two factors external to PS 84 also contributed. The first was the proliferation during 1967–68 of liberal critiques of the substance of teaching and learning in America, especially in central city schools. Widely read books and articles associated the inadequacy of urban education with "backward" methods that stressed student passivity, rote memorization, and the authoritarian structure of the classroom. Publicity was given to studies of British primary education which indicated that child-centered, informal methods were being success-fully employed to educate working-class and immigrant children. These writings helped shape the reformers' pedagogical ideas and provided them with a legitimacy they had not previously enjoyed.[23]

The second significant external factor was the mushrooming dissatisfac-tion with New York schools throughout the city and the rise of the citywide movement for community control. The Board of Education came under increasing attack during the 1967–68 school year from blacks and liberal whites concerned with education. Everywhere there was talk about "the failure of the system," and the legitimacy of the professionals declined precipitously. The Bundy panel criticized the schools for their inability to educate nonwhite children, for their rigidity, and for their insulation from parent and community influence.[24] On the West Side hopes were still high for community control of the schools in the Joan of Arc Junior High School complex, while the three experimental districts—Ocean Hill-Brownsville, IS 201 and Two Bridges—were already in operation and struggling to win power from the Board of Education and the professional unions.

These events had their effect at PS 84, where parents were becoming less willing automatically to accept the professional judgments of the school administration and the District Superintendent. They began to question the motivation of the educators, and to feel that educators were seeking to protect their own power and interests in the bureaucracy. The UFT became synonymous with opposition to the community control movement, and most of the teachers who had struck in the fall—including all those in the Freedom School—became disaffected with, and often openly hostile toward, the union. Perhaps most significantly, the parents, expecially those who constituted the Profile group, felt more and more that they had a legitimate right to have access to *their* school, to be informed of what was taking place within it, and to participate in the decisions which had previously been made by professionals free from parental input.

[22] In Karl Mannheim's sense of a body of ideas which describes and justifies a set of social situations and conditions which do not presently exist. "Utopias" rationalize the emergent interests of collectivities antagonistic to the status quo. Karl Mannheim, *Ideology and Utopia* (New York: Harcourt, Brace & World, 1936).

[23] See p. 97, footnote 13 above. Jonathan Kozol's critique of the Boston public school system, *Death at an Early Age* (New York: Bantam, 1968), won the National Book Award for that year.

[24] Mayor's Advisory Panel on Decentralization of the New York City Schools, *Reconnection for Learning* (Bundy Report), New York, 1967, *passim.*

The proposal for the reorganization of PS 84 indicated that the consciousness of parents and teachers had developed to the point where they could clearly conceptualize an alternative social structure. But the plan for reorganization also showed that the reformers had no political analysis which could realistically show the way to overturn the old order. The reformers still believed that change would depend upon the power of their ideas rather than on the mobilization of power. The proposal did, however, have the unintended consequence of further radicalizing parents and teachers by convincing them that the old regime was unreformable.

school officials
agree to moderate reform

The reformers submitted their proposal to the Local School Board and District Superintendent. Along with it was a petition of support signed by more than 150 parents. The LSB and Rosen responded by indicating their general interest in "any constructive innovation" but also the need to move slowly and above all to effect change with the cooperation of Mrs. Wertzel. Rosen, in fact, portrayed Wertzel as wishing "to be a close partner with . . . the interested teachers and representative parents in evolving the final plan which will be submitted to me for evaluation." [25]

Mrs. Wertzel, probably under pressure from Rosen to cool things at 84, agreed to carry on discussions with teachers and parents. In fact, she now claimed to have an innovative program of her own which involved an ungraded kindergarten and first grade. She thus openly recognized the need for change, and seemed to accept the general goals of the reformers. But her previous hostility toward pedogogical reform, her personal conflict with the teachers advocating change, her tactical errors, and the relative vagueness of her "moderate" program all managed to transform a potentially co-optive response into a radicalizing one.

The principal met twice with several parents and teachers. These meetings convinced the would-be reformers that Wertzel was "unwilling to enter into any kind of cooperative relationship" with them, and that she had no interest in implementing their ideas. Wertzel was perceived as being hostile and intransigent rather than conciliatory:

At this meeting, again NO responsibility or decisionmaking role was assigned to the parents by Mrs. Wertzel. Again, she asserted her total control over any program in regard to content, scope, and assignment of teachers and pupils. There is no role for the parents or the interested teachers. In fact, Mrs. Wertzel made it quite clear that the very teachers who had originally run the Freedom School, and who had submitted the infant school proposal to her and Dr. Rosen and the Local School Board, WOULD HAVE NO PLACE IN THE PROGRAM.[26]

[25] Letter to Mrs. Silver from Dr. Rosen, District Superintendent, June 10, 1968.

[26] Letter from a member of the PA Executive Board to the LSB, July 5, 1968. Capitalization in original. Professor Samson's description to us of her experiences as a consultant at PS 84 supported the factual account in this letter.

When the parents learned that Silver and Davis had submitted their resignations to the principal and planned to leave 84 for the more supportive environment of the IS 201 district, they mobilized against Wertzel. Led by the Profile group, some sixty to seventy parents picketed PS 84 on June 24, 1968. The pickets carried signs affirming support for Silver and Davis, attacking the poor quality of New York City schools, proclaiming that "the infant school must be saved," and demanding the "complete reorganization" of PS 84.

Despairing over working with the PS 84 administration, the reformers resorted to tactics which they themselves viewed as militant and somewhat illegitimate. The parents and teachers who comprised the urban movement at PS 84 believed themselves to be responsible reformers, not revolutionaries, and hoped—though did not necessarily expect—to have their cause recognized by some actors with the authority to effect change. In this case, these would be the District Superintendent and the Local School Board.

The District Superintendent, however, refused to take action acceptable to the parents. Rosen asserted that there was no problem at 84; that he had command of the facts (the parents and teachers being, by implication, in error); that there was only one possible way for change to occur at 84—with the principal and at the proper pace. He thus ignored the claim that the principal was opposed to change, implying that this could not be the case.

I *regret* your statement that Mrs. Wertzel rejected your suggestions. . . . I can state *without doubt* that Mrs. Wertzel is committed to working with parents and teachers toward the implementation of the ideas expressed by several of the teachers. As the responsible head of the school and as Chairman of the Working Committee her views must also be part of any discussion which takes place. Please give this effort your continuing cooperation so that the experience and background of the principal as well as the teachers and parents can become a part of the total plan. *The process cannot be hurried.* Understanding must be developed as a part of the total effort.[27]

The District Superintendent's letter involved several typical bureaucratic defensive maneuvers:

1. Denial of the asserted reality—forcing the client to prove his facts before further action can be taken.
2. Proposals for delay—often framed in terms of an argument that to "hurry" is technically impossible.
3. Asserting superior knowledge and expertise—assets with which the official, as a result of his special training, is well endowed, and which legitimize his power.

By implication, the official accused the petitioners of being in error, impatient, incapable of expert judgement, and otherwise unreasonable.

If the clients accepted his contentions, Rosen either defined the problem out of existence (since Wertzel would then have been cooperating) or gained a delay of several months, which would likely work to his advantage. If they

---

[27] Letter from Rosen to several parents, July 3, 1968. Ital. added.

rejected it, he still had complete power within his hands—some time would certainly pass before something else happened; and the client group might expend its energy trying to disprove his facts or simply disintegrate in the meanwhile. Where Wertzel was often clumsy and, by giving vent to personal animosity, undermined her own position, Rosen was self-controlled; he resisted pressure in a rational tone without name-calling or rancor.

The Local School Board made primarily a symbolic response to the demand for the infant school, as well as to the previously submitted Profile. There was very little that the LSB could do. Its powers were almost nonexistent before July, 1968—the month the Marchi Act went into effect.[28] In addition, the LSB was always afraid of creating controversy and jeopardizing its position with the Board of Education, thereby reducing its chance to get official power which might lead to real innovation in the district.

An invisible victory.   The parent-teacher movement believed that it had failed to get meaningful outside intervention. In fact, however, a major step toward innovation was taken at the end of the 1967–68 school year, the significance of which went unrecognized by reformers and defenders alike. In order to facilitate Mrs. Wertzel's introduction of her "moderate" program of ungraded classes, the District Superintendent appointed Professor Samson as teacher-trainer at PS 84. Her position was funded by a New York State program which helped urban schools to achieve racial integration. In District 5 this was known as the "Balanced Classroom Project," the aim of which was to develop teaching methods suitable for situations where tracking was eliminated to prevent de facto segregation. Professor Samson began working at PS 84 during the fall of 1968. Her activity constituted the "split in the elite" which made radical change possible. She was a political entrepreneur who both capitalized upon the external pressure which came from the parent movement and her own internal position as a fully credentialized professional. We will return to Professor Samson's role in the process of change later in this chapter.

the dynamic of radicalization

Rosen's tactics had their costs in pushing the parents toward more direct action by making them pessimistic about the possibilities of working within any part of the system. He and Wertzel, regardless of their contrasting styles, were alike in their unwillingness to make substantive concessions. And at this point the parents would have been satisfied only by such concessions, by significant changes in the structure of PS 84 and their relationship with the principal.

While the general political attitudes of 84 parents were probably to the

[28] A bill passed by the New York State Legislature, May 22, 1968, which somewhat increased the powers of the Local School Boards, in particular their right to "advise" district superintendents on such matters as principal selection and tenure.

left of most people in the city, they did not account for the specific movement at the school. These attitudes might also have supported a pro-professionalism and pro-Union stance.[29] Had the school administration been able to respond to the initial requests that it work with parents and permit some teachers to innovate in their own classrooms, it might well have prevented further deterioration of its position. Instead, however, demands reached the point where they involved the complete restructuring of the school. PS 84 was, by June 1968, in a state of organizational disintegration, a state which the principal and the reformers had helped to create and which the District Superintendent and LSB had been incapable of altering. The office of the principal had become embroiled in political controversy.

Here, the ideology of educational professionalism showed itself to be a two-edged sword. Under stable conditions educators like Rosen and Wertzel used the ideology rather effectively to maintain their power and autonomy by identifying threatening individuals and groups as making political demands or having interests in obtaining power. The legitimacy of would-be reformers was undermined and that of the bureaucrats was enhanced, for only the latter could be interested solely in educational goals. But because the educators sincerely held their ideology and role conception, they were inhibited from entering into bargaining relationships with groups demanding change even when such relationships became a strategic necessity. They were accordingly unable to establish mechanisms which could institutionalize and routinize conflict. Nor could the educators cultivate their own supporters from the parent body, since the mobilization of outside groups tended to undermine the political formula upon which their legitimacy rested. Thus, when reform groups became powerful enough to thoroughly destabilize the situation, to involve the educators in conflict and force them into overtly political roles, the professionals became tainted by their own politicization and found themselves with only limited resources for waging uninstitutionalized political battles.

Even under these circumstances, the principal might have remained at PS 84, supported by her legal status if nothing else. But her regime proved incapable of surviving the upheaval produced the next autumn by the 1968 UFT strike.

THE RETREAT OF THE ADMINISTRATION AND THE ESTABLISHMENT OF A NEW ORDER

The United Federation of Teachers struck the city schools on three separate occasions during the first months of the 1968–69 school year. The last of these strikes (almost six weeks long) was a catalytic event in the process of change

[29] It is important to see that there is no necessary correlation between what has usually been thought of as the political left in the United States and sympathy toward the goal of community control.

at PS 84. Parents and teachers broke into the building and worked together for more than a month in running a school for 500 of its 900 children. The Freedom School experience was repeated, though now on a much larger scale and *within* PS 84. Again parents and teachers grew closer together; again they discovered new possibilities for teaching methods and social arrangements. This experience of running their own school altered the consciousness of many parents. It both increased their disaffection from the manner in which 84 had traditionally been run; and provided them with an alternative model of what could be achieved within their own school, with their teachers and children.

The strike polarized social groupings both within PS 84 and at the district and citywide levels. Previous cleavages became reduced to one: pro- versus anti-community control. Moreover, it provided an emotional intensity to the entire conflict situation at 84 which facilitated the mobilization of the movement for change, while making the old regime a clearcut enemy which had to be deposed. It was either "us" or "them."

the movement grows and becomes
the de facto government

On the Thursday after the major strike began, the PA held an emergency public meeting to discuss conditions at 84. The Local School Board representative indicated that principals had been directed that "no school shall be closed without a call to the District Office; that a decision to close should be based solely on the safety of the children." [30] Then the UFT district chairman took the floor and argued for parental support of the strike. "The union," he asserted, was "only asking for fair play: hire and fire by legal means and on grounds of competence, not on the basis of attitudes which cannot be objectively determined." He claimed that "the teachers in the district were interested in talking to the parents"; that they were not "opposed to decentralization or to community control"; but that they were "strongly opposed to groups that threaten our rights to due process." The district chairman concluded by pointing out to the parents that "by keeping the schools open" they were "only prolonging the strike and hurting their own children."

In the discussion which followed, the parents uniformly expressed opposition to the union, to the strike, and to the union leader's arguments. They called the chairman a racist and the strike racist in motivation. Several parents declared that the rights of the union should be threatened, and that the movement for community control, if it was to make gains, required the defeat of the union. Others argued that "attitudes which cannot objectively be determined" had a great deal to do with the competence of teachers and administrators, and that one of the things which made their own principal incompetent was "her attitudes, her attitudes toward us as parents, toward our children, toward some of her own staff." Finally, the parents expressed

[30] Minutes, October 17, 1968.

resentment at the UFT Chairman's accusation that they were "only prolonging the strike."

Until Friday, October 18, PS 84 had been operating with twenty-nine of its normal complement of fifty teachers and administrators, and about 400 of its 900 children.[31] On that day the custodians' union announced that it would honor the picket line of the UFT and refuse to open the schools. Since only the custodians had keys to the buildings, Rosen and the LSB authorized parents to break into the schools. Now confronted with a second picket line, with the necessity of breaking down the door to gain entry to her school, and with hundreds of milling children and screaming parents, Mrs. Wertzel reportedly "went to pieces." The parents claimed that she fled the school without making provision for the children, crying hysterically that she could not return until the custodians did. Several parents then forced their way into the school, followed by the nonstriking teachers and children. One of these teachers, a black woman allied with the reformers, was appointed "teacher-in-charge," and the period of PA management of 84 had begun.

The strike facilitates radical action.   Under most circumstances, any action the parents contemplated taking—whether deposing the principal or instituting a curricular innovation—posed a dilemma. On the one hand, the immediate result of activity to disrupt the status quo was to throw the classroom or school (as the case might be) into disorder, to provoke hostility and invite reprisal against their children; in short, to incur highly tangible and immediate costs from activity which created conflict. On the other hand, the parents had little hope that reform could be effected without breaching the system's norms, without using power and producing conflict. Yet gains would come only in the future, and were, moreover, hardly assured. The people who advocated action were therefore always placed on the defensive, posed with the dilemma of resigning themselves to an unacceptable status quo or trying to upset it in the hope of replacing it with something better, being assured in the process only of creating disorder.

This difficulty for the would-be reformers was exacerbated by the fact that the costs of the status quo were less visible than those of any action they might take to change it. The ongoing system might have created many victims, but it did so slowly and silently. Revolution within the system was noisy and exposed, with the revolutionaries forced to bear the responsibility for their policies in a way which members of the established order did not.[32]

In the past this dilemma had often prevented parental action, as when the PA decided in the early spring of 1968 that they should stay with Mrs. Wertzel. But now, external forces had changed the social situation within 84 and the nature of the status quo. Almost half of the teaching staff had gone on strike. The principal, the parents believed, had been overwhelmed by events and was unable to keep control over the changing situation before she left.

[31] PS 84 School Attendance Registers, 1968–69.

[32] The dilemmas confronting activists here at the micro level are at least somewhat analagous to those faced by groups wishing to bring about significant change at the societal level.

Children were running through the halls, windows had been broken, some classes were badly overcrowded while teachers remained idle. Finally she had abandoned her school. PS 84 was already in a state of disorder, and so the parents could define their own actions as aimed entirely at restoring order, in other words, as conservative rather than radical.

The strike situation not only shifted the burden of proof from the movement to the old regime, but also facilitated the growth of the movement itself by providing new modes of recruitment. Since the movement became the de facto management of the school, it could ask parents to "come in to help keep things going," rather than, in effect, to help disrupt the administration. Parents acting in the immediate self-interest of their children would join forces with the movement, which was the source of ongoing educational services and stability. Many of these "service-oriented" recruits became politicized, first through their contact with the original PA activists, and then after the strike when the system they had established was threatened with elimination.

PA management.   The parents were ready and able to organize themselves and work to keep the school going. For the entire three weeks of the custodians' strike, parents stayed in PS 84 day and night. A group of fathers took turns sleeping in front of the open doors. A lunch committee organized and supervised a full lunch program. Parents called the home of every child enrolled at the school and managed to increase attendance from 300 on the first Monday after Wertzel left to an average of 500 by the following week. A planning group met daily with Mrs. Rexford (the teacher-in-charge) and a committee of teachers. Volunteers patrolled the halls and monitored the entrances to the building. They worked with particular teachers who were having trouble with discipline, and ran "cooling off" rooms to handle children who were disrupting classroom activities. They even swept the floors and cleaned the lavatories. All together more than 150 parents participated in some aspect of running the school, with about one-third of these doing something almost every day.

Everyone who participated at 84 during the weeks of the strike claimed to be moved by the experience. For the first time parents, administrators, and teachers were working together within the public school in an atmosphere of community. The PA President told a meeting of parents and teachers "how proud the parents all were of their teachers . . . that PS 84 had become like a family." [33] Teachers and parents fraternized both in and out of the building. As was the case during the Freedom School the year before, they resolved that they had to preserve what was happening. As one parent put it, "This school is now humanized; this is the whole difference; and we can't let it be taken away from us." [34]

In the absence of Mrs. Wertzel several innovations were instituted. Parent assistants were welcomed by a number of teachers, and the signs

[33] Minutes, October 25, 1968.
[34] Minutes, November 13, 1968.

which ordered parents not to enter classrooms or stand in the halls without the written authorization of the principal were removed. The parents established a community room where they could meet during the school day, drink coffee, and babysit for parent volunteers. The practice of having children line up in the school yard each morning and noontime to be marched into their rooms was eliminated. Parents and teachers ended the de facto segregation of several classes, and set up rooms which combined former Intellectually Gifted Children (IGC) and Citizenship classes, thereby bringing together bright white children with "disruptive" blacks and Puerto Ricans.[35] The four experimental classes being directed by Professor Samson were, for the first time, permitted the use of the corridor space adjacent to their rooms, an innovation which the principal and custodian had previously blocked. Teachers met regularly with the acting administrator and, along with parents, participated in making policy decisions.

For the teachers, the changes made under the new regime meant freedom to innovate, a redefinition of the parent-teacher role relationship, and the democratization and professionalization of the organizational power structure.[36] For the parents, the new arrangements meant that "de facto segregation was killed" and that they were experiencing "genuine community control: professional decisions being made cooperatively by professionals and the community . . . not eliminating professional discretion, but making it accountable to the interests and desires of the clients the professionals are supposed to serve."[37]

preparations for
the counter-revolution

The parents and teachers at PS 84 were convinced that Mrs. Wertzel would attempt to eliminate the changes which had been made. This belief, combined with strong attachment to the new regime, helped push the PA into a decision to ask for Wertzel's replacement. Two weeks before the strike was to end (at the termination of the custodians' strike) the PA Executive Board was already thinking about how to deal with the principal and the striking teachers:

Mr. A.:   We will have a real problem when the 900 children come back. We have to take the striking teachers back but don't placate them any more. We have everything arranged.

[35] Citizenship and Junior Guidance classes were created in order to isolate children with "behavior problems." They could be found in most New York City schools with large nonwhite populations. These classes had few white children in them. The IGC classes were supposedly intended for "gifted" children. However, their standards were often much lower in practice than in theory. Such classes then became devices by which to protect white children from their nonwhite classmates.

[36] For a general discussion of the professional and bureaucratic aspect of the elementary school teacher's role see Dan C. Lortie, "The Balance of Control and Autonomy in Elementary School Teaching," in *The Semi-Professions and Their Organizations*, ed. Amitai Etzioni (New York: Free Press, 1969), pp. 1–53.

[37] Minutes, October 25, 1972.

There is no excuse for disrupting the children again for the convenience of those who struck illegally. The teachers who come back will have to set up new classes.

Mrs. T.:   For the first time in memory we have had a meaningful relation with the professionals. The wishes of the parents have been articulated within the school and have actually influenced what happened. We know damn well that Wertzel will put a stop to this right away.

Mrs. S.:   This experience has shown us what our school could be. There are lots of things wrong here and with the system. So Wertzel isn't responsible for everything. But an awful lot must fall on her shoulders, a lot of blame.

Are we really afraid of what Mrs. Wertzel will do? The school is in better shape now than it ever has been. We have to fight for parent participation. Soon there will be a battle. She is going to come back and she will want the parents out. That would not be fair to the parents of the children. We must make a stand now.[38]

The Executive Board agreed that there was no way of working with Wertzel any more; that she should be removed.

The Board also resolved to maintain the organization which had been established during the strike; that is, to keep children in classes which were heterogeneous and not return them to their old, prestrike classes and teachers. This turned out to be an important tactical decision, since it forced Wertzel into taking the offensive and into making mistakes in the process. She became the one demanding change, and the parents could defend the new status quo in the name of tranquility and "the best interests of the children." They were able to turn the tables in the symbolic battle between institutional reformers and the old guard.

The PA Executive Board was unanimous in its decision to work for the removal of the principal, and it met frequently during the last two weeks of the strike to plan its strategy. The Board had reversed its position from that of the previous spring, when it had refused to officially endorse the Profile. This turnabout resulted almost entirely from altered consciousness on the part of its members, as ten of the twelve officers had also been on the Board in 1967–68. The decision was supported by a vote of forty-one in favor, with five abstentions, at an open meeting of the PA.

Statements by parents on the Executive Board illustrated the thinking of the activists:

Do you remember what we asked Dr. Rosen for when Mrs. Wertzel was hired? We wanted a principal with vision, with competence, with the ability to buck the system. Rosen knew what we wanted. He asked us to talk to Mrs. Wertzel, to start with this.

I've come to see that she has no time for black parents. Many times I've tried to meet with her. . . . She doesn't talk to me unless I am with a white group. At the beginning of October she said, and I won't forget it, "You people expect more than your children can do."

The Local School Board and Rosen must hear from those of us who changed our minds. We had supported her because we thought we might not be able to do any better. But now I just don't see how we could do much worse. . . . She has shown us a

[38] Minutes, October 31, 1968.

complete pattern of following the orders of the system, of perpetuating everything wrong with the system because she is a part of it and believes in it.[39]

During the final days of the strike the Parent Association prepared itself to fight for its innovations and against Mrs. Wertzel and the educational bureaucracy. The movement could be characterized as developed, in the sense that its organizational form and consciousness would remain more or less the same throughout the period of sustained mobilization. As mentioned previously, the leadership core in the Profile group and the old Executive Board used the strike as the opportunity to co-opt new cadres. These were disproportionately black. So by the time the Wertzel regime prepared to stage its return, the active center of the movement had not only expanded to forty or fifty people, but also overrepresented blacks in proportion to their numbers at the school.[40]

The PA's strategy was to rely upon the Local School Board. This board constituted what Michael Lipsky has called a "reference public," [41] and parents barraged it with demands for action. The PA collected 200 signatures on a petition demanding Wertzel's removal and presented it, along with letters documenting her alleged incompetence, to the LSB. One meeting with the Board was attended by seventy yelling parents. A committee met with a lawyer from Mobilization for Youth Legal Services, an anti-poverty law group, and was told that since Wertzel was untenured, her removal could be achieved by Rosen without the use of judicial or arbitration procedures.

THE ADMINISTRATION
RETURNS—AND FALLS

Mrs. Wertzel was confronted by the parents immediately upon her return to school after the strike. At a tense meeting attended by parents, the principal, Dr. Rosen and members of the Local School Board, the parents presented Wertzel with the demand that she resign. At the same time they manipulated the situation to demonstrate to the outside observers that the principal was irresponsible and incompetent.

Mrs. M. (President of the PA):   Speaking for the entire body of parents, I am telling you, Mrs. Wertzel, that we no longer want you to continue as principal of this school.

Mrs. Wertzel: I have been assigned as principal of this school and I intend to remain here until I am legally told not to remain.

Mr. T.:   We all know the real reason behind this strike. All the teachers who were out are racists. And you are a racist, Mrs. Wertzel.

Mrs. B.:   I want to ask Mrs. Wertzel why she wants to stay in a school where parents feel so opposed to her philosophy of what a school should be like.

[39] Minutes, November 12, 1968.

[40] See minutes, November 24, 1968.

[41] Michael Lipsky, "Protest as a Political Resource," *American Political Science Review*, LXII, December, 1968, 1144–58.

Mrs. Wertzel: I am principal of this school and I shall remain here until under due process I am subsequently removed.

Mrs. R.:   Many of us who supported you last year don't trust you any more. . . .

Mrs. Dodge (LSB Member):   I ask what Mrs. Wertzel plans to do?

Mrs. Wertzel: I am always willing to work with parents.

Mrs. Dodge: How would it be if Mrs. Wertzel would be willing to work with a parent group?

Mrs. T.:   And that group would be here all day long?

Dr. Rosen: What does that mean? Mrs. Wertzel can't have parents around here all day.

Mrs. T.:   We are talking about community control. This means professionals translating the needs of our children into appropriate action. We have to be present to assure that Mrs. Wertzel will understand the needs of our children and act accordingly. That's what we mean by community control and that's why we must be here. . . . And it is your professional job, Dr. Rosen, to see that professionals behave in a professional manner.

Mrs. Dodge: How many parents do you want in here all day?

Mrs. Wertzel (who had left the room for a few minutes):   I just asked Mrs. Rexford which parental functions should be maintained. She suggested patrolling the halls and helping in the lunchroom. It will be my pleasure to welcome you in that capacity.

Mrs. T.:   What else did Mrs. Rexford tell you? How about everything we learned about running this school and the over 500 students we took care of.

Mrs. Wertzel: 400 and something.

Mrs. T.:   LIAR!

Mr. T.:   Our first priority is to remove this principal.

Mrs. P.:   I want to know what is going to happen tomorrow.

Mrs. Dodge: Let's be fair, she just got back.

(At this point the meeting broke into general confusion, with much shouting back and forth. Mrs. Wertzel walked out.) [42]

bases of conflict

The fully developed consciousness of the political movement defined goals which were antithetical to the existence of the old regime. Simply put, what the parents wanted was incompatible with what the principal believed to be sound educational practice, and, indeed, with her continued governance of the school. The parents at 84 had several objectives, not all of which were fully articulated, or universally held. First, they wished to see Mrs. Wertzel removed from their school. The banner around which all of the parents could rally was one which proclaimed Wertzel's incompetence. Wertzel was a "bad principal" and "she had to go." But in saying this, the parents were sometimes unclear about whether they wished to replace Wertzel as a *person* or as a *type* of principal. The optimal short-term tactic for the parents was to emphasize the former, for they could then build a case for her incompetence which would permit Rosen to transfer her without having to face the more general political issues. Nevertheless, parents often referred to her as the wrong *kind* of principal, and most, but not all, of the parents

[42] Minutes, November 17, 1968.

hoped to replace her with someone who would transform the nature of the principalship. These parents were working for a political revolution, not merely a coup d'état.[43]

Second, the parents desired to preserve the changes that had been made in the structure of the school during the strike. Since most of these changes involved a basic revision in the social structure of PS 84, they constituted a social revolution. Preserving that revolution was by definition impossible without getting a new kind of principal, one who defined the role completely differently from the old type as represented by Mrs. Wertzel; for a new definition of the principal's role vis-à-vis teachers, children, and especially parents was itself the central element of the revolution.

Third, a minority of the parents who were mobilized during the strike—but nearly all of those who had been in the Profile Group and who sat on the (enlarged) Executive Board—spoke of achieving community control for PS 84. Everyone who used this phrase understood it to mean at least two things: (1) parents would have access to the school; and (2) they would exercise oversight through a set of procedures which would redistribute a certain amount of power in their favor. In this sense, the goal of community control clearly involved the redefinition of the role of principal so that the parents would become an important reference group for its occupant. It also implied that parents would routinely participate with the principal in making general policy decisions. Finally, community control meant that teachers would be encouraged to communicate directly with parents and be responsive to parental interests and initiatives.

There were two specific issues on which the overall conflict between the parents and the principal focused. One of these was the question of school organization, that is, of how teachers and children should be assigned to one another. During the strike, as we have previously discussed, the parents and the nonstriking staff had set up classes that were balanced racially, and they had instituted informal teaching methods in about ten classrooms. The nonstriking teachers, under the leadership of Mrs. Silver, created a "Transition Plan" which maintained most of the changes established during the strike, and gave the returning "UFT" teachers new classes, different from their original assignments. The Parent Association supported Silver's plan at a well-attended meeting held the night of November 18 by an overwhelming vote of 113 to 1.

The principal claimed that the post-strike arrangement in the school was educationally harmful because it "violated sound educational practices" and incorporated "untried methods" into too many classrooms. Wertzel wanted to return to the organization in effect before the strike began. In particular, she wished to eliminate a fourth grade class being taught by Mrs. Gold. This class was composed of half of a former Citizenship room, and half

---

[43] There are some significant differences between revolutions in societies and "revolutions" in organizations which are but a part of an institutional subsector. Nonetheless, it seems worthwhile to speak of fundamental changes in social structure, governance, etc. of organizations as revolutionary, since they do constitute major upheavals within a limited sphere.

of an IGC room. The principal claimed that Mrs. Gold was incompetent to teach IGC children, and that it was "unwise" to "force the kind of children who were in the IGC class to have their learning upset by disruptive and problem children." [44] The parents replied by asserting that learning was taking place in Mrs. Gold's classroom; that it was possible to teach heterogeneous groups with the "open, infant school" methods Mrs. Gold was using; and that Citizenship classes had been racist in their effect, while Mrs. Gold's class was integrated—an important consideration in its own right. Mrs. Wertzel, however, continued to stress the "bad educational effects" for the "better students."

The conflict over school organization involved a power struggle between parents and "their" half of the faculty against the principal and "her half." It also centered about the question of who should benefit and who should lose as a result of the UFT strike—the strikers who went out because they were opposed to community control in Ocean Hill, or those who stayed and created community control in PS 84. Finally, the conflict represented two opposing educational philosophies of how children should be grouped within schools, tracked by ability or heterogeneously.

The parents were able to preserve most of the organizational changes that occurred during the strike. Their success in blocking counter-revolution had important consequences. It buoyed them into believing that they had sufficient power to confront the administration directly, and gave them the confidence to continue their attack against the principal. It also demonstrated to the professional staff that the PA could protect them from the sanctions of the old regime. Innovation could no longer be blocked by bureaucratic superiors. The parent movement, by establishing itself as a power within the school, reduced the risks of innovation and, in fact, offered direct support to teachers willing to accept racially heterogeneous classes and/or to adopt informal teaching approaches. Under these conditions there was a general diffusion of innovative methods among professionals associated with the social circle of the original (high-risk taking) innovators.

The second post-strike issue arose from the demand by the parents that they be allowed to keep their community room, a demand which directly threatened the principal, who made every effort to thwart it. Her defense of professionalism drew a sharp line between parental participation and parental intrusion. The former was to be encouraged, while the latter was to be avoided at all cost. The community room represented a direct intrusion by the parents into the school. The political symbolism of the community room was to indicate that the parents had a right to be within the public school and to play some part in its governance. The practical political effect of the community room was to allow parents to hold meetings during the school day, within the school, at their own discretion. This helped them to have an insider's knowledge of events, to be a sounding board for the grievances of teachers, i.e., to create alliances which crosscut the bureaucratic authority structure. The principal evidently recognized the political potential of the

[44] Related by Mrs. Gold in an interview with the authors, November, 1969.

arrangement when she accused the parents of being "ensconced in the room, conniving and plotting with teachers." [45] The location of the community room in PS 84 was particularly significant in this regard. The room was by the school entrance, across the hall from the office, and it had in fact become a kind of counter-office, in which a parallel structure of school government was headquartered. The community room was an important step in the process of attaining community control, for it both figuratively and literally broke down the boundary defenses of the bureaucracy, undermining the meaning of inside and outside. As a parent put it in a PA meeting with the principal, District Superintendent, and members of the LSB:

We have found extraordinary value, educational value, in the presence of parents in the school—because of their support for children, their understanding of children. A community room changes the whole atmosphere in a school. It means that parents are always here to watch and to help. We become participants and the school is no longer alien territory for our children. [46]

The parents prevailed in the issue of the community room for much the same reason as they did in the conflict over reorganization. The principal was unable to organize a constituency to oppose the determined and mobilized movement. The Local School Board was sympathetic to the basic idea of community control; the Superintendent was unwilling or politically unable to bar the parents from the school through the use of police power; and the professional unions were weak throughout the district. By prevailing, the parents gained an organizational resource in the community room which permitted them to advance more effectively to the further goal of changing the professional governance and pattern of lay-professional interactions in the school.

**a bureaucratic defensive move:
the superintendent suggests
a fact-finding study**

The three weeks following the UFT strike were marked by conflict and turmoil at PS 84. The general tension in the school had apparently been communicated to many of the children, particularly to those in classes which Mrs. Wertzel was trying to reorganize and the parents to maintain intact. Discipline disintegrated: children ran through the halls; numerous false alarms were turned in; windows were broken. The principal and parents had noisy confrontations in front of children. Many teachers were openly flaunting direct orders from Wertzel; many were not speaking to one another. In short, PS 84 was no longer a viable institution.

The District Superintendent was compelled to face the situation, as he had not done the previous June. On December 6 he proposed the study which the Profile group had requested seven or eight months before. What was

[45] Minutes, November 22, 1968.
[46] Ibid.

needed, he declared, was "someone objective to act as a fact-finder to assess the situation . . . , [describe] key differences, consult experts, come up with recommendations." [47] Rosen suggested that a month-long study be conducted by Dr. Richards, staff director of the Jewish Board of Guardians West Side Mental Health Center. He would be assisted by an advisory committee drawn equally from the various parties at issue. The committee would have no authority to enforce its recommendations.

The Executive Board's initial reaction was one of disappointment and suspicion. It had wanted Rosen to remove the principal. The year before, an investigation of the facts at 84 would have been viewed as a major concession to their demands; now it was seen as too little, too late, just another delaying tactic designed to avoid direct authoritative action. The parents were suspicious of Rosen's choice of Dr. Richards, about whom they knew little; and they could not understand why the Superintendent and the LSB observers did not already know enough to come to a decision. Their suspicions were confirmed by the manner in which Rosen responded to their questions at his meeting on the sixth:

Mrs. D.:   This would have been a proper, rational way to proceed after the Profile was presented last spring. Now we have no time for leisure because the day-to-day condition is so serious.

Dr. Rosen: I assure you this is not an academic exercise. This is a serious proposal that resulted from professional consideration over several days.

Mrs. H.:   There are observations from several members of the LSB. Why aren't you informed enough to make a decision?

Dr. Rosen: I'm not.

Mrs. H.:   You are asking a great deal of the parents.

Dr. Rosen: I know.

Mrs. D.:   How do we operate in the meantime?

Dr. Rosen: You give the leadership of the school a chance to operate for a month. You do your activities as you have been doing. There would be no drastic change.

Mrs. D.:   But we need a drastic change. We have the fourth grade situation: Mrs. Wertzel is beginning departmentalization in order to reinstitute tracking and segregation. The children are rebelling now throughout the school. What shall we do?

Dr. Rosen: You cast your dependence on the administration of the school to carry out what is best.

Mrs. D.:   What is being done is directly opposite to what we think is right and proper.

Mrs. G.:   Four weeks is a long time in a child's life. They don't deserve this.

Mrs. H.:   The parents are always put on the defensive.

Dr. Rosen: Everything parents have said is noted. There are other things too. Your testimony is not the only testimony. . . . It is difficult to determine the situation; an objective person is needed.

Mrs. K.:   He can't be objective. He's being hired by you. He and you have your own interests to protect. We have ours. He'll see what he wants to see.[48]

[47] Minutes, December 6, 1968.
[48] Ibid.

The PA Executive Board unanimously agreed that they could not accept Rosen's proposal; that doing so would only provide him with more time to delay. Instead, most of the parents felt they should link their movement at 84 with that of the Joan of Arc Governing Board despite some reservations about the Board's effectiveness.

Many of the parents had come fully to reject the ideology of educational professionalism. Their consciousness—and the rational basis of the movement for community control at PS 84 and elsewhere—was articulated in a brief interchange at the Executive Board meeting on December 9:

Mrs. T.:   This is a political fight.

Mrs. B.:   I don't see why we should let ourselves be trapped into accepting the idea that a political position negates educational gains. There is no other way to implement educational change!

Mrs. H.:   It is a question of power. We want the Planning/Governing Board to have power to get a new principal. We are doing this to affect education here. You can't put education in one bag and power and politics in another. Our fight is political and it is educational.[49]

The Executive Board voted (with one member abstaining) to have the Planning/Governing Board begin a search to find a suitable replacement for Mrs. Wertzel, and to advertise immediately in *The New York Times* "for a principal for PS 84, a community-oriented, integrated school in Manhattan that will have a position available in February of 1969." In addition, the parents drafted a letter to Dr. Rosen, which demanded that the study of the school be conducted by the Joan of Arc Planning/Governing Board in consultation with the Parent Association, and that following the investigation, the Governing Board should make specific proposals for the reorganization of the school.[50] The District Superintendent nonetheless persisted in his proposal, attributing its rejection by the PA to his failure to "get across the basic purpose." The implication was that Rosen was advancing a rational suggestion in the interest of all, which could be rejected by reasonable people only because they had failed to understand.

confrontation and the
transfer of the principal

Shortly after the parents had rejected Rosen's proposal to conduct an unbiased investigation of PS 84, they learned that Mrs. Wertzel had expressed her willingness to accept a voluntary transfer, if such could be arranged. Until the District Superintendent could find another principalship for her, however, she intended to stay on at 84.

Several weeks passed, and still there was no position elsewhere for Wertzel. The parents met with Rosen and were informed that matters were out of his hands. The parents lobbied the Local School Board vigorously—

[49] Ibid.

[50] Letter to Superintendent Rosen from the PA Executive Board, December 9, 1969.

both in private and in several public demonstrations—and supplied it with
the legal opinion of an NAACP lawyer, who affirmed the Board's authority
to "terminate the services of a probationary principal [Mrs. Wertzel] on the
recommendation of the Local Superintendent with the approval of the
Superintendent of Schools." [51] In addition, a delegation from the PA met
with Milton Galamison, a member of the Board of Education and spoke with
an associate superintendent of schools at 110 Livingston Street (central
headquarters of the city system). But none of the other New York districts
wanted Wertzel, and the Board of Education showed no inclination to
transfer her to central headquarters, or to take other action. So the principal
remained on the job at PS 84.

The PA Executive Board concluded that a "massive march" on the
office of the District Superintendent was appropriate. More than sixty
parents attended a Local School Board meeting, where they learned that
Rosen had no intention of censuring the principal. In fact, he had recently
given her a "satisfactory" performance rating, as her second year on the job
at 84 had concluded that week and he was required to evaluate her work.
The parents reacted with fury. Their anger was exacerbated when Rosen
would provide no explanation for his rating of the principal, other than to
say, "I have evaluated her with my *professionally developed sensitivity.*" [52] The PS
84 parents thereupon more or less spontaneously decided to force the hand of
the LSB by refusing to leave the meeting hall until the Board had made a
statement of its intentions. The Board withdrew into private session with the
District Superintendent and then voted publicly (with Rosen's concurrence)
to "transfer Mrs. Wertzel to District Headquarters at the earliest date
feasible."

PROVISIONAL GOVERNMENT
AND VICTORY

The fact that Superintendent Rosen gave Mrs. Wertzel a satisfactory
performance evaluation complicated the situation at 84 and served to further
radicalize the PA. There was now no basis for the principal to be removed
from her salary line. In fact, when she was transferred to District Headquarters she took her line with her, being paid a principal's salary of more than
$20,000 to perform routine clerical work. Only two possibilities remained
open within the normal bureaucratic procedures: Mrs. Wertzel could find a
job elsewhere in the system and resign from her budget line, or an additional
budget line could be allocated to PS 84 by the New York City Board of
Education. Since Wertzel could not find a position at another school, the
Local School Board concentrated its efforts during the remainder of the
1968–69 year on getting the Central Board to provide 84 with funds to hire

---

[51] Letter from Elizabeth DuBois to the chairman of the Joan of Arc Planning/Governing Board,
January 16, 1969.

[52] Minutes, February 3, 1969. Emphasis added.

another regular principal. It expressed to the Central Board its own frustration at being unable to act authoritatively to settle the situation:

Under your decentralization resolution you delegated to us schools with serious problems, but delegated no powers sufficient to solve them. You place us in an untenable position, and one that we cannot accept.[53]

Central Headquarters did not answer for two months, at which time it ritualistically affirmed that "the position of Acting Principal of PS 84 can be filled by one of the present assistant principals by direction of the District Superintendent with the approval of the Local School Board." [54]

In spite of its misgivings the LSB was forced to accept the appointment of Mrs. Rubin, the assistant principal, as acting principal. The new principal was, from all indications, similar to the old. Mrs. Rubin was a more effective administrator than Wertzel and managed to have better relations with some of the staff. But she did not change the extremely conflict-ridden relations with parents. Rather, she attempted to make them accept the old system of signing in at the office and stating their business before gaining access to the school. She discouraged parent-teacher contact, accusing the parents of "disrupting the educational process by going into classrooms." [55] The community room was a continual source of friction. The principal refused to order the school janitor to clean it. She threatened several times to evict the parents; and informed them in the spring that, since she projected the need for ten first-grade classes the following autumn, they would probably have to give up their room "for the benefit of the children." During September 1969 when her enrollment estimates proved to be inflated, she attempted to transfer several teachers whom the parents had admired. In sum, then, Mrs. Rubin was, to the parents, yet another product of the old regime typified by Wertzel. Her appointment did not change the situation at 84 for the better, and involved no concession by the system to the substance of their demands.

the failure
of direct confrontation

The behavior of the District Superintendent in giving Mrs. Wertzel a satisfactory rating, thereby assuring that he could no longer remove her from the principalship of PS 84, and the ensuing unresponsiveness of the Board of Education, convinced the parents that working within the educational system was impossible. The parents saw some use, however, in confronting the system with the help of the Joan of Arc (JOA) Planning/Governing Board. The JOA Board, had one power resource the PS 84 Parent Association lacked—money. The Board had more than $20,000 on hand and was ready to use this sum to assist the parents. The strategy was for a committee of PS 84 parents

---

[53] Letter from Rhoda Lysenko, Chairman of Local School Board 5, to John Doar and members of the Board of Education, February 14, 1969.

[54] Telegram from the Superintendent of Schools to LSB 5, April 22, 1969.

[55] Minutes, April 8, 1970.

and Board members to select a suitable acting principal for the school, and then offer to give the Board of Education the money needed to pay his salary. If the Board of Education refused, the "community" would have the choice of trying to install its principal directly in the school, or of "setting up an office for him across the street to demonstrate the complete illegitimacy of the administration at PS 84." [56] A screening panel was established, and the parents put a great deal of effort into defining what they wanted in a principal, and into looking for a man to meet their requirements. But the LSB and District Superintendent reiterated the impossibility of recruiting a new principal for PS 84 "so long as Mrs. Wertzel occupies the budget line and 110 Livingston refuses to create a new line." [57]

A number of the most militant parents and several members of the Joan of Arc Board decided to confront the local authorities in the middle of April, two months after the "temporary" appointment of Mrs. Rubin. Led by George Jenkins, the black organizer recently hired by the JOA Board, some twenty parents occupied the office of the District Superintendent on April 16, 1969. Jenkins sat in Rosen's chair and answered the phone as "Superintendent X," while referring to Rosen as the "ex-superintendent." [58] Rosen suffered this public humiliation without taking counteraction.

Mrs. Lysenko, chairman of the LSB, arriving sometime after the sit-in began, tried to conciliate the parents. She agreed to wire the Board of Education demanding that a new position be authorized and stating the LSB's intention to use Joan of Arc money to pay the appointee. Within a week, however, the LSB reversed itself, claiming that the terms of the agreement had been imposed under duress. The Local School Board went even further in its turnabout. Ignoring its previous admission that Mrs. Rubin was unacceptable as principal, it distributed a mimeographed letter to the parents of PS 84 warning against "the illegal installation of a principal":

We want to assure you that the Local School Board and District Superintendent will use whatever means are necessary to ensure that the only principal or acting principal at PS 84 is one serving under a legal appointment. We will not allow any illegal placement. [59]

To the Board, legality was of great importance; accordingly it emphasized that "anyone who is asked to participate in or support any illegal action [should] consider carefully and understand that such acts will create tremendous disturbance in the school, harm its educational program and seriously upset the children." [60] To the parents, outcomes—results—could no longer be ignored. The procedures in the system, they felt, reflected everyone's interests but those of the system's clients. And now, the LSB was

[56] Minutes, April 20, 1969.
[57] Letter from the Executive Secretary of LSB 5 to the President of the PA, March 13, 1969.
[58] The events were witnessed by the authors.
[59] Letter to parents, c. April 20, 1969.
[60] Ibid.

itself demonstrating the "hypocrisy" of "those who have a stake in the status quo." [61] The President of the PA stated the attitude of most of the active parents during a special public meeting with the LSB at the end of April, 1969:

> The notice [distributed by the LSB] is inflammatory; and designed, by playing to parental fears of further disorder, to stampede the parents into approving the status quo—into approving as permanent principal a person whom members of the Local School Board and Dr. Rosen have themselves, in public statements and in letters to 110 Livingston Street, adjudged unsuitable to be principal of our school. . . .
>
> We are not outsiders. These are our children. Black, Spanish, white—poor, middle class, rich—they all need stability and the kind of solid education that the district office, Local School Board, and the entire educational establishment have NOT been able to provide for them.[62]

The question of what the parents would do once they had decided upon a candidate for the principalship turned out to be moot. They never had to confront the local school authorities, since, after great effort on their part in locating an acceptable man for the position, the candidate (for unknown reasons) failed to appear at a public meeting intended to introduce him to the community.[63] The contingent of police Superintendent Rosen had ordered in anticipation of "illegal action" proved unnecessary. The PA strategy of trying to confront the system through the help of the Governing Board had failed.

the elite innovator

Dr. Rosen, apparently in reaction to parental pressure, resigned from his position at the end of the 1968–69 school year. The Local School Board, on the advice of a screening committee representing parents and teachers from district schools, appointed Dr. Seymour Hammer to be District Superintendent. The new Superintendent had been the principal of a Harlem grammar school, where he received national recognition for radically improving pupil achievement. He was reputed to be an innovator and a maverick in the system. He took the job with the understanding that he would stay only one year "so I can't be co-opted." Dr. Hammer frequently stated his commitment to community control and his intention to "buck the system" to "make changes," and to "get away with whatever we can in making the schools more responsive to parents, and in making professionals perform." He, in effect, rejected the ideology of educational professionalism, and believed that many, if not most, decisions made within the schools were

---

[61] Minutes, April 8, 1969.

[62] Statement by the PA President, mimeo., April 28, 1969.

[63] The selection committee agreed upon a candidate who was then a principal in a small New Jersey city. This man had originally answered an advertisement placed by the Governing Board in *The New York Times*. He was interviewed twice in New York, and a delegation visited him at work in New Jersey. Everything was arranged when he failed to appear at his "presentation." The next day the Governing Board received a one line telegram stating that he had reconsidered.

"just as much political as they are educational." [64] He welcomed controversy and conflict, and from the start he assumed a stance more militant than that of the Local School Board. In most respects—in personal style, in the substance of his beliefs, and in the way he played his role—Hammer was the antithesis of Rosen. Operating within the same legal constraints as had Rosen, and working with the same Local School Board, Hammer effected a number of reforms in the district which would probably have been inconceivable the year before. (See Chapter Three.)

Six months after she had been transferred out of PS 84, Wertzel was given another principalship. Her budget line was therefore unoccupied. Hammer immediately "plugged" the line by appointing a qualified principal to it. This individual was on a two year terminal leave as principal of another school in the district. For the purposes of Board of Education bookkeeping, he was now listed as principal of PS 84, just as Wertzel had been, even when she was not actually in the school. Because no vacancy then technically existed for a regular (i.e. on-list) principal at PS 84, the District Superintendent could appoint an acting principal. Hammer thereby was able, in effect, to bypass the principal-recruitment procedures established by the Board of Examiners and to choose from a larger pool of candidates than could meet the city's (as opposed to the state's) qualifications.

Parents and school personnel select their principal.   The Local School Board had announced new screening-panel procedures at the end of October 1969. Each school would have a panel composed of one elected parent representative for every 100 children, two teacher representatives, one paraprofessional, and one member of the Local School Board. The District Superintendent would refer candidates to the panels. Although the de jure authority to make appointments rested with the District Superintendent and LSB (and ultimately with the Superintendent of Schools), Hammer and the Local Board let it be understood that they were delegating de facto power to the screening panels.

The PS 84 panel met several times during November and December. Altogether it interviewed fifteen candidates. Although the parents maintained an official position of favoring no particular applicant, most of them were predisposed toward Mr. Simon, whom Hammer had appointed temporarily to administer the school. Simon seemed to be the type of principal they wanted. He was committed to community control, wished to democratize the internal structure of the school, and believed strongly in the idea of open pedagogical methods. In addition, parents had the opportunity to see him perform on the job. It therefore came as no surprise when the screening panel chose Simon to be principal. The following week on January 26, 1970, the Local School Board unanimously approved his selection.

[64] Interviews, November and December, 1969.

Thus, the parents had attained one of their major goals for PS 84. They had not only removed two principals of the "old type" but had found someone who gave every indication of being the "new kind of principal" they desired. Success, in the end, depended upon the initiative of the District Superintendent. Had Dr. Hammer not taken over the job, the parent movement would probably have been unable, by itself, to place someone like Mr. Simon in the principalship. As organized and committed as the activist parents at PS 84 had become over the previous years, they were just not powerful enough to move the system without assistance from within the ranks of the bureaucracy.

The "revolution" at PS 84, like all revolutions, required a split in the elite.[65] In District 5 this split was made possible by the replacement of Dr. Rosen by Superintendent Hammer, a man who committed himself to the movement—the advocates of community control—instead of to the system and its old guard. Hammer was appointed, in large part, because Rosen had been harassed out of office, and the Local School Board was ready, under community pressure, to use this opportunity to appoint a new kind of professional. Superintendent Hammer was ready to comply with the parents' desires at once, whereas Rosen had responded to the parents with various tactics designed to protect the system. Parents had reasoned with Superintendent Rosen. But his role conception and political consciousness provided him with interests which were largely antithetical to those of the parents. The parents had sufficient power to push Wertzel into requesting a transfer, but not enough to compel the old Superintendent to remove her, or even to find her performance unsatisfactory. It was only when the larger community could effect a change in the professional governor of the district schools that the parent movement at PS 84 could finally attain success.

THE MOVEMENT AND
INSTITUTIONAL CHANGE

As we have seen, the political movement at PS 84 succeeded in altering the type of governance of the school, both by changing the role of the principal and by establishing procedures through which clients would have a major voice in professional recruitment. This required the assistance of an innovator from within the elite of the bureaucracy, Dr. Hammer, the new District Superintendent. The movement also changed pedagogical methods in the direction of informal or open education. Here too the role of a professional innovator (Professor Samson) was of crucial importance in translating external political pressure into new organizational policies and professional practices.

[65] Cf., Crane Brinton, *The Anatomy of Revolution* (New York: Random House, 1958), pp. 29–41.

the functions of the movement
and the professional innovator
in changing school practices

The origins of the specific ideas and forces associated with informal education at PS 84 were to be found in the Freedom School. Silver, Davis and several other teachers who had come together in the Freedom School became a source of new ideas within the school faculty. These teachers, who innovated in their own classrooms, sought to effect more macroscopic changes in the school as a whole. Their ensuing confrontations with the principal served further to propagandize an alternative model of classroom arrangements—really, an alternative ideology of education.

Without the presence of the parent movement it is doubtful that the Freedom School teachers would have been able to bring about radical transformation of pedagogical practices at PS 84. The parents protected the early innovators on the faculty from reprisals by the principal, at one point compelling the Local School Board to reverse a decision to transfer Davis and Silver out of the school. The parents took the initiative in observing Professor Samson's program in a Harlem school, and it was through their lobbying at district headquarters that the director of the Balanced Class Project asked her to become a teacher-trainer at PS 84. Above all, the parents applied continual pressure on Wertzel and then on Rubin to accept informal methods; while at the same time they helped reduce the power of both administrators to control events in the school, thereby *creating a situation where change could not effectively be prevented from the top*. Thus, the movement of parents and deviant professionals both presented norms and values counter to those of the traditionally structured school and checked the power of individuals authorized to enforce the old norms—the administration. Once the traditional methods and standards came to be challenged openly, many teachers began to experiment and to consider new pedagogical arrangements.

The political movement was able to negate the old order. But by itself it could probably not have established a lasting new one. It could not impose a coherent model of how to teach informally, structure classrooms, or evaluate success. It could not authoritatively assert which of the many experiments were moving in the right direction, which were not moving at all but merely represented the loss of all purpose in the classroom. It could not train teachers to utilize methods for which their previous professional education left them unprepared. Without these functions being fulfilled, not only would informal methods not have become institutionalized at PS 84, but a reactionary movement might well have developed which would have acted in the name of the children and their need to be educated. It was Professor Samson who played the professional leadership role which stabilized the situation while institutionalizing the potential gains of the revolutionary period.

Samson was a charismatic person who engendered the faith necessary to overcome considerable obstacles in moving toward an untried goal. Her personality, her expert status, and her ability to articulate a convincing justification for informal methods combined to facilitate the suspension of judgment demanded during the period of transition to a new order. Because she was a designated "teacher-trainer" she could legitimize the whole reform effort, giving it an official program name (informal methods) and an official initiator (herself). Thus, while she did not introduce informal methods into PS 84, she rationalized their introduction by functioning as the professional in charge.

She rationalized the process of innovation in another sense as well. She demonstrated how changes could be made realistically with the personnel and children at the school. She showed the principal how to do things which seemed to be impossible, for example, how to use the corridors for educational activities without violating fire laws. She provided teachers with the professional support and guidance which the parents could not give and the principals (first Wertzel, then Rubin) either could not or would not provide. A teacher who began using informal methods in 1968–69 spoke to this point:

Last year [1968–69] I taught a second grade with a roll of 32. It was a very rough class, with seven of the children picked as material for Junior Guidance. Things were going just terribly. I heard that a few teachers were trying open classes. I was somewhat hesitant, but I thought *anything* had to be better than my class, the way it was going. . . .

Anyway, I started, and I was a wreck. I worried all the time about whether I would ever straighten things out—you know, be able to maintain order without standing there screaming. I was anxious about whether I was doing the right things, whether the children were really going to learn, especially reading. . . . I was continually upset because everything seemed to be taking so long to accomplish—forever.

Mrs. Samson was holding meetings during the middle of the [1968–69] year and Rubin said anyone interested could go. So I did, and I got moral support and ideas, even though I wasn't one of the four people in the official program. I also talked to other teachers who were trying this and having troubles too. I guess we gave each other company. But without Mrs. Samson I don't know what would have happened. She showed me how to actually do things. How to handle a child who couldn't adjust. What to say in particular situations. She came in here and did things so I could watch.

It was still rough. It took until the spring [about six months] for the class to start functioning.[66]

While Professor Samson was a forceful person, her activity was that of the professional helper. She refrained from ordering; instead she tried to "show," to demonstrate how things could work. She assumed that only through the voluntary acceptance of change by the teachers would innovation actually be effected in the classroom. As she put it,

You see the teacher must want to change. When she wants to take a first step, she must be helped; but not forced to go on. If that first step doesn't show the teacher that

[66] Interview, Fall, 1969.

she is trying something with promise, you, as the change agent, have no hope and no right to push for more.[67]

Similarly, she dissuaded the principal from instituting change by administrative fiat:

There was a problem with the paraprofessionals. One of them was unalterably opposed to what was going on. So we had a meeting and did a very historic thing: we let the paraprofessionals decide which program they wanted to work in, and some switched. Wertzel objected, said that people couldn't have their choice of doing anything they wanted; but finally she agreed.[68]

Her helping or integrative approach[69] demanded strict attention to the educational aspects of the reform: "remaining politically neutral . . . not asking the principal for anything which isn't completely germane to the program . . . [and] always trying to be constructive and to emphasize ways of achieving overall education goals." This approach accounted for much of Professor Samson's success as an effective professional innovator who greatly facilitated the actual implementation of the programs demanded by the political movement.

Nonetheless, her effectiveness—not to mention her very presence in the school—was made possible by the political situation which the movement brought about. At other schools on the West Side and in Harlem where Professor Samson was working to restructure teaching methods, she made fewer gains than at 84. Her strategy of presenting teachers with an alternative demonstration model by first creating a "corridor program" during a small portion of the day had only limited success. Teachers at these schools remained generally committed to the traditional norms and ideology, and remained bound by the sanctions of viable organizational hierarchies. Under such circumstances Mrs. Samson, as the change agent, found it difficult, and often impossible, to establish the relationship necessary to her developmental (or integrative) strategy. Administrators who seemed initially more cooperative than Wertzel or Rubin prevented changes which Samson had been able to bring about at 84.

While Professor Samson operated within PS 84 with considerable political acumen, and understood the ways in which innovation could be prevented by the established authorities in an organization, her analysis of the process of change was—interestingly and perhaps necessarily—"rationalistic." She subscribed to the common model people use when they think about effecting change, a model which states that new forms will be adopted if they are "better" than old ones, if they are demonstrated to be superior.

[67] Interview, June, 1970.

[68] Ibid.

[69] Harold Weissman defines an "integrative strategy" for effecting change as one in which "the change agent works *with* the change target, solving problems, educating, and negotiating." Harold Weissman, "Educational Innovation: The Case of an External Innovating Organization" in *Service in the Mobilization for Youth Experience*, ed. Harold H. Weissman (New York: Association Press, 1969), p. 207.

The evidence from PS 84 and Professor Samson's own experience suggest, on the contrary, that innovations are not rejected or adopted only on their merits, but also on the basis of the distribution of interests and power within organizations. This is not to deny an important rational component to the process of change, but only to assert that by themselves the merits of a new program rarely are sufficient to guarantee its adoption.[70] Innovations usually demand the exercise of power by groups with an interest in them. In this case, a group with such an interest was the political movement at PS 84.

One of the leaders of the movement stated this very well in a letter written to *The New York Times*. The letter criticized an article[71] which provided a laudatory description of informal education at PS 84 but ignored the role of the political movement.

The article by Walter and Miriam Schneir on the open corridor at PS 84, though it provides a vivid description of learning at the school, glosses over a most crucial fact: the political struggle to change the school from a typical "grim and joyless" one into the place it has now become. This is most important, because the impression left by their account is that, somehow, the changeover just happened through the strength of will of Lillian Samson. It is true that Mrs. Samson played a large role in establishing the educational program. Had it not been for the political struggle, however, the soil at PS 84 would not have been able to nourish the seeds of the change.

It is important, therefore, that readers are aware of this struggle, for if they want to change their schools, and are faced, as we were, with the kind of traditional administrators, school boards, and boards of education who are resistant to change, they will not succeed, just as we would not have succeeded, had we not been able to mobilize large numbers of parents to change the power relationships (symbolized by the selection of a principal who is accountable to the parents). This change was made possible by a coalition of parents and teachers, and indeed, it was the teachers who first made the parents aware of how bad the school was, and who presented us with a proposal for an alternative. . . .

To ignore this fact is to mislead innocent parents who, armed with their copies of *Crisis in the Classroom*, will wander, starry-eyed, into the offices of their principals, and will expect their factories to become centers where learning is a joy. Before they embark they should be prepared for endless hours of meeting with indifferent officials, of endless delaying tactics, of promises that seem to offer a beginning but are, in reality, more of the same old stuff. They should be prepared to be called crazy, troublemakers, outside agitators, and the like. It will only be after they succeed that they will become a model for others to emulate.[72]

the fruits of victory

In the period after Mr. Simon's assumption of the principalship, PS 84 did become a "model for others to emulate." By the 1970–71 school year

---

[70] There is usually disagreement as to what the merits are. The possibility of value-free and objective analysis of a potential change is limited. The merits look different to individuals with different structural positions and interests.

[71] Walter Schneir and Miriam Schneir, "The Joy of Learning—In the Open Corridor," *The New York Times Magazine*, April 4, 1971.

[72] Letter to the Editor, *The New York Times Magazine*, April 4, 1971, from the President of the Parents Association. The letter was not published, but was distributed at PS 84.

more than two-thirds of the school's classrooms were organized along informal lines. The cover of *The New York Times Magazine* featured a picture of children tumbling in a corridor of PS 84. The lead article (to which the forementioned letter was addressed) declared that "today at PS 84, the visitor can see in operation the most dramatic . . . innovation[s] of the British primary schools." [73] Other schools in the district began to adopt informal methods. Superintendent of Schools Scribner and UFT President Shanker both endorsed informal pedagogy as a promising innovation. What was once a revolutionary idea became part of the officially acceptable program; though there remained open questions as to how far the innovation actually would extend elsewhere, and whether its routinization would not, as in the case of so many other programs, involve its dilution and ultimate subordination to status-quo interests.

PS 84 also became a model for a community-controlled school with a new type of principal.[74] The movement realized its ends in fundamentally altering the governance of the school. The Simon regime changed the relative power of professionals and parents to the benefit of the latter. The new principal declared that administrative decisions with regard to parent access, tracking and suspension policies, and a wide range of pedagogical matters had previously been, in effect, "a political choice to limit the power of parents over what happens to their children and to maintain the hegemony of so-called expert professionals over these matters. In reality, expertise has little to do with many decisions. . . . To assert the opposite is nothing but self-serving, even if professionals genuinely believe in their own arguments." [75]

Fully committed to community control himself, Mr. Simon gave parents the right to participate in school policymaking. He invited parent representatives to help him establish the organization plan for the 1970–71 school year, and allowed all parents to have a say in which teachers their children would get. He encouraged parents to come into classrooms and generally to participate in the life of the school. The community room was maintained and became established as a permanent lounge and meeting place. In addition, Simon continued to work toward implementing policies long demanded by the movement, which generally involved a shift in resources to the advantage of black and Spanish children.

The fall of 1971 marked the end of the mobilized period at PS 84. While parents continued to be involved in policy decisions, the PA ceased to constitute a political movement. It was demobilized and became an organization supportive of the administration. The office of the principal once again assumed a central controlling function. The role of principal was, however, redefined so as to include parents as a major reference group. In other words, the professional now saw himself as responsible to a parent

---

[73] Schneir and Schneir, "The Joy of Learning."

[74] This innovation has not, however, been discussed outside of the immediate community, nor has it received the blessings of Central Headquarters or the professional unions.

[75] Interview, July, 1970.

constituency, and the continued presence of parents provided a mechanism for assuring representation of their interests. The new order did not elicit the extraordinary commitment and mass participation of the communal days associated with the 1968 strike. But the regime constituted a major departure from that which governed PS 84 previously. In the case of PS 84 the demise of an urban political movement was a product of its triumph.

north side forces: a case of organizational transmutation

WITH GARY REDISH

5

North Side Forces, a community group based in Paterson, New Jersey, illustrates a third possible fate for an urban political movement. It neither succeeded nor failed; rather it changed its character to an extent that the label movement no longer described it accurately. Forces was conceived to be an organization which would simultaneously develop a political infrastructure in Paterson's North Side and support programs providing educational, health, and economic services. The constituency arising out of the service programs would provide the primary cadre for political mobilization; in this way the two endeavors would feed into each other. Ultimately North Side Forces did become the successful operator of several neighborhood programs including two day-care centers and a dental clinic, but the political militance of its early days vanished and its constituency remained oriented to its service function rather than becoming involved in political action. While the individuals associated with it offered a potential basis for militant organization, they did not constitute a viable political force.

The achievements of North Side Forces were considerable. By 1972, after four years of existence, Forces had obtained state funding for several of its projects while maintaining its financial independence through the voluntary contributions of a white suburban group of supporters. Its pre-school youth, recreational, and dental programs were satisfactorily serving their clientele and operating as training facilities where indigenous people learned paraprofessional and technical skills. The original, white president of Forces, Reverend Richmond Sears[1] had been succeeded in office by a black man from the neighborhood, and Sears was gradually disengaging himself from informal leadership in the organization so as to allow the dominance of community residents.

[1] Pseudonyms are used throughout.

North Side Forces' ability to gain and run a variety of service programs, however, did not extend to its most important substantive program—a low-income housing complex which it and its suburban allies tried to sponsor. Although the city government had initially approved the development, it subsequently vetoed the proposal despite the existence of seed money, carefully drawn plans, and available federal funding. The loss of the housing program reflected Forces' political failure—it could not marshall the power resources to force the city to overcome the legal technicalities which it used to reject the housing development. The resolution of the housing project issue revealed the general political impotence of the North Side community and demonstrated the pitfalls of the service approach as a means to political activation.

PATERSON'S NORTH SIDE

Paterson is an old industrial city located twelve miles west of New York City. It is the county seat of Passaic County and the third largest city in New Jersey with a population in 1970 of 144,824. Blacks officially account for 41,047 of this total; however, it is widely believed that the black population was greatly undercounted by the census. Of the slightly over 100,000 whites at least 20,000 are Spanish.

Paterson was founded in 1792 by Alexander Hamilton as a center for manufacturing. Located on the Passaic River just below the Great Falls—a spectacular 70-foot waterfall offering cheap power—its future as a major industrial center was confidently predicted. With Hamilton's assistance the Society for Establishing Usefull Manufactures, a group of prominent business leaders and public figures, set about developing the site. The Society, which was New Jersey's first chartered corporation, was granted control of the Falls and tax exemption. Its plans to produce a broad range of machinery and consumption goods never attained fulfilment, however, and eventually the various enterprises were sold to private companies.

During the nineteenth century a variety of industries made their home in Paterson. Most important was silk manufacture, and by the middle of the century Paterson silks had world renown. Although the silk industry declined by 1900, other manufacturing including locomotives and armaments took up the slack. Curtiss-Wright employed 17,000 aviation workers in Paterson during World War II, though it moved its operation to the suburbs soon after the war ended.

For much of this century Paterson was an important regional shopping center, and its large central business district still boasts several department stores. The growth of giant suburban shopping malls, however, has meant that patrons use the new interstate highway that bisects Paterson to leave the city to shop rather than to seek the amenities of its downtown. Gradually the central business area has been taken over by bargain stores selling odd lot merchandise, discount pharmacies, and the other retailers that move in to service the immobile poor when quality stores move out.

Since 1945 Paterson has seen the steady decline of both its industrial and commercial base. Visually, with its great old riverside mills dominating the landscape, it reminds one of New England's now desolate textile-producing cities. But socially it more closely resembles Newark. For the exodus of workers and middle-class citizens which left the New England mill towns depopulated has, in Paterson, freed space for an influx of blacks and Puerto Ricans seeking relatively cheap housing in the tight northern New Jersey market. This process of exchange of population reached its peak during the decade 1960–1970 when, despite a stable overall population figure, the white population declined from 122,000 to 103,000.[2] The poverty of the remaining population, despite a few enclaves of residential affluence, is attested to by a median family income of $7,088 in 1970 as compared to $11,674 for the rest of the county excluding the city of Passaic. The median family income for blacks living in Paterson's ghetto areas is approximately $6,185.[3]

Paterson is less well known than nearby Newark, which has become a nationwide symbol of urban decay. Its problems, however, are no less acute, and its relative obscurity means that it lacks even what meager benefits Newark obtains as an object of national attention. Paterson's own riots in 1967 went largely unheeded; its municipal administration is wholly dominated by whites; and planning for future development shows little concern for the housing needs of poor residents:

Paterson has about 75 percent of . . . [Passaic] County's obsolete housing stock; all of it urgently requires rehabilitation or replacement. In recent years, the City has been building about 50 housing units a year, . . . while it needs 17 times that many. Just to meet the relocation requirements of the downtown renewal program will require an estimated 200 units a year.[4]

In 1972 Paterson elected a new, conservative white mayor openly unsympathetic to minorities who called for the ending of federal social and rehabilitation programs in the city.

Paterson thus differs sharply from New York, the locale of the two other organizations described at length here. It has less of a commitment to minority improvement; it has little traditional political activism by neighborhood groups; and it offers less glamor to those who succeed in gaining the limelight. To work for community power in Paterson is to labor in a very obscure vineyard.

The North Side, or Riverview, District of Paterson contains approximately 10,000 residents cut off from the rest of the city by the Passaic River. By 1970 this formerly white working-class neighborhood was 75 percent black; the white population mainly had Spanish surnames. Except for a large low- and middle-income housing project on its periphery, the North Side

---

[2] U.S. Department of Commerce, *Census Tract; Paterson-Clifton-Passaic, N.J.: Standard Metropolitan Statistical Area; 1970 Census of Population and Housing*, p. P-1. This figure includes Latins.

[3] Ibid.

[4] Regional Plan Association, "The Potential of Paterson as a Metropolitan Center in Northern New Jersey," *Regional Plan News*, No. 92, February, 1972, 19.

neighborhood is characterized by two and three story frame dwellings crowded together along narrow, dusty streets. Besides the projects, virtually all the housing is of prewar vintage. On any warm evening the sidewalks are filled with family groups and unattached men seeking freedom from the heat and crowding indoors.

The only public transportation in the area is sporadic bus service, which takes the residents across the river where they must make connections if they wish to leave the city to get to jobs. Most North Side residents are ill educated and unskilled. The median grade completed is the eighth, and only 17 percent have graduated from high school. Median incomes within the two census tracts which comprise the area were $5,397 and $6,669 in 1970.[5]

The North Side's only political representative is a single alderman who, under Paterson's strong mayor form of government, has been powerless to advance the interests of his constituency. Until the emergence of North Side Forces no organization spoke for the area at meetings of the municipal administration, the planning board, the school board, or other agencies whose activities directly affected the neighborhood. Although Paterson does have a poverty agency and a Model Cities office, these organizations are located on the other side of the river and largely ignore the poor black and Latin community living on the North Side.

ORIGINS OF NORTH SIDE FORCES

The political vacuum, great poverty, and absence of social programs on Paterson's North Side indicated an obvious need for community organization. Nonetheless, no organization appeared until the disbandment of a white Methodist congregation in the area proved to be a catalytic event in the formation of the Ecumenical Association for Urban Concerns, later to be called North Side Forces.

Reverend Richmond Sears, a white graduate of the University of Iowa and Drew Theological Seminary in Madison, New Jersey, came to Paterson in 1964 as pastor of Christ Church. The church served Methodist, German-language worshippers on the North Side who, according to Sears, "were feeling the impact of the neighborhood and weren't anxious to do anything about it."[6] A black minister, Reverend Joe Booth, worked with Sears as co-pastor until 1968 in an effort to integrate the church. "Whites in the congregation said it was okay for blacks to join their church, but on their own terms," Sears recalled.[7] In summing up his attempt to integrate his church, Sears concluded that it was foredoomed to failure:

Many creative things happened in this period [1964–68], yet the integration model was clearly a failure. Why? Many in the congregation welcomed—and on occasion

[5] U.S. Department of Commerce, *Census Tract*, pp. P-60–61 and P-67.
[6] Interview with Gary Redish, March 30, 1972.
[7] Ibid.

actively sought—black participation, but always with the assumption that to integrate is "for them to become like us." All at a time when awareness of the black man's unique cultural and historical existence was at one of its most turbulent and creative stages! This latent contradiction surfaced, and added to this was the fear and hostility among whites created by riots and demonstrations that reached their peak in 1968–69.[8]

Given the seemingly unstoppable demographic changes affecting Paterson, it was inevitable that regardless of the Methodists' strategy toward integration, there would eventually be no congregation left for the church to guide. The process was hastened by several incidents involving Christ Church and Calvary (Methodist) Church, also on the North Side. Calvary became divided over a proposal of its pastors to provide day-care facilities on its premises for black neighborhood children. At the height of the dispute, which provoked an exodus of many members of the congregation, the church burned down and the remaining members joined Christ Church. Thereafter the deepening involvement of Sears and Booth in local racial issues, culminated by Booth's publicly referring to "phony white liberals" in the congregation and Sears' arrest after organizing a neighborhood demonstration against the police, led the white Methodists still in the area to demand the removal of both ministers. When the bishop refused their request, they voted in September 1968 to disband the Christ Church congregation.

Richmond Sears and his wife, Lisa, who had taken an important role in the church's integration efforts, elected to stay on the North Side and establish an "urban ministry." Joe Booth moved from the neighborhood to join a government-sponsored poverty program. Then Sears decided to use the Ecumenical Association for Urban Concerns (EAUC), a nonprofit corporation which had been established to run the Calvary day-care facility, as the organizational basis of their effort. The Searses received a commitment from the Methodist Church to continue Richmond Sears' salary while he acted as head of EAUC.

goals

The original goals of EAUC derived from the Searses' involvement with the Ecumenical Institute, an interdenominational Chicago organization directed at making the church relevant to inner-city needs. The couple had been on an Ecumenical Institute-led retreat in 1966, and now that Reverend Sears no longer needed to carry the responsibility of a congregation, he and his wife could devote their full energies to implementing the "Fifth City" model of urban action evolved by the Institute.

The Fifth City model identified three causes of the "inner-city crisis":

1. The negative self-image of the black man, attributable to the wounds inflicted by whites.
2. The absence of local structures allowing blacks to take advantage of technological abundance.

[8] Report to Northern New Jersey Board of Missions, March 2, 1972, mimeo.

3. The lack of means for participating in social decisionmaking processes.[9]

The method for attacking these problems was community organization in a limited geographical area: "It is black power flowing into and through the local processes toward radical alteration of the situation." [10]

Key to the operation of the model was the development of a cadre of individuals who would play a leadership role in recruiting a larger group into the activities of the organization. The initial cadre in Paterson consisted only of the Searses and a few blacks who had previously participated in the affairs of the church. The minister and his wife, however, were acutely conscious of the necessity that the leadership group be composed of blacks, and intended as much as possible to restrict their own roles to fund-raising and technical assistance. Community interest and involvement would arise from the participation of individuals in the various service-providing agencies established under EAUC; political power would develop naturally from the formation of functioning community structures and from a coalition with other organizations in Paterson aiming at black power.[11]

Initial emphasis was on education and in particular the implementation of the once controversial preschool, which formed the basis of the cadre's outreach efforts. Parents of preschool children and indigenous staff members comprised the core of the community organization. As EAUC spawned additional structures, these too were supposed to perform simultaneously the functions of providing services and acting as centers of neighborhood solidarity and power mobilization. The stress was on black self-help and independence from funding agencies. While individual units of the organization might receive governmental assistance, the organization itself operated without governmental support. There was thus an obvious need to develop some other basis of funding, and from the beginning EAUC attempted to build a white suburban constituency to provide financial and technical aid.

impact of the church

In the spring of 1969 the Ecumenical Association for Urban Concerns shed its religious-sounding title and acquired the new name North Side Forces. While its activities were entirely secular, its headquarters continued to be in the old church parish house, its first president was a white ordained minister, and its principal financial support came from church-related organizations. This religious association lent a certain sanctity to the organization's activities, and undoubtedly Sears' religious beliefs had a significant impact on his behavior. Community members, perhaps with some justification, regarded him as a saint, and his clerical position exempted him from the suspicions often directed at would-be leaders in the ghetto. It also

[9] Testimony of the Ecumenical Institute, *Hearings before the Subcommittee on Government Research of the Committee on Government Operations*, U.S. Senate, 90th Cong., 2nd sess.

[10] Ibid.

[11] Report to Board of Missions.

permitted him to play a role not usually open to whites in black neighborhoods.

Church involvement had been an important factor in Southern civil rights activity, particularly in relationship to actions led by The Reverend Martin Luther King (a Baptist) and the Southern Christian Leadership Conference (SCLC). While the role of churches has been less evident among blacks in the North, clergy have nonetheless been involved in a number of community organization attempts. For instance, in Rochester the community organizing activities of Saul Alinsky were underwritten by a coalition of churches, and a number of ministers were important among the local black leaders. In the movement for community control of schools in New York City there was also significant clerical involvement. A Catholic priest, the only white on the Ocean Hill-Brownsville governing board, was one of its principal organizers and most radical members. The group which pressed for community control at IS 201 centered around the Chambers Baptist Church, and both the minister's wife and the assistant pastor served on the IS 201 governing board.

In the case of North Side Forces the Methodist Church played a roughly analogous role to that of the federal government in some of the cases described in Chapter Two or, to a lesser extent, the Board of Education in the instance of Joan of Arc; it functioned as an outside agency that provided the push causing the local organization to come into existence. There is no question that without the initial support of the church and the personal efforts of Reverend Sears, North Side Forces would never have been born.

ORGANIZATIONAL GROWTH
AND THE
DECLINE OF MILITANCE

During the end of 1968 and the beginning of 1969 there were a number of militant demonstrations and scuffles with the police in Paterson. Sears and several of the black participants in Forces were involved in these activities and some were jailed. The ambitious stance of the organization was reflected in the title of its newspaper, *The North Side Weapon*, which was circulated to 5,000 people. But, according to Sears,

There has been a lot of disillusionment over the failure of leadership at that time [1968–69]. We worked very closely with SCLC which had a strong local chapter then. The local power structure pretty much decimated the leadership of that organization. . . . I'm often impressed how little it would take to shake up a city like Paterson. Looking at 68–69, I think we could do a lot. But a lot of blacks look back and say it didn't work, I'm not going to do that again. I don't know why. We almost brought the city to the brink then.[12]

[12] Interview with the authors, June 18, 1972.

By the end of 1969 confrontation tactics had petered out. *The North Side Weapon* ceased publication due to lack of funds and workers. North Side Forces had been an element in a citywide movement demanding changes in the police and city administration favorable to blacks; once that citywide effort faded, Forces turned to the task of building its own neighborhood structure. Here the focus was on developing programs rather than recruiting members into a political organization, even though in 1970 the Forces board voted to organize the community politically:

We made the decision two years ago to go the community organization route. But we've never really realized that vision. . . . There are some male social clubs in the neighborhood. If we had a paid organizer we could tie into them. We would need a hard-nosed ghetto black for it.[13]

While the direct political mobilization aspect of Forces' efforts diminished, program development flourished. In October 1968 the Paterson Ecumenical Pre-School (PEP-I), an all-day child care center, was established. It was supported by tuition payments from parents based on ability to pay, contributions by suburban church members, and assistance from the Methodist Church. It had a number of aims including parent involvement, the teaching of black pride, and the provision of skills. Neighborhood residents were interviewed and selected to be teachers. The most important criterion for hiring was ability to relate to children, and except for the position of director, formal academic credentials were not required.

For several years PEP was in dire financial straits. Since no federal or state funds were allocated to the school, church and suburban donations had to be scraped up each month to keep it in operation. Fund-raising was mainly the province of Sears and Jack Wilson, Forces' Youth and Community Director. In 1971–72 this pattern of private funding ended when the New Jersey Bureau of Children's Services granted Forces $132,000 to develop a second day-care center (PEP-II) for children whose mothers were in the Welfare Incentive Program (WIN). In addition, the Passaic County Child Care Coordinating Committee awarded PEP-I a three-to-one matching grant of up to $68,000.

In September 1969 the Northside Health Council was formed to plan for comprehensive health care for all community residents. The following year Forces purchased a building to be used as a health center; the down payment of $1500 was donated by a suburban church. In 1971 the Methodist Church gave $15,000 to support the opening of the center, and as a first step a dental program was initiated to provide full dental care at a cost of $25 per family a year. The Bergen County Dental Association and the Department of Dentistry of Fairleigh Dickinson University provided dental supplies as well as volunteer dentists. The clinic was administered by two neighborhood residents, including the wife of the president of Forces, who were trained as dental assistants at Fairleigh Dickinson.

[13] Ibid.

Forces was less successful in sponsoring activities for teenagers, and its youth program became moribund for a long period due to "lack of leadership and heroin"; it was revitalized in 1972 with a $15,000 grant from the state. Its program for elementary school age children, however, was much more productive, due largely to the efforts of Jack Wilson, a black college graduate who joined the Forces staff in 1971. Wilson, who described himself as an adherent of the philosophies of Martin Luther King and Imanu Baraka (Leroi Jones), felt strongly that middle-class blacks had a duty to serve in the ghetto. He therefore turned down more lucrative employment opportunities to work for Forces on an extremely meager salary; his wages derived first from a small church grant and then from monthly contributions by suburban church members and the proceeds of folk music concerts he gave himself.

Wilson ran an after-school and summer recreation program for children in 1971 and 1972. With only volunteer assistance he mounted a session for fifty children, which included sports, swimming, frequent trips to museums, theaters, and other culturally enriching places, as well as remedial educational exercises. The program had an informal, somewhat haphazard quality, summed up in this account of a Wilson-led excursion to Chinatown:

'Twas a cold and windy day when the children from the neighborhood walked through Chinatown. For many it was the first look at the culture of another people. . . . Mr. Jack, trying to be frugal and not pay for parking, lost the van on one of the side streets which became a major concern for all because the lunches were left inside. . . . The children fried rice and had tea as part of the oriental study, which will conclude with a trip to the museum. Then on to a study of African culture.[14]

In another incident the program's newly acquired used van was taken away and destroyed by a contractor who after months of delay had finally been persuaded to clear a lot for use as a playground adjacent to the program's facility.

In addition to his roles as fund raiser and youth director, Wilson edited a two-page mimeographed newsletter that initially appeared weekly, then sporadically. Unlike the *North Side Weapon*, *Forces in Focus* was not militant in tone. Instead it was a chatty little sheet that brought residents up to date on activities in the various programs, new schedules for the day-care center's school bus, and public events of interest to blacks; it also provided notes on black history and appeals for greater neighborhood involvement in Forces' activities. North Side Forces succeeded no better than the New York groups in obtaining access to major media. The *Paterson News*, the city's only daily, gave no coverage to Forces' activities; according to Wilson it was "reactionary and not favorable to anything positive about the black community." *The Record* (Bergen County), the largest circulation paper in the county, ran a few articles about Forces, including a feature article devoted to Jack Wilson, and *The New York Times* in 1972 presented a three-column complimentary article chronicling Forces' various endeavors. For any but the most sporadic coverage, however, the organization had to depend on its own resources.

14 *Forces in Focus*, mimeographed newsletter of North Side Forces, No. 9, December 1, 1971.

The newsletter, which was circulated free to Forces' membership and also made available in local gathering spots such as stores and laundromats, constituted Forces' principal effort to reach the community at large. The size of the organization remained small, with 250 dues-paying members, of whom about 75 ever came to meetings or participated actively in any way; many were in arrears for the minimal dues. Of the active members the great majority were parents of children in the preschool or on the staff of one of the programs. Monthly meetings of the organization were usually attended by ten to twenty people, mainly the hard core of activists who held positions on the governing board, and staff people. Despite continual requests for volunteers to assist in clean-up endeavors and operation of the thrift shop, few community residents were willing to perform such chores. Jack Wilson commented ruefully on the propensity of unemployed neighborhood men to stand around and watch as he and children in the recreation program struggled to move heavy pieces of debris from the land surrounding the youth center.

leadership

Official responsibility for the governance of North Side Forces rested with its executive board; in addition, the preschool, health program, and housing corporation, which will be discussed below, had separate governing bodies. Two-thirds of the membership of these boards consisted of community people, all of whom were black except for the Searses. Community members were predominantly female. While a few of the board members were on welfare, most were employed either as teachers in the preschool or as paraprofessionals in the public school. The noncommunity members of the boards were either drawn from professional circles in Paterson or the suburban "friends" of North Side Forces. The former were a mixed racial group; the latter were white. The officers of all the executive boards except the housing corporation were black with the exception of the Reverend Richmond Sears, who was initially president of the North Side Forces board and subsequently stepped down to the post of treasurer.

Sears was replaced as president of Forces by Tom Dempson when Sears insisted that his continuation in the post was inappropriate. Dempson, a black man in his middle thirties, lived in the middle-income housing project on the periphery of the neighborhood. He had been injured in an industrial accident and supported himself on his disability allowance; this permitted him to be free days and to devote considerable time to the organization. Dempson was a highly effective public speaker and a professed militant; he suffered, however, from administrative inexperience, and he found little support for his more radical proposals. He confessed that the newness of his organizational job placed him at a disadvantage; he lacked the skill and assurance of veteran organizers and would despair when meetings were sparsely attended or calls for action went unheeded.

There was a good deal of tension between Dempson and Jack Wilson, the youth director, which finally contributed to Wilson's resignation in the fall of 1972. Wilson had been a key figure in the alliance with suburban whites, frequently representing the Forces organization at meetings of its white supporters. While working on the North Side Wilson would adopt a ghetto *patois,* but on his missions to the suburbs he would sound very much the middle-class college graduate. Dempson felt that the reliance on whites for support necessarily resulted in an injury to black pride and solidarity, while giving whites undue influence in the organization. Another element which probably undermined the relationship between the two men was Wilson's superior educational attainments and social status. Dempson felt that these made Wilson into an outsider even though he had taken up residence in the neighborhood; he also probably felt envious of them and of Wilson's evident popularity in the community. These sentiments expressed themselves in demands that Wilson restrict himself to a narrowly defined staff role rather than a leadership function.

Sears attempted to play a mediating role between Wilson and Dempson. His position, however, was extremely difficult since his whiteness and church connections made him suspect to Dempson. But Sears very much wanted North Side Forces to become self-sustaining and felt that this could happen only under indigenous black leadership of the sort provided by Dempson. Although Sears was the principal figure in North Side Forces for the first several years of its existence, by 1972 he had reduced his participation considerably and hoped that he could soon leave the organization altogether.

Sears, Dempson, Wilson, some of the preschool teachers, and several women in the neighborhood constituted the cadres of North Side Forces. Of the latter the most significant was Marylou Jones, a former welfare mother who now worked in the public school administering the lunch program. In personal style she very closely resembled the black female activists of the movement for community control of schools in New York. She was flamboyant, highly verbal, and humorous; she could claim with justice to be an authentic voice of the black ghetto. While she was less open about her antipathy to whites, she tended to side with Dempson in his rivalry with Wilson. She was not, however, willing to endorse militant protest action, and would cite the death of her son, who jumped or was thrown from an upper story window of the police station, as evidence of the price exacted from protestors. At a meeting in which Dempson proposed that Forces mount a demonstration against the city administration for disapproving its housing programs, Mrs. Jones countered: "I ain't sitting in for nobody. It doesn't do any good anyhow. I've been through it all, and what difference does it make?" [15]

Most of the energies of the leadership group were devoted to planning and administering the service programs. It was content to work in scruffy surroundings and to maintain low salary levels for staff. By 1972 the Forces budget had increased to a projected $200,000, more than double the previous year's expenditure. This money was being spent as directly as possible on

[15] Meeting of Century 21 Housing Corporation, June 21, 1972; from notes of the authors.

programs; thus far North Side Forces has managed to avoid the investment in overhead which characterized so many of the officially sponsored poverty programs. There were no smart offices, fancy equipment or well-paid clerical staff. Projects were not used as an excuse for the creation of unneeded jobs. While the Forces leadership group admitted disappointment in the lapse of its original political objectives, it felt proud of its accomplishments in the service sector. Its political weakness, however, contributed directly to the failure of its most important "service" program—its proposal to build low-income housing in the neighborhood.

CENTURY 21: THE LIMITS
OF ADVOCACY PLANNING

The most pressing need in the North Side community was housing, and early in the history of Forces Sears investigated ways in which the organization could address itself to the area's housing problems. He saw improved housing both as necessary to community well-being and also as the strongest available rallying point for community sentiment. Since there was almost no desirable housing in the entire neighborhood, it was an issue which affected everyone. It was also an area in which his suburban contacts could prove especially useful.

In December 1969, forty members of the Archer United Methodist Church of suburban Allendale toured the North Side ghetto under Sears' guidance. The group was shocked by what it saw and decided to organize a nonprofit corporation in order to qualify as a sponsor under the federal low-income housing subsidy program. The original Archer group joined with a large group of suburban churches in the housing venture. By 1972 about two dozen churches and fair housing groups were participating in the Suburban Task Force, which had as its principal aim the funding of the housing operation. Capital was raised through the selling of stock at $20 per share in the newly formed Century 21 Housing Corporation and through direct contributions by church groups. In addition the Task Force sponsored a number of fund-raising parties, theater trips and other events.

Part of the money ($5,000) raised in this fashion was used to hire the advocacy planning firm of Jones and Schmidt, which was given the task of specifying the requirements for sponsorship of a federal program, selecting sites in the North Side suitable for housing, and outlining their advantages and disadvantages. By the spring of 1971 the possible sites had been narrowed down to an unused, overgrown playground owned by the Paterson Housing Authority adjacent to a public housing project and an area across the street occupied by several old houses. Jones and Schmidt proposed a phased 100-unit development on the two sites, permitting relocation from the group of houses into the new buildings across the street and the replacement of the preempted recreational land. Funding would be under Section 236 of the federal Housing Act of 1968. This plan was presented to the city, which responded as follows:

Our information indicates the land [occupied by the playground] is still in the name of the City of Paterson Housing Authority. The land use controls adopted under the approved Urban Renewal plan exist for a 40 year period. However, pending determination and clarification of the City's ability to sell land being used for public purposes, it will be the City's intention to do everything possible to make the proposed public use (playground area) available for housing purposes as proposed.[16]

Upon receiving this positive response, the housing corporation proceeded to retain a legal firm and began interviewing architects suggested by the planning consultants. Neighborhood people participated actively in the architect selection process, and eventually a black firm from New York was hired. In December the Paterson Board of Finance passed a resolution naming Century 21 as the developer of the North Side area, and early the following year Paterson Model Cities agreed to lend Forces $20,000 in seed money to assist the project.

In May, however, the city stated that it could not legally sell the playground site to Century 21. Its original designation as recreation land for the Christopher Columbus Public Housing Project meant that if Paterson sold the land the federal Department of Housing and Urban Development (HUD) could require Paterson to reimburse it. Furthermore, Paterson was applying for "green acres" money from the state, and under the green acres program for recreational development the land had to be reserved for park purposes. At the same time the city received a letter from HUD denying permission to build the proposed housing because the project's small size did not meet guidelines in effect at that time. HUD argued that the poor condition of the surrounding dwellings would soon cause the new development to become a slum. This situation led Model Cities to withdraw its offer of seed money.

After more than two years and the investment of thousands of dollars, Century 21's housing plans were aborted. The efforts of the corporation's attorney to iron out the difficulties with the city's legal staff were unavailing, even though he felt that the obstacles were far from insuperable and could be overcome relatively easily with strong support from the city. The main stumbling block was the playground designation of the principal site; but the land was not being used for that purpose, was part of a parcel intended to serve low-income housing needs, and would eventually be replaced. There was no other site on the densely settled North Side which would have accommodated even a 100-unit project without extensive demolition.

North Side Forces' political impotence was revealed at a meeting of Century 21 held in June 1972 to consider a strategy for persuading the city to ease the way for the housing proposal. The meeting was attended by twenty representatives of the suburban churches, ten blacks from the North Side community, Dempson, Sears, and representatives of the corporation's legal and planning consultants. Dempson and Mrs. Jones explained that Forces had no influence at all in city hall. While the last mayor had been at least sympathetic, he had resigned to become New Jersey Commissioner of

[16] Letter from Mayor Lawrence F. Kramer to Century 21 Housing, September 30, 1971.

Community Affairs and his replacement showed no interest in their situation. None of the candidates in the forthcoming city election came from the North Side or was likely to promise support for the housing program. Forces did not have a sufficiently viable constituency to offer a bloc of votes to a mayoral candidate in return for support, and there was no alternative political authority to which it could appeal. There was every sign that the city administration wanted to develop Paterson in such a way as to make it unattractive to low-income residents; first priority in development under urban renewal was for the central business district, and hardly any provision had been made for relocation of displaced residents. Dempson proposed that Forces should attempt a sit-in at the mayor's office, but his argument received no endorsement from either the other blacks or the whites present at the meeting. Some of the suburbanites proposed publicizing Forces' plight in the Bergen *Record* and making representations to their congressional and legislative delegations. These proposals were eventually implemented but to no visible effect. The subsequent election of the most conservative of the five mayoral candidates scotched any hopes Century 21 might have had for renewed consideration at city hall.

The inability of Forces to obtain serious attention for its housing program indicated the limitations of advocacy planning as a strategy for poor people's groups. The production of a highly sophisticated plan by the consulting firm, the great amounts of time spent by members of Century 21 on the planning process, and the availability of professionals competent to negotiate with the city in technical terms did not affect the ultimate outcome of the endeavor. Century 21's experience supported Frances Piven's assertion that advocacy planning was an insufficient asset to produce a reallocation of resources:

In one city after another, local groups in Model Cities neighborhoods are involved in the technical dazzlements of planning, some to prepare plans, others to compete with counterplans. But there is little being built in these neighborhoods. Nor are locally prepared plans likely to change the pattern. A plan, of itself, is not force; it is not capable of releasing the necessary federal subsidies or of overcoming the inertia of the city agencies. Quite the contrary, for those people who might otherwise have become a force by the trouble they made are now too busy.[17]

Century 21, however, did not corroborate the either/or premise of Piven's argument. Its members were not inhibited by participation in the planning process from becoming "a force by the trouble they made"; they would not have made trouble regardless. Without the assistance of the advocate planners Forces would not have been able to formulate a set of demands; there is little reason to think the organization would have been better off in the absence of the planning effort. Yet technical expertise without political power was, exactly as Piven contended, "not capable of

---

[17] Frances Fox Piven, "Whom Does the Advocate Planner Serve?" in *The View from Below: Urban Politics and Social Policy*, eds. Susan S. Fainstein and Norman I. Fainstein (Boston: Little, Brown, 1972), p. 232.

releasing the necessary federal subsidies or of overcoming the inertia of the city agencies." The housing issue demonstrated not the flaws of planning but rather of a strategy of concentrating exclusively on services.

The total extent of Forces' constituency was the necessarily very limited number of people it could serve; its name was barely known outside of this small stratum of the North Side population. Whereas the housing program had been intended to enhance the reputation of North Side Forces, it instead became a symbol of its ineffectiveness and the general powerlessness of the black community. This almost total lack of political resources came as a shock to the white church members who had participated actively in the housing corporation, and who were unaccustomed to finding themselves in such a position. The seeming illogic of the city's refusal to work for a low-income housing program that would cost it virtually nothing stymied them, but they could think of no effective response. Dempson was inclined to blame the suburban influence for Forces' docility in the face of adversity, although there was no taste for protest action in the black community either. The considerable involvement of a group of middle- and upper-class whites in the activities of an impoverished black community group does, however, raise some interesting questions concerning the results of this kind of coalition, and in the next section we shall examine in more detail the role of the white allies of North Side Forces.

THE SUBURBAN TASK FORCE

Sears' insistence on involving white liberals in the activities of North Side Forces derived from his history of participation in the Southern civil rights movement. The splintering of that movement and the slogan of black power which caused its disintegration led him to emphasize the importance of maintaining blacks in leadership positions. But he saw a role for sympathetic whites in providing financial support, voluntary labor, technical assistance, and political influence. Because of his vision, North Side Forces represented an unusual fusion of black power and black–white coalition.

The relationship between Forces and Sears' suburban contacts was formalized by the establishment of the Suburban Task Force in connection with the Century 21 housing corporation. The efforts of the Task Force, however, extended beyond housing to financial contributions for various purposes including Jack Wilson's salary, volunteer work in the youth program and the organization's thrift shop, and the opening of suburban homes for various activities. Thus, residents of exclusive communities would hold fund-raising open houses and make their swimming pools available to black children bussed in by the youth program.

By 1972 the Task Force numbered 387 (mainly enrolled as families) exclusive of clergy. Eighty families constituting 152 individuals responded to a mail questionnaire inquiring into their backgrounds.[18] Of the respondents

[18] This survey was devised and administered by Gary Redish in June 1972.

two-thirds (105 men and women) had college degrees, nearly half of whom had attended graduate or professional school. Only four men and thirteen women had not attended college at all. Forty-three percent reported family incomes exceeding $25,000 a year; of the twenty families earning less than $15,000 a year eleven were retired and on pension. Almost the entire sample of men had prestigious occupations. Twenty-five were professionals, four owned their own businesses; thirty-eight were executives or managers; two held government jobs; five were retired; and six gave no answer. Many women were employed, with the largest number (15) working as teachers. Sixty percent of the families responding had heads of household over forty years of age. Only one family had ever lived in Paterson, and 60 percent had come to New Jersey from out of state. Three-quarters of the respondents reported having visited the North Side Community at least once, although less than half said that they had attended a Task Force meeting or function.

The group, not surprisingly, was overwhelmingly Protestant. More than fifty families indicated that at least one of their members had served as an officer in a church group, and more than half the families had become connected with North Side Forces through their religious affiliation. Most of the respondents were active in political or civic groups as well.

The Suburban Task Force provided Forces with an unusual resource. While the amount of funding it sustained was small by the standards of government support or foundation grants, it was largely without strings and responsive to emergency needs. These factors gave Forces greater flexibility and scope for experimentation than was available to organizations subject entirely to the rigid procedures of formal grant application. Task Force members were available upon request for a variety of jobs including training a neighborhood resident to keep the organization's books, offering free legal counsel, and maintaining contacts with county and state (although not city) officials.

The relationship between the suburbanites and the community members of Forces differed from that which characterized the integrated civil rights organizations of the early sixties. Except for Sears and some board members, whites did not belong to Forces itself and thus did not compete with blacks for jobs or prestige. But neither were they prohibited from activity, as occurred in a number of organizations using the slogans of black power. Rather, whites largely played the role of allies with their own separate organizational structure. Sears and Wilson conscientiously acted the part of liaison men, so that the whites did not feel neglected or unwanted. Forces was thereby able to capitalize on the enthusiasm of liberal whites who sought to involve themselves with black liberation beyond simply placing checks in the mail. The expulsion of whites by the Student Nonviolent Coordinating Committee (SNCC) and the Congress of Racial Equality (CORE) had resulted in the dissipation of white support and eventually the disintegration of the organizations. North Side Forces, on a small scale, indicated a way in which blacks could use the good intentions of white liberals with minimal, though by no means nonexistent, tension.

ORGANIZATIONAL TRANSMUTATION

North Side Forces evolved from a small organization intent on gaining community power to a much larger, service-oriented body. Although it did not fulfill some of its earlier objectives, it nonetheless effectively operated a series of programs in a neighborhood which had been almost totally neglected by other agencies. In many respects, despite a much lower level of funding, it closely matched the community development model visualized for the Community Action Programs (CAPs) of the War on Poverty. Neighborhood residents were involved in the planning and execution of bureaucratic services in their own community; staff positions were filled wherever possible by local people, who were selected for their ability to communicate with clients and who received on-the-job training where necessary; the organization operated with an absolute minimum of bureaucratic red tape.

As was the case with the CAPs, programmatic success had no necessary connection with political action. Individuals involved in day-to-day program administration tended to devote their time and talent to administrative chores. Programs grew larger, and increasing numbers of people became dependent upon them as employees or clients; political activity came to jeopardize their status. In a situation where program gains were obvious and militance had high risks, co-optation became the almost inevitable result. While Forces members retained an ideological commitment to the redistribution of power and were acutely aware that they lost their housing program due to lack of political initiative, they continued to play essentially bureaucratic roles.[19]

The development of Forces into a quasi-governmental agency occurred despite the housing issue, which both provided a tangible goal and revealed clearly the unsympathetic nature of the city administration. There were several reasons, however, why the Forces leadership could not convert the housing question into a basis for mobilization rather than the symbol of Forces' political defeat.

First, the Forces leadership, while holding an ideological diagnosis which attributed the poverty of the North Side to the powerlessness of its inhabitants, did not itself actively proselytize its viewpoint. Its appeals to the community were limited to rather mealy-mouthed exhortations in *Forces in Focus*:

We need your help. As you read this, something is happening in your community, which together we can save. Demolition without representation or relocation, crime (both nuisance and serious), drug addiction, garbage in our streets—the list can go on

---

[19] Roche and Sachs distinguish between "bureaucrats" and "enthusiasts" in social movements: "While the bureaucrat tends to regard the organization as an end in itself, to the enthusiast it will always remain an imperfect vehicle for a greater purpose." J. P. Roche and S. Sachs, "The Bureaucrat and the Enthusiast: An Exploration of the Leadership of Social Movements," *Western Political Quarterly*, VIII, June, 1965, 249.

and on. Alone, it seems to be impossible to handle, but Unity of People changes all that. As residents, each of us has an investment to protect. By participating in a community organization that is by no means fancy, things begin to happen.[20]

When residents continued in their state of apparent apathy or hopelessness, no further efforts were made to reach them.

Second, while the organization had funds for programs, it had none for political organizing staff. As was the case with the Joan of Arc Board, none of the local leadership had the talent or experience for this kind of activity. Even the original CAPs had money available for organizing; and Joan of Arc was able to raise such financing from foundations. By 1970 foundations would not make grants of this sort since they would endanger their tax position; some of the suburban friends might have been willing to make contributions to support a paid organizer, but it was unlikely that sufficient money could have been raised in this way. Without a professional organizing staff Forces was unable to develop a mass base. It had clients, but few of them regarded the organization in any other light than a place to leave their children or get their teeth filled.

Third, the North Side community had a low base level of mobilization. There was a complete lack of political organizations, street corner speakers, underground newspapers, and protest actions. The few militants were exhausted by earlier struggles and had largely withdrawn from political activity. The black community of Paterson resembled the white in its tendency to lose its upwardly mobile members to the surrounding suburbs or the big cities. Paterson offered few rewards for either the economically or politically ambitious.

North Side Forces presents a contrasting case to Joan of Arc in that, while it similarly failed as a political movement, it succeeded as something else. Both groups illustrate the tension between organizing and service-providing functions. For Joan of Arc, however, the objective of gaining power remained foremost, and its inability to achieve that goal caused its disintegration. North Side Forces, which began with an equally strong emphasis on power and services, soon became totally absorbed in the maintenance and expansion of programs and ceased, except in the private rhetoric of its leaders, to be a political movement.

[20] *Forces in Focus*, No. 11, December 15, 1971.

patterns of
participation and
consciousness

6

The case studies of Joan of Arc, PS 84, and North Side Forces attempted to capture the dynamics of urban movements and to analyze events without destroying the flow of the actual stories. Now our approach will change to addressing certain theoretical topics, with evidence drawn from our own investigations and those of others. These topics can be grouped in three main areas, to each of which we devote a chapter: first, the nature of involvement by individuals in urban movements; second, the relationship between the internal structure of these movements and their ability to attain external goals; and, finally, the larger significance of urban political movements, both for the groups they purport to represent and for understanding American political institutions.

In considering the nature of individual involvement we will discuss the motivations of movement participants, their political consciousness, and the ways in which each interacts with activity and behavioral experience. A full explication of the theoretical issues associated with participation and consciousness also requires us to raise a question which our evidence has so far addressed only in part. Why have some people become involved in movements while others have not? It is one thing to say that urban movements have their social basis in lower- and working-class minority groups, and another to understand the forces which lead some of their members to participate in movement activity and deter others from doing so. Our research has focused on movements and those who *did* join them, rather than on collectivities and the variety of political activities in which their members engage. Nonetheless, we want to raise the issue and consider such research findings as may help throw some light upon it.

Were sufficient evidence available, a theoretical exposition of the nature of participation in urban movements would attempt to answer all the following questions:

1. What kinds of people develop political ideas consonant with movement activism? From which collectivities have they been drawn? How do they differ from other people in these collectivities?
2. What kinds of people have actually participated in movement activity? How did they come to join? What was their initial consciousness? What were their personal motivations and how did these change over time?
3. How does developed consciousness differ among movements depending on issue areas, targets, and overall political environment?
4. What is the interactive process among movement recruitment, activity, and the motivation and political consciousness of adherents?

Some of the data already presented is germane to these questions, although none of it permits more than suggestive or illustrative answers. In addition, we have evidence about activists in the movement for community control of schools which provides further information about the social background and motivations of those involved in urban movements. The next section will be devoted to the exposition of this material. In the latter part of the chapter we will try to make some generalizations about the pattern of participation in urban movements as a whole. These will be based upon evidence from the various case studies and from the work of other researchers. The reader should be warned, however, that there is little published data available to help answer these questions; our conclusions are therefore drawn with caution and are quite circumscribed in their scope.

As we discussed in Chapter Two, the movement for community control of schools created some of the most divisive political conflict in the recent history of New York City. The indigenous leadership in that movement centered about two of the three demonstration-district governing boards, those of Ocean Hill-Brownsville in Brooklyn and Intermediate School (IS) 201 in Harlem, and, to a lesser extent, the insurgent group attempting to gain community control for the Joan of Arc schools. Participant observation at Joan of Arc, and in-depth interviews with a large proportion of the members of the three governing boards, provide us with information about the kinds of people who were involved in these groups.[1]

THE JOAN OF ARC
PLANNING/GOVERNING BOARD

The Joan of Arc Board consisted entirely of parents of public school children.

---

[1] Data on the social backgrounds and consciousness of members of the Ocean Hill-Brownsville and IS 201 Governing Boards were collected under the auspices of the Institute for Community Studies, Queens College, City University of New York. Some of these findings are reported in Marilyn Gittell *et al., Demonstration for Social Change* (New York: Institute for Community Studies, 1971).

Of the eleven active members of the Board, four were black, two Puerto Rican, and five white; seven were women; five were lower- or working-class, and two more marginally middle-class. Their status as parents was a primary identification; they viewed parents as an adversary or interest group with a common enemy of educational professionals. The members, however, always saw racial identifications as of equal importance to client ones, and, in fact, believed themselves to be advancing first and foremost the interests of minority group parents and children.

The JOA activists all took a strong personal interest in the education of their own children. Except for one who thought it financially out of the question, the white members flirted with the idea of putting their children in private schools, but kept them in public school because they believed in racial integration and the social value of a public education. Still, they felt guilty about subjecting their children to what they considered the dismal failure of the New York school system, and they became involved in trying to improve that system.

The two Puerto Rican women were less willing than the whites to tolerate the costs to their children of keeping them in public school, and both had succeeded in sending some of their children on scholarship to private schools. One of these, when explaining her involvement in education, said:

I want my children to become important people. I want them to be a doctor, or lawyer, or professor. I am very involved in seeing that they get a good education. I want them to succeed.[2]

Three of the black women did not consider private schools to be an alternative for them. They were very passionate about the need for parents to participate in their children's education and made great efforts to be physically present in the schools. One had quit her more remunerative job as a medical technician to work as an educational assistant so that she could better supervise her children's schooling:

The schools are my whole life. I spend almost all my time on the schools. I would like to return to my career as a medical technician, but I can't spare the time from the schools.

This same woman had gone to the trouble of mimeographing a history of her conflicts with school authorities over her children and distributing it to anyone expressing an interest.

Opponents of community control characterized their antagonists as power seekers. Albert Shanker, president of the United Federation of Teachers (UFT), referred to critics of the 1969 Decentralization Law in the following terms:

The provisions of the law are deeply disturbing to some groups—to those who hoped to parlay small but tightly organized and well financed minorities into control of the

[2] Unless otherwise indicated all quotations and background information on participants are drawn from interviews with the authors.

schools, to those who hoped to use that control as an instrument for ulterior political ends, to those who in local situations have already used it to divert funds from education to patronage.[3]

The JOA Board, like other activist educational groups, found the Decentralization Law "deeply disturbing." Its members did indeed seek power for parents in the schools. But the allegation that they wished to do so for "ulterior political ends" was a misrepresentation.

The most important motive leading people to participate in the JOA Board was a desire to improve the quality of the schools their children attended. They undoubtedly also received extrinsic rewards—psychic income from feeling that they were defending a good cause, reassurance from being part of a group. A member remarked: "Until I met . . . others who were fighting for the schools, I felt alone and depressed." Only one in any way saw the Board as a direct vehicle for future political advancement:

Being on the Governing Board has made me restless. I feel that if I'm good at the Governing Board job, I shouldn't be spending my days in a printing plant. I do have political ambitions, but I prefer to leave them vague at the moment.

Another said political office might be a possibility in the distant future and two members thought that they might some day run for a place on the District 5 Local School Board. The remainder professed a desire to stay "involved" but had no ambition for office. Typical answers to the question, "What are your plans for future involvement in the community?" were:

I don't think about the future much.

I don't plan these things. I want to remain involved. But I don't have any personal ambition for power—I recognize that this is a defect for this kind of work.

I have another nine years of involvement in front of me—until my youngest child finishes school. But I certainly don't want to run for office.

I enjoy being involved very much and I will continue in some way to be involved. But I'm not sure how.

Lack of desire for public office was one indicator of the relatively low priority that personal power held as an incentive for JOA members. Another was their minimal level of organizational activity. Only four of the eleven were active in organizations other than the West Side Parents Union and their school parent associations (PAs); only three had ever taken an active part in a political organization. Of the five who did participate in other organizations, one and occasionally another participated in the Democratic Party; one was a trade union officer and also an officer of the tenants' committee in a large cooperative apartment complex; one worked in church and community organizations; and one was active in a Puerto Rican organization. Three members belonged to other organizations besides the Governing Board but were not active in them.

[3] Letter to the editor, *The New Republic*, November 15, 1969, p. 30.

Table 6-1

Organizational Affiliations of JOA Members[a]

	N
No affiliations	4
Affiliated but inactive	3
Active in other organizations:	
In one other organization	1
In more than one other	3

[a] Excluding educational organizations.

Almost all the JOA members considered partisan political organizations irrelevant to the achievement of community control. On the West Side most politics has been citizens' politics. The activities of the political clubs declined in the sixties, and many of the important community leaders had only nominal ties with the political parties. While a few of the JOA members belonged to the reform Democratic clubs, most regarded even these "clean" political groups as suspect—the province of ambitious middle-class lawyers who used them for personal ends.

patterns of involvement:
two types

JOA Board members fall into two categories according to the extent of their organizational affiliations. These categories seem to have subjective correlates in the motives and consciousness of the members. The two types, which are labeled here *educational specialist* and *community activist*, are also applicable to the IS 201 and Ocean Hill-Brownsville Boards. The educational specialist type predominated among the elected parent representatives of all three boards.[4] The six (out of eleven) JOA members who were specialists limited their civic activities almost entirely to education. Usually they had been concerned with schools for years and had participated in PA's and various ad hoc educational groups. For these members initiation into the political world was a product of election to the Governing Board; and they were attracted to membership almost entirely through their substantive interest in education rather than out of a more general tendency toward voluntarism. By and large public life did not appeal to them. None of the four members who indicated that they might some day wish to run for a political or educational office was an educational specialist.

While participation in an insurgent group forced the educational specialists to take questions of power into account, they would have preferred to operate in a depoliticized atmosphere. As one of them put it:

[4] The total of five community activists on the JOA Board includes the one appointed member and another member who had formerly been active in other organizations but had ceased to be at this time.

At the time of the [Governing Board] election it looked like recognition . . . was a good possibility. If I had known the future I would not have wanted to be on the Governing Board. I had become very interested in what was the substance of good education in this community. I would not have been interested in a purely political job.

Although outside observers have thought that most of the community control adherents originally became activated through the community action programs (CAPs) of the federal poverty program,[5] this hypothesis was not borne out by the New York experience. Rather, a number of parents, many of them lower-class, had been long concerned with improving the schools their children attended both through racial integration and structural reform. The institutionalization, temporary though it was, of the community governing boards offered what looked like an opportunity for them to play a more effective role in influencing the educational system.

Five of the JOA members moved into educational activism as a natural progression from other organizational work, but even they had a history of interest in education. On the Joan of Arc Board these community activists had typically been involved with housing or civil rights groups; in Harlem and Ocean Hill they had participated as well in antipoverty organizations, although most of the poverty agency people were appointed members *ex officiis*. In many lower-class areas of New York the neighborhood housing councils and poverty agencies form an organizational infrastructure similar in certain respects to the service clubs of suburbia. While they differ from middle-class organizations in their interests and programs, they resemble them in providing opportunities for individuals who enjoy community work and like to speak at meetings or sit on committees.

The community activists, as would be expected, had more organizational skills (such as public speaking and negotiating) than the educational specialists. Their consciousness included more elements of a community-control ideology; they saw closer links between educational activism and a general set of political remedies. In addition, they were more likely to aspire to leadership roles, both on the Governing Board and through officeholding. The community activists had more frequent contacts with people of influence, and they did not shy away from situations involving the use of power. Within the type of community activist, however, there was a range in terms of political interest and aspirations for power. Roughly this range extended from those who were either not personally ambitious or sought only educational office to those who desired political position. The latter, comprising only two individuals, were the most consistently active members of the Board, the most frequent public speakers on its behalf, and the ones most likely, because of their positions on the Board and Parents Union, to be called to confer with the District 5 Local School Board or Superintendent.

A brief description of three representative members of the JOA Board should aid in providing insights concerning the membership characteristics of

[5] Cf. Gittell, *Demonstration for Social Change*, p. 15.

the Board. These three individuals are lower- or working-class nonwhites who exemplify the two types outlined above. They differ from the middle-class members of the same type primarily in that they are less well educated and correspondingly less sophisticated and cosmopolitan. They are, however, equally articulate, albeit somewhat more emotional in their approach. They have been chosen as prototypes in preference to the middle-class members because they more closely correspond in background characteristics to participants on the other governing boards, who will be similarly classified as educational specialists and community activists.

Educational specialist.   Mrs. M., a Puerto Rican who grew up in East Harlem, had lived on the West Side for fifteen years. The education of her three children was her dominant concern, and she eventually managed to get two of them into experimental schools, one run by the Catholic Church and the other by Hunter College. She was deeply involved with the schools for nine years through the PAs, serving in various official capacities including two terms as president. She took a job as an educational assistant in the JOA district and attended night school at City College under the paraprofessional program. Although still only in her freshman year, she looked forward eventually to obtaining a bachelor's degree.

Except for a brief membership in the Reform Democratic Club, Mrs. M. had only taken part in school-related organizations: "I am not a joiner." Before becoming a Governing Board member she had no personal contacts with city or foundation officials. She was a founding member of the West Side Committee for Decentralization of Education (WSCD), and when the WSCD dissolved itself, she "reluctantly" ran for the Governing Board. Mrs. M. felt her activities on the WSCD obliged her to run as an example to others, but she "knew it would be time-consuming and frustrating." She estimated that she devoted at least twenty-five hours a week to activities connected with the Board, on which she served as treasurer. She tried to involve others in the Board's goals, mainly through telephone calls and personal contacts: "I have been calling people for years to come to meetings which have produced nothing." Although she was pessimistic about mobilizing West Side parents sufficiently to make them a powerful educational influence, she did not think this was an impossible goal.

Mrs. M. received little personal satisfaction from her organizing activities and expressed irritation at the JOA Board's tendency to talk rather than act. She was more enthusiastic about her work in the school as a paraprofessional and enjoyed being with children and directly contributing to their education. While she viewed community control as a means for redistributing power, she tended to see this power exclusively in the educational domain rather than as general political power and looked to community control as a method specifically for the improvement of education. Within this realm she tried to represent the "general feelings and attitudes of parents in schools where achievement is low." She felt she had to speak in the interests of "the unaware, uninvolved, nonparticipant group in the community."

Community activists.   Mrs. F., a black member of the JOA Board, was at the low end of the range of community activists in terms of aspirations for power and political orientations. Like Mrs. M. she had been active in the PA since her children entered school and had held a number of PA offices. She too was extremely caught up in her children's education and had covered the walls of her public-housing apartment with framed pictures painted by her daughter and awards won by her children. She claimed to know personally, through her job as a paraprofessional and her family contacts, two-thirds of the children in the community's schools. She had held offices in the Methodist Church organization, participated in the Protestant Council, been chairman of the Riverside School Health Program and president of the Frederick Douglass Houses Civic Association. On her wall was a certificate of merit from the City of New York in appreciation of her services in housing improvement. Since becoming a Governing Board member, school activities had preempted most of her time.

Mrs. F., despite her extensive community work, did not belong to a political club and took no part in partisan politics. She did not feel that the political party organizations could contribute to her goal of improving conditions in the community, particularly for black and Spanish residents. Although she had a greater variety of contacts within the community than did Mrs. M., she also had no personal access to city agencies and foundations. She obviously enjoyed working within the community, speaking at public meetings, and talking with parents. She had worked as a parent coordinator in District 5 the previous year when her job had been to set up meetings in people's homes to talk about education and human relations. She continued on her own to use all possible opportunities to speak to parents and to interest them in what happened in the schools. Involvement to her was both a necessity, if the schools were ever to improve, and an ideal. Indeed, she argued that participation by parents in school activities should be compulsory; only through participation could people become educated to know their own interests and thus to make rational demands.

At the other end of the continuum among community activists in terms of aspirations for power and political orientations were the two individuals who occupied leadership positions—the Board's chairman and the executive director of the West Side Parents Union (WSPU). These two members customarily chaired meetings, spoke to outside groups, and were well known within the community. They tended to view their endeavors as more inspirational than manipulative, aimed at organizing or advancing the community rather than at getting something immediate out of higher-ups. Thus, the JOA chairman, who had once run for state assemblyman on the Liberal ticket, told us: "I have come to believe in organization and education of the people as opposed to wheeling and dealing, lobbying in the legislature."

In large part Mrs. W., the WSPU executive director, resembled her counterparts on the Ocean Hill and 201 Boards. Like most of the more political members she was not an elected parent representative but rather became a member by virtue of her position in another organization. Like all the Board members she had been an active participant in the PAs for a number of years; in addition she belonged to the Riverside Reform Democratic Club and was chairman of its educational committee as well as being a representative to the Democratic County Committee. She devoted most of her time to school affairs, mainly in her capacity with the Parents Union. She was the only Governing Board member arrested in the sit-in in the District 5 Superintendent's office over the suspension issue, and she had been very persistent in trying to get District 5 to change its policy on suspensions. Eventually she was appointed to the District 5 committee on disciplinary policy.

Although Mrs. W. had only limited contacts with higher-ups in the city's administrative echelons, she nonetheless had more access than the other members (except the chairman), and had sat in on conferences with the Mayor and Superintendent of Schools. In addition, she had personal contacts with foundation officials and had attended a number of leadership training sessions sponsored by foundations, from which she felt she came back "clearheaded, with many new ideas."

Mrs. W. felt limited in her activities by the small sum of money available to her under the WSPU's foundation grant. She thought that poor people could not be organized unless they were reimbursed for participation. She was in the WSPU's storefront office every day to assist parents, and she tried to make the Parents Union into an intermediary with the school bureaucracy, a service-providing organization which would also function to recruit supporters for the JOA Board. She frequently accompanied parents with grievances in their confrontations with school personnel. The WSPU differed from the traditional political clubhouse in its antiestablishment objectives and in its tenuous connection with city authorities. Mrs. W., however, tried to make it serve a similar function of providing private citizens with access to officialdom. Although the WSPU did not carry much weight beyond the district level, Mrs. W. did succeed in forging links with the District 5 Board and staff, particularly after Seymour Hammer became District Superintendent.

Mrs. W. was one of the few Governing Board members who saw the future more positively after her Governing Board experience than before it: "I feel I can do more. Training has broadened my outlook. It has given me many new ideas." She was the only JOA participant who, when asked what her greatest dissatisfaction had been, mentioned a specifically political event: "I have been most dissatisfied with the Decentralization Law and the cuts in welfare . . . with the reactionary swing these days . . . Proccacino and Marchi." [6]

[6] Respectively the Democratic and Republican candidates for mayor in 1969. Both were viewed as conservatives.

THE OCEAN HILL-BROWNSVILLE
AND IS 201
GOVERNING BOARDS

Interviews with governing board members at Joan of Arc, Ocean Hill, and IS 201 provide information concerning the social basis of the movement for community control of schools in New York City and the substance of its ideology. The data on the Ocean Hill and IS 201 Boards offer additional insights to those gained from the analysis of the Joan of Arc Board, since these boards were drawn from homogeneous ghetto areas and thus present a more typical recruitment pattern for urban movements. The Ocean Hill and 201 Boards are treated separately here partly for convenience and partly because combining them with Joan of Arc would have resulted in disguising the effects of the different recruitment situations. This section describes the backgrounds of all the participants on the Ocean Hill and IS 201 Boards and then examines the motives and political consciousness of the parent and community members.

The Ocean Hill and 201 Governing Boards both had three categories of memberships: parent representative; community representative; and teacher or supervisory representative. (See Table 6-2.) Parent and teacher members each represented a particular school and were elected, respectively, by the parents and faculty of that school.[7] The supervisors in the complex voted for the supervisory representatives; and the Governing Board selected the community representatives from among candidates suggested by community organizations. In addition, the Ocean Hill Board had a university representative, a white professor from Brooklyn College who was selected by the Board.

The data presented here is based on interviews with seven parent and community members on the Ocean Hill Board and eleven on the IS 201 Board. In its first two years (1967–69) the Ocean Hill Board had a total of twelve parent and community members, five of whom could not be contacted or refused interviews. Where the data is available, background information is provided for the five who were not interviewed. The eleven interviews of IS 201 parent and community members account for all except four of the fifteen members of the Governing Board in these categories. Again, where available, some background information is supplied concerning those members who were not interviewed. (Eleven teachers and supervisors on the two boards were also interviewed but data on these individuals will generally be omitted in the following analysis.)

social backgrounds

Although the great majority on the two governing boards was black,

---

[7] Twenty-three percent of those eligible voted in the IS 201 election. Accurate figures are not available for Ocean Hill-Brownsville on voting turnout.

Table 6-2

Composition of Ocean Hill-Brownsville and IS 201 Governing Boards by Membership Category (January 1968)

	N
OCEAN HILL	
Parent Representatives	7[a]
Community Representatives	4
Teacher Representatives	4[b]
Supervisory Representatives	1
University Representatives	1
IS 201	
Parent Representatives	10[c]
Community Representatives	4
Teacher Representatives	5
Supervisory Representatives	1

[a] One from each school in the complex, except IS 55, a new school which had not opened at the time of the election.

[b] Only four of the eight faculties elected teacher representatives.

[c] Two from each school in the complex.

there were several white members among the teacher and supervisory representatives, as well as one white community representative in Ocean Hill-Brownsville—a priest. (See Table 6-3.) Puerto Ricans were somewhat underrepresented on the Ocean Hill Board as compared with their proportion of the school population. The Ocean Hill-Brownsville schools were 27 percent Puerto Rican, 70 percent black, and 3 percent "other" (i.e. white) during the 1967–68 school year,[8] but only two governing board representatives were Puerto Rican. The proportion of Puerto Ricans on the IS 201 Governing Board corresponded closely to their numerical strength in the school community; in the categories of parent and community representative, Puerto Ricans were more than proportionately represented. The ethnic composition of the IS 201 Complex in 1967–68 was 20 percent Puerto Rican, 79 percent black, and 1 percent "other." [9] Yet, the Puerto Rican community representative felt that Puerto Ricans had been shortchanged:

The 201 experience became identified as a black question; it became a black-oriented issue. Puerto Ricans protested, at first kindly, then vehemently. They felt underrepresented on the teaching and administrative staffs, felt that there were insufficient Puerto Rican parents on the Governing Board. The situation polarized to the point where Puerto Ricans withdrew; they feared participating. Confrontations with the city did not help to attract Puerto Rican parents, who were frightened by them.

[8] Derived from Institute for Community Studies, Queens College, *New York City School Fact Book* (New York, 1969), pp. 206–7.

[9] Ibid., pp. 197–98. Many Puerto Rican children go to parochial school; consequently, they are a smaller proportion of the school population than of the total East Harlem population.

Table 6-3

Composition of Ocean Hill-Brownsville and IS 201 Governing Boards by Membership Type, Sex, and Ethnicity[a]

TYPE OF REP.	SEX (N)		RACE/ETHNICITY (N)		
	Male	Female	Black	White	Puerto Rican
Ocean Hill-Brownsville					
Parent	0	7	7	0	0
Community	4	1	3	1	1
Teacher	2	2	4	0	0
Supervisory	3	0	1	1	1
University	1	0	0	1	0
Total	**10**	**10**	**15**	**3**	**2**
IS 201					
Parent	1	9	7	0	3
Community	3	2	4	0	1
Teacher	0	7	4	3	0
Supervisory	0	1	1	0	0
Total	**4**	**19**	**16**	**3**	**4**
Total, Both Districts	**14**	**29**	**31**	**6**	**6**

[a] This and succeeding tables describe all representatives for whom information is available, including those who left the boards and, where they existed, their replacements. Thus, the total number described may exceed the number that served on the boards at any one time.

Both boards were predominantly female, although their chairmen were male. The number of men never equalled the number of women on the Ocean Hill Board, even though due to turnover the totals in Table 6-3 indicate the same number of men and women. The proportion of men on the IS 201 Board increased to 35 percent by the spring of 1970.

Parent members of both boards with one exception were lower-class women. The IS 201 chairman, a former janitor, described himself as a "full-time educational activist"; while on the Governing Board he started a firm to assist community education groups in formulating programs. All the female parent representatives who worked, except one who was a beautician, were paraprofessionals in the schools. The number of paraprofessionals was especially striking at 201, where a majority of the parent members held these jobs. In Ocean Hill most of the parent members called themselves housewives and several of them probably were on welfare. Only two of the parent members, both at 201, had completed high school; one of these was attending community college.

The community representatives on the two boards were a varied group in comparison to the parents. They were much more highly educated; many had middle-class incomes; and by virtue of the positions which they occupied, they had more previous experience in dealing with political issues. Both boards had clergymen among their community members, but the influence of

Table 6-4

Education and Occupation of Parent Representatives on the Ocean Hill-Brownsville and IS 201 Governing Boards

	OCCUPATION (N)			EDUCATION (N)		
	House-wife	Parapro-fessional	Other	Some H.S.	H.S.	Some College
Ocean Hill Brownsville	4	3	0	7	0	0
IS 201 [a]	0	5	2	5	1	1
Total	4	8	2	12	1	1

[a] Two parent representatives who refused interviews are not included in the tally for IS 201.

religious organizations was significantly greater at IS 201, where the Chambers Baptist Church served as a community rallying point for protests against the Board of Education's plans for the intermediate school. One community representative was the assistant minister of the church; another was the wife of the pastor. In addition, one of the teacher representatives had close ties with Chambers, having worked in the educational programs of the church before becoming an art teacher.

Table 6-5

Education and Occupation of Community Representatives on the Ocean Hill-Brownsville and IS 201 Governing Boards

	OCCUPATION (N)				EDUCATION (N)			
	Community worker	Clergy	Politi-cian	Business-man	H.S.	Some College	College	Grad. School
Ocean Hill-Brownsville	2	2	1	0	1	0	0	4
IS 201	3	1	0	1	1	2	0	2
Total	5	3	1	1	2	2	0	6

Most of the community representatives had been connected with various poverty and settlement programs in the areas; only one had an occupation that was not directly concerned with community improvement or assistance. The Ocean Hill community representatives included the director of a community recreation center; the district's state assemblyman (a lawyer); a minister; a priest; and a staff member of a community action agency (CAA) concerned with education. The 201 Board had three CAA directors; these headed a housing agency, a multipurpose agency, and an educational improvement project. In addition, there were a minister and a real estate salesman.

The community members of the Ocean Hill-Brownsville Board had been active participants in educational affairs in the area well before the election of the Board. Several had been on the "independent local school board," which had been formed in 1966 when the community found it had no spokesmen on the District 17 Local School Board.[10] All the community representatives on the 201 Board had been involved in the initial protests over the segregated opening of IS 201.

patterns of participation

Parent and community members[11] of the two demonstration governing boards found participation to be a natural outgrowth of previous involvement. Typical answers to a query concerning past activity were:

I have been involved in trying to improve the schools for the past twenty years, mostly by myself. I attended Open School Week and PTA meetings. . . . I worked as a volunteer in the schools for the past fifteen years, and I was one of the first paraprofessionals in the classroom.

I have been involved in attempting to improve the schools for six years. I began by attending PTA meetings and was appointed chairman of the construction committee the first night I attended a meeting. My wife made me come because of the problems she and the child were facing in the school.

When my son started kindergarten six years ago I saw that there was a need for parents to help in the schools. I became active in the PA. I helped out with plays and costumes in the school, and I liked it so much that I asked the principal to let me know when there was a school aide opening. I have had this job as an aide for the past three years. The Governing Board election made me see the possibility of participating in a new project. I saw the need for help in the schools and I wanted to help—to do my part.

The parent members universally had begun their participation in school affairs through the PA; a few of them had also joined other parents' groups such as the independent school board in Ocean Hill or the HARYOU (a community organization) parents committee. The great majority of the parent representatives, however, had restricted themselves to the PA.

While some of the community representatives had children in local schools, the majority did not. They became involved in educational activities in various ways. The clergymen sponsored education and community service projects in their churches and participated in the early planning of the

[10] Carol A. Wielk, "The Ocean Hill-Brownsville School Project: A Profile," *Community Issues* (published by the Institute for Community Studies, Queens College), I, February, 1969, 4–5.

[11] This section is based on interviews with four community and seven parent members of the IS 201 Governing Board and four community and three parent members of the Ocean Hill-Brownsville Governing Board.

demonstration districts. Those who were staff members of community agencies similarly found that participation in educational controversies developed out of their jobs. The Puerto Rican executive director of the East Harlem Tenants Council, a government and foundation financed agency devoted to solving housing problems and planning neighborhood development, explained:

I have been involved in schools since 1962 when people first began to think of the potential of local school boards, if they had control over money and curriculum. In 1963 there was the first public argument between Yorkville and East Harlem, which were part of the same local school district. Since that time I have participated in the East Harlem Coalition for Community Control, which had its base in the Tenants Council, and planning for the IS 201 Board. The Tenants Council is sponsoring the East Harlem Pilot Block, a federally funded redevelopment program. It is to contain a community-run private school aimed at providing that student achievement can be improved, and I've been negotiating with the New York City Educational Construction Fund about this.

None of the parent representatives, and only two of the community representatives, contemplated elective office. One of these was already a state assemblyman; after the 1970 community school board elections he became chairman of the local school district into which Ocean Hill-Brownsville was absorbed. As a professional politician he was unique among governing board members in the demonstration districts and Joan of Arc and eventually took a stand strongly opposed to the rest of his Board.[12]

While most parent and community members expressed a desire for greater involvement in educational improvement, involvement was usually seen as a service rather than a political activity. It was interpreted to mean working with children. Thus, one male member commented:

Being on the Governing Board has encouraged my plans for greater involvement in the community. . . . I would like to become active in recreational programs and with juvenile delinquents. I want to work with youth and help prevent delinquency and drug addiction.

The majority of the women interviewed wished to work in the schools, either as volunteers or paraprofessionals. Two or three, in addition, mentioned with some zest their determination to continue the political battle. For instance, one Puerto Rican woman declared:

Sometimes I think I am going to quit in frustration. But I love to fight for my rights. I want to stay on the Board. They don't have enough fighters.

[12] Assemblyman Wright split with the rest of the Governing Board during the confrontation over the transferred teachers, and during the following year ceased attending Governing Board meetings. Partisans of the demonstration district boycotted the 1970 community school board election, and a faction headed by Wright gained a majority on the District 23 Board with less than 5 percent of those eligible voting in the election. Wright's group was hostile to the continuation of the Ocean Hill-Brownsville district in even attenuated form. On July 8, 1970, *The New York Times* reported that Wright's office was raided and vandalized by a group of teenagers who opposed the dissolution of the demonstration district.

A few others, in contrast, felt too weary to continue:

I was tired as hell when I started. I'm more tired now. I would really like to move out of New York into a place where problems are not of the same magnitude. I have just about given up here. The only thing that would change New York City is a revolution, a bloodbath. This might come, but I would hate to be here. . . . I think I am too old to lead a revolution. The youth consider me an old fogey because I am more patient. I couldn't lead a revolution. I have the fears that come from age, education, maturity.

If any of the board members thought of themselves as revolutionaries, they did not admit it.[13]

As on the Joan of Arc Board, most of the parent members of the IS 201 and Ocean Hill-Brownsville Boards limited their organizational memberships to groups concerned with education. According to the typology described earlier, almost all of them would be classified on the basis of their affiliations as educational specialists rather than community activists.

Table 6-6

Organizational Affiliations of Parent Members of the IS 201 and Ocean Hill-Brownsville Governing Boards[a]

	N
No affiliation	7
Affiliated but inactive	2
Active in other organizations	1

[a] Excluding educational organizations.

In contrast the community representatives had a wide range of affiliations. Since their membership on the boards was the result of their prior organizational positions, this was to be expected. Thus, all of them fit the category of "community activist." The community representatives differed sharply from the parent members in that most of them engaged, at least on occasion, in overtly political activity.

Educational specialists and community activists on the two demonstration district boards resembled strongly those of corresponding type at Joan of Arc. Two members of the IS 201 Governing Board who exemplify each type will be described here in detail so as to illustrate the similarities between the participants in the different districts and also to show the effects of the specific milieux in which the participants found themselves.

Educational specialist.   Mrs. B., a black parent representative from one of the elementary schools in the 201 complex, had lived in Harlem for

[13] Two of the people who refused interviews were among the most militant of the Ocean Hill-Brownsville members; it is thus possible that the professed revolutionaries were not included in the interview sample.

twenty-five years. She came to New York from the South, where she had completed the eleventh grade—"In the South that's as far as you went"—and became active in educational affairs when her oldest child entered school: "I involved myself. I attended meetings and volunteered for duties." She was elected president of her school's Parent Association and then became chairman of the planning committee for the demonstration district. Although she belonged to the tenants' organization where she lived and to the NAACP, she was active in neither. She became a Governing Board member "because I felt that I should be involved in anything affecting my school. I felt that I was needed to inform the parents about what was happening with the Governing Board." Mrs. B. spent all her spare time, which she estimated at ten to twenty hours a week, on Governing Board matters.

Through her earlier participation in school affairs, she encountered some of the people who were to serve with her on the Governing Board; she met the rest while on the planning committee. Her membership on that committee and on the Board did not bring her into personal contact with city officialdom, but she did participate in general meetings of the Board with governmental officers and the Board of Education.

Mrs. B. explained what her experience on the Board meant personally:

I felt somewhat limited in what I could say [at Board meetings], because I didn't always know what to do. I was inexperienced in this kind of organization. I didn't want to put my two cents in when I was unfamiliar with the issue. I tried to be sure of myself when I said something. I would ask questions.

I was educated on that Governing Board. It was a daily education. I learned a lot about education. I started out not knowing how things were organized, what they were called. . . . Yes, I increased my political knowledge too. But I saw too much of it [politics]. I saw that leaders lie. I'm not a politician. Too much politics shouldn't be in the schools.

I'm looking for togetherness in this community. The Governing Board is trying to increase the skills and knowledge of children. They are trying to reach the children. I feel that a real sense of community is possible. I think this community can become a really modern area. But I am concerned about all areas. I am concerned about humanity.

Mrs. B. was somewhat ambivalent about the use of confrontation tactics:

The teachers in Ocean Hill-Brownsville were not willing to accept Negroes being put in some of the drivers' seats. This caused a lot of confusion. The whites rebelled; the blacks pushed. . . . Parents on the Governing Board were trying to do what was best.

[In 201] the [UFT] teachers tried to provoke an issue because they were unwilling to accept the concept of the Governing Board. We weren't trying to hurt teachers or to take someone's job. . . . The boycott tactics by the parents were effective. They did good. But they did damage too. The damage was done when outsiders came in.[14]

---

[14] Mrs. B. refused to elaborate on the nature of these outsiders except to say they were people attracted by crisis who came from "outside the area."

Along with almost all the other members she attributed the Board's inability to achieve its objectives to its inexperience and the community's unfamiliarity with it:

We lacked know-how in communications. Most parents didn't really understand what the Governing Board was trying to do. . . . But before the Governing Board the children here were being destroyed.

She concluded: "They came in, and then they left, and now they're taking the district away from us. And we're sad."

Community activist.   Mrs. C., the wife of a Harlem minister, was director of an education project funded with federal money. Her agency sponsored tutoring by college students in the homes of Harlem children, ran parent and teacher workshops, and handled parents' grievances with schools, the Welfare Department, and other city services. While she did not become an official member of the 201 Board until the fall of 1969, she belonged to the original planning group and participated in picketing, boycotts, and negotiations on its behalf; she knew all the members of the Board before becoming one herself.

Mrs. C. had finished two years of college in the South. Her own three children had originally attended public school in East Harlem, where she had lived for thirteen years, and she had been elected president of the PAs of two schools. Now, however, her two younger children received scholarships from a private school, and her oldest was in college: "Finally my children ended up in a private school [Fieldston]. But I'm fighting for all children. I'd prefer to have my children in a good public school."

In addition to her PA activities and her job, Mrs. C. had participated in school affairs through the Harlem Parents Committee and through an education group sponsored by her church. She was also active in a variety of political and community organizations: she was among the founders of an insurgent Democratic Club; was on the board of several community agencies (the East Harlem Development Corp., MEND, the East Harlem Youth Organization), and the board of the Voices of East Harlem, a well-known singing group; she also was a trustee of her church, which was very active in the community. Mrs. C. had a long history of participation in the civil rights movement, having marched at Selma and picketed many times in New York: "I've been in the whole trick bag."

Mrs. C. estimated that she spent from five to twenty hours a week on matters specifically related to the Governing Board, but that many of her other activities also touched on things of concern to the Board. She had met individually with city officials through her job, in addition to her contacts as part of Governing Board delegations.

When asked why she became a Governing Board member, Mrs. C. responded:

I didn't want or not want to be on the Governing Board. The complex is part of my community. Since I'm concerned about my community and about education, it was only natural. . . . I always was in the schools asking questions. Being a Governing Board member does not make me any different. I do what I'm always doing.

She did not think that her service on the Governing Board had affected her plans for the future especially:

I get tired. But I don't think it changes my plans. Frustration and tiredness get me mad as hell. I get pissed because we have to waste so much time proving to bureaucratic structures that we know how to do certain things. . . . In the white community bureaucrats assume it's there.

People often ask me to run for political office. But I don't want to.

When I started out, I wanted to accomplish as much as I could. So many things have happened. You just go on from one thing to the next. I never had any set, long-range program.

Along with almost all the Governing Board members, Mrs. C. regarded her membership as a personal education:

This was a new ballgame for all of us.

The Governing Board discusses all kinds of things that relate to education, and if we don't understand it we stay until we do.

I took a course in remedial reading. I've never had to use it. I had to learn to be a fund-raiser instead. . . . You have to learn to be a politician and how to deal with political people.

When asked to evaluate the Governing Board's effectiveness, Mrs. C. replied:

The IS 201 Governing Board is a group of intelligent articulate people. . . . Asking me if we have succeeded educationally may be putting us in the same bag as the Board of Education does. We do have some excellent programs. But education is a slow process. The complex needs more time than it's had to show valid results.

Mrs. C. concluded by explaining why she felt the complex needed to survive:

We need to change the whole system of public education. Headway is being made in the complex since the Governing Board became able to recruit teachers and evaluate programs.

I have become more radical if radical means innovative. I see the need for more changes than I did at first.

She did not like resorting to street demonstrations and school boycotts, though she had frequently engaged in such tactics. She hoped that the Board could use more "sophisticated" methods of pressure in the future.

Poor people have to sort of respond to the inevitable. Until people in communities like mine build up their economic and political strength, we're still at the mercy of forces beyond our control. Only if we organize will we get these people [governmental officials] to listen to us. It's not just a thing of communications. They only hear the people with some punch.

My views are constantly changing about everything. Right now [February 1970] what we're thinking about is the survival of the complex and the best education for kids. My views about this haven't changed. But my views on tactics change constantly.

The interviews with Mrs. B. and Mrs. C. show their similarity to the members of the Joan of Arc Board. Mrs. B. was typical of the educational specialists on all three boards. Mrs. C., as the female director of a community service agency, represented the modal type among the community activists, but this group was more varied than the other. There were more men among the community activists than among the educational specialists; there was also a greater range of occupation and educational background, and more variation in personal style, ranging from forceful and flamboyant to staid and respectable. By and large the educational specialists all maintained an air of propriety. Many in both groups, however, would mention that they did not drink and led quiet lives. Predictably the community activists were more articulate and more accustomed to responding to questions than the specialists.

Effect of locale.   The situations in which the educational specialists on the various governing boards found themselves did not differ in any important essentials. Because these people limited their interaction with the political environment to their participation in school affairs, they were all operating in a similar context. For each of the educational specialists the governing boards represented the principal vehicle for civic action. The educational specialists, with the exception of a few in Joan of Arc, had roughly similar backgrounds and led similar civic lives regardless of where they lived.

In contrast, the community activists had different opportunities in different places. On the West Side even those most active had very limited access to officialdom and participated in relatively few organizations. This could be attributed to the low level of nonwhite organization in that area and the dominance of political life by whites. In Harlem the great number of black community organizations meant that anyone willing to be active had a large choice and that many groups were competing for one's allegiance. Heads of community organizations in Harlem played a greater role as spokesmen for their communities than did their counterparts on the West Side and seemed to enjoy somewhat better access to the city administration. In Ocean Hill-Brownsville, where there was a less well-developed organizational infrastructure than in Harlem, the community activists fell between those in Harlem and the West Side in terms of the range of activities available to them, the amount of their political experience, and the extent of their access to higher officials.

political consciousness

The ideological positions expressed by the IS 201 and Ocean Hill Governing Board participants did not differ significantly from those of the Joan of Arc members. The following quotations are excerpts from typical statements made by parent and community representatives on the boards. The sample of board members interviewed is probably not representative of the entire population since the most publicly militant members of the Ocean Hill Board did not grant interviews. Nevertheless, the excerpts constitute a reasonable portrayal of the thinking of the active members of the IS 201 Board (members not interviewed were mainly those least involved with the Board)[15] and of the modal position on the Ocean Hill Board.

diagnoses

The most difficult aspect is the inability of administrators in politically sensitive posts to understand the need for change, the need to be sensitive to outside communications. The biggest obstacle to change is the failure of administrators to concern themselves with output instead of internal politics and their job status. People have no understanding of how to educate non-middle-class, nonwhites. The Board of Education fails to understand that different methods must be used on poor children who suffer from simultaneous, related needs caused by the multiple effects of poverty. (Community representative, IS 201)

If the kids don't learn to read in the first or second grade, forget it! But teachers will not adapt to new curriculums; they don't like it. It makes it hard to make improvements. (Parent representative, IS 201)

I don't look at Ocean Hill as a parochial problem any more. Its problem is a general one—that of educating and including the masses. . . . The power structure is not concerned with making the experiment work. The UFT will make no compromises with the community—it is not concerned with community welfare. (Community representative, Ocean Hill)

I am very pessimistic with respect to the viability of the political and educational structure to foment change. My participation in the educational arena has made clear to me that the concept of lay control of education [through the Board of Education] is merely a front for the perpetuation of the established political structure. (Community representative, Ocean Hill)

remedies

The most effective way to educate children is through the involvement and participation of parents and community. . . . The Governing Board has been effective in a number of interconnected ways. First, it has been politically effective. There must be a strong political push to create pressure for change. This has led to effectiveness in education. The Governing Board has set up a system that works better than the previous one. It has reduced apathy toward the schools. It has made education a matter of concern to the previously uninvolved—to many people. It has united and organized the community to fight. (Community representative, IS 201)

[15] Those who could not be contacted or refused interviews in 201 included only two highly active members, one a parent and one a community representative. Several observers familiar with the 201 Board, however, considered them to be similar in attitudes to the majority of the members.

I have become more pessimistic. The white power structure will not provide meaningful change. But at the same time I have become more optimistic that parents have gained from experience. Things have got to get better. I have developed a tremendous scepticism about whites in this movement. They are helpful up to a point, but they will cut you off without blinking. Yet, the alternatives to white help are not clear. . . . I'm not as idealistic as I once was. I had looked forward to massive federal funds, to the type of programs where people would really be involved, where they would upgrade a really downtrodden people. But look what happened. (Community representative, Ocean Hill)

I now understand that the forces of change are 95 percent political, 5 percent professional. . . . I feel more strongly about community control now. The community should take any measure which is honestly directed at better education of children. I would support boycotts, demonstrations, strikes, removing of children from school (as a last resort), political pressure and involvement. . . . The Puerto Rican people tend to be very conservative. *El Diario, The Daily News* influence the population on broad national issues. But the Puerto Rican community is militant about housing, narcotics, jobs, cleanliness. There is an impediment [to action] because you cannot move faster than the population is willing to move. . . . But there is flexibility for change. For example, I led a march of 450 Puerto Ricans on the police station even though this is the kind of action that is usually opposed by Puerto Ricans. It is necessary to propagandize, inform, mobilize. Leaders must be careful not to isolate themselves. . . . There is a marked difference between the black and Puerto Rican populations in terms of their potential for organization around the issue of education. Schools are a greater issue for blacks—more of a national issue for blacks. But the Puerto Rican community can be organized around schools. (Community representative, IS 201)

At this stage of the game I have learned that we lack the key resource for fighting—money. The Board of Education has set the stage for a good intra-community fight between the pro and anticonfrontationists. If it had adequate funds, the Governing Board could fight on the educational level. McCoy [the Unit Administrator] now emphasizes educational results. With money he can show positive educational progress to the community. Showing educational progress is the only way to organize the community. Parents don't want a fight, they want education. . . . Parents now resent keeping their children out of school. They will have to go a different route. (Community representative, Ocean Hill)

Parent and community representatives on the Ocean Hill and IS 201 Governing Boards all favored the break-up of the central educational bureaucracy as the only way to end the immobility of the system. Many attributed educational failure to inadequate personnel and argued that community control was necessary if the schools were to recruit teachers and supervisors responsive to the needs of the black and Puerto Rican communities. Some explained the behavior of the schools within a larger social and political framework of racial discrimination, poverty, and the domination of the city government by the "power structure." Others dealt with the educational system in specific terms and did not see it through a general political ideology.

Everyone emphasized the need for far-reaching innovations in the way children were taught; although there were differences concerning what kinds of innovations were desirable. Most parents on the boards were not able to be specific concerning the particular changes they would like to see within the classroom. Many of the representatives in the two demonstration districts, as in Joan of Arc and PS 84, looked back to the days of the 1968 school strike for a model of how schools could be run. To them the strike period was a time when all the teachers in the school were deeply involved in their work, and parents participated freely in the running of the schools:

I thought the school strike last year was beautiful. The only tragedy was that it ended. It gave parents a chance to do their thing. It gave parents knowledge of their own worth. It taught them that they could make it on their own. It is sad that things are normal again. The teachers who fought last year are now falling into the same old bureaucratic ways.

Most of the members were cynical about political parties and politicians. While they considered the separation of politics and education to be a desirable end, they viewed the present educational system as permeated with concessions to political interests. They recognized—and regretted—that they had to use political techniques themselves in order to change the system.

Most members justified their use of confrontation tactics as a necessary response to attempts by the Board of Education and United Federation of Teachers (UFT) to "sabotage the districts." Many hoped that they would no longer need to resort to such militant measures in the future. They felt that parents disliked keeping their children out of school and that children were disrupted by the school boycotts. None admitted that they would initiate violence.

Members of the demonstration district boards, like those of the Joan of Arc Board, had deep commitments to their communities. Few of them felt that their positions as board members required them to balance interests or advance some kind of "public interest." Rather, they intended to change the outcomes of the educational process so as to increase the benefits going to poor blacks and Puerto Ricans. They were usually the first to admit that they were inexperienced and did not know how to achieve that aim. But they felt that the initial step had to be restructuring the school system so that it was responsive to the needs of the collectivities they represented.

It is possible to doubt the sincerity of many of the respondents—at least some had mixed motives and perhaps saw the governing boards as presenting an opportunity for jobs or power. But for most, membership developed out of their previous attempts to obtain a decent education for their children. The dissatisfaction of the board members with the New York educational system was real enough, and the frustrations of participation meant that membership had its costs. One does not have to believe that the governing board members, had they obtained long-term authority, would have been altruists in order to trust the sincerity of their belief in community control. The opportunities for corruption are much greater for those within the system than for those trying to change it. The governing board members were reformers with only limited successes—their chief reward had to be the pride resulting from the belief that they were laboring for a just cause. In the long run they perhaps stood to profit materially; but for the present their rewards were mostly intangible.

PATTERNS OF PARTICIPATION AND CONSCIOUSNESS IN URBAN POLITICAL MOVEMENTS

Earlier in this chapter we listed four general questions about the pattern of participation in urban movements which we would like to answer. The problem, however, is that beyond our own work there is relatively little known about urban movements per se, or about the set of phenomena most closely related to them—the civil rights movement in the North, the more activist Community Action Agencies (CAAs), and, farther afield, the Southern civil rights movement. Indeed, even were we to accept data about recruitment, motivations, modes of participation, and consciousness of members of *any* political movement as relevent to our case, we would find a dearth of useful studies. The most reasonable course in such a situation is to state from the outset what kinds of evidence are not germane and what kinds are available to be used with caution. The substance of a general discussion about urban movements inevitably, then, becomes circumscribed and aimed primarily at suggesting questions or issues.

If we had sufficient evidence about urban movements as a type it would be interesting to compare them with other movements in order to gain some insight into general movement processes. We cannot, however, use these other movements to provide data about urban political movements. Knowing the attributes of members of the Social Credit Party in Quebec, to cite an example about which some evidence is available,[16] does not tell us anything about inner-city activists in the United States. The same may be said for student radicals, about whom there is more data.[17] Movements with different ideologies, functioning in different institutional settings and under divergent historical conditions, are no more likely to be of a kind than are any other social phenomena. The only theoretical perspective which permits the use of data gathered under markedly dissimilar conditions is the psychological or psychoanalytic, which assumes that there is a movement type of personality which appears everywhere and molds movement activity wherever it arises. But this assumption takes for granted precisely what must be demonstrated.[18]

[16] See Maurice Pinard, "Poverty and Political Movements," *Social Problems,* XV, Fall, 1967, 250–63; "Mass Society and Political Movements: A New Formulation," *American Journal of Sociology,* LXXIII, May, 1968, 682–90; *The Rise of a Third Party: A Study in Crisis Politics* (Englewood Cliffs, N. J.: Prentice-Hall, 1971).

[17] Cf. Kenneth Keniston, *Young Radicals* (New York: Harcourt, Brace & World, 1968); and *Student Activism and Protest,* eds. Edward W. Sampson and Harold A. Korn (San Francisco: Jossey-Bass, 1970). See also footnote 38 below.

[18] See Appendix, pp. 254–57, for a discussion of the psychological theory of social movements.

There are two main sources of "hard" data describing the political activities of urban minorities during the recent past. One set arises from the urban riots of the mid-sixties. Following the Los Angeles riot of 1965 there were a number of sociological studies of who participated in civil disturbances, what their motivations were, how they compared with nonparticipants and so forth.[19] The thousands of rioters who were arrested or detained provided a captive audience for federally funded survey research. The obvious question, however, is whether rioting is similar to movement activity. Except for the fact that the riots were contemporaneous to urban movements, we have no reason to expect that riots and political movements are similar in etiology, patterns of participation, motivation or consciousness. Studies which treat riots, rebellions, political violence, and a variety of social and political movements as interchangeable phenomena assume a likeness without providing evidence to prove it.[20]

The second data set is a product of the Community Action Programs (CAPs) of the War on Poverty. During the period 1965–68 about one thousand local Community Action Agencies (CAAs) were established throughout the country. Each program was required by the Office of Economic Opportunity (OEO) to have a research and evaluative component. OEO also funded several scholarly comparative studies, notably the "20-city study" carried out at Brandeis University[21] and the "100-city study" conducted by the National Opinion Research Center of the University of Chicago.[22] The CAA data, while more useful than information on participa-

---

[19] See Louis H. Masotti and Don R. Bowen, *Riots and Rebellion* (Beverly Hills, Calif.: Sage Publications, 1968); Nathan Cohen, *The Los Angeles Riots: A Socio-Psychological Study* (New York: Praeger Special Studies, 1970); Seymour Spilerman, "The Causes of Racial Disturbances: Tests of an Explanation," *American Sociological Review*, XXXVI, June, 1971, 427–42; and Clark McPhail, "Civil Disorder Participation: A Critical Examination of Recent Research," *American Sociological Review*, XXXVI, December, 1971, 1058–72.

[20] See the discussion and citations provided by Eisinger, who concludes: "A number of scholars argue that recent ghetto violence, while politically motivated, was expressive in nature, while some preliminary survey evidence shows that most actors who engage in protest activities, conventionally defined, do so for instrumental purposes." Peter Eisinger, "The Conditions of Protest Behavior in American Cities," *American Political Science Review*, LXVIII, March, 1973, 14.

The most significant recent example of an analysis that attempts to deal with all types of militant political action is Ted Robert Gurr, *Why Men Rebel* (Princeton, N. J.: Princeton University Press, 1970).

[21] Reports 1–5 under the general title, "Community Representation in Community Action Programs," Florence Heller School, Brandeis University, Waltham, Massachusetts, February 1968–March 1969, mimeo.; these reports are also available from the National Technical Information Service, Springfield, Virginia, classified under No. OEO-CG68-9499-A/2; David M. Austin, "Patterns of Participation: A Report on a Study of Community Representation in Community Action Programs," Heller School, Brandeis University, 1969, mimeo; David M. Austin, "Resident Participation: Political Mobilization or Organizational Cooptation?" Heller School, Brandeis University, May 1970, mimeo. Some data from the Brandeis study have been published in Stephen M. Rose, *The Betrayal of the Poor* (Cambridge: Schenkman, 1972).

[22] James J. Vanecko "Community Mobilization and Institutional Change: The Influence of the Community Action Program in Large Cities," in *Planned Social Intervention*, ed. Louis A.

tion in civil disturbances, is limited in several ways. The large majority of CAAs were service-providing organizations rather than political movements; at most 10 percent of the agencies involved themselves in conflict activity and might be considered as a data source on urban movements. Many evaluation studies were conducted by entrepreneurial firms rather than academic institutions and can better be characterized as rationales to the funding agency than serious political or sociological analyses.[23] In addition, a number of the evaluation studies have never been publicly circulated.[24] Thus, while the War on Poverty activities are only partly related to the subject of our concern, the potential usefulness of the millions of dollars worth of research on that effort is further limited by what seems to us a disappointing output.

Besides the analyses of civil disturbances and CAAs there are few investigations of nonwhite collective action in the North. In part, the lack of work on northern organizations results from the loss of coherence as the civil rights movement turned North in the mid-sixties, as well as its antiwhite bias, and perhaps most significantly, the methodological difficulties of gaining access to small, ephemeral groups engaged in movement-type activity. Thus, while there is some evidence on modes of participation in the Southern civil rights movement[25]—even this tends to focus on students, who are more accessible to academics—not much can be said with any certainty about the

Zurcher, Jr. and Charles M. Bonjean (San Francisco: Chandler, 1970), pp. 253–75; James Vanecko and Bruce Jacobs, "The Impact of the CAP on Institutional Change," National Technical Information Service, Nos. PB-192-967 and 968, n.d., microfiche; Bruce Jacobs, "Community Action and Urban Institutional Change," National Technical Information Service, No. PB-193-967, August, 1970, photocopied.

[23] There are some exceptions: Ralph M. Kramer, *Participation of the Poor* (Englewood Cliffs, N. J.: Prentice-Hall, © 1969); Kenneth Clark and Jeannette Hopkins, *A Relevant War Against Poverty* (New York: Harper & Row, 1970); Dale Rogers Marshall, *The Politics of Participation in Poverty* (Berkeley: University of California Press, 1971); Louis A. Zurcher, *Poverty Warriors* (Austin, Texas: University of Texas Press, 1970). Zurcher's study provides the most extensive data on participants, but because they derive from a CAA in Topeka, Kansas with a target population which included many Indians, they are not useful to us. See also Don R. Bowen and Louis M. Masotti, "Spokesmen for the Poor: An Analysis of Cleveland's Poverty Board Candidates," *Urban Affairs Quarterly*, IV, September, 1968, and Zurcher and Bonjean, *Planned Social Intervention*.

The following unpublished studies of individual cities also contain useful data: Wayman J. Crow and James R. Johannsen, "Organizing the Poor in their Neighborhoods," Western Behavioral Sciences Institute, 1150 Silverado, La Jolla, Calif., October 15, 1969, mimeo (a study of CAAs in San Diego); and Lawrence Northwood, "The Development of Social Welfare Action in a Growing Ghetto: A Study of Block Organizations in the Anti-Poverty Program," National Technical Information Service, No. PB-184-528, n.d., photocopied (study of Seattle CAP).

[24] These are theoretically available from the National Technical Information Service. However, there is no topical arrangement of studies which, instead, are filed among tens of thousands of other documents according to contract numbers. The Office of Economic Opportunity has never, to our knowledge, published a master listing of the studies which it commissioned.

[25] Donald Von Eschen, Jerome Kirk, and Maurice Pinard, "The Disintegration of the Negro Non-Violent Movement," *Journal of Peace Research*, III, 1969, 216–34; "The Conditions of Direct Action in a Democratic Society," *Western Political Quarterly*, XXIII, June, 1969, 309–25; "The Organizational Substructure of Disorderly Politics," *Social Forces*, XLIX, June, 1971, 529–44.

Northern situation. Lipsky's work on rent strikes,[26] Weissman's on Mobilization for Youth,[27] and Silberman's discussion of Alinsky[28] are the most significant empirical studies. These, however, concentrate on organizational dynamics and tell us little about the social characteristics, modes of recruitment, motivation, and consciousness of activists.[29] Given the limited availability of other sources, the discussion which follows will briefly recapitulate evidence from the various case studies, mention other work where germane, and suggest some plausible hypotheses based on our own primary data.

social attributes of activists

The social characteristics of participants in urban movements are a product of two closely related factors: the collectivities from which movements develop and the types of people within those collectivities who are willing to risk political activity. Because of the emergent properties of movements it is not fruitful to distinguish between who is recruited into an ongoing movement, as opposed to who creates movements. Urban movements have been too undeveloped and unstable to offer the kind of recruitment data which might be gathered about, say, the French Communist Party, or the NAACP.

If we emphasize solely the question of which collectivities have given rise to urban movements, we will come to the seemingly tautological conclusion that they have been lower- and working-class minority groups. After all, our focus has been almost exclusively on efforts to advance the interests of these collectivities and on movements based largely, but not entirely, within them. There is, however, some data which indicates that most locally-based movements have in fact mainly represented minority groups. Peter Eisenger[30] presents quantitative evidence on the incidence of protest activity, which he defines as marches, demonstrations, sit-ins, picketing, etc. Since these activities are typically associated with some kind of movement substructure, we may use them as an indicator of the presence of political movements, though one which is not entirely satisfactory. Eisenger surveyed newspaper accounts of protests from a random sample of 43 cities with populations between 100,000 and 1,000,000 (N = 141) during a six-month period in 1968.

[26] Michael Lipsky, *Protest in City Politics* (Skokie, Ill.: Rand McNally, 1970).

[27] Harold H. Weissman, *Community Development in the Mobilization for Youth Experience* and *Individual and Group Services in the Mobilization for Youth Experience* (New York: Association Press, 1969).

[28] Charles Silberman, *Crisis in Black and White* (New York: Random House, 1964).

[29] Some useful evidence along these lines may be found in Richard Young, "The Impact of Protest Leadership on Negro Politicians in San Francisco," *Western Political Quarterly*, XXII, March, 1969, 94–111. Studies by Brill and Ellis also provide data, though the first is severely limited by the idiosyncrasy of the case, and both are of questionable reliability; see Harry Brill, *Why Organizers Fail: The Story of a Rent Strike* (Berkeley: University of Califoria Press, 1971) and William W. Ellis, *White Ethics and Black Power: The Emergence of the West Side Organization* (Chicago: Aldine, 1969).

[30] Eisenger, "The Conditions of Protest Behavior in American Cities."

His key finding is that blacks predominated in protest activities: "In those instances in which the race of the protestors was identified (95 out of 120 cases), 49 (52 percent) were composed entirely of blacks, 21 (22 percent) were mixed black and white, and 20 (21 percent) were exclusively white. . . . Mexican-Americans were responsible for the remainder. . . ."[31] His data give us at least an inkling of the relative proportion of movements which are homogeneously black, integrated, and all white. Only the last category would likely be unrepresentative of the kind of locally based activity we have called urban political movements.

Another way to phrase the question of who participated in urban movements is to ask how activists compare with the communities in which movements have emerged. Here we can consider several dimensions: class, race, sex, "rootedness." The evidence provided by our case studies points to the generalization that movements to some extent "cream" their communities in terms of class, but that this process does not go much beyond excluding the *lumpen*—not the most poor, but primarily drug addicts, pimps, unattached youths and unemployed single men. Several members of the demonstration district Governing Boards were on welfare, as were some of the mothers at PS 84. The Morningside squatters were among the poorest people in the community. The education of parent representatives on the Governing Boards (few had graduated high school) was typical of East Harlem and Ocean Hill-Brownsville. The socio-economic status of activists at Joan of Arc and PS 84 was roughly reflective of that of the upper West Side and the parent body at 84 respectively. The same may be said for North Side Forces (with the exception of the minister who founded it).

Some more tangential evidence also suggests that movement leaders are reasonably matched in terms of class to their communities. Richard Young found that black protest leaders in the San Francisco area tended to be heterogeneous in class background, only somewhat overrepresenting upper strata—in sharp contrast to black officials who were drawn primarily from the best families.[32] Bowen and Masotti present data from a study of indigenous candidates for CAP target area organizations (TAOs) in Cleveland which show that the educational backgrounds—a good indicator of class—of the 48 candidates reflected those of a sample of 500 community residents, except for the absence among the candidates of the least educated (less than eighth grade).[33] Wayman Crow indicates that participants in activist TAOs in the San Diego area were drawn from roughly the same economic levels as their neighbors.[34] Similarly, Gove and Costner found only moderate overrepresentation of better-off residents in CAP neighborhood organizations in Seattle,[35] as did Kramer in San Francisco.[36] According to

[31] Ibid., pp. 16–17.

[32] Young, "The Impact of Protest Leadership," p. 100.

[33] Bowen and Masotti, "Spokesmen for the Poor," p. 109.

[34] Crow, "Organizing the Poor," p. 8.

[35] Walter Gove and Herbert Costner, "Organizing the Poor: An Evaluation of a Strategy," in *Planned Social Intervention*, eds. Zurcher and Bonjean, pp. 275–88.

[36] Kramer, *Participation of the Poor*, pp. 190–91.

Dale Rogers Marshall, community representatives on the Los Angeles TAO which she observed were similar in class to their constituencies.[37] The weight of evidence from these studies and our own cases points to the hypothesis that urban activists are fairly similar to nonactivists in class background; while creaming does take place in the recruitment of movement leadership, it is not very extreme. Thus, unlike the recent Southern civil rights and student movements, urban groups do not seem to have been led by "outsiders" or by only the best-off indigenous people.[38]

Except for a tendency toward the underrepresentation of Latins, the forementioned studies also show that the racial composition of the leadership echelon is similar to that of their communities. The meaning of this finding is limited by the fact that many groups arise in homogeneously nonwhite areas where there is no possibility of interracial membership. Nonetheless, there does seem to be reason to believe that race is not a key discriminator in determining organizational involvement in heterogeneous communities, and that when class is held constant, blacks are no *less* likely to be activists than are whites. A study based on a national sample of urban blacks showed that more lower-class blacks than lower-class whites belonged to organizations and that the relationship between education and membership was weaker for blacks than for whites.[39]

In addition, comparisons of groups in Detroit and Chicago indicated that when socio-economic status was controlled, blacks were more likely than whites to be politically active.[40] Dahl found that New Haven blacks were disproportionately represented both in local political organizations, and in campaign and electoral work.[41] Another study of the participation of blacks in voluntary associations, excluding unions and churches, concluded:

[37] Marshall, *The Politics of Participation*, p. 47.

[38] The work of Von Eschen, Kirk, and Pinard on the sit-in movement in Maryland shows that for most of its history the movement tended to recruit students rather than adults, geographical outsiders rather than natives, and "ideologues" rather than average citizens. The authors conclude: "In short, the movement was small, disunified, and unrepresentative." Von Eschen, Kirk, and Pinard, "The Conditions of Direct Action," pp. 310–11.

Studies of the social background of student radicals indicate that they were predominantly the children of the most affluent and best educated Americans. See, for example, David L. Westby and Richard G. Bramgart, "Class and Politics in the Family Backgrounds of Student Political Activists," *American Sociological Review*, XXI, October, 1966, 691; Glen Lyonns, "The Police Car Demonstration: A Survey of Participants," in *The Berkeley Student Revolt*, eds. S. M. Lipset and Sheldon S. Wolin (New York: Doubleday, 1965), p. 521; S. M. Lipset and Philip G. Altbach, "Student Politics and Higher Education in the United States," in *Student Politics*, ed. S. M. Lipset (New York: Basic Books, 1967), p. 218; William A. Watts and David Whittaker, "Free Speech Advocates at Berkeley," *Journal of Applied Behavioral Science*, II, January–March, 1966, 53.

[39] Anthony Orum, "A Reappraisal of the Social and Political Participation of Negroes," *American Journal of Sociology*, LXXVII, July, 1966, 36.

These findings differ from those summarized by Milbrath, who notes: "It has repeatedly been found in nationwide studies in the United States that Negroes participate in politics at a much lower rate than whites." Lester W. Milbrath, *Political Participation* (Skokie, Ill.: Rand McNally, 1965), p. 138. Orum's data, because of his controls on class, are more refined than the earlier studies cited by Milbrath.

[40] Orum, "A Reappraisal," p. 37.

[41] Robert Dahl, *Who Governs?* (New Haven: Yale University Press, 1961), p. 294.

Our findings strongly support Myrdal's thesis that American Negroes belong to a far greater number of formal voluntary associations than whites. We found this true for Negroes at all social class levels when compared to their white counterparts, but it was especially true of lower-class Negroes.[42]

Since we do not have additional evidence of the effect of race on participation rates in urban political movements per se, we cannot go beyond stating that there seems to be nothing about black culture or social structure which precludes political activation besides those factors which militate against mobilization by any collectivity, especially one which is relatively poor.

In each of our lengthy case studies, women were predominant among movement leadership, though not always in the top position. This is partially explained by the fact that Joan of Arc, PS 84, IS 201 and Ocean Hill-Brownsville involved educational politics, an arena within which women constitute the main attentive public and where we should expect to find them highly active. However, there is reason to believe that women have been overrepresented in all kinds of movement-type activity, especially in groups which are predominantly black. Most of the studies of TAOs in the Community Action Program found high female involvement. The "20 city study" concluded that "the membership of CAA neighborhood associations, as is true of most neighborhood associations, is predominantly composed of women." [43] Gove and Costner[44] and Northwood[45] identified a similar situation in Seattle, as did Crow in San Diego, where he found that two-thirds of the members of community action councils (TAOs) were women.[46] Bowen and Masotti reported that 36 of 43 candidates for Cleveland TAOs were female in neighborhoods which were evenly divided in sex.[47]

The most elaborate of the War on Poverty research efforts—the "100 cities study"—attempted to identify local leaders at the most "grass-roots" level.[48] Its procedure was to ask a random community sample of 40 individuals in each target area to name two people who "seem to be doing something" about local problems, and who "seem to know a lot of people in the area." [49] These local influentials—called "quick pass leaders"—were then sampled randomly, with a total of 630 interviewed. Fifty-one percent of the quick pass leaders were black and 36 percent white, with the remainder Latin or unidentified. Forty-four percent of all the leaders were women. While sex was not cross-tabulated with race, it seems reasonable to assume that more than half of the black leaders were female. Taken together, our evidence points to the conclusion that among the urban lower strata, and particularly among blacks, movement type activity has not been a male

[42] Nicholas Babchuck and Ralph V. Thompson, "The Voluntary Associations of Negroes," *American Sociological Review*, XXVII, October, 1962, 652.

[43] "Community Representation in Community Action Programs," Report No. 5, p. 56.

[44] Gove and Costner, "Organizing the Poor."

[45] Northwood, "The Development of Social Welfare Action in a Growing Ghetto."

[46] Crow and Johannsen, "Organizing the Poor in their Neighborhoods," p. 7.

[47] Bowen and Masotti, "Spokesmen for the Poor," p. 108.

[48] Jacobs, "Community Action," pp. 235 ff.

[49] Ibid.

haps because of the effect of urban bureaucracies on day-to-
the high involvement of women as paraprofessionals in these
igh maintenance costs (especially in time) of indigenous
..ural factors among blacks, women have played a major role
..an political movements. Whether for these reasons or for other factors
which may be related more to the personal and institutional sexism of
"normal" political structures, the recruitment of women to urban movements
represents a major deviation from the typical pattern in the United States.
Milbrath's assertion that "the finding that men are more likely to participate
in politics than women is one of the most thoroughly substantiated in the
social sciences" [50] thus appears to require some revision.

The generalization that urban activists are not very different from their
neighbors in terms of class, race and sex suggests that *within* particular
communities, social-structural variables do not differentiate movement
members from the politically inactive. It may also be possible, though, that
more complex indicators of structural position would be correlated with
activity. Sociologists concerned with other movements have attempted to
employ concepts such as marginality, rootlessness, and status conflict to
explain why people become participants. Such qualitative evidence as we
have seems to show, however, that rather than being in some way socially
unusual, participants in urban movements have been well integrated into
their communities. All of the CAA studies point to this conclusion. Bowen
and Masotti, who were explicitly concerned with the "centrality" (vs.
"peripheralness") of the Cleveland TAO candidates, concluded that activists
were "wired in" to their communities, were "central" rather than "peripheral
types," and did not seem in any way marginal.[51] While we are able to
identify at a macroscopic level the social collectivities which have given rise
to urban movements, and the specific structural and institutional factors
which have contributed to their development, we suspect that even complex
structural attributes of individuals are weak predictors of participation or
nonparticipation in urban movements. It seems more fruitful to identify
persons recruited to movements on the basis of their consciousness and
personal life history (their occupational and political "careers," etc.). This
conclusion is consonant with our rationalistic interpretation of urban
movements.

patterns of involvement:
two types

The material presented earlier suggests that there are two basic
patterns of recruitment into educational movements, which we identify as

---

[50] Milbrath, *Political Participation*, p. 135.
[51] Bowen and Masotti, "Spokesmen for the Poor," pp. 93–95.

educational specialist and community activist. The former is associated mainly with parents who have a history of involvement with their local schools, and who have relatively little experience with noneducational organizations, general reform efforts, or political groups. The latter type characterizes individuals who come to educational issues from a past history of political activity and organizational affiliation. The identification of these ideal types raises two kinds of questions. First, do we find that movements in other issue areas also involve specialists and community activists? And second, how inclusive are the types—do they encompass such dimensions as motivations and political consciousness; can we, for example, think of them in the same way as Merton does of "locals" and "cosmopolitans?" [52]

The evidence from the various case studies shows the presence of specialists and community activists in several different kinds of organizations. At PS 84 a majority of the parents and teachers who worked for reform (especially those who were not in the top leadership) could be classified as specialists. In fact, once their movement had attained its specific goal it disappeared entirely, with only the minority of community activists remaining mobilized. The efforts at community control of health facilities involved mostly specialists. One reason for this was the high participation in movement activities of paraprofessionals working in health delivery agencies. North Side Forces and the Morningside Squatters recruited people who were interested mainly in specific changes in housing policy and in being able to acquire social services for themselves and their neighbors. In both movements, however, the leaders were community activists. We can also point to oppositionist groups such as the Cooper Square Development Committee which presented various mixes of the two types, but a tendency toward a specialist majority. Only further research will show whether the types are recurring across a large range and number of urban movements.

The theoretical importance of the specialist and community activist types would be enhanced if they captured a relatively large number of attributes of individuals. We believe that this may be the case. Specialists and community activists, we hypothesize, differ in their mode of recruitment into movement activity, their motivations for continued participation, and their political consciousness. The specialists tend to be individuals whose social location brings them into contact with reform efforts. They are the parents of school children who must interact with teachers and principals; patients of hospitals or paraprofessionals within them who cannot ignore bureaucratic policy; welfare recipients who depend upon agency output; people who need

---

[52] While both of Merton's types of influentials resided within the town he studied and limited their activity thereto, the cosmopolitans tended to be oriented to the larger society, to its culture and ideas, to be concerned with several substantive areas (in Merton's terms, to be *polymorphic* as opposed to *monomorphic*), and to have a wider range of organizational affiliations than the locals. The very different context of Merton's study precludes the direct application of his hypotheses to urban activists. However there does seem to be some similarity between our specialist and community activist types and his locals and cosmopolitans, respectively. See Robert K. Merton, "Patterns of Influence: Local and Cosmopolitan Influentials," *Social Theory and Social Structure* (New York: Free Press, 1957), pp. 387–420.

sing or who are confronted with city officials who regulate their ᵽjects. As we discussed in Chapter One, urban minority groups are ..ᴜᴏ close dependence on and contact with governmental bureaucracies. It is this factor which helps produce the mass (such as it is) of members in urban movements.

The motivation of specialist members is the desire to change particular agency policies and redirect benefits.[53] Thus, they tend to see such goals as replacement of a school principal or the vetoing of an urban renewal plan as ends in themselves rather than part of a larger attempt to change the structure of power. Combined with these motivations is a consciousness which tends to be relatively unintegrated. They have some radical ideas, especially with regard to their particular institutional target, but these ideas are not well structured into a developed radical ideology. The specialists have difficulty in tying their specific grievances to general diagnoses and in seeing close connection between the particular remedies for which they are striving locally and universal remedies for their collectivities. The specialists unlike the community activists do not usually have highly developed political consciousnesses.

The community activists differ from the specialists along each of the three dimensions of recruitment, motivations and consciousness. Community activists have a history of participation in a range of voluntary associations; they are joiners. They become involved in movement activity either because they consciously seek to create it or because their leadership position in an organization thrusts them into it. The minister who began North Side Forces exemplifies the former, while Mrs. C., the community activist member of the IS 201 Board described earlier, epitomizes the latter. The community activists view themselves as reformers working for "the people." They want to obtain power and benefits for their communities; they differ from the specialists in having programs and fairly abstract political goals.

Although the motivations of the community activists are diverse, they, more than the specialists, seem to enjoy the power which comes from occupying leadership roles. Yet, significantly, while the community activists are much more politically motivated than the specialists in the sense that they work for an explicit political program and that they strive for individual and group power, *both* types of participants seem to be estranged from traditional urban political institutions. Even the most political types in the movements tend to differ from politicians.[54] While a few have participated in local political clubs, community activists are not usually recruited from among party workers, nor do they typically go from movement activity to party politics.[55] The world of urban political movements is relatively separate

---

[53] The particularism of the specialists is not the same as that of participants in machine politics. The movement specialists rarely receive tangible personal benefits, such as income or jobs. Moreover, they usually rationalize their activity in collective rather than individual terms.

[54] See Richard Young's study of the difference between "protest leaders" and politicians in the San Francisco area. Young, "The Impact of Protest Leadership," pp. 100–104.

[55] Kramer comes to the same conclusion about activists in Bay area TAOs. Kramer, *Participation of the Poor*, p. 257.

from that of urban party politics. This, as we shall argue in the next chapters, has significant implications for urban political life.

The community activists tend to place organizational work in a broader context than do the specialists. They frequently use the term "community control" in a way which identifies this strategy as a general remedy for the condition of minority groups. While only a minority of community activists have a fully developed ideology, the activists as a whole tend to be more politicized and politically sophisticated than the specialists. They view themselves as political actors self-consciously striving to implement political programs.

These characterizations of specialists and community activists must be viewed as quite tentative. While our ideal types seem to be a useful starting point in developing a theoretical analysis of urban activists, they raise questions for which we do not now have answers. There is the basic question of whether patterns of recruitment, motivation and consciousness are correlated with organizational affiliations—as we have suggested—and cluster into the specialist and community activist types. In addition, one might ask whether the two types of activists are as distinct from one another as both are from the large majority of inner-city residents who never become involved in movement activity. This is an issue of degree, but with qualitative implications. Finally, is there a specific pattern of transition from being a specialist to a community activist? Do more radicalized specialists become activists, or are there separate patterns of recruitment such that the kinds of people who initially become involved as specialists remain specialists even after a prolonged experience of movement activity? [56] This last question raises the complex matter of the effect on consciousness of participation in urban movements—the effect of praxis on theory.

participation and consciousness

While movement activity can only begin when some critical mass of individuals possesses a nascent alternative consciousness, radical actions do not suddenly erupt after enough people have radical ideas. Rather, as the case studies—especially PS 84—have indicated, there is an interactive relationship between consciousness and action and a process of radicalization which depends upon specific experiences and events. The initial basis of involvement of individuals in urban movements may become less significant in determining their actions after they have participated in the movement for a period of time; in turn movement participation helps create the very experiences which alter their consciousness. Often, individuals have become

---

[56] Merton raises—and leaves unanswered—similar questions concerning influentials who operate only within one sphere (monomorphics) and those who function within several (polymorphics): "Under what conditions does the influential remain monomorphic? Is this a stable type—or is it rather a stage in the development of influence, such that the monomorphic in due course tends to become polymorphic?" Merton, "Patterns of Influence," p. 414. The relevance of Merton's questions to our own is enhanced by his suggestion that the locals tend to be the monomorphics and the cosmopolitans the polymorphics (p. 414).

involved in organizations which are not recognized as movements and through their experiences in the organizations have found their ideas and their activities radicalized. This appears to have happened to some neighborhood boards of Community Action Agencies. At PS 84 our evidence shows in great detail how the consciousness of activists changed as a result of external events (the UFT strikes), the responses of bureaucratic officials to demands for change, and the growth of their own organization and power. Experience on the Joan of Arc, IS 201 and Ocean Hill-Brownsville Governing Boards—none of which were clearly seen as movement organizations at the start—frequently radicalized the consciousness of participants.

In general we can identify at least three forces that arise from activity and facilitate changes in consciousness (which, in turn, help determine activity). First, the emergence or appearance of leaders with alternative ideologies can contribute to the radicalization of activists both through direct contact and socialization and through engagement in activities which could not have taken place without conscious leadership. The paid organizer of the Joan of Arc Board performed both these functions.

Second, the experience of certain catalytic events can bring about sharp changes in thinking. Such events may involve the experience of a "utopia" in the form of social arrangements which would not normally exist; the sudden collapse of established authorities due to their inability to enforce official norms or to provide expected services (or both); intransigence and counterattack by officials such as the firing of an agitator or the use of police violence; and the initiation by targets or third parties of reform efforts which have the unanticipated consequence of contributing to movement mobilization.

PS 84 exemplifies these catalytic events. The reform-minded nucleus of parents and teachers experienced a "utopia" first during the Freedom School, then during the 1968 UFT strike, each of which was made possible by a situation partly extrinsic to that of PS 84 (i.e., the factors which produced the two strikes). The 1968 strike precipitated the collapse of the institutional structure of the school, and the behavior of the principal in the face of difficult circumstances undermined her authority vis-à-vis teachers and parents. Mrs. Wertzel's attempt to fire the faculty ring-leaders precipitated the first picketing of PS 84 in June of 1967; and Superintendent Rosen's "unreasonableness" in giving Wertzel a "satisfactory" performance rating was the final step in the radicalization of movement participants. The attempt by the District Office to co-opt the reformers at 84 by introducing a teacher-trainer (Prof. Samson) backfired when Samson herself became a source of leadership and a resource for the reform movement.

The third force influencing the consciousness of movement participants is the nature of the movement's adversaries, and the form which conflict with them assumes. While different types of targets—e.g., school officials, health workers, welfare agencies—will affect movement activity and consciousness in different ways, all targets of urban movements have certain characteristics in common. These involve a general structural insulation from client participation in organizational decisionmaking; the manning of most official positions by whites while most clients are from minority groups; and finally, the adherence to universalistic norms by target agencies and the use of Progressive political formulae by their officials when in combat with urban movements.

The specific ideas of movement leaders have been molded by the way in which the targets of urban reformers embody the structural legacies of Progressivism, and by the necessity to create a new organizational basis to reform Progressive institutions. Thus, the targets of urban movements have affected the consciousness of movement participants in two related ways: collectively through the general structural and ideological character of the institutions which impinge upon the lives of inner-city residents; and individually through the combat interactions which the target officials help to shape (including the catalytic events which they may create). The cumulative effect of the many microscopic encounters between movements and their opponents is to propagate certain ideas both to their potential recruits and potential enemies. These encounters create a political situation —a definition of contending social actors and interests—which in turn becomes a confining condition on each further mobilizing effort and movement-target interaction.

The effect of movement participation upon participants cannot be described without knowing the state of mobilization at a given time, the resources which a group possesses, and the kinds of activities which it is capable of undertaking. An event which might be catalytic if an organization has high visibility is a nonevent in the absence of a propagandizing capacity. If a momement has reached a certain stage in size and power, the behavior of a bureaucratic opponent who defends his agency by ignoring reformers may further the mobilization of activists; but if a movement is very weak, being ignored may be its coup de grâce. We see that on the one hand the objective state of a movement helps determine whether leaders will have resources, events will be precipitated or capitalized upon, opponents will *have* to answer movement demands or not. Yet, on the other hand, this objective state is in good part defined by the quantity and quality of individual participation. If many people participate and are willing to incur large costs, then at the social level we may describe the movement as relatively strong. The nature of activity by each individual who is or may be mobilized thus helps to create the aggregate situation (the objective state of the movement) which itself affects the consciousness and activities of individuals. In no area of social and political analysis is it clearer than in the study of political movements that the subjective and the objective, ideas and action, individual behavior and aggregate structure, are interrelated with one another, are in fact different aspects of the same phenomenon.

The usual outcome of the interrelationship between participation and consciousness is not a process of radicalization. To the contrary, the resources of minority activists are limited and inefficient, while the defenses of their opponents are usually sufficient to fend off most attacks from below. The presence of a dominant American ideology of liberalism and the conditions which make collective action irrational[57] means that political movements are the exception, not by any means the rule. And when movements have emerged, as many did in the 1960s, they have been relatively short-lived. They developed to a point and then underwent a cycle of demobilization, produced by the tangible costs and psychological frustration of participation, by the modesty of the gains which even the most developed urban movements could achieve.

[57] "Irrational" in terms of the relationship of costs to benefits as described in Chapter Seven.

mobilization
and power

7

We are concerned with whether the mobilization of urban minority groups can change the distribution of social benefits in their favor. This question really breaks down into two parts: how can minorities be organized; and what must their organizations do in order to obtain their external goals? Here we examine the kind of organizational behavior that determines whether urban political movements can mobilize resources and transform them into effective power.

Although we utilize an analytic distinction between consciousness and action, we do not intend to imply a stage theory of the development of movements. Smelser, for example, argues that there is a temporal sequence to the determinants of collective behavior such that raised consciousness, or generalized belief, precedes action.[1] In contrast, we see continuous interplay between consciousness and action and consider that all activities of movements have a dual effect—they both reshape or reinforce the consciousness of members and potential members, and attack target organizations or social groups. We therefore wish to identify the processes by which movements can both use their initial resources effectively and develop additional resources through attracting new participants and increasing the commitment of present ones.

We premise our approach to the question of the development of collective power on an economic or exchange model, according to which a political resource is any factor which can be used to obtain desired ends for the individual or group expending it.[2] Political resources are equivalent to

[1] Neil J. Smelser, *Theory of Collective Behavior* (New York: Free Press, 1962), pp. 18–19, 292–95.

[2] The economic or exchange model of power is presented most rigorously by Talcott Parsons in "On the Concept of Political Power," in *Class, Status, and Power*, eds. Reinhard Bendix and

capital in the real economy. Like capital they may exist in a variety of forms, ranging from money, votes, and patronage to organizational skills, loyal adherents, and moral authority. As in the economy, resources can be saved, invested, and consumed. The function of a political movement is to provide a vehicle for the aggregation of individual resources so as to obtain collective ends. It is an investment institution analagous to a joint stock company, and like such a company it must attract investors, maintain their confidence, and show a profit:

The argument is that interest group origins, growth, death, and associated lobbying activity may all be better explained if we regard them as exchange relationships between entrepreneurs/organizers, who invest capital in a set of benefits, which they offer to prospective members at a price—membership.[3]

The economic model assumes that individuals will contribute their resources to a joint venture only when it profits them to do so—in other words, when the benefits of joining outweigh the costs. This assumption signifies two important difficulties for those seeking to organize individuals for collective action. First, an individual considering joining an action group cannot calculate his benefits with certainty unless he knows what other similar individuals intend to do.[4] Because the effectiveness of the action group depends on some minimum level of participation, the decision of each individual to participate requires an estimate of the number of others who will make positive decisions. But their decisions in turn depend on his. For group organizers to overcome the reluctance created by uncertainty, they must persuade potential supporters that the movement is an expanding enterprise.

This necessity, however, confronts the second logical problem involved in collective action. While small size leads to high risk and low effectiveness, large size produces apathy and few incentives for individual participation. If a movement succeeds, members of the collectivity it represents can benefit from its gains without having participated in the movement.[5] Such gains

---

Seymour Martin Lipset (New York: Free Press, 1966), pp. 240–65. See also Mancur Olson, *The Logic of Collective Action*, rev. ed. (New York: Schocken, 1971), pp. 9–16; Anthony Oberschall, *Social Conflict and Social Movements* (Englewood Cliffs, N.J.: Prentice-Hall, 1973), pp. 157–63; Robert Salisbury, "An Exchange Theory of Interest Groups," *Midwest Journal of Political Science*, XIII, February, 1969, 1–32; Peter M. Blau, *Exchange and Power in Social Life* (New York: John Wiley, 1964), esp. chap. 5; and Robert Dahl, *Who Governs?* (New Haven: Yale University Press, 1961), pp. 223–301.

[3] Salisbury, "An Exchange Theory of Interest Groups," p. 2.

[4] Davis and Palomba compare the situation of potential participants in a boycott to that of the two prisoners in the "Prisoner's Dilemma," a well-known game involving decisionmaking under uncertainty. In the payoff matrix of this game both prisoners stand to lose unless they can coordinate their behavior, but even with collusion neither can be sure that the other will behave so as to maximize mutual gains. J. Ronnie Davis and Neil A. Palomba, "The National Farmers Organization and the Prisoner's Dilemma: A Game Theory Prediction of Failure," in *Planned Social Intervention*, eds. Louis A. Zurcher, Jr. and Charles M. Bonjean (New York: Chandler, 1970), pp. 467–73.

[5] See Olson, *The Logic of Collective Action.*

constitute public goods, and they are equally available both to those who made them possible and to those who passively awaited them. Therefore, as Mancur Olson shows, it is not in the interest of any individual to incur costs that will only have a small incremental effect on collective benefits, unless he knows that his unique personal contribution will permit the action group to achieve its goals:

> *The achievement of any common goal or the satisfaction of any common interest means that a public or collective good has been provided for that group.* The very fact that a goal or purpose is *common* to a group means that no one in the group is excluded from the benefit or satisfaction brought about by its achievement.[6]

Only in quite small organizations can individuals be persuaded that their contribution is so significant as to relate to collective benefits directly.[7] Thus, even while group size is positively correlated with effectiveness, increasing size means that individuals are less likely to feel that their participation is crucial to the attainment of the collective good.

These dilemmas arise from a disjunction between a rational calculation of individual as opposed to group interests. Such a disjunction exists for all collective bodies including the state:

> And just as a state cannot support itself by voluntary contributions, or by selling its basic services on the market, neither can other large organizations support themselves without providing some sanction, or some attraction distinct from the public good itself, that will lead individuals to help bear the burdens of maintaining the organization.[8]

Olson here cites the difficulties of ensuring loyalty which face such powerful institutions as the nation-state or organized religion. Yet these organizations, even without the provision of sanctions and selective individual benefits, have great advantages over political movements for attracting support. The weight of custom and habits of loyalty can cause people to act without calculating their private interests. Most Americans will vote in presidential elections, even though the kind of rational assessment of interests described by Olson would justify their abstention. Political movements, on the other hand, must sidetrack individuals from their accustomed ways; accordingly even while their principal strength arises from the voluntary activities of their adherents, they are seriously handicapped relative to established institutions in attracting such voluntarism.

The obstacles to radical collective action by rational individuals then are large, and the task of organizations which seek to overcome them is heavy. It is little wonder that the movement organizations we have examined are small in size and short of life. We can, however, identify four significant factors which serve to overcome these obstacles and which explain why

[6] Ibid., p. 15. Ital. in original.

[7] Ibid., pp. 53–65.

[8] Ibid., pp. 15–16.

political movements ever exist at all. First is the possibility of obtaining specific material rewards even from participating in opposition movements:

It was, and still is, possible to make a viable career as a spokesman for radical or militant groups, from appearances on television shows, conferences, workshops, seminars, lectures, magazine stories, and university appointments, once mass media publicity had catapulted a vocal dissenter into the national limelight.[9]

The availability of these kinds of rewards is limited, and participants in the organizations we studied have little chance to obtain wide renown. Yet there are exceptions. George Jenkins, the paid organizer of the Joan of Arc Board, advanced from that position to become the director of a well known, foundation-supported advocacy planning firm, despite his lack of a college degree. One of the members of the PS 84 parents group managed to acquire a publishing contract for a book on the struggle there.[10] A number of the activists in the New York movement for community control of schools were invited to give paid lectures, were interviewed on television, and sent on foundation-sponsored retreats. Even without exposure to the national limelight there are some career opportunities in urban radicalism.

Second, while opposition organizations have few material benefits to offer, they may become a source of symbolic rewards. Participants can enjoy the virtue of having fought the good fight; they can have the emotional support of others in similar circumstances; and they can feel sufficient identification with the group that they interpret collective gains as being also individual ones. Olson's construction of the model of individual interests tends to exclude such identification as irrational, but his definition of rational interests seems unduly constricting and artificial.

Third, ideology is a persuasive device which leads individuals to understand the connection between their individual and group interests, so that rational calculations will be made in terms of social rather than individual good. One function of radical ideology is to reduce the dissonance between individual and collective rationality.[11] The economic model of rationality assumes that the criterion for individual rationality must be

[9] Oberschall, *Social Conflict and Social Movements*, p. 161.

[10] Hannah Hess, *The Third Side of the Desk* (New York: Scribner's, 1973).

[11] The difference between radical political movements and chiliastic ones arises from the character of their justifications, from the reasons they offer for individuals to forego selfishness for a cause. Spiritual movements call for individual sacrifices to insure propitious actions by supernatural forces. The ideology of urban radicalism, in claiming that individual mobility for urban blacks is chimerical, aims at explaining to its public why the sacrifices of participation are justified. Judgment as to whether participants are "true believers" depends on the validity of the ideological justifications present. It is not true, as Eric Hoffer contends, that "the fanaticism which animates them[the fanatical Christian, Mohammedan, nationalist, Communist, and Nazi] may be viewed and treated as one." Hoffer, *The True Believer* (New York: Mentor Books, 1951), p. ix. The displacement of private affects onto public objects is more or less reasonable depending on the correctness of the diagnosis which explains individual circumstances by social causes and the appropriateness of the proposed collective remedy. Cargo cults are irrational not because of the emotionalism they evoke but on account of the false premises from which they evolve.

individual self-interest, an assumption arising out of liberal utilitarian social philosophy which insists that social good can only be defined in individualistic terms. Both conservative and radical theorists reject this formulation, refusing to accept the atomized individual as the starting point for all social evaluations. If the liberal dichotomy of individual and society is not wholly applied, then individual action to incur group benefits becomes rational.

Fourth, and within the confines of the unmodified rational model, obstacles to collective action are reduced when risks are low or benefits high.[12] Lowering of risks results either from previous activities of members of the collectivity or from the loosening of social control mechanisms. Both these factors operated at PS 84, where the movement snowballed, thereby legitimizing participation in it, and where the established authority became immobilized, losing its normative control over school personnel. The extent of benefits that can be won through political action depends partly on how successful the movement has been in forcing up the stakes. Thus, the demands at PS 84 were originally for limited pedagogical experimentation and subsequently for fundamental changes in the governance of the school. Benefits also depend on the type of institution under attack. The discretionary benefits that can be yielded by a school or health service may be relatively intangible or marginal to the well-being of the participants; in contrast, welfare authorities and housing agencies have significant material rewards to dispense. The example of the Morningside Squatters is one where very substantial benefits—decent apartments for those who formerly had none—acted as a potent incentive to participation.

The strategies used by opposition movements are aimed at accumulating and using resources to improve the benefit/risk ratio and thereby to mobilize to meet the movement's external goals. We devote the remainder of this chapter to a discussion of the kinds of resources available to poor people's movements, the effectiveness of strategies used to develop and employ them, and the process of bureaucratic change. Our case studies, while far from conclusive in terms of indicating workable strategies, do illustrate positive and negative results associated with various approaches. Even if we knew the total number of organizations which employed each approach and did or did not achieve desired results, we would not know the correct strategy in each set of circumstances nor would we be safe in making the inference that the most successful strategy of the past would prove most useful in the future. Our aim here is not to predict which strategies will most likely be used nor which will have the best results but rather to outline the logical implications of different strategies. We consider the case studies to be suggestive of these implications, but our method of approaching them is not strictly inductive. The case studies do not adequately represent all urban movements, but they do offer a starting point for the development of arguments concerning the meaning of various strategies.

---

[12] See Oberschall, *Social Conflict and Social Movements*, pp. 162–63, where he discusses the changes in behavior associated with different "risk/reward ratios."

THE RESOURCES OF URBAN MINORITIES

The economic model of power does not assume that political resources are fixed in amount. Instead, like capital, additional resources can be created through the investment of existing ones. The ability to mobilize[13] slack resources is not restricted to any particular social stratum. As expressed by Robert Dahl the concept of slack resources in liberal democracies implies that citizens at the bottom of the social hierarchy could, if mobilized, exert much greater influence than they normally do: "Most citizens have political resources they do not employ in order to gain influence over the decisions of public officials; consequently there is a great gap between their actual and potential influence." [14] Power, according to this view, is not a zero-sum game, and the capacity of lower strata to mobilize power resources means that increasing the assets possessed by groups at the bottom need not reduce the assets of those at the top.

As in the economic system, how one interprets the meaning of increased "wealth" within the power system varies sharply according to point of view and underlying political philosophy. Increments in the standard of living of the poor need not change their position relative to the rest of society. Similarly mobilization of their power resources, if it provokes counter-mobilization, may result in an increase in the amount of power in the system as a whole without changing the relative position of various groups.[15]

Our concern with the relative position of the nonwhite urban lower classes leads us to examine the kinds of resources available to them. Can their organizations exploit resources which are not also available to their adversaries? They have at their disposal their numbers, their occupation of a "turf," moral appeal, and on occasion friends in high places. But none of these resources is as effective or reliable as money, an asset which such organizations might be able to raise once established, but which is almost always initially lacking. Thus, lower- and working-class minority groups seeking power operate with the same disadvantage as the impoverished economic entrepreneur who needs some capital before he can make more.[16]

[13] Amitai Etzioni defines mobilization as the "process by which energy that is latent from the viewpoint of the acting unit is made available for collective action." Amitai Etzioni, *The Active Society* (New York: Free Press, 1968), p. 388.

[14] Dahl, *Who Governs?*, pp. 305–6. See also Parsons, "On the Concept of Political Power"; Etzioni, *The Active Society*, pp. 395–97.

[15] Dahrendorf claims that authority is always a zero-sum game in which the winners dominate and the losers submit. Ralf Dahrendorf, *Class and Class Conflict in Industrial Society* (Stanford: Stanford University Press, 1959), p. 170. We do not agree with Dahrendorf that those in subordinate positions are without authority, but we nonetheless feel that relative position is more important than absolute potential.

[16] See Michael Parenti, "Power and Pluralism: A View from the Bottom," *Journal of Politics*, XXXII, August, 1970, 527.

Power resources are not completely interchangeable, and some tend to have low efficiency. For example, it is difficult for urban movements to convert the resource of numbers into power. Elections occur infrequently, rarely present clearcut issues, and the more significant ones are held over a larger geographical area than that controlled by the movement's public. Protest marches and other forms of direct action relying on a show of numerical strength tend to lose their impact when repeated. The effective disposition of large groups of people requires an excellent communications network, which in turn depends on organizational ability, media access, and funds. The success of urban political movements requires a combination of favorable historical circumstances and organizational momentum, but such momentum is hard to gain when one's starting point is at the bottom. The various strategies adopted by urban political movements are ways in which they have attempted to convert their relatively meager and inefficient resources into power. We look now at some of these strategies.

protest activities

Opposition movements must rely primarily on a strategy of protest to press their claims on social institutions. Protest activities permit the focusing of grievances, create martyrs, communicate the existence and desires of the protestors to both their immediate targets and a wider audience, and threaten social stability. They demand an answer and those in authority usually must respond in some way to the changed situation created by protest. Demonstration and threat are the forms of political action most available to people outside the normal channels of communication and influence. The leaders of community organizations realize that in order to achieve momentum they must capitalize on whatever issues are available.[17] But, as Alinsky asserts: "A grievance . . . *only becomes an issue when you can do something about it. . . .* Actually there are very few issues and every organizer knows this." [18] Unless protest tactics bring quick victories, continued requests for participants in such activities will soon evoke little response.

The Joan of Arc Board illustrates the difficulties of a small organization seeking to follow a protest strategy. The Board never became salient enough to its public to mobilize a great many people, and its inability to attract a

---

[17] Warner Bloomberg, Jr. and Florence W. Rosenstock, in an article on the Community Action Program, characterize the "social action-social protest model" as one that requires the dramatization of local issues:

> Cooperation and collaboration with most existing agencies is . . . likely to confuse rather than clarify . . . underlying conflict. . . . Organizers, therefore, must use every opportunity to bring latent conflict to the surface, to intensify it, and to aid the poor in developing and using whatever power resources can be developed by those who have little money.

Warner Bloomberg, Jr. and Florence W. Rosenstock, "Who Can Activate the Poor?" in *Power, Poverty, and Urban Policy,* eds. Warner Bloomberg, Jr., and Henry J. Schmandt, *Urban Affairs Annual Reviews* (Beverly Hills, Calif.: Sage Publications, 1968), p. 322.

[18] Marion K. Sanders, *The Professional Radical: Conversations with Saul Alinsky* (New York: Harper & Row, 1970), p. 70. Ital. in original.

large following diminished its appeal. Although the apparent frequency of demonstrations in American cities seems to belie the point, persuading people to incur the costs involved in demonstrating remains difficult. A movement must reach a critical mass before most sympathizers will perceive their risks in taking to the streets to be less than their potential gains. Harold Weissman, in his analysis of Mobilization for Youth, comments:

> One success leads to another. A successful organization develops an image of power; this power is then imputed to the organization, and then the organization actually becomes more powerful and better able to attain its goals.[19]

As the organization acquires an image of power, participation in it appears less like a gratuitous act and more like effective action. More people join, and the organization becomes more potent. Conversely, as was the case with Joan of Arc, futile protest leads to a cycle of demobilization; sympathizers become deterred from action, not least because they do not wish to look like fools associated with a hapless cause.

The critical factor determining the success of protest organizations in attracting followers is their effect on their target. This, as we have discussed, depends on their organizational strength, but it results from other causes as well. These include the reactions of third parties and the form of defense used by the target.

Third parties.   For political movements which do not represent majority collectivities, the positive support, or at least neutrality, of influential groups (third parties) is crucial.[20] A protest strategy, while drawing attention to the protestors, may alienate outsiders who are abstractly sympathetic. Movement leaders are forever caught in the dilemma of needing to publicize their moral appeal through tactics unacceptable to their allies. An article about the Joan of Arc Board by a member of the New York City Board of Education sharply delineates the problem:

> Take the example of the Joan of Arc complex which wanted to become a demonstration district. Several of us on the Board favored this. . . . Our logic was beginning to convince the few Board members needed to give us the seven votes for bringing this about in the face of enormous local and administrative opposition.
>
> But, at the public meetings, a small group of frustrated . . . women . . . kept violently disrupting the general meetings to get their views heard regardless of the agenda which frequently included similar problems in other sections of the city. . . . Actually, of course, they made it impossible for us to win the needed votes. . . .[21]

---

[19] Harold H. Weissman, "Problems in Maintaining Stability in Low-Income Social Action Organizations," in *Community Development in the Mobilization for Youth Experience*, ed. Harold H. Weissman (New York: Association Press, 1969), p. 176. Michael Lipsky in "Protest as a Political Resource," *American Political Science Review*, LXII, December, 1968, 1156, speaks of a "resource threshold" that a group must cross in order to command attention.

[20] The success of the Southern sit-in movement depended heavily on the intervention of third parties. See Donald Von Eschen, Jerome Kirk, and Maurice Pinard, "The Conditions of Direct Action in a Democratic Society," *Western Political Quarterly*, XXII, June, 1969, 309–25.

[21] *Manhattan Tribune*, February 15, 1969, p. 13.

The difficult position of movement leaders is exacerbated by the constant need to demonstrate to their supporters that they have not "sold out": [22] "The leader whose organizing appeal requires militant rhetoric may obtain eager press coverage only to find that his inflammatory statements lead to alienation of potential allies and exclusion from the explicit bargaining process." [23]

Defenses against protest.   Michael Lipsky identifies six ways in which target groups—usually administrative agencies—can thwart the demands of protest organizations:

1. Target groups may dispense symbolic satisfactions.
2. Target groups may dispense token material satisfactions.
3. Target groups may organize and innovate internally in order to blunt the impetus of protest efforts.
4. Target groups may appear to be constrained in their ability to grant protest goals.
5. Target groups may use their extensive resources to discredit protest leaders and organizations.
6. Target groups may postpone action.[24]

Two additional defensive strategies may be placed on the list:

7. Target groups may ignore protest organizations, thereby avoiding the kinds of controversies that attract media coverage.
8. Target groups may give communities the appearance of authority without its substance, thereby forcing them to discredit themselves through attempting actions that they cannot carry out.

Examples of all these defenses abound in the major cases described in Chapters Three to Five, as well as in the briefer ones chronicled in Chapter Two. The response of the New York State Legislature to the movement for community control of schools in New York City represented an instance of *symbolic satisfaction.* The Legislature passed a law called the Decentralization Act and named the existing large local school districts "community school districts." But it gave the community school boards hardly any additional powers; eliminated the demonstration districts which had been the focus of the movement; restricted foundation support, which had been the only source of independent local funding; and established a complicated election procedure intended to produce community school boards that could not be

[22] George Brager, in another analysis of Mobilization for Youth, comments that conflict over the maintenance of a militant strategy caused acute dissent within the organization. External opposition, rather than contributing to internal solidarity, precipitated division. George Brager, "Commitment and Conflict in a Normative Organization," *American Sociological Review,* IV, August, 1969, 483–91.

[23] Lipsky, "Protest as a Political Resource" p. 1152. See also Ralph H. Turner, "The Public Perception of Protest," *American Sociological Review,* XXXIV, December, 1969, 815–30.

[24] Lipsky, "Protest as a Political Resource" pp. 1155–6.

dominated by community control forces.[25] While militant parents' groups boycotted the elections, the Legislature was quite successful in satisfying spokesmen for the general public that the law represented genuine progress toward decentralization and community participation.[26]

The granting of *token material satisfactions* occurred in a number of cases. The Cooper Square Association eventually obtained a small number of the housing units they had called for under the Alternate Plan. The demands by Joan of Arc parents for a replacement elementary school were answered by plans to provide a building for half the children in the old one. The original outcry by PS 84 parents for a revamping of the school was met by state funds to provide for an educational consultant.

School systems and health suppliers have proved particularly adept at displaying *"innovative" programs* as evidence of their adaptation to reformist demands. The plethora of demonstration projects and experimental programs attest to the ways in which bureaucracies can contain change and display evidence of progress without structural upheaval. Thus, the Denver Neighborhood Health Center produced new programs, made services more accessible, and called upon local people for advice but resisted any major changes in the traditional professional–client relationship. Charles E. Wilson, the first unit administrator appointed by the IS 201 Governing Board in New

[25] The United Parents Association (UPA) analysis of the 1970 elections (mimeo, n.d.) for community school boards in the four outer boroughs found:

> In 6 districts with a population of Black and Puerto Rican pupils ranging from 30 to 48 percent, only 2 of the 54 school board members are non-white. In 8 districts which are predominantly Black and Puerto Rican, the majority of each board is white. These 14 of the 25 districts show a gross under-representation of Black and Puerto Rican parents. . . . Only 5 districts can be characterized as having elected community school boards which are fairly representative of the racial composition of the schools which they represent.

[26] *The New York Times* was more than willing to accept the law and the statements of the new Board of Education at face value:

> Polemics about the "destruction" of the demonstration districts not only distort the truth but undermine the prospects of civic peace and educational reform. Since the special districts will become part of larger units whose population is in sympathy with many of the educational experiments, there is no reason to fear that the gains they have already achieved will be jeopardized. . . .
> The need now is to make the system work, which it surely can if it is not sabotaged. Too much concern with new organizational patterns would obscure the true goal of decentralization: liberation of the schools from the straitjacket of bureaucracy. (*The New York Times*, December 24, 1969, p. 24.)

The *Times* had originally condemned the same law in the following terms:

> The New York City school decentralization bill is a bad measure patched together in an outrageous travesty of the legislative process. . . .
> It is hardly surprising that the new law has been cheered by the United Federation of Teachers and this city's organized school supervisors. . . . Nor is it surprising that it has already been denounced by virtually everybody else. . . .
> Furthermore, abolition of the demonstration districts can only serve as an additional reminder that the opponents of any extension of power within the local communities even on an experimental basis, are the real winners in this political contest. (*The New York Times*, May 2, 1969, p. 42.)

York, commented on the "innovativeness" of the Board of Education in establishing the demonstration school districts:

Although the establishment of the demonstration districts caused tumultuous opposition and bitter conflict, the Board of Education's approach should not be regarded as either innovative or imaginative. Ocean Hill-Brownsville and the 201 district were already virtually untenable enclaves. . . . What was imaginative was the effectiveness with which the cards were stacked against the success of the local communities. What was innovative was the clever way in which agreements were entered into without any care for long-standing precedents or union claims. Imagination and innovation were defensive weapons to protect the Educational Establishment.[27]

Demonstrations which never become systematically implemented allow political and bureaucratic bodies to impress third parties with their responsiveness at the lowest possible risk and expenditure of resources. As Peter Schrag wryly remarks about the Boston school system:

The system is now fairly littered with demonstration projects and experiments, head starts, preschools, enrichments, compensatory programs, second chances, reading laboratories, summer reviews, pilot schools, team teaching trials, and a whole host of other departures. . . . But so far, the system's long list of changes . . . has had almost no effect on educational substance for most of the children most of the time. . . . The innovations tend to remain well encapsulated, like droplets of oil on still water.[28]

Governmental agencies typically, and often truthfully, claim they have *no authority* to satisfy protestors. The refusal of the City of Paterson to permit North Side Forces to construct low-income housing is typical of such claims. The inability of the New York Board of Education to change the structure of the city's school system and the statement by District Superintendent Rosen to the PS 84 parents that he was inhibited by law from replacing their principal are other examples. The fact that Rosen's successor managed to do so indicates the way in which flexibility under the law can often be a matter of bureaucratic discretion.

Discrediting of protestors is almost always the initial defensive reaction of target groups. The Mayor of Oakland labeled the demands of the Black Strike Committee as "totally irresponsible." The United Federation of Teachers accused adherents of the Ocean Hill-Brownsville Governing Board of anti-Semitism. When George Jenkins spoke on behalf of the Joan of Arc community, members of the New York Legislature argued that he did not really represent that community. The absence of generally accepted legitimizing devices for community leadership makes it extremely vulnerable to the charge that it speaks for no one but itself. In contrast to government officials whose appointment or election follows legally established procedures, movement leaders can only assert their representativeness. There are no devices for investing them with the authority which officials possess automati-

[27] Charles E. Wilson, "Year One at I.S. 201," *Social Policy*, May/June 1970, p. 11.
[28] Peter Schrag, *Village School Downtown* (Boston: Beacon Press, 1967), pp. 70–72.

cally; even if their demands are in the interest of their constituency, movement leaders have few ways of offering proof of their status as legitimate spokesmen.

   Postponement of action is a strategy which comes naturally to bureaucracies even when not under attack. The elaborate bureaucratic procedures surrounding urban renewal meant that the Cooper Square association had to keep pressing its cause for over a decade. The New York City Board of Education postponed deciding on the status of the Joan of Arc Governing Board until the Legislature acted. The District 5 Local School Board refused to act on PS 84 until a study was completed. Since governmental bodies have much greater confidence that they will exist indefinitely than do their adversaries, time usually works on their side. Sometimes, however, failure to respond can increase tensions and further counter-mobilization. At PS 84, parents refused to accept a study as a substitute for action and increased their incitement of the administration.

   The price of *ignoring protest organizations* may similarly be increased tension and greater dissent. But small, weak organizations are often very vulnerable to inattention since they rely on the publicity surrounding open conflict to attract sympathy. While the Episcopal Church attempted unsuccessfully simply to outwait the Morningside Squatters, the New York City Board of Education was quite effective in evading interaction with the Joan of Arc Board. Joan of Arc members could not even get appointments with members of the Board of Education, and when they finally succeeded in arranging a meeting with that Board's president, he did not hesitate to cancel it without making a new one. Members of the Ocean Hill and IS 201 Governing Boards also complained of extreme difficulty in obtaining appointments with the Mayor and Board of Education, who would subsequently attempt to discredit them for acting without consultation.

   West Oakland Model Cities, the Cooper Square Association, the Ocean Hill and IS 201 Governing Boards, and North Side Forces were all at various times given the *appearance of authority* without real power of execution. West Oakland rebelled when its Model Cities delegates were told to operate through intermediaries rather than participate directly in decisionmaking at the city level themselves. Although Cooper Square early received official designation as a housing council under urban renewal legislation, it soon found that it could still be bypassed by the Mayor's office. The demonstration governing boards discovered that their powers over education did not extend to personnel. North Side Forces, like Cooper Square, received designation as a housing developer and broadcast its new status to the community only to discover that it was powerless to proceed. The discrepancy between claimed position and real authority inevitably reduced the public credibility of these bodies.

Counter-responses.   While the institutional targets of urban political movements usually begin from a position of relative strength, protest organizations do have some effective counter-responses to their defensive tactics. The most obvious is to maintain a level of disorder sufficient that policy makers must react. The risk involved, as Ocean Hill-Brownsville demonstrates, is that the authorities will respond by total denial, using the disorder to justify their action to the general public. If, however, the target group is internally divided and contains individuals sympathetic to the protest movement, these sympathizers can capitalize on the disequilibriated situation in order to press the claims of the protest group. Thus, the Morningside Squatters were able to take advantage of supporters within the Episcopal hierarchy who opposed the eviction of poor people for a home for the aged. These supporters eventually managed to persuade the Church to provide heating for the squatters.

At PS 84 and Lincoln Hospital, professional staff provided leadership for the movement. The PS 84 parent group had supporters within the school staff from the start. The resort to bureaucratic defense techniques by the principal heightened divisions in the teaching staff, and teachers who desired educational innovation refused to implement the directives of the school administration. The effectiveness of bureaucracies in coolly responding to outside agitation depends on their presenting a united front. If internal coherence does not exist, then such strategies as tokenism, postponement, and indifference become impossible to employ. Moreover, internal dissension leads to a decline in legitimacy vis-à-vis outsiders as each side within the organization seeks to discredit the other.

When continued protest action reaches a point where the target institution cannot continue its normal functioning, as happened when the squatters occupied the Morningside buildings or when the activities of the Ocean Hill-Brownsville Governing Board precipitated the school strike of 1968, the target organization must decide whether or not to repress the protestors. Use of outright repression, however, can be quite costly in terms of public sympathy. The Episcopal Church, for instance, declined to present an image of itself forcibly evicting poor Latin squatters. The New York Legislature did eventually eliminate the Ocean Hill-Brownsville demonstration district, but not without considerable public reaction and a further decline in the legitimacy of the educational system among blacks. Sometimes protest is so effective in disturbing established institutions that they lose their authority and cannot repress their opposition. Mrs. Wertzel, the principal of PS 84, attempted to fire dissident teachers and suppress the parent movement, but she could not make her will prevail. Similarly the Oakland municipal government could not reestablish its authority over West Oakland once the Model Cities Assembly had become its de facto government.

Even when governmental organizations refuse to capitulate to protest demands, continued harassment may produce victory by attrition. Bureaucratic personnel are often unaccustomed to stressful situations. At PS 84 Mrs. Wertzel seemingly lost control of herself and fled the school during the teachers' strike; she became hysterical during confrontations with dissenters; and while the cause of her eventual resignation was never specified, she apparently found it difficult to maintain her stability in the face of continued unrest. Likewise, Superintendent Rosen of District 5, who had to contend with constant criticisms, demonstrations, sit-ins, and crises at individual schools, submitted his resignation. He, unlike Mrs. Wertzel, had managed to maintain a calm surface and use most of the standard bureaucratic defenses. Nonetheless he found his role distasteful and unprofessional, and retired to a professorship in a graduate school of education.

The use of protest as a political resource requires that movement leadership ensure an adequate supply of protestors. Thus the strategic questions of organizing a following become of equal importance to questions concerning its use; as in all organizations task performance depends on organizational maintenance. As we noted earlier, effectiveness in goal attainment is itself an important contributor to an organization's ability to attract participants. Since, however, activity must begin before goals can be met, and also because individual rationality will cause people to prefer that others take the risks that will achieve group goals, organizations must find methods of directly inciting and maintaining participation. The groups we studied relied on three major mobilizing strategies—utopian appeals, professional organizers, and service provision—which we now analyze.

utopian appeals

An ideology can explain to individuals why they should make sacrifices for the benefit of the group. While we have previously discussed the kinds of justifications offered by urban activists in general, we are concerned here with the specific impact of different types of appeals. In other words, within the broad context of the remedies prescribed by movement leaders, what are the tactical effects of different emphases?

The most interesting comparison in this respect is between PS 84 and Joan of Arc. The quest at PS 84 for community control was always tied to substantive educational demands for the open classroom and a "new kind" of principal. The Freedom School constituted a utopia for many parents who equated its achievement at PS 84 with a revolution in the teaching of children. Parent activists knew why they sought power, and their conviction that the triumph of the parents group would mean the institutionalization of new educational methods invigorated them.

The Joan of Arc Board refrained from promising utopia. The Board members themselves were not convinced that their victory would be more than a first step toward improvement of education in the district. Because they saw community control as only a prerequisite to educational change, they lacked the messianism of the PS 84 parent leaders. The Joan of Arc Board failed to present an image of itself as likely to create a new educational system once it gained power; it thus could not evoke a sense of unambivalent enthusiasm for its cause. The Board's public was not concerned just with getting a more responsive school system; it wanted one that would provide educational results. The outcome was that while many sympathized with community control, few were sufficiently excited about it to make personal sacrifices. Moreover, sceptical observers questioned whether "community representatives" were necessarily less power hungry than the present occupants of authoritative positions. By not offering specific programmatic benefits the Board could not explain what advantages the community could gain from its activities, even if it produced a change in who ran the schools.

Most leaders seeking to develop urban political movements resemble the Joan of Arc Board in that they do not promise a new world. They are inhibited from doing so for several reasons: first, the minority status of lower- and working-class nonwhites means that the most they can hope for is greater equity within American society; this hardly amounts to the good life, and in fact the amount of improvement might be no more than marginal. Second, minority leaders lack a clear formulation of desirable social policy; while certain programs such as subsidized housing or government jobs have obvious benefits, the exact nature of equal education or improved welfare services remains unclear. Third, most movements focus on particular issues and are thereby faced with a contradiction between their overall analyses and tactical necessity. Ideologies of black power or community control declare that the condition of the poor results from general social conditions of racism and economic inequality. Changes in the school system or the administration of health services or welfare or justice would not in isolation affect the underlying bases of dissatisfaction. The need for leaders to focus on local issues, however, means that urban political movements expend their energies on obtaining objectives which their own analysis causes them to regard as only partial remedies.

The constraints on making utopian appeals constitute a serious drawback. For the PS 84 group the belief in the open classroom as an educational solution was crucial to its success. Other urban organizations lacking this kind of romanticism are hard put to tap the energies which went into the movement at 84. The importance of utopias has for good reason been emphasized by some theorists of radical political movements. Sorel argues for the usefulness, indeed the necessity of a vision of an idealized future:

And yet without leaving the present, without reasoning about this future, which seems for ever condemned to escape our reason, we should be unable to act at all. Experience shows that the *framing of a future, in some indeterminate time,* may, when it is done in a certain way, be very effective . . . ; this happens when the anticipations of the future take the form of those myths which enclose with them all the strongest inclinations of a people . . . ; and which give an aspect of complete reality to the hopes of immediate action by which, more easily than by any other method, men can reform their desires, passions, and mental activity.[29]

Sorel suggests that such utopianism need not detract from correct observation of reality and denies that the inevitable discrepancy between achievements and vision is necessarily injurious:

It must be admitted that the real developments of the Revolution [i.e. the Protestant Reformation] did not in any way resemble the enchanting pictures which created the

---

[29] Georges Sorel, *Reflections on Violence,* trans. T. E. Hulme and J. Roth (New York: Crowell-Collier and MacMillan, 1961), pp. 124–25. Ital. in original.

enthusiasm at its first adepts; but without those pictures would the Revolution have been victorious? [30]

He thus argues against the Marxist formulation which accused the utopian socialists, in their descriptions of socialist life, of "drifting off into pure phantasies." [31]

Marxism substituted for utopianism the laws of scientific determinism. Socialist theorists no longer needed to spell out the future if that future was inevitable, and revolutionists could evoke popular enthusiasm with the "scientific" assurance of proletarian triumph alone. But given a situation of historical indeterminacy, and in our present case the existence of poor odds of success, the absence of "enchanting pictures" places important limits on the ability to attract a mass following.

the professional organizer

A permanent paid staff constitutes a considerable mobilization resource for a community organization, although not one without drawbacks. [32] In a poor community few people can afford to devote their time to organizational work. But without a core of fulltime people an organization lacks coordination in its activities and enough manpower to carry out its program. Because a staff receives individual benefits, it will persist in its efforts during periods of discouragement or quietude, maintaining a sufficient organizational skeleton to allow interested people to remain informed about current events, encourage potential recruits to enlist, and provide an infrastructure around which to mobilize for the next crisis.

The staff also provides skills in organization, research, and communication that are not usually possessed by volunteers. Community organization and lobbying require techniques that do not come naturally to people just because they are reformers. Like most skills they develop only with practice; the inexperienced members of a neighborhood group need all the help in this respect that they can get. Moreover, if the community organization does not have at its disposal fulltime people who can generate programs on behalf of the group, it can only react to its opposition rather than taking the initiative.

Simply remaining in contact with their constituency requires leaders to spend large amounts of time and effort convening meetings and talking with people. Even then the number of constituents who can be personally contacted is quite small. Regular communication requires the publication of

---

[30] Ibid., p. 125.

[31] Frederick Engels, *Socialism: Utopian and Scientific* (New York: International Publishers, 1935), p. 36.

[32] Studies of community groups repeatedly find that the stability of the group depends on the existence of a paid staff. See Lipsky, "Protest as a Political Resource," p. 1150; Peter Marris and Martin Rein, *Dilemmas of Social Reform*, 2nd ed., (Chicago: Aldine, 1973), p. 186; Ralph M. Kramer, *Participation of the Poor* (Englewood Cliffs, N.J.: Prentice-Hall, © 1969), pp. 225–26, 229, 236–37; Weissman, "Problems in Maintaining Stability in Low-Income Social Action Organizations," p. 165; Charles E. Silberman, "The Potential for Community Organization," in *The View from Below: Urban Politics and Social Policy*, eds. Susan S. Fainstein and Norman I. Fainstein (Boston: Little, Brown, 1972), pp. 270–75.

frequent newsletters, the cultivation of ties with media representatives, and the fulltime availability of spokesmen for the group. Only in rare instances can the communications function be effectively fulfilled without paid staff.

The professional organizer who seeks to shape a neighborhood into an effective political force is a comparatively new phenomenon. His origins derive from two rather disparate sources: social work and allied professions, and union organizing. Within the social work profession "community organization" has for some time formed part of the standard curriculum. Its aims, however, have usually not been political. A social worker specializing in community organization coordinated agencies such as the Community Chest or a day-care council or attempted to involve people in neighborhood associations.[33]

Some social workers connected with the early poverty programs did develop a more radical view of community organization.[34] They have been joined by members of other professions which serve the poor. For example, corresponding to the concept of the social worker as engaged community organizer is that of the city planner as advocate: "Under the more recent and multidisciplinary models [of advocacy planning], political mobilization of the poor is viewed as a *sine qua non* for successful negotiation of the ghetto-developed plan." [35] Similarly, physicians attached to ghetto hospitals and lawyers working for legal aid services often construe their roles as extending beyond technical functions to fostering political militancy.

In rejecting the concept of the unbiased professional, many of the organizers with roots in the traditional helping occupations were influenced by the Saul Alinsky model, which arose directly from the experience of trade union organization. Historians of the American labor movement have contended that the growth of unionism depended critically on the professional organizer:

Once the initial fever of union enthusiasm had spent itself among the previously unorganized workers, the success of organization depended in large measure upon the availability of full-time, paid, professional organizers and adequate funds for organizing purposes.[36]

Alinsky changed the locus of organization from the factory to the neighborhood, where:

"[The organizer] becomes a catalytic agent transmuting hidden resentments and hostilities into open problems." His job is to persuade the people to move—to be

[33] See Harold L. Wilensky and Charles N. Lebeaux, *Industrial Society and Social Welfare* (New York: Free Press, 1965), p. 296; Harold H. Weissman, *Community Councils and Community Control* (Pittsburgh: University of Pittsburgh Press, 1970), chap. 7.

[34] See Harold H. Weissman, "Social Action in a Social Work Context," in Weissman, *Community Development*, p. 181.

[35] Sherry R. Arnstein, "Whom Does the Advocate Planner Serve? . . . But Which Advocate Planner?" in *The View from Below*, eds. Fainstein and Fainstein, p. 233.

[36] Milton Derber and Edwin Young, *Labor and the New Deal* (Madison: University of Wisconsin Press, 1957), p. 20.

active, to participate, in short to develop and harness the power necessary to change the prevailing patterns. "When those prominent in the status quo turn and label you an agitator, they are completely correct, for that is, in one word, your function—to agitate to the point of conflict." [37]

Silberman's discussions of Alinsky's tactics emphasizes the role of the professional organizer in building a common consciousness among previously apathetic community members. Although, as the case of PS 84 demonstrates, this function is best performed by highly involved volunteers, such individuals are frequently missing in impoverished neighborhoods. Joan of Arc presents a situation where the indigenous leadership lacked the time and skill to mobilize a following; until the Board hired George Jenkins (its organizer) it tended to await initiatives from its public rather than taking them itself. The result was inaction and a deterioration in image. After the Board's fumbled attempt to force reform in the junior high school a witness to the proceedings complained:

They looked ludicrous. They're supposed to be leaders. Why are they looking for us to tell them what to do? How can anything get done if no one is ever willing to put himself on the line to see that it gets done.

In contrast, when Jenkins saw an opportunity for a sit-in in the Superintendent's office and realized that the parent demonstrators were at a loss concerning what action to take, he immediately seized command. As one of the parents commented: "Jenkins was giving the word at the demonstration. . . . None of us did so."

The part played by the Columbia student organizers in leading the Morningside Squatters offered an instance of the complete fulfillment of the staff organizer's role. The students facilitated the move-in by lining up the participants and arranging support services for them. For a period they also acted as negotiators on behalf of the group, as well as setting up meetings, running the treasury, and seeing to building maintenance. Their endeavors to develop a cadre of leaders among the squatters succeeded, and eventually they were able to withdraw completely from their leadership function.

The role played by Jenkins at Joan of Arc, however, reflects the tensions endemic to the professional organizer's position. Foremost among them is the problematical nature of his legitimacy, which tends moreover to threaten the legitimacy of the sponsoring group. In playing a leadership role, the organizer may force others into considerable risk. Yet he is not an elected representative, and the public he is exhorting to action frequently notices that he is being paid for what they must do gratis. Successful organization evidently requires the presence of workers who receive tangible rewards in both income and career advancement from their organizing efforts. [38] The

[37] Silberman, "The Potential for Community Organization," p. 279. Internal quotations are from an interview with Saul Alinsky.

[38] Marris and Rein, in the *Dilemmas of Social Reform*, assert: "Spontaneous protest is too sporadic;

very existence of these rewards, however, makes the organizer appear self-serving and less legitimate than those who can make no private gain from their public activities. The problem is magnified when the organizer's salary comes from a source outside the community or when the organizer is also a professional in fields such as medicine, social work, or planning. The mistrust by West Oaklanders of the advocate planners employed on their behalf by Model Cities, or the board of the Denver Neighborhood Health Center of the "liberal" medical staff, was exacerbated by the outside ties of these professionals, which meant that they had divided loyalties.[39]

The organizer is usually accountable to a board or other executive body, and ultimately he can be fired. But this accountability is post hoc and not very useful for directing the organizer at the time of crisis. Many of the situations in which he finds himself require discretion and improvisation—the organizer is hired to seize opportunities. The outcome is that members of the sponsoring body lose their knowledge and control of the organization's daily functioning and become dependent on their staff. Thus, Jenkins gradually assumed the dominant role at Joan of Arc. Although he believed he should educate the community not dictate to it, he considered that his most controversial actions were educational and thus not undemocratic even though executed without consultation.

The maintenance of a paid staff has the further undesired consequence of putting community organizations in the fund-raising business. A neighborhood group can perhaps raise enough money locally to pay for supplies and the rental of an office, but staff salaries are almost always beyond its means. Even a small staff costs a great deal. The Joan of Arc Board spent nearly $40,000 in ten months, and it never funded a major service program. Much of the staff's time and energy become devoted to the search for funds, and programs are shaped to meet the demands of outside sponsors:

[The] very existence [of community action organizations] was dependent upon their ability to write proposals that reflected what their sponsors wanted to hear rather than what they were actually doing. The extraordinary adaptability of ABCD [Boston's poverty agency] demonstrated on many occasions, and the opportunism which accompanied it, were not idiosyncratic. This is the law of life for organizations of this type—organizations that lack permanent financing and assured status within some established institutional hierarchy, organizations constantly in search of patrons who will put up the money to pay the rent.[40]

Thus, while a professional organizing staff may be an essential resource

---

soon discouraged by frustration, it lacks the power of sustained bargaining. If the poor are to attract the able organizers they need, the defence of their interests must offer a career which rewards the ambitious with growing prestige and power" (p. 186).

[39] Lisa R. Peattie describes the problem for the advocate planner of deciding to whom he or she should be responsible in "Drama and Advocacy Planning," *Journal of the American Institute of Planners*, XXXVI, November, 1970, 405–10.

[40] Stephan Thernstrom, *Poverty, Planning, and Politics in the New Boston* (New York: Basic Books, 1969), p. 166. See also Marris and Rein, pp. 175, 183; Charles E. Silberman, *Crisis in Black and White* (New York: Random House, 1964), pp. 352–55.

for the development of urban political movements, it has important liabilities. Some of these drawbacks apply also to the other main strategy for achieving organizational stability—the provision of services.

service provision

A number of community organizations, including the more militant Community Action Agencies, have regarded the provision of services as a path to developing a constituency and maintaining its support. The services approach represents an effort to overcome the logical problem presented by Mancur Olson—that it is irrational for individuals to incur costs in order to obtain public goods. According to Olson an organization must attract members either through coercion (e.g. compulsory dues check-off) or selective incentives, that is, particular benefits to individuals:

An organization that did nothing except lobby to obtain a collective good for some large group would not have a source of rewards or positive selective incentives it could offer potential members. Only an organization that also sold private or noncollective products, or provided social or recreational benefits to individual members, would have a source of these positive inducements.[41]

The offering of services ranging from day-care and free breakfasts to addiction counseling and assistance with the welfare office thus constitutes the provision of selective incentives.

But the experience of a variety of organizations points to the tendency of the service function to absorb all others. In a study of neighborhood organizations established under the federal poverty program Nathan Cohen comments:

Most of these projects have had their greatest success in involving people around their interest in services, self-help, and mutual aid. The attempts to move from this level to programs of social action and protest have met with less success. . . . There is greater emphasis on seeking a personal than a collective escape.[42]

Similarly, Weissman asserts:

Low-income organizations . . . can be stabilized by social activities or by providing social services to members and others, but such stability will not necessarily lead to social action. Ultimately, if organizations of low-income people design their own programs, the organizations will devolve into a neighborhood social group with a heavy emphasis on the provision of individual services.[43]

[41] Olson, *Logic of Collective Action,* p. 133.

[42] Nathan E. Cohen, "Building a Social Movement among the Poor," in *Neighborhood Organization for Community Action,* ed. John B. Turner (New York: National Association of Social Workers, 1968), p. 56.

[43] Weissman, "Problems in Maintaining Stability in Low-Income Social Action Organizations," p. 174.

For an organization to provide services, it must have a dependable staff. Effective services depend on time, coordination, and reliability. The maintenance of this staff, as was true for an organizing staff, requires funds. Organizations offering services are thereby led into the pitfalls of the fund-raising effort described earlier. Moreover, the provision of services is extremely expensive. Besides staff, it may require the rental of space for clinics and day-care centers, the acquisition of transportation, the purchase of equipment, and the like.

The rapid increase in the budget of North Side Forces indicates the costliness of the service approach and the way in which reliance on government funding seems inevitable. North Side Forces did manage to exploit a liberal suburban constitutuency so as to maximize its independence. The fact that it was offering recreational programs and hot lunches undoubtedly appealed to the suburban donors more than a program of militant action. To this extent the service activities did not diminish the resources that might otherwise have been available for political effort. Nonetheless, the operation of the various youth and health enterprises absorbed all the time and energy of the staff, making the question of the availability of funds for other purposes academic.

The rationale of using services to mold an active following does not seem to work itself out in fact. Once individuals develop an interest in the maintenance of facilities like day-care centers they will defend their continued existence. But loyalty to the service program does not often become transferred to a more general cause. Many kinds of services, such as intercession with school or welfare authorities, are one-shot efforts, and the individuals benefiting from them do not feel bound to the organization which assisted them. Moreover few people can be serviced by relatively small, nonbureaucratized organizations. The nature of selective incentives derived from services is that they are disaggregative rather than unifying.

The services approach, then, while successful in attracting poor people to community organizations, has failed to create organizations with a political purpose. The transmutation of North Side Forces from an organization with radical objectives to an operator of programs with few political implications is typical. The offering of services by counter-institutions, while useful in itself when the institutions are flexible and responsive, is a weak mobilizing device. Ironically the activities of the government in providing services in ways found unsatisfactory by community spokesmen has proved to be a stronger force for community mobilization.

CLIENTS AND PUBLIC
SERVICE BUREAUCRACIES

The targets of urban political movements have most frequently been the urban service bureaucracies rather than ostensibly political institutions. In the first chapter we discussed the reasons why these "progressive" bureaucracies precipitated hostility among their clients, and in the last chapter we deal with the general political effects of the choice of local bureaucratic targets. Here we examine the factors in the institutional environment of the nonwhite urban lower classes which cause them to select public service bureaucracies as their targets and look at the impact which their strategies for mobilizing power have or are likely to produce at the local level.

One important reason for the concentration on bureaucratic targets is the inappropriateness of the political arena, as defined by electoral competition, for the pursuit of the kinds of remedies sought by movement leaders. The issues which rally opposition among inner-city dwellers are traditionally outside the political realm. American political parties concern themselves little with education, housing, and welfare problems. Even New York's Reform Democratic Clubs, which initially intended involvement in these areas, early had their committees on local problems atrophy.[44] The only community bodies that deal with the everyday relations between poor people and government bureaucracies are not partisan organizations but civic action groups such as housing councils, parent associations, and private social service agencies. The groups operate in a different milieu from the political parties, and individuals involved in them see little connection between electoral politics and their concerns. Leaders of urban political movements, as we indicated in Chapter Six, were participants in civic groups rather than party activists. Thus, the leadership of urban movements did not have preexisting ties with the political parties and was not inclined to look to them as effective vehicles for the expression of their interests.

The attenuated political infrastructure of most cities, resulting from the destruction of the old ward machinery by Progressive reform, means that political organizations are frequently the personal organizations of candidates, and there is often no party machinery to be captured. At-large election procedures for councilmen and huge legislative districts preclude success except for those able to mount a citywide (or in New York, boroughwide) campaign. The path of running candidates directly for office is thus difficult to follow. One reason for establishing community control as an objective is that it would create accessible political offices. In its absence, however, grass-roots organizations have mostly abstained from electoral activity.

The difficulty of winning elections is one factor in explaining why movement organizations do not run candidates for election. This obstacle, however, did not prevent radical groups in the past from forming their own party and seeking, sometimes successfully, local political offices (although it should be noted that the Socialist Party of the turn of the century was operating in the era of small electoral districts, and the costs of campaigning have increased considerably since the radical thrust of the thirties). In other countries and in the United States during other periods, the radical political party was the key institutional representation of the interests of subordinate

---

[44] See James Q. Wilson, *The Amateur Democrat* (Chicago: University of Chicago Press, 1962), Chapters Five and Seven; and Joseph Lyford, *The Airtight Cage* (New York: Harper & Row, 1966), Chapter Seven.

groups pressing for changes in the social system.[45] But contemporary urban radicals are largely too pessimistic to place their hopes in a political party pledged to overhauling American society. Adherence to a party as an organizational weapon when that party has no immediate prospect of victory requires a high level of ideological commitment and faith in ultimate triumph. The pragmatism and concentration on local issues characteristic of urban political movements precludes the sort of appeal that could build an ideological party.

Albert Hirschman, in a discussion of the strategies available to clients of declining institutions, asserts that they have a choice between "exit" and "voice." [46] Exiting means taking one's business elsewhere; voice refers to articulating demands for change. In theory the political party should be the vehicle through which a movement can most effectively exercise its voice:

Because of the weak organization of the [political] movement, it tends to be very fragile, breaking up when some of its primary objectives have been accomplished. It is in the transformation of the movement into a party . . . [that] political leaders in movements [seek] to transform the restless sweep of public energy, liberated by and flooding through the political sector of social life, into something more stable and permanent.[47]

The American political tradition, however, is hostile to programmatic or ideological parties.[48] Despite some precedents for leftist third parties, urban radicals face a system of political institutions which both structurally discourages the formation of new ideological parties and depicts them as absurd if impotent or mortally dangerous if even mildly successful.[49]

[45] The main successes of the Socialist Party in the United States were at the local level. In the decade 1911–1920 Socialist candidates won elections for mayor or other major municipal offices in 174 cities and towns, including Berkeley, Schenectady, Milwaukee, and Minneapolis. The same decade saw the election of 150 Socialist state legislators. James Weinstein, *The Decline of Socialism in America, 1912–1925* (New York: Random House, 1967), pp. 116–18. In contrast, there is to our knowledge only one professed radical, Congressman Ron Dellums of California, holding a major political office in the United States today.

[46] Albert O. Hirschman, *Exit, Voice, and Loyalty* (Cambridge: Harvard University Press, 1970), Chap. 1.

[47] David Apter, *The Politics of Modernization* (Chicago: University of Chicago Press, 1965), pp. 205–6.

[48] William N. Chambers identifies the American liberal tradition, its relative economic abundance, and "an ingrained pragmatic tendency" as the basic factors which "make American politics less oriented to ideology than the politics of many other nations, and American parties less significant in performing continuing policy-making functions than parties elsewhere." He argues also that these factors inhibited the development of third parties. William N. Chambers, "Party Development and the American Mainstream," in *The American Party Systems,* eds. William N. Chambers and Walter Dean Burnham (New York: Oxford University Press, 1967), p. 28.

[49] Louis Hartz notes: "The American liberal community contained far fewer radicals than any other Western society but the hysteria against them was much vaster than anywhere else." He observes that the absolutism of American liberalism, when confronted with the Communist menace, caused deportation of radicals to be an instinctive reaction: "After all in a land where Communism is truly 'alien,' what is more sensible than to get rid of it simply by throwing out

thout the option of voice within the regular political arena, urban
s are left only with the power to exit—that is, to act as a voting bloc
to whichever major party most accedes to their demands. This has
largely been the strategy of the American trade union leadership. But as in
any market situation the use of exit to insure responsiveness to the consumer
requires effective competition among "producers." Given the absence of
ideological conflict between the major parties, and in fact, the lack of any
party competition in most American cities, the threat of exit becomes a weak
one.

The exit strategy is particularly ineffective as a way of influencing the
public bureaucracies that are the primary targets of urban political
movements. The clients of these bureaucracies cannot exit in the sense of
removing themselves from their jurisdictions. Nor can they employ the
electoral form of exit to force bureaucratic change. The classical model of
bureaucratic control in a democratic society portrays bureaucracies as
governed from the top by political appointees who are themselves ultimately
responsible to the electorate. But a combination of inertia, job tenure, and
civil service regulations means that, even if bureaucratic clients could,
through electoral power, change the people at the top, political control of the
bureaucracies is too remote for such changes to make a vast difference at the
bottom where the interface between client and organization is located.[50]

The direction taken by militant organizers of the poor has been
determined by a variety of historical factors operating at the national and
local levels. For the moment we are concerned only with those inputs which
affect local activities and which establish the constraints governing the
specific choices made by would-be leaders within inner-city communities.
Here the overriding factors which have shaped their efforts have been their
low potential effectiveness in the arena of party competition, both as a power
within the regular parties and as a third force; and their sensitivity to the
policies followed by public and quasi-public providers of services, making
these agencies both most immediately responsible for their plight and also
most susceptible to their demands. The choice of mainly bureaucratic targets,
however, limits the strategies available to urban political movements. The
following discussion focuses on the causes for the apparent lack of responsiveness of urban bureaucracies, especially as exemplified in the educational
system, and looks at the ways in which outside pressure can produce changes
in organizational behavior.

---

the men who brought it over." Louis Hartz, *The Liberal Tradition in America* (New York:
Harcourt, Brace & World, 1955), pp. 300, 201. In the case of black militants, where
deportation is largely not an option, a form of internal ostracism seems to occur. There is
simply no place for them within the political framework. Even the remnants of the old radical
political parties—the Communist and Socialist Parties—have not made the black struggle
their own. And significantly, physical exile has been the fate of many Black Panther Party
leaders.

[50] Marris and Rein, in the epilogue to the second edition of *Dilemmas of Social Reform* (p. 277)
identify this problem of political communication as the most obviously frustrating flaw of the
social service structure.

client groups
and institutional change

There are two important and differing explanations of the failure of public bureaucracies to innovate. The first explains bureaucratic stasis in terms of the latent functions it serves for dominant strata in the society as a whole:

Bureaucracy . . . can be taken to reflect the interests of the dominant social classes. The apparent irrelevance of social services, judged by the needs of the poor, could have a harsher explanation than the devotion to ritual of organization men. It may suit the needs of the middle classes, whose well-being would be threatened by more generous and effective service to the poor.[51]

According to this explanation, bureaucratic outcomes result from the distribution of interests and power in society, with the benefits of social policy accruing to those who control power resources. Because the poor have few resources at their disposal, they are relatively unable to command benefits from government.

The alternative explanation for bureaucratic incapacity is specific to the nature of governmental organization. While this explanation is sometimes used to supplant the first, the two are not contradictory, and there is good reason to suppose that both operate. According to this second mode of thought, the determining factor which diverts governmental bureaucracies from concentrating on producing outputs acceptable to their clienteles is the absence of bankruptcy as a consequence of malfunction. Public enterprise is largely exempt from the negative sanction of diminishing profit or financial demise caused by the exit of dissatisfied customers; in other words, public bureaucracies are free of market constraints.[52] Indeed, innovation is often irrational for members of public bureaucracies, since it usually leads to dislocation within the organization:

Ritualism in such a context, if one considers the actor's frame of reference and not the whole organization, must be viewed as conformity to what is expected from him and

---

[51] Ibid., p. 45.

[52] In a study of a large county social welfare agency W. Richard Scott observes:

> The client's interests did not always take precedence, because the [social] worker was under considerable pressure to follow supervisory directives, and all his decisions were expected to conform to federal, state, county, and agency regulations. In a very real sense, the client's interests were defined in large part by the agency. It is true that clients were "free" to refuse to follow the directives of their case-worker, but to do so was to forfeit their claim to assistance. And, unlike the more traditional professional-client relationship, the client did not have the option of turning to another professional: the agency possessed a monopoly in the dispensing of public welfare funds and services.

"Professional Employees in a Bureaucratic Structure: Social Work," in *The Semi-Professions and Their Organization*, ed. Amitai Etzioni (New York: Free Press, 1969), pp. 126–27.

no longer as over-conformity. It is the rational response and not a "professional deformation." [53]

Instead of the reward system of the market, there is a different mechanism of rewards and punishments that places a premium on risk avoidance. The existence of job security and the absence of the profit motive mean that the "customers" of the bureaucracy have no sanctions over its personnel. On the other hand, the bureaucrat is motivated by a desire to get along with his associates and to advance up the administrative hierarchy; thus peers and administrative superiors become significant reference groups for him.[54] Innovation in private industry normally occurs because enterprising individuals are willing to take risks in the hope of future gains (industries that are so large as to control their market display risk avoidance characteristics similar to those in public bureaucracies). But in public administration, the likelihood of future gains for individuals who press for change is very small.

It is important to remember that *systems* do not adapt to changing circumstances, that adaptations are brought about *by people*. Thus, when one speaks about responsive structures, one really means structures which provide both incentives for change and leverage such that it is possible for individuals in key positions to affect the system. As we have already discussed, public bureaucracies offer few such incentives. In addition, there are few positions within the organizational hierarchy with sufficient power to bring about change. The presence of a centralized authority in most municipal systems does not mean that the highest echelons have the power to reorganize the system. On the one hand, the infusion of additional resources and major changes in institutional structure require legislative action. On the other, control over agency employees is really quite weak. Virtually all subordinate employees have guaranteed tenure; promotion is largely according to seniority, credentials, and the passing of exams; and many middle-level personnel are in crucial positions that permit them to control the flow of information concerning program implementation. Thus, even in very highly centralized organizations, the paradox of authority described by Crozier applies:

This centralization of authority . . . seems associated with the whittling away of the content of authority; everything seems to be in the hands of the director, who is the only one whose power is legitimate. Yet, although his authority may be considered

---

[53] Michel Crozier, *The Bureaucratic Phenomenon* (Chicago: University of Chicago Press, 1964), p. 199.

[54] See Michael Lipsky, "Toward a Theory of Street-Level Bureaucracy," paper presented at the annual meeting of the American Political Science Association, September 1969. Lipsky asserts that even though the "street-level bureaucrat" is in day-to-day contact with his clients, they are not as significant agents of socialization into the bureaucratic role as are other members of the bureaucracy. Two books, Gerald Levy, *Ghetto School* (New York: Bobbs-Merrill, 1970) and Estelle Fuchs, *Teachers Talk* (Garden City, N.Y.: Doubleday, 1969), describe the process by which idealistic teachers succumb to ritualism and cynicism. See also Crozier, *The Bureaucratic Phenomenon*, p. 191.

absolute, he is in most cases helpless, and the amount of actual control he can exercise is extremely small.[55]

We see then that in addition to general social interests and social values that militate against improvements in services for minority groups, we can identify a number of factors inherent in centralized public bureaucratic structures that severely inhibit innovative behavior. Responsiveness is discouraged by the recruitment into civil service jobs of people with high risk avoidance; the socialization of new recruits by socializing agents with little interest in change; the lack of material incentives for innovation; and the structural rigidities of a system where no level has the power to affect other levels of the organization profoundly.

The forceful intervention of clients destabilizes a bureaucracy's informal normative structure. Clients can change little directly themselves, and a united bureaucracy determined to resist their attack through the use of every available strategy is usually invulnerable. Crisis, however, forces administrators to evaluate consciously those practices which they have followed habitually; it may become rational, in terms of bureaucratic survival, to do something rather than nothing, and even doing nothing now requires some thought. Most important, from the viewpoint of those within the bureaucracy clients become a third party in relation to their own internal struggles just as, from the outside, sympathizers within the bureaucracy become a potential resource for client groups. Thus, for those bureaucrats who are constrained by extant institutional norms and have remained suppressed dissidents, or for those who seek scope for professional experimentation, the presence of an active client movement may facilitate breaking away from old routines, as some of our case studies show.

Dissatisfaction with old methods was expressed by a number of teachers and supervisors actively involved with the movement for community control of schools. The central focus of these school personnel was what happened in the classroom, and their principal emphasis was on the need to enlarge the leeway of school staff to innovate educationally. They did not give up their belief in the dominance of professionals in determining school policy, but, as one teacher asserted:

To make needed changes in East Harlem, you have to have an organization such as the IS 201 Board. But the Board right now can only make changes if it operates extra-legally. . . . The principal barrier to change is the traditionalists. These are people in power who are making their reputations on existing methods. The lesson of last year is that if you want to do something, you have to go ahead and do it.[56]

The success of the parent movement at PS 84 resulted from an alliance between teachers seeking pedagogical freedom and parents desiring both a new educational program and a new system of power within the school. The process of organizational change at 84 began with a split within the

---

[55] Crozier, *The Bureaucratic Phenomenon,* p. 81.

[56] Unless otherwise indicated, all quoted statements are from interviews with the authors.

professional staff and a subsequent polarization which encouraged a number of teachers to become converted to the cause of the initial rebels. The destabilized situation in the school and the collapse of old norms and patterns of authority gave freedom to entrepreneurial types among the professionals. The entrepreneurial role was played partly by members of the regular school staff, but most forcefully by Lillian Samson, the consultant hired to institute informal classroom methods. Within the fluid situation presented by PS 84, Professor Samson used the carrot of state aid and the stick of parental and staff rebellion as backing in her bid for additional support from the administration. She provided assistance to teachers so that they could transform their initially timid experiments into full-fledged innovations. She sold her product skillfully, so that teachers and parents, matching her enthusiasm, were willing to devote enormous time and energy to making the new classroom techniques work. Her activities exemplified the general model of the administrative change agent who designs strategies to enlarge his or her resource base so as to effect fundamental change.

As power within the school shifted to the innovating teachers and their parent allies, resisting elements in the staff either were forced to leave the school, departed of their own accord, or succumbed to the new set of norms. Neutral teachers, now that deference to parents and informal educational methods were officially sanctioned, began to adopt the new modes. The change in the constellation of vested interests, such that traditional patterns of behavior were no longer in congruence with patterns of psychological or material rewards and punishments, meant that diffusion of innovation could take place without hindrance.[57]

According to the diffusion model, change comes about when individuals emulate innovations that they see operating successfully elsewhere. Diffusion begins to take place when adopting a new mode of action no longer involves much risk—results are fairly predictable, and opposition to change is not severe. At PS 84 a majority of the teachers in the school began to employ open classroom methods once the new, community-selected principal took office, even if they were not formally part of the infant school program. Thus, the adoption of change "on its merits" began to operate once the social supports for the old system disintegrated, and new supports took root. The merits of the change became clearer to most teachers as social rewards began to be associated with adopting the new methods, rather than with maintaining the status quo.

At the district level[58] the various parent movements had succeeded in precipitating the resignation of the district superintendent. His replacement, Dr. Hammer, was able to overcome the obstacles, related earlier, to change from the top for two reasons. First, Hammer saw his appointment as a temporary one intended to shake things up. Thus, he made no effort to

[57] See Everett M. Rogers, *The Diffusion of Innovation* (New York: Free Press, 1962), esp. chaps. 2 and 7.

[58] In this context it is important to remember that the size of a local school district in New York City approximated that of the entire school system of Syracuse.

develop the kinds of relationships with unwilling subordinates that would be necessary if he were to remain in the post for the long run. He was willing to expend all his capital at once because his was a one-shot effort. Second, he went directly to parents for support in his circumvention of normal personnel procedures in appointing acting principals throughout the district. The acting principals, because of their tenuous position and because they were originally beholden to parent groups for their appointment, continued to regard clients as an important constituency. The result of original parent mobilization was the establishment of parents as an important reference group and a resource for the activist Superintendent to use in maintaining his control.

Similar interactive processes between clients and professionals occurred at Lincoln Hospital, where the ongoing thrust for change remained centered in the staff. At IS 201, teachers who served on the Governing Board reported that it was their initial interest in classroom experimentation that caused them to become active in the district. A teacher who was hired by the district when it was first designated as an experimental complex recalled her motives in teaching there and then becoming involved in the movement for community control:

I took a teaching job in 201 because I knew I could not function in a traditional school. Once I got there I went to lectures on the experimental district. I didn't *want* to be on the Governing Board, but I disagreed with the policy stands of the teacher candidate from 201, and I decided to run against her. . . . My greatest satisfaction has been working with parents in a close situation and realizing that despite differences in outlook and education, it is very possible as black people to put aside personal differences and work toward a common goal.

Another black, long-time teacher in the 201 district, who had previously participated only in conservative professional associations, commented on her Governing Board experience:

I was in my own little shell before. I just rode through the community on my way home to the Riverton Apartments [a Harlem middle-income apartment complex]. As a Governing Board member I really got into the community. . . . I joined the Governing Board because there was nothing relevant under the old system. Schools had to have personnel who were closer to the children, mentally and physically. . . . Now teachers have much more freedom to try out new things. The principals encourage experimentation. . . . I didn't know how much politics there was in education. . . . I didn't know that things weren't done according to rules, that pressure and influence could bring extra money. I am practically a revolutionary now.

Thus a political movement can alter the bureaucratic environment sufficiently both to change the consciousness of personnel and to provide strategic resources for innovators within the bureaucratic hierarchy. The success of the movement depends upon at least a few individuals within the bureaucracy responding to the altered organizational environment and splitting from the old guard. A process may then be set in motion whereby entrepreneurial types seize opportunities for innovation, opponents of change are forced out of their positions or bypassed, recruitment of new personnel attracts individuals seeking less traditional posts, and new attitudes and modes of behavior diffuse among the previously uninvolved.

Short of extensive democratization of bureaucratic institutions, bureaucratic change cannot be a simple response to pressures from beneath. There is no reason to assume that bureaucrats will react constructively to a crisis created by client rebelliousness; it is quite likely that they will respond with panic, defensiveness, and symbolic gestures. The key role of client groups in forcing change is to provide resources for those among professional cadres who are willing to risk new ways of doing things but are thwarted by organizational sanctions. The availability of a power resource in the form of a mobilized client group, however, does not guarantee that anyone will wish to use it or can use it effectively. Thus, while one can explain some examples of bureaucratic change ex post facto by pointing to the effect of grass-roots activity, one cannot predict that similar future efforts will necessarily produce a desired response.

The strategies and targets selected by urban political movements mean that the impact of their mobilizing efforts depends primarily on the activities of bureaucratic personnel and only ultimately on the policies of those officially entrusted with political decisionmaking. The examples of movements for community control of education and health indicate that grassroots mobilization can cause institutional change by concentrating on proximate local targets. The diversion of energy into these channels, however, results in the disaggregation of political demands and the limiting of national effects. Nevertheless, it is questionable whether, given the strategic alternatives of urban political movements, their ideology, and their recruitment basis, a more concerted form of action is possible.

a functional
assessment

8

Urban political movements are vehicles by which minority groups have attempted to address their social problems through collective political action. Movements have sought to act as agents of political socialization, as interest articulators, and as means of creating and utilizing power. Each of these functions is also performed by routine or normal institutions in a liberal-democratic society—by political parties, electoral competition, and legislative bodies. The existence of urban movements and the reasons given by members for participation, however, attest to the inadequacy of routine political institutions for serving the needs of urban minority groups. Urban movements have constituted an attempt by minority group activists to perform functions which other institutional forms have served inadequately.

The rise of urban movements should not be interpreted as necessary or inevitable. While all lasting structural forms are maintained in part because they are functional for at least some set of actors, many needs are unfulfilled or performed badly by available social and political structures. The political needs of urban minority groups were not well served prior to the rise of movements in the 1960s. The appearance of movements was not only a result of minority group perception that new forms had to be created; it also resulted from forces outside the control of movement leaders. Thus, the interpretation that movements fulfill functions not being served by other institutions should be freed from any teleological implications.

In addition, the identification of the functions which movement structures perform for minority groups does not tell us how well movements actually do fulfill these functions. Urban movements are limited in their effectiveness because of their own characteristics and because of the larger political situation within which they must operate. Indeed, under present circumstances no political structures are likely to serve the needs of urban minorities very well since these collectivities are triply plagued by low income and class standing, by being racially outcast, and not least, by constituting an electoral minority in a democratic system.

A basic institutional vehicle for linking the activities of government with the needs, demands, and interests of particular collectivities is, according to modern democratic theory, the political party. The party is the instrument which rationalizes the process of elections in large societies by recruiting candidates, defining policy positions, and orchestrating the activities of elected representatives both within the legislature and between it and the executive. The importance of the party is especially great for collectivities whose members are relatively powerless as individuals, since the party is the institutionalized means for converting numbers into power. The mere existence of parties does not, however, mean that they in fact perform the functions which, in theory, they might. *The failure of the American political parties and the choices they make available at times of election to reflect the needs of urban minority groups is one of the functional voids which urban movements have sought to occupy.*

Since urban minority groups are, as the name implies, national minorities, we might expect their needs to be advanced by a national party in which they were united with a larger group on the basis of class interest. This party would attempt to minimize racial and ethnic differences, reconcile conflicting interests among its various constituencies, and direct national governmental policy in an egalitarian and welfare-state direction. Of course, this is an idealization of how the party would function, especially in the face of considerable ethnic and racial divisions within the lower strata. But we should not forget that the absence of an effective socialist party in the American experience has, itself, eliminated an institutional source of propaganda and leadership which might have changed the major polarities in the direction of class division. As we have previously discussed, the present American party system includes no socialist alternative of more than trivial strength:

Nothing, indeed, is clearer than that the two major American parties are and always have been overwhelmingly middle-class in organization, values, and goals. From a European point of view, they can hardly fail to appear exquisitely old-fashioned, as nineteenth-century anachronisms.[1]

America had the first developed democratic party system in the world. By about 1840 the national parties had assumed their current form. But the American parties did not move in the direction of the mass-membership, programmatic parties which evolved in Europe toward the end of the nineteenth century. This, in effect, is equivalent to saying that a powerful socialist party never emerged here, for the left-wing European parties had a considerable influence in making center and right-wing parties more popularly rooted and programmatic. The course of historical evolution of the

[1] Walter Dean Burnham, "Party Systems and the Political Process," in *The American Party Systems,* eds. William Nisbet Chambers and Walter Dean Burnham (New York: Oxford University Press, 1967), pp. 280–81.

American parties has led a number of analysts to speak of their "arrested development" and their failure to function as a regularized mechanism of linkage between ordinary citizens and their government. In particular, the parties have not offered policy alternatives addressing the problems which have arisen as a result of the major social trends of this century—industrialization, urbanization, the emergence of an estranged nonwhite minority, and the decline in significance of legislative bodies in the face of growing bureaucracies, both public and private. Lowi makes the case—perhaps a bit too strongly—when he concludes:

> It is as though parties, having no institutional involvement with public policy, were under no pressure to alter the system in ways which each new public problem might require. In fact, the existing system can be presumed to be a vested interest of party leaders.[2]

The limited ability of the major American parties to represent the interests of the lower classes in the national government is replicated at the local level. Here it might be more appropriate to speak of retrogression and not merely arrested development. The political machine did provide linkages between the urban masses and city hall, even though machine structures were incapable of advancing programs or of acting in the collective interest of the people whose votes were a source of machine power. The institutional reforms of the first decades of the century destroyed the party infrastructure which integrated city neighborhoods into the decisionmaking process. The machines which functioned so as to deter the mobilization of the lower classes were largely replaced by Progressive institutions which altogether proscribed any mass input into local government. The social composition of urban political elites shifted in favor of the educated and professional classes. This was the case in city councils, school boards and the management of various service bureaucracies. The dual concomitants of Progressive reform were thus the insulation of the governmental center from the neighborhoods and the hegemony over the center by the middle class. As Samuel Hays puts it, "One observes a gradual exclusion of local community leaders from the decision-making process which, in turn, involved a gradual exclusion of direct representatives of lower socio-economic groups."[3] The rise of Progressive institutions meant that "a functional system of representation in a cosmopolitan upper-middle-class context had replaced a geographical system of representation which had involved leaders from all segments of the . . . socio-economic structure."[4]

---

[2] Theodore J. Lowi, "Party, Policy, and Constitution in America," in *The American Party Systems*, eds. Chambers and Burnham, p. 275. Internal reference is to Samuel P. Huntington, "Political Modernization: America versus Europe," Paper presented at the Annual Meeting of the American Political Science Association, Washington, D.C., 1965.

[3] Samuel P. Hays, "Political Parties and the Community-Society Continuum," in *The American Party Systems*, eds. Chambers and Burnham, p. 180. Also see Hays' article, "The Politics of Reform in Municipal Government in the Progressive Era," *Pacific Northwest Quarterly*, LV, (1964), 157–69.

[4] Hays, "Political Parties," p. 181.

In many cities Progressive reform eliminated the electoral functions of the political parties by instituting nonpartisan elections. But even where elections continued to be partisan, the parties did not integrate the new urban masses into the local political system. Urban minority groups in particular tend to be underrepresented both as individuals in the party leadership and as collectivities in party programs.[5] Those who benefit most directly from the party organizations are the cadres of those organizations and other already powerful groups.

The failure of urban minorities to find their interests represented in government is aggravated by the atrophy of the legislative branch of government in relation to the executive. The rise of great, centralized bureaucracies accountable in only remote ways to elected representatives means that party and electoral institutions cannot control the emergent centers of power. There is an absence of representative institutional forms which operate directly on the behavior of urban bureaucracies. Bureaucratic structures have tended to be controlled internally rather than by the mayor's office or city council. What we see in American cities is not only a partisan politics which is not functional for urban minorities but one which is increasingly irrelevant to the actual sources of power. The universalistic bureaucracies which the Progressives hoped would put an end to undemocratic, personalistic politics have themselves moved beyond the control of normal political structures. *Representation of the interests of bureaucratic clients directly within urban agencies (not just indirectly through influence on elected officials) constitutes a second function which has not been adequately performed for urban minority groups and which movements have attempted to serve.*

A description of the functions unfilled by extant political institutions cannot in itself describe the mechanisms which bring new structures into being. Throughout this study we have tried to show the forces which have led individuals to create the structural forms we call movements. Moreover, functional analysis tends to take needs for granted, or at least to view them as things which adhere in social arrangements rather than being themselves highly variable and defined by consciousness and ideology. Thus, the increased solidarity of blacks and Latins as social groups and their expectations of being represented in local government and of benefiting from its policies created the needs which existing institutional mechanisms could not serve. Movement leaders have sought to develop a consciousness among minority groups that would create increased demands on governmental institutions, undermine their legitimacy in the eyes of blacks and Latins, and show the rationality of movement activity. Political leaders, in other words, work to develop the needs which old structures then cannot serve and to themselves supply the new structures which can serve them. Since these new structures are political movements dependent upon mobilization and collective action, the process of creating needs and structures occurs simultaneously. For this reason ideas and consciousness are crucial factors in accounting for the rise of new forms.

[5] Michael Parenti, "Power and Pluralism: A View from the Bottom," *The Journal of Politics*, XXXII, (1970), 528, discusses the failure of political parties in Newark to represent the poor.

Accepting the argument that urban movements function to serve unfulfilled needs—with the aforementioned caveats on functional analyses— we should like to know the ways in which they do so and with what effect. The next sections consider urban movements in their functions of representation or interest articulation, and of interest aggregation or vehicles for mobilizing power and pressing claims on governments. In addition, urban movements will be placed within the context of the American political tradition as we consider the historical forces which have given rise to movements and the potential of urban movements as a remedy to the situation of urban minorities.

URBAN MOVEMENTS AS NEW
STRUCTURAL FORMS: DO THEY
REPRESENT THEIR CONSTITUENCIES?

Representation is a function performed by political structures which articulate the interests of their constituencies. The function of representation is to link society with the state or, put in somewhat different terms, social masses with political elites. The precise nature of the representative function in both its normative and empirical senses has long been one of the central concerns of political theory. Here, we will only consider quite briefly the ways in which a structural form may be said to be representative and then ask whether urban movements can and do perform different types of representative functions.

Hanna Pitkin in *The Concept of Representation*[6] provides a useful classificatory schema for the several dimensions or aspects of the representative function. She distinguishes among:

1. *Formal representation,* meaning that one is a representative by virtue of the position one occupies or the election procedure to which one submits. This view of representation specifies nothing about the behavior of the representative while in office. "Within the limits of his authority, anything that a man does is representing. . . ."[7] Through an act of election, or selection by an elected official, the public entrusts itself to the representative's judgment. Both an initial, mandating appointment and a method for calling the representative to account after some term in office are necessary for formal representation.

2. *Descriptive representation,* meaning the representative is like his constituency. "[Representing] depends on the representative's social characteristics, on what he *is* or is like. . . ."[8]

3. *Symbolic representation,* meaning the representative is an object of identification for his

[6] Hanna F. Pitkin, *The Concept of Representation* (Berkeley: University of California Press, 1967). Robert Lyke applies Pitkin's schema to the movement for community control of education in his article, "Representation and Urban School Boards," in *Community Control of Schools,* ed. Henry M. Levin, (Washington, D.C.: Brookings Institution, 1970).

[7] Ibid., p. 39.

[8] Ibid., p. 61.

constituency. "A political representative is to be understood on the model of a flag representing the nation. . . ."[9] An example of an almost purely symbolic representative would be Adam Clayton Powell during the term when, because of congressional action, he was never physically present in Washington. Symbolic representation involves "emotional, affective, irrational psychological responses."[10]

4. *Substantive representation,* meaning that the representative acts for his constituency. The representative is acting on behalf of his constituents when he is either doing what they want or what is best for them, in terms of their interests.[11] There are thus two dimensions of substantive representation, which may sometimes be in conflict: (1) mandated representation[12] and (2) interest representation.

Only urban movements which have arisen from elected bodies provide *formal representation.* The demonstration district and Joan of Arc governing boards, target area organizations of the Community Action Program, the Parent Association Executive Board at PS 84 are examples of movement organizations which received the mandate of a formal election. Even in these cases, however, we may ask if the mandate was for the status of movement leader, or for one which became transformed in such a direction after occupancy. Because the nature of office was frequently unclear at the time of election, the second condition of formal representation, the presence of a mechanism of accountability, is especially significant. There have been few situations, however, in which political movements have lasted long enough for leaders chosen once through elections to stand again. Among our cases this happened only at PS 84. Most urban movements probably do not have well defined mechanisms for establishing a mandate and maintaining accountability, so that in general, movements are not formally representative of larger constituencies.

This fact must be evaluated within the larger context of competing institutions. Relatively few local officials are elected. While most governmental employees are in some way accountable to such officials, accountability may be attenuated to the point of nonexistence for bureaucrats fully protected by civil service regulations. In fact, civil servants almost always oppose the creation of institutional structures intended to produce formal representativeness—witness, for example, the extreme antagonism of the police to the establishment of civilian review boards. Most bureaucrats are not formally representative of any constituency, whether the citizens of a city, their clients, or the residents of the geographical area they serve; however minimal the formal representativeness of urban movements, their bureaucratic targets are even less representative in this sense.

The evidence presented in Chapter Six regarding the social attributes of movement participants and their relationship to their communities may be viewed from the perspective of *descriptive representation.* Our general finding is

[9] Ibid., p. 92.

[10] Ibid., p. 100.

[11] Ibid., p. 145.

[12] The distinction between these two dimensions of substantive representation and the terms mandated and interest are our own.

that movement activists have been similar to their nonactivist neighbors in social background characteristics. Although there has been some creaming in the recruitment of movement leaders, its actual extent seems quite small. Compared with the recruitment pattern of elected officials and bureaucrats, urban movements have been more descriptively representative of minority group constituencies. As we noted earlier, nonwhites have been unable to use elections to place individuals with similar social attributes into office; nor do incumbents of administrative positions represent minorities proportionate to their number in the general population. This applies not only for agency heads and highly educated professionals but also for policemen, building inspectors and other "street level" bureaucrats.

The greater descriptive representativeness of urban movements than other governmental structures means that representatives with social backgrounds similar to those of their constituents will tend to act more on their behalf than will individuals with contrasting backgrounds. This is especially true when representatives interact daily with their constituents, have similar life styles, occupy similar statuses—in short, have the same structurally based interests as those they would represent. While descriptive representation does not necessarily assure responsiveness, the presumption is that it increases its likelihood. This presumption underlies the efforts of urban radicals to achieve community control. We have found little in urban movements themselves to suggest that movement leaders have become separated from their constituencies. Their descriptive representativeness has, indeed, contributed to the functionality of movement structures in articulating the interests of urban minority groups, although it has limited their access to high levels of decisionmaking where they have little established entrée.

Pitkin's third dimension of *symbolic representation* reflects the function of the representative as an object of identification and symbolic attachment. Urban movements usually function in this way, and many of their slogans—black power, community control—as well as their leaders and tactics have stood for the aspirations and psychological needs of nonwhite constituencies. Surely the day has passed in which machine politicians like William Dawson can be viewed as the prime example of symbolic representation for blacks, although the leaders who hustle the white power structure and reap great personal gain may still be symbolically representative of at least some blacks. Deciding how well each of these alternatives, collective movement and individual hustler, function to represent minority groups symbolically, brings us to the empirical problem of actually employing this dimension and to some difficulties of functional analysis itself.

Beyond the use of plausible assertions, the only way to determine how well several alternative structures or objects function as symbolic representatives is either to use survey research to examine the identifications of a particular collectivity or to accept collective mobilization, voting for a candidate, or some other behavior as indicative of functionality. The first course, besides being difficult to carry out empirically, does not distinguish symbolic from other forms of representation. The second course is theoretically confused, since leaders and movements are not passive objects. Ideas and leaders function to make particular structural statuses salient to members of collectivities, to determine the social bases of their identifications. To cite an example, the movement leaders at PS 84 altered the social identifications of parents and professionals so that the major structural polarity became pro-versus anti-community control. At the same time they functioned as symbolic representatives of the forces for community control. In other words, they created the needs which they then fulfilled. Urban political movements as emergent structural forms have functioned to transform the consciousness of nonwhite collectivites and to diffuse political beliefs which in turn have made them symbolically representative of many nonwhites.

The most important question we must address here is the degree to which movements have functioned as *substantive representatives* of what minorities want (*mandated representation*) and of what their social situation implies they should want (*interest representation*). As we indicated above, surveys of constituents (or better, potential constituents) are the most appropriate way to answer the question of how well urban movements function as mandated representatives of nonwhite collectivities. Unfortunately, not much work has been done along these lines. The most sophisticated research to date was carried out by Rossi and his associates.[13] Their findings provide a good deal of evidence about the loss of legitimacy of public service bureaucracies, but tell us little about attitudes toward urban movements or toward their program of community control.

We do have available, however, two sources of information which are germane to the question of mandated representation. The first is a study of resident attitudes toward the public schools and community control of schools in the Ocean Hill-Brownsville district at two points in time: in 1968 a year after the demonstration districts began to operate, and in 1970 when they were about to be eliminated. The second study is of neighborhood residents and community leaders in seven areas of New York City. It uses longitudinal survey research to examine directly many of the questions of representation we have been considering. Since this study is at a preliminary stage, we will only be able to present some limited data from a sample of residents in two areas of Brooklyn. The findings of both the Ocean Hill and New York neighborhood study, while by no means conclusive, do support the conclusion that urban movements have functioned as mandated representatives and have fulfilled needs for minority groups not now being served by other structures.

Two surveys indicate both that the movement for community control of schools represented the expressed will of the majority of parents in Ocean Hill-Brownsville and that support for it increased between 1968 and 1970. The first survey was a random sample of 212 parents with quotas from each of the schools in the district. The results were published in the Niemeyer Report.[14] The second survey was similarly drawn, included 214 parents, and

---

[13] These findings were presented in Chapter One, p. 4.

[14] Advisory and Evaluation Committee on Decentralization to the Board of Education of the City of New York ("Niemeyer Committee"), "An Evaluative Study of the Process of School

was conducted by the National Opinion Research Center of the University of Chicago (NORC).[15] Questions on the NORC survey were intended to repeat some of those asked two years earlier in order to approximate a longitudinal study. While we do not know how many of the individuals who comprised the 1970 sample were also polled in 1968, examination of both sets of parents indicates a high degree of similarity in social background characteristics.[16]

Several of the questions on the surveys were designed to discover whether parents found the administration of the demonstration district more responsive to the community than the regular educational hierarchy. One item, asked on the 1970 but not on the 1968 questionnaire, inquired:

In general, do you think that the [Board of Education downtown/local Governing Board] tries to do what most of the parents in this district want, what only some parents want, or acts pretty much on its own?

A majority regarded the local governing board as representing the wishes of most parents; and only 15 percent considered that it acted on its own. The figures were almost reversed for the Board of Education. (See Table 8-1.)

Table 8-1

Parent Assessment of Representative Nature of School Officials (Ocean Hill-Brownsville, 1970)

	NEW YORK BOARD OF EDUCATION (in percent)	LOCAL GOVERNING BOARD (in percent)
What most district parents want	22	50
What only some parents want	24	30
Acts on its own	47	15
Not sure	7	5

Decentralization in New York City," mimeo, July 30, 1968, chap. 4. The Institute for Community Studies of Sarah Lawrence College conducted the survey in cooperation with Louis Harris and Associates. The interviewing was apparently done in May-June, 1968, after the Ocean Hill Governing Board had ordered the involuntary transfer of thirteen teachers and six supervisors.

[15] This study was directed by the Institute for Community Studies of Queens College. Some of the survey data is presented in a publication of the Institute: Frances Gottfried, "A Survey of Parental Views of the Ocean Hill-Brownsville Experiment," *Community Issues*, II, October, 1970. However, our figures are taken directly from the original marginals provided by NORC.

[16] Seventy-one percent of the 1968 sample and 80 percent of the 1970 sample were black, with 24 and 16, respectively, Puerto Rican; 68 percent of the 1968 sample had completed less than eleven grades of school (29 percent less than nine) while 70 percent of the 1970 sample had been similarly educated (26 percent completed less than nine years); 54 percent of the first sample and 57 percent of the second had income of less than $5,000.

The following item was asked on both surveys:

If you were concerned about a school problem and contacted [the New York City Board of Education/Local Governing Board/Unit Administrator] yourself, do you think they would try to do anything about it, would listen but try to avoid doing anything, or would pretty much ignore you and try to dismiss you as soon as possible?

There are striking differences between the 1968 and 1970 polls in the assessment of responsiveness of the local governing board. Approximately three quarters of the respondents in the second survey (as opposed to about half in the first) felt that these local officials would try to help them. In contrast, only about 30 percent in either poll gave the same evaluation of the Board of Education. (Table 8-2.) Virtually no one felt that he would be completely ignored by local officials, while about a quarter of the respondents felt they would be ignored by the Board of Education.

Table 8-2

Assessment of Responsiveness of School Officials by Ocean Hill-Brownsville Parents

	NEW YORK CITY BOARD OF EDUCATION (in percent)		LOCAL GOVERNING BOARD (in percent)	
	1968	1970	1968	1970
Understand/try help	27	34	56	76
Listen/do nothing	36	36	14	15
Ignore	23	25	6	2
Not sure	14	5	24	7

Several items on both surveys were addressed at determining whether parents agreed with the ideology of the community control movement; in particular, at whether they believed that citizens should directly influence the running of the school system. They were also asked if they felt that "the people" had sufficient influence in the school system at large (NORC survey only) and in the demonstration district. All the replies show that the great majority thought that "the people" should have more influence on school policy in New York. The responses show a much greater satisfaction with the situation in the demonstration district than in the city. (Table 8-3.)

Another item in the 1970 survey indicated that a majority favored the continuation of the demonstration district, and only 6 percent felt they would be pleased if the district was abolished. This assessment was in keeping with the overall findings of the two surveys, which showed greater approval of the outputs of the demonstration district than of the total system and widespread agreement that the community should be more influential in the making of school policy. The consistently low percentage of parents expressing opposi-

Table 8-3

Assessment by Ocean Hill-Brownsville Parents of Influence of "the People" in Running the Schools

	1968 (in percent)	1970 (in percent)
AMOUNT OF INFLUENCE IN THIS DISTRICT		
Too much influence	19	12
Too little	46	43
Right amount	16	36
Not sure	19	7
COMPARED TO BEFORE THE GOVERNING BOARD WAS ESTABLISHED		
More influence now		65
Less		8
Same		16
Not sure		10
AMOUNT OF INFLUENCE IN CITY		
Too much influence		5
Too little		76
Right amount		16
Not sure		2

tion to community control indicated that the movement did have the mandate of parents, although groups opposed to the movement frequently impugned the representative character of the governing boards and their supporters. An advertisement placed in *The New York Times* during the teachers strike, for instance, described the people who were attempting to keep the transferred teachers from entering the schools as follows:

There is good reason to doubt that these "community representatives" are in fact representatives of the Ocean Hill-Brownsville community. Their core appears to be a group of 50 to 100 individuals who turn up at one school after another throughout the city to harass and intimidate teachers.[17]

But even in this most controversial of all actions, the NORC survey showed 50 percent of the community sample expressing support of the Governing Board and only 24 percent agreeing with the teachers' viewpoint.[18] And the survey data suggest that the number of parents endorsing the community

[17] Paid advertisement of the Ad Hoc Committee to Defend the Right to Teach (Michael Harrington and Tom Kahn, co-chairmen), "The Freedom to Teach," *The New York Times*, September 20, 1968; reprinted in *Confrontation at Ocean Hill-Brownsville*, ed. Maurice Berube and Marilyn Gittell (New York: Praeger, 1969), p. 121.

[18] The question was phrased as follows: "Last year there was a controversy between the teachers' union and the Ocean Hill-Brownsville school districts. From what you've heard or read, do you tend to support the local Governing Board and Unit Administrator or the teachers?"

control movement's general objectives while having reservations concerning the particular tactics it followed was much higher.

Our second source of data on mandated representation derives from a study of neighborhood residents and leaders in New York City being conducted by the Bureau of Applied Social Research of Columbia University. Evidence from a sample of 238 residents of 24 randomly selected blocks in a low income section of Brooklyn which is about 80 percent black indicates high feelings of inefficacy at the local level. Thus, 68 percent of the respondents thought they could do "little or nothing" about a proposed law which they felt was "unfair or harmful." [19] And 55 percent believed they could do "very little" or "nothing" when "a person has been treated unfairly by the city government."

A sample of 238 residents from another poor Brooklyn area which was 30 percent black and 45 percent Latin responded very similarly to these items. In this neighborhood we have data from an additional item which relates directly to governmental bureaucracies:

How much influence do you think the people of this neighborhood have on the way city government services are run in this area—would you say a lot of influence, some, a little, or none at all?

Seventy-seven percent answered "a little" or "none at all." In both neighborhoods respondents expressed high levels of dissatisfaction with the quality of city services, so that their perceived inefficacy meant that they could not alter an unacceptable situation.

Finally, residents were asked a question which is somewhat indicative of their attitude toward community control:

How much influence do you think people in this neighborhood *should* have on the way city government services are run in this area—would you say a lot of influence, some, a little, or none at all?

In the first neighborhood 50 percent of the sample said they should have "a lot of influence," and 39 percent "some"; in the second these figures were, respectively, 39 percent and 46 percent.

While the data from the New York City Neighborhood Study is sketchy, it does point to a perception by minority groups that existing mechanisms for affecting local bureaucracies are inadequate and that movement in the direction of community control is desirable. Together with the evidence from the Ocean Hill-Brownsville parents, it shows that our analysis of urban movements as fulfilling a function of mandated representation is backed up by at least some hard empirical data. Of course, it is

[19] "Suppose New York City was considering a law you thought was unfair or harmful. How much do you think you could do about that—a lot, some, a little, or just about nothing?" Data from this study are presented in a working paper entitled "Four Communities," New York City Neighborhood Study, Bureau of Applied Social Research, Columbia University, January 1973, mimeo.

possible that New York City is atypical in its government or that residents there are unique in their political radicalization. We do not think this to be the case—Rossi's data for example show a high level of black alienation from urban bureaucracies in other cities, and Eisinger reports many incidents of protest in a sample which did not include New York.[20] There is reason to believe therefore that urban political movements have reflected the sentiments of a significant number of nonwhite residents in many American cities.

A full sociological analysis of urban movements as representative institutions should ask how well they function to represent the actual interests of nonwhite collectivities as opposed to their conscious desires. The determination of actual or objective interests, however, produces a theoretical morass—which includes some of the problems we have noted in discussing symbolic representation. Since the members of a collectivity may simultaneously occupy many social statuses—e.g., black, poor, parent, bureaucratic client—an overall assessment of their objective interests demands an empirical analysis both of the structural forms which determine the wealth and power resources associated with each status and of the relative importance of the various statuses in determining the aggregate of material benefits received by individuals. Once objective interests have been identified—and these change with alteration in social structure—we can appraise the functionality of movement structures in advancing these interests.

Any attempt to assess urban political movements in terms of the criterion of *interest representation* is necessarily value laden. It depends upon an evaluation of the ideology of movement leaders, a judgment that cannot be made without reference to basic political values and unprovable assumptions. The core beliefs underlying urban political movements are that minority groups are the victims of a racist society, and that the amelioration of their situation depends upon collective mobilization and the employment of pressure against governmental institutions. We accept this diagnosis as generally valid and feel that, in fact, these movements do represent the interests of their constituents.

Urban political movements, however, constitute a remedy with significant drawbacks. These hinge upon the use of a conflict strategy and the choice of public service bureaucracies as primary targets. In the first place, because bureaucratic reform depends upon elite innovation, too much pressure from below may be counterproductive—it discredits would-be professional reformers instead of providing an external constituency for internal reform; its outcome is frequently immobilization rather than innovation. In the second place, attacks against the agencies which service the ghetto and their politicization jeopardize the routine provision of public services. Once the professional hegemony over the granting of public services is undermined, other (white) collectivities may begin to question the

---

[20] Peter H. Rossi et al., "Between White and Black: The Faces of American Institutions in the Ghetto," in *Supplemental Studies for the National Advisory Commission on Civil Disorders* (New York: Praeger, 1968); Peter K. Eisinger, "The Conditions of Protest Behavior in American Cities," *American Political Science Review*, LXVII, March, 1973.

allocation of benefits, and relative group power instead of group needs may become the sole criterion for determining who gets what. In such a situation, minority groups may be at a serious disadvantage. Finally, by embroiling service bureaucracies in conflict and undermining their legitimacy, movements may also be destroying the resources available to the agencies most concerned with the condition of the ghetto. Minority groups share a common interest with welfare bureaucracies in an expansion of public revenues allocated to social welfare. Bureaucracies under attack from below cease to be effective advocates in the state legislature and federal government. Since resources for the poor must come from the public fisc, a strategy of antagonizing public officials can be extremely costly.

Thus, to conclude that urban political movements do, in fact, articulate the interests of their constituents requires that we accept their costs as unavoidable. We do so primarily because we see no alternative structural form which can function more effectively in the interest of urban minority groups, given the larger context of American politics. Within this larger context, however, we must now ask the question of whether the interests articulated by urban political movements can be aggregated so as to create a force for change beyond the most local level.

URBAN MOVEMENTS AND NATIONAL INTERESTS

The structure of urban movements protects them from succumbing to the tendencies toward rigidity and oligarchy that afflict large, stable organizations.[21] But the virtues of responsiveness and representativeness are mainly produced by the small size and instability which constitute the chief weakness of these movements in their efforts to achieve external goals. Low organizational capacity, the risks of participation, orientation toward narrow issues, and the decreasing incentives to individual activity caused by increasing group size[22] all limit the magnitude of these bodies. Yet even movements which have succeeded in sparking mass revolutions have consisted mainly of collections of small disconnected groups. Oberschall observes that:

In revolutionary situations there is a tremendous outpouring of words, pamphlets, posters, and meetings, but communication and influence take place in small groups of

[21] S. M. Lipset, when studying the Typographical Union, found that the iron law of oligarchy prevailed most strongly in the largest (national) unit. He concluded: "The monopoly which an incumbent administration has over the channels of intraunion communication is lessened considerably in most union locals. There, a small group of individuals with relatively few resources may reach entire memberships with their propaganda." S. M. Lipset, Martin A. Trow, and James S. Coleman, *Union Democracy* (New York: Doubleday, 1956), p. 397.

[22] As we discussed in Chapter Seven, Mancur Olson's analysis shows that it becomes less rational for individuals to participate in organizations producing public goods when they are large than when they are small. Mancur Olson, *The Logic of Collective Action*, rev. ed., (New York: Schocken, 1971), chap. 2.

neighbors, coworkers, associates, and so on. . . . Contemporary research has discovered the great importance of small groups and local influentials in routine mass communication processes. Their importance is perhaps even greater in the period of mobilization for collective behavior episodes.[23]

Our case studies, Eisinger's findings on the level of participation in protest activities,[24] and impressions gathered from newspaper accounts and discussions with activists all suggest that the size of contemporary urban movements, except in rare instances of peak mobilization, does not exceed a few hundred, and that the stable core of activists seldom goes beyond fifty. Groups of this size cannot, except in the most unusual circumstances, hope to have more than a highly specific and localized impact.

Our analysis of urban movements leads us to hypothesize that they will not become much larger. In major cities with a high level of radical consciousness there will be more groups rather than larger ones. Once groups go beyond the number that can participate directly in an open meeting, they require an elaborate infrastructure to maintain communications, allocate tasks, and dispense individual rewards. The level of financial support and organizational ability required for operations of this scope is considerable, and their source is at the moment nowhere apparent. Aggregation of the interests embodied in the variety of small-scale movements is not the result of links which they have created with each other. Most of them work in isolation, rooted in their neighborhoods and engaging individuals with few outside ties. To the extent that all the various small movements for community control and improved social services add up to a single force for institutional change, their consolidation rests in the perception of outsiders, who see the common goals of a multitude of efforts despite their origins in a variety of sources.

There are two conceivable modes through which the demands of minority groups might be concerted at citywide or national levels. The first is through a mass movement of the urban poor, and the second is through the development of a national coalition which would unite the interests of minority groups with those of other collectivities. The possibility of the former is impeded by the organizational obstacles we have described, but might nonetheless arise under the leadership of a charismatic individual. Marcus Garvey and Martin Luther King managed to inspire thousands of people to activity, although not long-term participation. Whether another such person may appear and maintain mobilization long enough to gain major concessions from the national government, or have sufficient organizational abilities to develop a coherent, stable framework for ongoing participation, is an unanswerable question at this time.

The second possibility, that of a national coalition, is less dependent on

---

[23] Anthony Oberschall, *Social Conflict and Social Movements* (Englewood Cliffs, N.J.: Prentice-Hall, 1973), p. 174. Brinton makes a similar comment concerning the role of small groups before the French and American Revolutions. Crane Brinton, *The Anatomy of Revolution* (New York: Random House, 1958), pp. 87–89.

[24] Eisinger, "The Conditions of Protest Behavior in American Cities," p. 17.

fortuitous events and thus more open to systematic analysis. The forging of such a coalition depends only partly on the minority groups that would participate in it. It would be largely the result of the attitudes and strategies of potential partners, even though these would in some measure be determined by the stance of minorities toward them. Efforts to achieve working-class unity across racial divisions have so far borne little fruit. The "natural" alliance of the poor with the working class is severely limited by racial antagonism. This hostility is created partly by prejudice. It is also rooted in the manipulation of the lower strata to exploit divisions among them by those who profit from such divisions; and in the real threat which, given the current distribution of resources and capitalist structure, the aggressiveness of minority groups presents to those who occupy the rungs just above them on the social ladder. While the racial prejudice of the working class has been mitigated in this century in association with rising levels of education, tensions over jobs and "turf" continue to be exacerbated by thrusts toward minority job quotas, integrated housing, and school desegregation. The ideology of movement leaders further militates against coalition by emphasizing the racial rather than class basis of solidarity among urban minority groups. Cross burning and other overt acts of racial hostility have diminished, yet the essential vision of minorities as competitors rather than allies has not been abandoned by the white working class.

Divisions among the lower strata could be overcome through the acceptance of a unifying, class-based ideology. Such an ideology, however, has never taken firm root in the United States, and short of economic collapse there is little reason to predict it now. In our discussion of the political machine we asserted that it confined the development of a socialist party through providing an alternate institution representing lower-class interests in a manner stifling to the growth of class bonds. The interests of workers are now aggregated largely through the trade unions, which function similarly to frame working-class demands in narrow terms. We see, for example, little pressure from unions for a national health care plan or for income redistribution. Instead, they prefer to bargain for health care and wage increments within industry contracts, thus delivering benefits to their own workers and no one else. Except for the protection of trade union rights, organized labor pursues a political program only halfheartedly and rarely frames its desires in ideological language. Union officials see little advantage to themselves in a mobilized working class, and besides leaders of the few unions such as the United Farmworkers which represent primarily minority workers and have a leadership drawn from the ranks, they do little to elicit mass enthusiasm for general causes. The refusal of union elites to devote themselves to raising working-class consciousness and propounding broad political demands means that the only significant social structure which could provide an institutionalized basis for class action abstains from doing so. As in the case of the machine, the role of unions can be explained by general factors in American social development. But similarly the fact of union behavior restricts future possibilities and reinforces the tradition of nonideological politics.

The absence of a labor-based mass party has meant that urban minorities have had few alternatives at the local level besides movement-type organizations through which to press their demands. Urban political movements in their redistributive goals (although less so in their antibureaucratic aims) resemble socialist parties. The expression of these goals in structures outside the realm of routine politics results from the absence of more suitable structures of interest aggregation. At the national level urban minorities have not been able to develop alternative political structures. They form a component of the Democratic Party, but the substantial role played by organized labor in that body and the continued importance of Southern Democrats in Congress inhibits that party's capacity to express the interests of nonwhites.

The forces dividing minority groups from whites with whom they share a similar class situation have caused them to find their chief national allies among Progressive idealists drawn from the upper middle class. This alliance began during the New Deal, but its implications did not become fully apparent until the 1960s when foundation and federally sponsored efforts directed specifically at the urban poor commenced. Then the incompatibility of interests between upper class reformers and the deprived lower class began to reveal itself within both the Democratic Party and the government.

Piven and Cloward attribute the federal poverty program and other similar measures to a pragmatic recognition by ruling elements of the Democratic Party that they must cement the allegiance of black voters:

A way had to be found to prod the local Democratic party machinery to cultivate the allegiance of urban black voters by extending a greater share of municipal services to them, and to do this without alienating urban white voters. It was this political imperative that eventually led the Kennedy and Johnson Administrations to intervene in the cities.[25]

According to their view programs to aid the urban poor were a co-optative response to the threat of defection at the polls and disorder in the streets.

While this may have been the intention of the Democratic strategists— and such an intention does not exclude a sincere concern with the welfare of the poor—the programs set in motion a chain of events that not only integrated many potential ghetto leaders into the system *but also* precipitated the growth of urban movements. The urban movements we examined were aided by the provision of crucial funds or the development of leadership cadres through programs sponsored by the government, foundations, or churches. Opposition to the programs grew among those who felt threatened by their radicalizing force,[26] even while left-wing critics decried their debilitating effects on militant leaders:

[25] Frances Fox Piven and Richard A. Cloward, *Regulating the Poor* (New York: Pantheon, 1971), p. 256.

[26] Moynihan describes the process as follows:

Over and again, the attempt by official and quasi-official agencies (such as the Ford Foundation) to organize poor communities led first to the radicalization of the middle-class persons who began the effort; next to a certain amount of stirring among the

Over a period of time . . . federal intervention had the effect of absorbing and directing many of the agitational elements in the black population. . . . From the perspective of integrating blacks in the political system, the Great Society was a startling success.[27]

Piven and Cloward contend that the black militance of the period was not caused by federal intervention. Rather it was caused by

a population [in the inner city] that was extremely volatile and politically rebellious—not because it had been aroused by federal funds and federal rhetoric . . . but because of the traumatic dislocations it had suffered.[28]

We cannot disprove Piven and Cloward's assertion, nor their contention that black militants were diverted from the streets, where they would have been more effective, to the meeting rooms. We interpret the history of the 1960s differently, however, and see the development of articulate leadership and movement organizations as arising in part directly out of programs to aid the poor. While the relationship between the programs and militant action was complex, their presence brought previously nonexistent political and financial resources into the ghetto, provided a forum for dissidence and rewards for protest action, offered legal services to protesters, and stimulated the development of radical ideology. Piven and Cloward argue that the federal intervention came as a response to disorder rather than causing it, but in fact the major pieces of Great Society legislation preceded both the main period of rioting and of active community organization. At the very least the War on Poverty was a catalytic event, giving rise to a new analysis of their situation by urban minorities. Moreover, the decline of militant action that has occurred under the Nixon Administration seems to indicate that lack of commitment by the government to an antipoverty program has a more calming effect on militance than does a co-optative strategy. Successful protest action depends on a vulnerability in the opposition due to the presence of individuals at least partly sympathetic to the protesters' cause. Established governmental institutions can almost always outlast dissent if they are unified on a strategy of resistance or repression. The

poor, but accompanied by heightened racial antagonism *on the part of the poor* if they happened to be black; next to retaliation from the larger white community; whereupon it would emerge that the community action agency, which had talked so much, been so much in the headlines, promised so much in the way of change in the fundamentals of things, was powerless. . . . Just possibly, the philanthropists and socially concerned intellectuals never took seriously enough their talk about the 'power structure.' Certainly, they seemed repeatedly to assume that those who had power would let it be taken away a lot easier than could possibly be the case if what was involved was *power.*

Daniel Patrick Moynihan, *Maximum Feasible Misunderstanding* (New York: Free Press, 1969), pp. 134–35. Ital. in original.

[27] Piven and Cloward, *Regulating the Poor*, p. 276.

[28] Ibid., p. 272.

poverty programs were reflective of a supportive attitude toward the poor within the government, and associated with it were individuals at various levels of government who leaned toward a more radical view than was embodied in actual policy. The result was an encouragement of movement activity which capitalized on divisions inside the government and which avoided total suppression through the presence of sympathizers in authoritative positions.

The attempt by the modern Progressives to build a constituency among urban minorities backfired. Reform of the Democratic Party, led by the McGovern forces, produced in 1972 a far larger representation of urban blacks in the National Convention than ever before. But the alliance between inner-city blacks and suburban liberals was uneasy. Blacks were distrustful of the personal style of the McGovern people and felt that the issues of the Vietnamese War, the environment, and women's rights, which were the primary concerns of the suburbanites, were of secondary importance to them. The subsequent election showed that while those blacks who voted, voted overwhelmingly Democratic, most blacks found the two candidates insufficiently attractive to vote at all.[29] The triumph of the Democratic left wing in 1972 caused a considerable desertion of the white working class from its traditional political allegiance; the Nixon landslide victory indicated that this was a price the Democrats could not afford to pay.

Urban movements were only one, and not the most important, of many factors contributing to the Republican victories of 1968 and 1972. The War in Vietnam and the riots of the mid-sixties both weighed more heavily in creating distrust of the Democratic regime. Minority groups seeking to use the movement structure to force concessions to themselves were the victims of historical forces which they did not control. But unquestionably black disquiet in the 1960s, as expressed in civil disorders and street crime, demands for school and neighborhood integration, conflicts over control of new federal programs and old urban bureaucracies, and refusal to accept the legitimacy of established authority became lumped together in general public attitudes. Opposition politicians exploited this sentiment, while oldtime liberal supporters began to back away from the tide they had at least in part created.

By linking themselves with minority groups, Democratic liberals became associated in the minds of many with street crime and ghetto riots. Even though the radicalism associated with some of the federal programs would probably have ultimately been absorbed through a combination of institutional response and individual co-optation, it provoked counter-mobilization and feelings that minority groups were being given too much. The popular reaction to urban disorder was not to buy off the lower classes but to repress them. Whatever truth there might or might not be in the connection frequently made between ghetto lawlessness and the rising expectations

---

[29] According to a Joint Center for Political Studies (JCPS) survey of predominantly black inner-city precincts and wards in 24 major cities, 87 percent of the voters in those areas voted for McGovern. JCPS, however, calculated that nationwide only 41 percent of blacks of voting age voted in the 1972 presidential election. *Focus*, publication of JCPS, Washington, D.C., I, December, 1972, 7–8.

stimulated by antipoverty programs, many people became determined to prevent future encouragement of such expectations. President Nixon's dismantling of the Office of Economic Opportunity, the community mental health centers, and other programs involving participation of the poor meant the end of institutions which had provided at least an arena for mobilization if not a direct incentive to it. The 1969 revision of the Internal Revenue Code, which effectively stopped foundations from financing community groups, further suppressed the liberal-minority alliance by jeopardizing the tax-free status of foundations and threatening their officials with criminal penalties if funds were determined to be supporting political action. As assertion of the needs of minority groups became increasingly risky for politicians and foundations, the lack of shared material interests between minorities and their upper class allies meant that there was little basis beyond moral appeal for continued ties.

Urban political movements developed in response to a perception that only pressure tactics could force changes in ongoing institutional structures. These movements have frequently resorted to direct action, and the threat of violence has been implicit in their activities. A sustained campaign of actual violence might have forced greater responsiveness—although greater repression seems the more likely outcome. The left-wing argument, however, that the effort to achieve local organization meant a diversion of militant leaders from their best strategy misses the point that the effective employment of violence requires organization and the delineation of goals, both to attract supporters and coerce the opposition. The development of guerrilla organization confronts many of the same problems as does that of nonviolent movements; and to the degree that the risks of violent action are greater, the possibility of attracting participants other than to sporadic outbursts of rage is less.

The conclusion that the mobilization of urban minority groups into nonviolent movements provoked reaction and the loss of outside support does not imply that minorities would have been better off quiescent, or that they would have profited more from concentrating exclusively on the electoral process. The winning of political office by candidates drawn from minority groups will not change the overall position of those groups unless they also can mount enough pressure to change the policy alternatives presented in elections. The experience of the immigrant lower class with the machine demonstrates that descriptive representation does not assure the substantive representation of broad constituency interests.

We have explained the nature of contemporary urban movements in terms of the urban dialectic: The structure of the political machine partly created and partly reinforced a system of representation whereby the urban poor did not have their interests articulated on a class basis. The antithesis to the machine—Progressive reform—both destroyed the political infrastructure of most cities and contributed to the growth of the large impersonal bureaucracies which the minority poor presently find unresponsive to their needs. Urban political movements arose in opposition to Progressive reform and have tried to recreate a political structure through which the lower classes can press their demands. These movements resemble the machine in their localism and some of their procedural aims, but they differ from the machine in their substantive goals. They have adopted from Progressivism an emphasis on widespread community participation in politics and on the public service role of government. Many of the public interest norms of Progressivism have been retained even while their application has been challenged. Urban political movements are an attempt to move outside the machine-progressivism dichotomy that has dominated urban politics in this century so as to obtain a form of government and set of social policies more representative, in all the senses described in this chapter, of urban minority groups.

These movements cannot be called a success. Many of them have not been able to withstand internal disaffection or diversion from their stated goals. Externally they have largely not managed to exploit local issues for broader purposes. The political and numerical weakness of urban minorities has caused them to concentrate their demands on local targets. Here the need to appeal to followers on the basis of narrowly defined issues has resulted in movements oriented toward highly specific goals. Within the limits of this arena, however, they have made some gains. Most important, they have assisted in forcing local governmental institutions to consider constituencies which they had previously ignored, and this consideration has resulted in an improvement in public services in some instances and, at the least, the halting of such policies as indiscriminate urban renewal. At the national level the advances are more doubtful. While urban minorities have achieved greater representation within the Democratic Party, they have lost ground in the government itself. The Republican Administration in Washington constitutes a swing of the pendulum away from concern with the deprived, both ideologically and in the actual substance of policy. It has also produced a decline in the strength of urban political movements, as national policies have been implemented on the local level. The replacement of federal programs categorically directed at the poor by revenue sharing terminates policies that stimulated the growth of political agitation by minorities.

We do not, however, consider urban political movements to be purely a historical phenomenon. The situational factors and consciousness which produced them in the 1960s have not disappeared, and we expect their resurgence in the presence of a more sympathetic national government. A Democratic victory would not result in the attainment of the demands of minority groups. Democrats have been burned by their association with urban radicals, and the increased power of minorities within the party will be balanced by wariness among white professional politicians. But a different atmosphere in Washington would provide a new incentive to radical movements among the poor. While urban movements have constituted a possible synthesis of earlier political forms, they are not a final synthesis, and in white counter-mobilization their own antithesis has appeared. Just as the earlier forms of the machine and Progressivism have lingered on, we may expect that urban movements and also white antagonism to them will continue as important factors contributing to an enduring state of tension in American cities.

social and
political movements

appendix

The literature on social and political movements provides a rather large set of definitions, concepts and theoretical approaches, many of which contradict one another. It is the purpose of this appendix to give a general overview of that literature. In so doing it will both describe the concepts which are necessary for analyzing urban political movements and the theoretical positions which underlie the preceding chapters. The discussion below will consider the definition of social and political movements, the conditions under which they arise, their structural forms, and their functioning.

DEFINITION OF POLITICAL MOVEMENTS

The presence of social discontent,[1] if it is based only in individual awareness of a disjunction between *what is* and *what should be*, does not assure that a force for social change will arise. Individual dissatisfaction may expend itself through acts of personal dissipation or criminality, or it may produce apathy and withdrawal. It becomes difficult, therefore, to predict when, if ever, the discontent perceived by an outside observer will express itself in the form of concerted group action to achieve a new order.

---

[1] Many sociologists would use the word "strain" where we have employed "discontent." See, for example, Neil J. Smelser, *Theory of Collective Behavior* (New York: Free Press, 1962), p. 47. Anthony Oberschall, *Social Conflict and Social Movements* (Englewood Cliffs, N.J.: Prentice-Hall, 1973), p. 23, presents a useful discussion of Smelser's concept. Wilbert E. Moore uses "strains" and "tensions" synonomously; see his *Social Change* (Englewood Cliffs, N.J.: Prentice-Hall, 1963), p. 3. Rush and Denisoff use the terms "strain," "dysfunction," "structural contradiction," and "dilemma" more or less interchangeably. Gary B. Rush and R. Serge Denisoff, *Social and Political Movements* (New York: Appleton-Century-Crofts, 1971), p. 186.

For many years analysts wondered why American blacks, long the victims of social injustice and clearly aware of their maltreatment, remained politically quiescent. Arnold Rose, in his 1948 condensation of Myrdal's *The American Dilemma,* commented concerning blacks at that time:

The protest motive is ever present and in some degree it has reached practically all American Negroes. But the protest motive is limited mainly to the spreading of certain ideas about how things *should* be. Few Negro individuals are in a position to do anything practical about it. Everyone has to get on with his own life from day to day. He has to accommodate. The Negro protest is thus mainly suppressed and turned inward.[2]

Beginning in the early 1960s, however, we witnessed a period of sustained black activism directed at the social, cultural, and political institutions maintaining inequality.

When such a period of action caused by the efforts of an identifiable social group does occur, we call the agent of change a social movement. In formal terms, *we define a social movement as an emergent group which proposes to innovate and depends for its success upon the conversion of a social collectivity into an action group.*[3]

Social movements are often treated in the social science literature as one form of "collective behavior," a concept used also to designate fads, crazes, panics and other kinds of nonpurposive group behavior. For those interested in intentional social change, however, it is precisely the purposefulness of social movements that makes them important. We therefore concentrate on the aspects of social movements which make them distinct phenomena, and in particular we emphasize that subset of social movements which we designate as *political* movements. We do, however, use the terms political and social movements somewhat interchangeably, since all political movements are social movements even though all social movements do not have political goals.

A political movement is a type of social movement in which the innovation intended requires a change in the authoritative allocation of values or in the process by which such allocative decisions are made.[4] In other words political movements attempt to change the distribution of public goods or the method by which public institutions distribute benefits. In this sense, innovation may be politically conservative or politically radical, depending on the groups participating in the movement and their goals. Movements attempting to bring back monarchies or halt the construction of low-income housing are aiming at

---

[2] Arnold Rose, *The Negro in America* (Boston: Beacon Press, 1948), p. 250; ital. in orig.

[3] All the common definitions of a social movement include the elements of change and group activity. See W. Bruce Cameron, *Modern Social Movements* (New York: Random House, 1966), p. 7; Herbert Blumer, "Social Movements," in *New Outline of the Principles of Sociology,* ed. A.M. Lee (New York: Barnes & Noble, 1951), p. 199; Ralph H. Turner and Lewis M. Killian, *Collective Behavior,* 2d ed. (Englewood Cliffs, N.J.: Prentice-Hall, 1972), p. 246.

[4] This description of a political movement derives from David Easton's definition of politics as "the authoritative allocation of values for a society." David Easton, *A Framework for Political Analysis,* (Englewood Cliffs, N.J.: Prentice-Hall, 1965), p. 50.

significant changes in the mode or outputs of government even though their aims may not be called innovative in the more ordinary meaning of that word. "Innovation" here refers to deep-seated change, regardless of its direction.

Significant *innovation*, in this sense, as opposed to simply new programs, experiments, or inventions, never occurs without resistance. Its essence is change in the structure of institutions, and such change means that people with vested interests in the current structure must lose some of their benefits. Where the structure of social institutions has been formed over a long period and has acquired traditional legitimacy, change will be resisted even by those who would not lose materially from the disregard of custom. Thus, for instance, many whites fear school desegregation even when it would not affect them directly.

Social movements are *emergent*[5] phenomena, never assuming a permanent form. Throughout their lifespan movements are likely to change in size and structure, alter their strategies, and develop their ideology in response to changes in situation and internal support. Movements are explicitly goal directed and are constantly either succeeding or failing to meet their objectives. Each success or failure will affect aspects of the movement's structure and behavior. Tactical decisions tend to have quick repercussions with large impact on organizational development. A movement differs from more stable, routinized organizations in existing almost entirely through its activity rather than through a defined organizational structure. Thus, expansion or contraction of activity produces immediate and powerful feedback effects on organizational size, coherence and morale. These in turn have a significant relationship to the level and effectiveness of action, and so on.

Movements are necessarily the products of a *collectivity*. The collectivity consists of individuals with shared statuses or social conditions. In other words, members of the collectivity have certain interests in common, which provide a basis for action. These interests, however, need not be manifest; that is, their existence does not depend on the awareness of members of the collectivity:[6]

The nature of social organization determines the life-chances of the individual *whether he is aware of this social determination or not.* . . . Consequently individuals whose life-chances are similarly *affected by* similar objective social conditions are said to have a *common interest* whether they perceive any such interest or not.[7]

[5] We have borrowed this term from Rush and Denisoff, *Social and Political Movements*, p. 252.

[6] Dahrendorf designates collectivities defined on the basis of common latent interests as "quasi-groups," which he distinguishes from interest groups. His term "interest group" is the equivalent of our action group. Ralf Dahrendorf, *Class and Class Conflict in Industrial Society* (Stanford: Stanford University Press, 1959), p. 180.

[7] Isaac Balbus, "The Concept of Interest in Pluralist and Marxian Analysis," *Politics and Society*, I, February, 1971, 167. Ital. in original. Balbus is here summarizing the Marxian conception of interest.

An *action group* is characterized by solidarity and program. It is born when members of a collectivity recognize common grievances, reach agreement on means of remedy, and began to incur costs in order to achieve their goals. An action group as used here is identical to what Max Weber called a "party":[8]

"Parties" live in a house of "power." Their action is oriented toward the acquisition of social "power," that is to say, toward influencing a communal action no matter what its content may be. . . . Party actions are always directed toward a goal which is striven for in planned manner. This goal may be a "cause" (the party may aim at realizing a program for ideal or material purposes), or the goal may be "personal" (sinecures, power, and from these, honor for the leader and the followers of the party). Usually the party action aims at all these simultaneously.[9]

An action group may be what is normally labeled a political party, that is, a group which participates in contests for public office, or it may aim at controlling governmental outputs without actually obtaining office. While all movements are action groups, all action groups are not movements. The party which seeks only personal rewards is an action group but not a movement since its attempt to gain power does not derive from a program of social change.

Since deprivation and unhappiness with one's lot are present in all societies at all times, one must ask when this situation gives rise to organized pressures for change. In the next section we look generally at the prerequisites for the formation of political movements.

THE ORIGINS OF
POLITICAL MOVEMENTS

Movements are, as we noted earlier, emergent phenomena. Because they are always in process of becoming, it is difficult to pinpoint their beginnings. Do three people meeting to discuss ways of overthrowing the government constitute a movement? What about a streetcorner orator and his audience? If an organization begun by the three people or the streetcorner orator turns into the Communist Party or the CIO, we would most likely describe the original meeting or speech as the start of a movement. But if the group or speaker never attracts public notice, we might withhold the label.

The birth of movements is the result of an interactive process. It requires that some members of a collectivity perceive their social position as unjust and identify the fault as associated not with themselves as individuals but with their collective position. The perception of injustice arises from changes in both the objective position of the collectivity and in subjective

[8] We will use the term "party" in the common meaning rather than in Weber's, which, since it defines action groups, is more general.

[9] Max Weber, "Class, Status, Party," in *From Max Weber*, eds. H. H. Gerth and C. Wright Mills (New York: Oxford University Press, 1958), p. 194.

reactions to them. The feeling of being unjustly treated by society is called relative deprivation and is derived from comparisons with the positions of other collectivities or individuals which serve as reference points. Relative deprivation facilitates the development of an ideology which can explain the social situation of the collectivity and point to available means of redress. But relative deprivation is, in turn, intensified through group contact with an explanatory system that apportions blame and proffers solutions. In this way, the interests of a collectivity and ideas which define those interests interact to increase the group's relative deprivation and to effect the spiral of mobilization which creates action groups and political movements.

An additional element in the creation of a movement consists of the events and individuals which present themselves at a historical moment. These comprise the leaders and spokesmen for the incipient movement, those of opposing groups, and the incidents through which they all play their roles. The continuous feedback of events onto the situation of the collectivity and the development of its ideology completes the circle of causality in the formation of movements.

relative deprivation

Virtually all theorists trace the origins of movements to a change in the situation of the collectivity from which they spring. A collectivity may long suffer extreme misery without its giving rise to social action because its condition coincides with its expectations. The introduction of a new factor in its situation, however, may cause a divergence between perceived reality and expectations, which we designate relative deprivation.

The magnitude of a relative deprivation is the extent of the difference between the desired situation and that of the person desiring it (as he sees it). The frequency of a relative deprivation is the proportion of a group who feel it.[10]

A number of writers have tried to identify the kinds of historical changes which provoke relative deprivation. Perhaps most influential has been de Tocqueville, who argued in *The Old Regime and the French Revolution*:

It is a singular fact that this steadily increasing prosperity [in France before the Revolution], far from tranquilizing the population, everywhere promoted a spirit of unrest. The general public became more and more hostile to every ancient institution, more and more discontented; indeed, it was increasingly obvious that the nation was heading for a revolution.[11]

James C. Davies concludes that revolution is most likely after a reversal of a steady improvement in objective conditions. He describes the curve of need satisfaction in this situation as forming a J shape, while expectations

[10] W. G. Runciman, *Relative Deprivation and Social Justice* (Berkeley: University of California Press, 1966), p. 10.

[11] Alexis de Tocqueville, *The Old Regime and the French Revolution,* trans. Stuart Gilbert (New York: Doubleday, 1955), p. 175.

continue as a monotonically increasing upward line. The result of the change in direction of the need satisfaction curve is a sudden sharp divergence between expectations and satisfactions.[12]

Tocqueville's and Davies' theories both relate relative deprivation to a situation of rising expectations. Other theorists, notably Marx, who predicted the uprising of the proletariat on the basis of its ever increasing emiseration, see the source of relative deprivation in a deterioration of conditions.[13] Still another version of the deteriorating conditions hypothesis traces the origins of movements to a loss of accustomed rights and privileges or downward social mobility. Thus, Rudé, in his discussion of the French Revolution, asserts:

At every important stage of the Revolution the *sans-culottes* intervened, not to renovate society or to remodel it after a new pattern, but to reclaim traditional rights and to uphold standards which they believed to be imperilled by the innovations of ministers, capitalists, speculators, agricultural "improvers," or city authorities.[14]

Explanations of the sources of American rightwing movements generally attribute them to fears of status loss. Daniel Bell, for instance, considers that the forces of bureaucratization and technological change which characterize modern society "are deeply unsettling to those whose values were shaped by the 'individualist' morality of nineteenth-century America."[15]

Seemingly altruistic reform movements like American Progressivism can also be explained as a reaction to the threat or reality of status deprivation. The Progressives proclaimed themselves as acting in the public interest and usually belonged to a privileged social class with apparently nothing to gain from their noblesse oblige. Despite their ostensible disinterestedness, however, the Progressive reformers were seeking to restore values which they perceived as threatened by, on the one hand, corporate capitalism, and, on the other, the immigrants and the machine. "Progressivism, in short, was to a very considerable extent led by men who suffered from the events of their time not through a shrinkage of their means but through the changed pattern in the distribution of deference and power." [16]

[12] James C. Davies, "Toward a Theory of Revolution," *American Sociological Review*, XXVII, February, 1962, 5–19; and "The J-Curve of Rising and Declining Satisfactions as a Cause of Some Great Revolutions and a Contained Rebellion," in *Violence in America*, eds. Hugh Davis Graham and Ted Robert Gurr, Official Report to the National Commission on the Causes and Prevention of Violence (New York: New American Library, 1969), pp. 671–709.

[13] Karl Marx and Friedrich Engels, *The Communist Manifesto* (New York: International Publishers, 1948), p. 16. This prediction has sometimes been formulated in the slogan "The worse the better." Davies refers to an antithetical passage in Marx where he makes a rising expectations argument in "Toward a Theory of Revolution," p. 5. But G. D. H. Cole, in *The Meaning of Marxism* (Ann Arbor, Mich.: University of Michigan Press, 1948), p. 116, contends that Marx intended emiseration to refer to an absolute not a relative condition.

[14] George Rudé, *The Crowd in the French Revolution* (New York: Oxford University Press, 1959), p. 225.

[15] Daniel Bell, "The Dispossessed," in *The Radical Right*, ed. Daniel Bell (New York: Doubleday, 1963), p. 21.

[16] Richard Hofstadter, *The Age of Reform* (New York: Random House, 1955), p. 135.

Both common sense and an examination of historical cases point to the conclusion that an incongruity between reality and expectations can arise from a number of different objective and subjective factors.[17] In a general discussion of the origins of movements, it is sufficient to say that the feeling of grievance which is the first element in the crystallization of consciousness arises from relative deprivation. At this point members of a collectivity are, in Gurr's words, "strongly susceptible to ideological conversion." [18] Relative deprivation alone, however, does not suffice to explain the origins of political movements, nor why feelings of discontent should be channeled into innovative political action rather than, say, riotous behavior or religious expression. "Economic and political class consciousness [for example] obviously does not emerge as a simple reaction to the position of a group in the economic and social structure." [19] We must, therefore, examine other factors to see when relative deprivation becomes a source of collective political activity.

the role of ideas

The ideology of a political movement develops from the meshing of discontent with specific ideas. These ideas follow a life cycle of their own and may originate in sources independent of the actual movement. Although political ideas are produced within the constraints of the historical epoch and social position of the thinker, some individuals are less closely hemmed in by the intellectual boundaries of a particular society than others.[20] This relative freedom has permitted theorists to formulate concepts which express the consciousness of as yet unformed groups:

Every age allows to arise (in differently located social groups) those ideas and values in which are contained in condensed form the unrealized and the unfulfilled tendencies which represent the needs of each age. These intellectual elements then become the explosive material for bursting the limits of the existing order.[21]

This "explosive material" may be gathered from a variety of sources by the leaders and propagandists of nascent political movements to justify their

[17] This conclusion is reached by Gurr in his chapter on the social origins of relative deprivation, Ted Robert Gurr, *Why Men Rebel* (Princeton: Princeton University Press, 1970), pp. 92–122; and by Geschwender in his attempt to explain radical consciousness by means of cognitive dissonance theory. James A. Geschwender, "Explorations in the Theory of Social Movements and Revolutions," *Social Forces*, XLVII, December, 1968, 127–35.

[18] Gurr, *Why Men Rebel*, p. 121. The concept of susceptibility is central to Hans Toch's theory of the formation of social movements: "When a person searches for meaning, he can be defined as 'susceptible' to social movements. A *mild* increase in susceptibility would involve a slight lowering of sales resistance to available solutions." Hans Toch, *The Social Psychology of Social Movements* (Indianapolis: Bobbs-Merrill, 1965), p. 12. Ital. in original.

[19] Seymour Martin Lipset, *Agrarian Socialism* (New York: Doubleday, 1968), p. 57.

[20] See Karl Mannheim, *Ideology and Utopia* (New York: Harcourt Brace & World, 1936), pp. 158–59.

[21] Ibid., p. 199.

aggrievement, rally a following, and act as a focus for demands. The reactive process through which ideas become ideologies is complex and not always easily predictable.

The Bolshevik Party's revolutionary program offers a most important historical illustration of the lifting of a set of ideas from its original context to form the basis of a new ideology. Marx's theory of revolutionary socialism evolved out of the Western European experience of capitalist expansion. It eventually became the doctrine of the Socialist Parties in Russia despite Marx's own pessimism about the possibility of revolution in a country which had not yet reached the full development of bourgeois capitalism.[22] Marxist ideas, however, were modified to fit the Russian situation. Marx's analyses of capitalist society, historical materialism, and the revolutionary role of the proletariat were welded with Lenin's argument concerning the revolutionary party to form the basis of the Bolshevik ideology.

Similarly in France the far left revolutionaries seized upon preexisting ideas which fit their situation even though these ideas did not arise from it:

The ideas which the sans-culottes proposed during periods of shortage were not always highly original. In the majority of cases they had already been expressed, sometimes in a different form by orators from different sections of the montagnard bourgeoisie, who had themselves borrowed these ideas from the common store of eighteenth-century philosophical thought, to which Rousseau had made such a significant contribution.[23]

The theories of Rousseau, like those of Locke in England, reflected the period in which they were written, formalized what were perhaps the thoughts of many, and were subsequently partially extracted to become the ideology of as yet unmobilized collectivities.

The emergence of the ideology of the various movements for community control of urban institutions resembles the preceding examples. Demands for community control developed primarily in response to local political situations. However, ideas of writers such as Fanon[24] and Carmichael and Hamilton,[25] particularly as they related to "internal colonialism," provided a rationale for goals that evolved originally out of reactive political strategies. Another different source of intellectual support for the movement may be

[22] Until the 1880s, Russian radicals, although familiar with Marxist thought, agreed that Marx's description of the proletarian revolution was inapplicable to Russia and mainly accepted a populist doctrine which emphasized the role of the peasants. "Marxism began to win adherents only when, as a consequence of repeated failures of populist movements to attain their ends, faith in the ideas and methods of those movements weakened. Then there was resumed that quest for 'an algebra of revolution.' " Samuel H. Baron, "Plekhanov and the Origins of Russian Marxism," in *Readings in Russian History*, II, ed. Sidney Harcave (New York: Thomas Y. Crowell, 1962), p. 81.

[23] Albert Soboul, *The Parisian Sans-Culottes and the French Revolution, 1793–94*, trans. Gwynne Lewis (New York: Oxford University Press, 1964), p. 64.

[24] Frantz Fanon, *The Wretched of the Earth* (New York: Grove Press, 1963).

[25] Stokely Carmichael and Charles V. Hamilton, *Black Power* (New York: Random House, 1967).

found in the Jeffersonian rationale of local self-government, as well as from a number of modern critics of bureaucracy.[26]

The struggle for political control of Northern urban institutions and its accompanying ideology occurred after the apparent exhaustion of the antecedent set of ideas associated with black liberation. The assassination of Martin Luther King, following his failure to carry the civil rights movement to the North, and the seeming irrelevance of federal equal opportunity legislation to the Northern situation comprised a historical context that "demanded" a new approach. Simultaneously, the cumulation of years of large-scale migration of blacks in hopes of a better life in the North, and rising expectations created by the civil rights movement and federal legislation resulted in a volatile situation among Northern blacks.[27] A set of ideas, some arising from the American democratic liberal tradition, some from the anticolonial struggle abroad, and some deriving from the specific conflict became available. In numerous local controversies over the control of individual schools, hospitals, or occasionally whole municipalities, the occasion arose to generalize discontent through the set of ideas which become the ideology of community control. The interaction between theory and practice produced at this moment a perception of shared discontent, an explanation of its cause, and a political "solution."

the historical moment

Often in the history of political movements there is an identifiable moment when the movement appears to crystallize, when a number of individuals suddenly discover what they have in common and wherein lies the source of the injustice they feel. Although the individuals may long have been susceptible to new ideologies and unconsciously undergoing a process of conversion, an issue or event, even a speech or magazine article, precipitates a new consciousness. Participants in a variety of different movements have reported this experience. One woman in a letter to a women's liberation magazine writes:

We [my husband and I] decided on some sort of an equal partnership, and I am going to begin college come September. Well, I was a little scared, and the whole idea was still a little fuzzy. I was just beginning to get myself together when I bought *Ms*. It was like an explosion. Suddenly I came fully to my senses. It was an awakening of the person within me.[28]

[26] Alan A. Altshuler, *Community Control* (New York: Bobbs-Merrill, 1970). Chap. 2 sets forth the ideological framework of the movement for community control.

[27] In a comparison of blacks in the South and North, Gittell and Krupp state that "Where discrimination is high and the Negro is poor and uneducated, his expectations will be low and unresponsive to changes in conditions." Marilyn Gittell and Sherman Krupp, "A Model of Discrimination and Tensions," in *Riots and Rebellions*, ed. Louis H. Masotti and Don R. Bowen (Beverly Hills, Calif.: Sage Publications, 1968), p. 79. Reports of survey research on Northern blacks also support the hypothesis that improving conditions creating rising expectations are associated with increased discontent. Don R. Bowen, Elinor Bowen, Sheldon Gawiser, and Louis H. Masotti, "Deprivation, Mobility, and Orientation Toward Protest of the Urban Poor," in *Riots and Rebellions*, p. 199; Murray Edelman, *Politics as Symbolic Action* (Chicago: Markham, 1971), p. 107.

[28] Letter to the Editor of *Ms*., July, 1972, p. 45.

Malcolm X compares the suddenness of his insight into the condition of blacks, acquired through the teachings of Elijah Mohammad, with the conversion of Paul on the road to Damascus:

Many a time, I have looked back, trying to assess, just for myself, my first reactions to all this. Every instinct of the ghetto jungle streets, every hustling fox and criminal wolf instinct in me, which would have scoffed at and rejected anything else, was struck numb. . . . I remember how, some time later, reading the Bible . . . , I came upon, then I read, over and over, how Paul on the road to Damascus, upon hearing the voice of Christ, was so smitten that he was knocked off his horse, in a daze. I do not now, and I did not then, liken myself to Paul. But I do understand his experience.[29]

Sometimes the underlying dispute between social groups jells in a particular issue; Rudé's depiction of the spread of political radicalism in eighteenth-century London describes this process:

It was inevitable that political radicalism, once reborn, should arouse a response among the unenfranchised "lower orders." There were the precedents of the Good Old Cause and of the 'levelling' movement and Shaftesbury's Green Ribbon Club, of which the memory, though long submerged, had survived in popular tradition. Besides, there was the deep-felt belief in the Englishman's "birthright" and "liberties" and the hatred of "Popery and wooden shoes," which, though they might find an outlet in xenophobia and religious intolerance, might equally well be harnessed to a radical cause. In addition, there were other demographic and social factors, such as the rapid rise of London's population and its development into a unified capital city. The ground was thus well prepared. But, equally, there had to be an issue around which a movement could take shape.

The issue was the "Wilkes affair," and the slogan "Wilkes and Liberty" became for nearly a dozen years the rallying cry of City merchants, London's labourers and craftsmen, and the freeholders and householders of Westminster, Middlesex and Surrey.[30]

Political organizers seek to precipitate and capitalize on strategic errors of the opposition in order to create mobilizing issues. The Birmingham marches led by Martin Luther King exemplify the creation of an issue in this fashion. The failure, or inability, of Sheriff "Bull" Connor to respond peaceably to the nonviolent marchers led to widespread news portrayals of children being knocked over by fire hoses. The result, as well as making the general public sympathetic to the marchers, was to solidify black identity and make the Southern Christian Leadership Conference (SCLC) into the organizational focus of the Southern civil rights movement.[31]

Occurrences such as the jailing of Wilkes or the use of fire hoses in Birmingham are *catalytic events* which make manifest and give meaning to

---

[29] *The Autobiography of Malcolm X*, with the assistance of Alex Haley (New York: Grove Press, 1964), p. 163.

[30] From *Paris and London in the Eighteenth Century: Studies in Popular Protest* by George Rudé. Copyright © 1966 George Rudé. Reprinted by permission of the Viking Press, Inc.

[31] See Howard Hubbard, "Five Long Hot Summers and How They Grew," *The Public Interest*, No. 12, Summer, 1968, 3–8.

underlying historical currents.[32] Because many events can precipitate the birth of a movement, the way an event is treated by potential leaders as well as by leaders of the opposition crucially affects whether or not it becomes significant and the kinds of action it provokes.[33] Leaders affect events both through their participation in them and also through providing a symbolic interpretation of them. The symbolic interpretation causes the public to see the event not just as a thing in itself but as representing something larger and more general; events such as the Haymarket Massacre or the bombing of the Birmingham church are not just crimes committed by certain individuals against other individuals, but come to *stand for* the general oppression of laborers or blacks.[34] Leaders like Gandhi or Martin Luther King become symbols in themselves of the collective aspirations of their followers.

Thus individuals and events often make their most important contribution to the interactive process which creates political movements through their symbolic effects. On the one hand, they provoke responses with stimuli that depend upon collective predispositions created by relative deprivation and nascent ideology. On the other hand, leaders instill in the collectivity the belief that it is relatively deprived; they seize ideas and attach them to collective interests, thereby creating the ideological basis for group action. When the interaction reaches a level such that members of the collectivity become organized into an action group, we say that a movement has formed. Once a movement comes into being it takes on certain structural characteristics common to the type, but its phenomenological essence prevents it from being fixed in character or easily defined.

THE STRUCTURE OF
POLITICAL MOVEMENTS

The fluidity of political movements and their differing objectives mean that there are structural variations both between movements and within them at different points in time. As a result, we tend to have a number of contradictory images of how a movement looks. Perhaps the first which springs to mind is that of the unruly mob:

On the 20th April a major affray took place at Middleton, where Daniel Burton's power-loom mill was attacked by several thousands. The mill was assailed with volley

---

[32] Other historically significant catalytic events include the calling of the Estates General by Louis XVI, the British Stamp Act, the refusal of Rosa Parks to sit in the back of a Montgomery bus, and the Kent State shooting.

[33] Investigations of the starts of riots all discover one precipitating event, usually indistinguishable in its facts from many other events that are routine daily occurrences. *Report of the National Advisory Commission on Civil Disorders* (Washington, D.C.: U.S. Government Printing Office, 1968), p. 68.

[34] They are what Edelman calls "condensation symbols," which he defines as evoking "the emotions associated with the situation. They condense into one symbolic event, sign, or act, patriotic pride, anxieties, remembrances of past glories or humiliations, promises of future greatness: some one of these or all of them." Murray Edelman, *The Symbolic Uses of Politics* (Urbana, Ill.: University of Illinois Press, 1964), p. 6.

upon volley of stones, and its defenders replied with musket fire, killing three and wounding some more. On the next morning the threatening crowds assembled in ever greater strength, and were joined at mid-day by—"a body of men, consisting of from one to two hundred, some of them armed with muskets with fixed bayonets, and others with colliers' picks, [who] marched into the village in procession, and joined the rioters. At the head of this armed banditti a *Man of Straw* was carried, representing the *renowned* General Ludd whose standard-bearer waved a sort of red flag." [35]

Another picture is that of the revolutionary conspiracy, highly disciplined and secretive, waiting in the wings to seize power. The classic example, and the one which has inspired much of the existing writing on political movements, is the Bolshevik Party:

In Lenin's view the party must be the "vanguard of the proletariat." It must lead the working class, as the working class must lead other classes into revolution. . . . The party must not follow the "elemental" movement of the workers, must not become a "tail" to the working class, but must lead the workers forward, understanding their true interests better than they themselves. The party must be a band of "professional revolutionaries," bound by an iron discipline. Quality must come before quantity. No one must be admitted to the party who would not completely subject himself to its leaders and put the claims of the party on his time and efforts before all others. [36]

Besides the romantic depictions of movements as the creators of mass uprisings or perpetrators of revolutionary coups d'états are yet two other images: the movement as mobilizer of reactionary sentiment warning the world against Communism at home, sex education, or fluoridation; and the movement as originator of progressive measures, pressing for prison reform, public libraries, and compulsory education.

[The meeting] . . . started with a prayer for the Lord's help in the fight against "the humanistic godless effort to destroy the sanctity of the home and the well-being of the children of America." And following that there was the pledge of allegiance, and following that the national anthem. Then the chairman stepped up to the podium to announce that something special was coming. . . .

Up at the podium appeared now a little blond-haired girl wearing a party dress. . . . "Ah am a child," said the voice. "In me lies the hope of the future. . . . Protect me, for Jesus said, 'Let the little children come unto me.' " The voice went on to say something about protecting parents and teachers too, and then closed with a reverent, "Thank you, God, for the beauty and wonder of our children." . . .

Thus, began the opening rally of the National Convention on the Crisis in Education, a gathering of delegates from parents' groups in twenty-two states that had vowed to combat sex education in the public and parochial schools and, while they were at it, to prevent school integration through bussing, to forbid psychological testing of students, to halt teacher sensitivity training sessions, and to get prayer back into all the nation's classrooms. [37]

[35] Account of Luddite rioting in Lancashire; E. P. Thompson, *The Making of the English Working Class.* Copyright 1963 by Pantheon Books, A Division of Random House, Inc., pp. 567–68; internal quote from *Leeds Mercury*, April 25, 1812; ital. in original.

[36] Hugh Seton-Watson, *From Lenin to Khrushchev* (New York: Praeger, 1960), p. 24.

[37] Mary Breasted, *Oh! Sex Education!* (New York: Praeger, 1970), pp. 246–47.

Sol Cohen depicts a contrasting gathering devoted to educational change:

Shortly after the election, on December 11, 1894, a small group of society women met in Mrs. Valentine Mott's Victorian drawing room to form a ladies' auxiliary to Good Government Club E, one of the most energetic of the numerous anti-Tammany groups in the city at the time. . . . To help Club E reform the New York City school system, they organized the Woman's Association for Improving the Public Schools. In April 1895 the WAIPS formally severed itself from Club E. This step was taken, we are informed, "to sever the Association from even this slight connection with politics." [38]

Each image of the movement evokes a picture of the typical member— uncouth worker; revolutionary intellectual; crewcut rugged individualist; genteel reformer. Also associated with each image is an organizational type, ranging from unstructured to highly centralized; and a normative status, running from illegality to mere unorthodoxy. In this section we examine the structure of political movements in terms of organizational form and normative status. Then we shall ask whether the structure of political movements is rooted in rational or irrational motivations.

internal organization

Movements must have some form of internal organization if they are to act. The essence of a movement's activities is to convert an unorganized collectivity into an organized one. In the case of outlawed revolutionary movements, this has often meant the creation of tightly disciplined cells to permit mobilization and oppositionist activities. Above-ground movements usually contain a looser kind of organization, following the typical pattern of selecting a governing board and employing staff with responsibility for various tasks. Regardless of whether organization is loose or tight, there must be some way of coordinating individual actions. Movements here resemble all other forms of ongoing social action, ranging from economic corporations to governments to garden clubs, in the necessity of control mechanisms for continued functioning.

Nonetheless, many scholars have attempted to differentiate movements from other forms of political activity on the basis of the presence or absence of organizational structure. The result has been considerable confusion, as illustrated in the following passage from the *Encyclopedia of the Social Sciences:*

Social movements are a specific kind of concerted-action groups; they last longer and are more integrated than mobs, masses, and crowds and *yet are not organized* like political clubs and other associations. A social movement *may,* however, *be comprised of organized groups* without having one overall formal organization (for example, the labor

[38] Sol Cohen, *Progressives and Urban School Reform* (New York: Bureau of Publications, Teachers College, Columbia University, 1964), p. 2.

movement, which comprises trade unions, political parties, consumer cooperatives, and many other organizations).[39]

Heberle seems here to argue first that movements are relatively disorganized, then that they may be highly organized but lack a single overarching organization. They are not like political clubs but may include within them political parties. One can, however, think of examples of movements operating under a single central control, such as many of the colonial independence movements; one can also think of groups such as the major American political parties that are not movements but are characterized by minimal central direction.[40]

Herbert Blumer takes what seems to be an evolutionary view of the organization of social movements:

In its beginning, a social movement is amorphous, poorly organized, and without form; the collective behavior is on the primitive level . . . and the mechanisms of interaction are the elementary, spontaneous mechanisms of which we have spoken. As a social movement develops, it takes on the character of a society.[41]

Again, counterexamples come quickly to mind. While the organizational structure of a movement rarely remains stable, there is little evidence of unilinear development. The international communist movement oscillated throughout its history between a highly organized, elitist structure and a looser "popular front" type of organization. The American civil rights movement could trace its origin to the Niagra Movement where the National Association for the Advancement of Colored People (NAACP) was formed. Its beginning was neither formless nor primitive; during different periods it moved between greater and lesser degrees of unity and of mass mobilization. It has been characterized by both spontaneous and highly planned acts in no particular chronological sequence but rather in response to varying circumstances.

Another view of movement organization arises from the attempts to explain "totalitarian" social movements.[42] These writings portray alienated

---

[39] Rudolf Heberle, "Types and Functions of Social Movements," *International Encyclopedia of the Social Sciences*, 2d ed., XIV, (New York: Free Press, 1964), p. 439. Ital. added.

[40] Roger Brown calls revolutionary movements a form of collective behavior, then makes the categorical statement that "the behavior from which collective behavior is to be distinguished includes all those social actions that are organized or institutionalized" (p. 713). Having made this statement, however, he classifies the Black Muslims during the period of Malcolm X's ascendancy as a revolutionary movement, describes the Black Muslims at length, and finally admits: "A social movement like the Black Muslim is much more formalized and organized than is a crowd and there is some doubt in my mind whether such movements should be considered collective behavior" (p. 728). Roger Brown, *Social Psychology* (New York: Free Press, 1965). Smelser also classifies movements as a form of collective behavior and stresses that such behavior is "not institutionalized." But he then emphasizes the importance of organizations such as parties, pressure groups, and clubs to the development of "norm-oriented" movements. Smelser, *Theory of Collective Behavior*, p. 274.

[41] Blumer, "Social Movements," p. 199.

[42] See, *inter alia*, Hannah Arendt, *The Origins of Totalitarianism* (New York: Harcourt Brace & World, 1958); Erich Fromm, *Escape from Freedom* (New York: Rinehart, 1941); William Kornhauser, *The Politics of Mass Society* (Glencoe: Free Press, 1959); Robert Nisbet, *Community and Power* (New York: Oxford University Press, 1953).

individuals who are unable to integrate their lives into the institutions of mass society:

There are countless persons today for whom the massive changes of the past century have meant a dislocation of the contexts of function: the extended family, neighborhood, apprenticeship, social class, and parish.[43]

They join mass movements because they are unable to attach themselves to the normal mediating organizations of mass society.

Mass movements in this view are not necessarily disorganized, but their organization is of a different type from that of groups which operate within the accepted pluralistic framework. They demand the submission of the individual to the group, particularly to the leader of the group:

The first mechanism of escape from freedom . . . is the tendency to give up the independence of one's own individual self and to fuse one's self with somebody or something outside of oneself in order to acquire the strength which the individual self is lacking. Or, to put it in different words, to seek for new, "secondary bonds" as a substitute for the primary bonds which have been lost.[44]

Movements which have developed in response to individual alienation and anomie, according to the mass society view, rely on emotional bonds and identification with the charismatic leader rather than bureaucratic or democratic modes as the basis for organizational direction and unity.

None of the mass society authors argue that all social movements are totalitarian or partake of the characteristics they describe. Nonetheless, their implication is that in a pluralistic democracy social movements differ from other intermediate groups in substantial, negative ways. For instance, Lipset, writing in the same tradition, claims:

These characteristics [of psychological impoverishment associated with the lower class] also reflect the extent to which the lower strata are *isolated* from the activities, controversies, and organizations of democratic society—an isolation which prevents them from acquiring the sophisticated and complex view of the political structure which makes understandable and necessary the norms of tolerance.[45]

This seems to mean that lower-class movements would almost certainly carry the mass characteristics described above. However, even in his discussion of the middle-class movements of Populism and Progressivism, Lipset implies a lack of sophistication and complexity:

On the political level they [Populism and Progressivism] showed a strong distrust of parliamentary or constitutional democracy and were particularly antagonistic to the

[43] Nisbet, *Community and Power*, preface to 1962 Galaxy edition, pp. xi-xii.

[44] Fromm, *Escape from Freedom*, p. 141. The precursor of the mass society theorists was Gustave LeBon, who in 1895 argued that in a crowd men forsake reason and responsibility. "By the mere fact that he forms part of an organized crowd, a man descends several rungs in the ladder of civilization." Gustave LeBon, *The Crowd* (New York: Viking, 1960), p. 32. Freud based his analysis of group psychology on LeBon's observations. Sigmund Freud, *Group Psychology and the Analysis of the Ego* (New York: Bantam, 1960; orig. pub. 1921).

[45] Seymour Martin Lipset, *Political Man* (New York: Doubleday, 1960), p. 104. Ital. in orig.

concept of party. They preferred to break down the sources of partisan strength and create as much direct democracy as possible through the introduction of initiative and referendum, and through easy recall elections.[46]

Movements according to this view are suspect because they seek to inject the mass directly into decisionmaking and tend to avoid bargaining and compromise.

As illustrated by Lipset's writings, the mass society theory of social movements has the interrelated implications that movements lack complex organizational structures and that they are rooted in irrational psychological needs. These implications have recently received considerable criticism. Two articles, in particular, attack the mass society argument, especially as it is extended to movements other than the Nazis. Gusfield makes the general argument that

extremist politics is developed and conducted by well-structured groups, representing discrete and organized parts of the social structure, acting to secure goals related to group needs. While such groups are alienated from the existing political institutions, they are not socially disintegrated or unrelated to the society and its political framework in which their values receive short shrift.[47]

Von Eschen, Kirk, and Pinard, supporting their theoretical conclusions with data from the Southern sit-in movement, find that "disorderly politics has an organizational substructure dragging people into activity just as does routine politics." [48] They point out that: (1) participants in direct action movements are not less likely than others to join organizations; (2) without a developed organizational substructure, strong movements would be unlikely to arise; (3) many movement organizations participate in both disorderly and routine politics; (4) organizational involvement does not always reduce alienation. Whether this occurs depends on whether the organization is able to generate power." [49] They attribute alienation not to lack of organizational integration but to objective conditions of powerlessness and deprivation.[50]

[46] Ibid., p. 169.

[47] Joseph R. Gusfield, "Mass Society and Extremist Politics," in Rush and Denisoff, *Social and Political Movements*, p. 50.

[48] Donald Von Eschen, Jerome Kirk, and Maurice Pinard, "The Organizational Substructure of Disorderly Politics," *Social Forces*, XLIX, June, 1971, 530.

[49] Ibid.

[50] Sherif argues that while the joining of social movements implies alienation, the end result is not chaos but a form of organization. Once the movement takes shape, "much of the activity involves planning, office work, communication, recruitment, and training, during which the character of collective behavior becomes more deliberately planned, coordinated, and executed." Muzafer Sherif, "On the Relevance of Social Psychology," *American Psychologist*, XXV, February, 1970, 144–56.

Saul Alinsky stresses the need for careful organizational work if mass movements are to be effective in their search for power: "People don't comprehend the months of tedious, boring organizational work done by organizational staffs. The only thing that keeps the staffs going is an understanding of organizational structure and what they're doing it for and why." Saul Alinsky, "Directing Urban Discontent," in *Urban America: Crisis and Opportunity*, eds. Jim Chard and Jon York (Belmont, Calif.: Dickenson, 1969), p. 143.

Our research has found urban political movements to be rooted in organizations which participate in both "disorderly" and routine politics. Although movement sympathizers, like voters for established political parties, may participate in organizationally sponsored activities without actually joining, leadership almost invariably operates through some kind of organization. One cannot, therefore, distinguish between movements and other political action groups such as parties or pressure groups on the basis of organizational structure, and our study of movements focuses on the activities of defined organizations.

"Normality." Movement organizations use both regular and extraordinary channels for influencing political outcomes. It should be remembered that both the Nazi and Communist Parties participated in elections, and that pressure groups have been known to bribe officials. Thus, whether or not a group participates in legal or illegal activities is not a clearcut criterion for differentiating between movements and other political groupings.[51] The way the public will perceive a political movement, however, constitutes a complex question.[52] Actions such as marches and rallies carry different meanings depending on whether they benefit the high school football team or the Black Panthers. The congregation of large groups of people, when they are hostile to established authority, always carries with it an implicit threat. Other forms of direct action used by movements—for instance, strikes, boycotts, and picketing—may be legally protected but are often interpreted by the general public or beleaguered officials as illegitimate.

Movements are often forced by their situation to resort to extraordinary, although not necessarily illegal, methods to force responses to their demands. Hodgkin, in differentiating between national independence movements and parties, comments:

The strategy of the congress [i.e., movement] is, in general, aggressive—expressed in such terms as "the struggle against imperialism," "la lutte contre la colonialisme"—and may involve any or all of the recognised techniques of popular pressure: national boycotts, general strikes, civil disobedience, mass demonstrations, press campaigns, as well as petitions, deputations and agitation through traditional channels. . . . [The strategy of the party] is, in most cases, more flexible and gradualist—directed towards

[51] Almond and Powell comment ruefully that it "would be convenient" if one could construct a typology relating type of group to form of action, but they are forced to dismiss the possibility. Gabriel A. Almond and G. Bingham Powell, Jr., *Comparative Politics* (Boston: Little, Brown, 1966), p. 74. Lukács states: "There are, it is true, periods in every revolution when a *romanticism of illegality* is predominant or at least powerful. But . . . this romanticism is quite definitely an infantile disorder of the communist movement. It is a reaction against legality at any price and for this reason it is vital that every mature movement should grow out of it and this is undoubtedly what actually happens." Georg Lukács, "Legality and Illegality," in *History and Class Consciousness*, trans. Rodney Livingstone (Cambridge: M.I.T. Press, 1971), p. 256.

[52] See Marvin E. Olsen, "Perceived Legitimacy of Social Protest Actions," and Ralph H. Turner, "The Public Perception of Protest," in Turner and Killian, *Collective Behavior*, pp. 225–30 and 231–43, respectively; also Allan A. Silver, "Official Interpretations of Urban Riots," in *Urban Riots*, ed. Robert H. Connery (New York: Random House, 1969), pp. 151–63.

the use of electoral machinery and representative institutions as the main means of securing or retaining power.[53]

Lack of legitimacy in the eyes of the general public is essential to the continuation of the political movement as a political movement rather than as an accepted part of the political establishment. "Nonlegitimacy invites repression; but if protest becomes legitimate it ceases to be viable protest" [54] —that is, it becomes co-opted. Because movements are demanding a new order, they must escape from politics as usual or see their goals seriously compromised.

Rationality.   Because participants in political movements refuse to accept the results of politics as usual, they appear irrational to many observers. In the United States especially, refusal to compromise is seen not only as wrongheadedness but also as a violation of widely cherished beliefs concerning the proper way of conducting political conflict. Fundamental to the American political formula[55] is a faith in tolerance:

Tolerance in a society of competing interest groups is precisely the ungrudging acknowledgment of the right of opposed interests to exist and be pursued. This economic conception of tolerance goes quite naturally with the view of human action as motivated by interests rather than principles or norms. It is much easier to accept a compromise between competing interests—particularly when they are expressible in terms of a numerical scale like money—than between opposed principles which purport to be objectively valid. The genius of American politics is its ability to treat even matters of principle as though they were conflicts of interest.[56]

If, indeed, participation in social movements is irrational, then the willingness of individuals to participate must be explained on grounds other than those of sensible pursuit of logically selected goals. The most common explanation for outwardly irrational behavior is that it arises from psychic needs. In this interpretation individuals join social movements in order to project neurotic impulses onto public objects. Thus, Harold Lasswell states that the "political type . . . [displaces] private motives . . . on public objects, rationalized in terms of public interest." Lasswell claims that "power is expected to overcome low estimates of the self"; and that it is men

[53] Thomas Hodgkin, *Nationalism in Colonial Africa* (New York: New York University Press, 1957), p. 144.

[54] Rush and Denisoff, *Social and Political Movements*, p. 267.

[55] Mosca defines the political formula as the "legal and moral basis, or principle, on which the power of the political [i.e. ruling] class rests" (p. 70). "The political formula must be based upon the special beliefs and the strongest sentiments of the social group in which it is current, or at least upon the beliefs and sentiments of the particular portion of that group which holds political preeminence" (p. 72). At any historical period the political formula defines political rationality. Gaetano Mosca, *The Ruling Class*, trans. Hannah D. Kahn (New York: McGraw-Hill, 1939).

[56] Robert Paul Wolff, "Beyond Tolerance," in *A Critique of Pure Tolerance*, Robert Paul Wolff, Barrington Moore, Jr., and Herbert Marcuse (Boston: Beacon Press, 1965), p. 21.

"indoctrinated . . . with a political mission" (i.e., ideologues) who most fully exemplify the type.[57]

According to their critics, movements seek a perfect world which rational men know is unobtainable. Unwillingness to compromise results from an inability to recognize the social necessity of consensus. An article by Egon Bittner best sums up this formulation:

If, however, we postulate that the definitive characteristic of radical movements is that they are inspired by doctrines and beliefs that seek to impose a unified, internally consistent schema of interpretation upon a world of heterogeneous meanings, a schema necessarily disconfirmed in practical experience, and if we assume that the cited organizational solutions discredit the disconfirmation and thus protect the validity of the doctrine in the eyes of believers as well as the unity and continuity of the movement, then we must consider the contingent problem of finding persons most suited to participate in it.

A variety of characteristics commonly associated with participation in radical movements such as origin in a socially displaced stratum of the society and the personality traits of dependence, rigidity, sado-masochism, and others, appear to fit the solution of organizational tasks of the movement.[58]

The assumption that individuals join social movements out of neurotic impulse underlies research attempting to associate a single personality type with both right and left wing movements. Milton Rokeach, for example, argues:

In ideological movements, time perspectives appear to be typically future-oriented. The past hardly exists, and the present is unimportant in its own right. . . . It is the future that counts and the suffering and injustice existing in the present is sometimes condoned, even glorified, for the sake of securing some future heaven, Utopia, promised land, Platonic or classless society. . . . The major function served by closed systems is to defend the self or the group against anxiety. The central feature of anxiety, as distinguished from fear, is a dread of the future, for the future is the most ambiguous and unknowable medium in man's cognitive world. It follows that attempts to cope with anxiety should involve a deemphasis of the present and a preoccupation with the future. It also follows that persons characterized as having relatively closed systems should manifest not only more anxiety but also more future-orientation than those with relatively open systems.[59]

[57] Harold D. Lasswell, *Power and Personality* (New York: Viking, 1948), pp. 38, 39, 41. Smelser asserts that all forms of collective behavior have connected with them a "generalized," or "exaggerated" belief containing irrational elements: "A norm-oriented movement involves elements of panic . . . , craze . . . , and hostility." Smelser, *Theory of Collective Behavior*, p. 271. Curie and Skolnick criticize Smelser for being biased in his attribution of irrationality to all collective behavior. Elliott Curie and Jerome Skolnick, "A Critical Note on Conceptions of Collective Behavior," *The Annals*, CCCXCI, September, 1970, 34–45. Smelser's rejoinder appears in the same issue, pp. 46–55.

We discuss the conflict between individual and social rationality in Chapter Seven.

[58] Egon Bittner, "Radicalism and Radical Movements," *American Sociological Review*, XXVIII, December, 1963, 939.

[59] From chap. 20 of *The Open and Closed Mind* by Milton Rokeach (New York: Basic Books, 1960), p. 367. See also Edward A. Shils, "Authoritarianism: 'Right' and 'Left' " in *Studies in the Scope*

Systematic research on the personality characteristics of movement participants has, for reasons of access, been performed most extensively on students involved with radical causes. Thelma McCormack, commenting on studies performed before 1950, notes that research on the radical personality has moved from regarding the radical as irrational and maladjusted to considering him as a superior example of adjustment.[60] A more recent review article states that since 1920 hundreds of reports on student attitudes have shown a correlation among intelligence, academic achievement and left political orientation.[61] An article on the Free Speech Movement (FSM) at Berkeley concludes that "few college students in general can match the positive development of those personality characteristics that distinguish student activists from their college contemporaries." The authors of the Berkeley article indicate that the high scores of FSM members on complexity and autonomy scales demonstrate "more interest in intellectual inquiry, greater tolerance for ambiguity, greater objectivity, and more independence of thought." [62]

While findings on student radicals may be unique to that group, or reflective of observer biases, the evidence is sufficient to permit movement participants at least a presumption of psychological innocence. For a movement to be declared irrational, evidence must be presented regarding the particular case.[63] N. R. F. Maier draws the sensible conclusion that some movements are more rational in their appeals than others. He distinguishes between movements that capitalize on aggression arising from frustration and those which are directed toward obtaining specified goals. The latter are characterized by the relative absence of fanatics and a more responsive leadership.[64]

---

and Method of the "Authoritarian Personality", ed. Richard Christie and Marie Jahoda (Glencoe: Free Press, 1954), pp. 31–34; and the mass society theorists cited above (footnote 42). Eric Hoffer's description of the "true believer" embodies the thesis of the association between personality disorder and participation in radical movements most strongly:

> There is a fundamental difference between the appeal of a mass movement and the appeal of a practical organization. The practical organization offers opportunities for self-advancement, and its appeal is mainly to self-interest. On the other hand, a mass movement, particularly in its active, revivalist phase, appeals not to those intent on bolstering and advancing a cherished self, but to those who crave to be rid of an unwanted self.

Eric Hoffer, *The True Believer* (New York: New American Library, 1951), p. 21.

[60] Thelma H. McCormack, "The Motivation of Radicals," in *Collective Behavior*, eds. Ralph H. Turner and Lewis M. Killian (Englewood Cliffs, N.J.: Prentice-Hall, 1957), p. 439.

[61] Christian Bay, "Political and Apolitical Students: Facts in Search of a Theory," *Journal of Social Issues*, XXIII, July, 1967, 77.

[62] James W. Trent and Judith L. Craise, "Commitment and Conformity in the American College," *Journal of Social Issues*, XXIII, July, 1967, 39.

[63] Similarly, Chalmers Johnson accuses of psychological reductionism those who refuse to distinguish between acts of political violence resulting from the needs of an abnormal personality and those generated by personal tensions arising from a disequilibriated social system. Chalmers Johnson, *Revolutionary Change* (Boston: Little, Brown, 1966), p. 77.

[64] N. R. F. Maier, "The Role of Frustration in Social Movements," *Psychological Review*, XLIX (November, 1942) 591–92.

Our own examination of urban political movements contains a presumption of individual rationality. We also assume that attempts by the relatively deprived to improve their position through group action represent at least an initially rational approach, and that movements cannot be a priori distinguished from other political action groups by a standard of rationality. As long as action continues to be goal directed, and the goals remain justifiable in terms of group interests, we consider these movements to have a primarily rational basis even if some proportion of their participants are solving their private psychological problems through public action.

THE FUNCTIONS OF
POLITICAL MOVEMENTS

Our concept of a political movement—a body which seeks to change the distribution of social benefits through the conversion of a social collectivity into an action group—defines the phenomenon through its functions. There are two crucial elements in the definition: (1) the mobilization of support; and (2) the effecting of change. The presence of both these elements is necessary for a collectivity to be designated as a movement.[65]

The latter element distinguishes movements from other kinds of political action groups. Parties and pressure groups also attempt to mobilize support; when they press for change, they merge into movements depending on the scope of the changes they demand. Sorauf lists the functions of parties as mobilizing voters behind candidates for election; organizing the policymaking machinery of government; acting as a propagandist for political attitudes, ideas, and programs; and (especially for parties outside the United States) providing a framework for developing group solidarity, usually through sponsoring affiliates such as social clubs and providing services.[66] Except for organizing the policymaking machinery of government—a function restricted to parties with majority parliamentary representation—movements may engage in all the functions of parties and always perform the latter two.

The functions of pressure groups include manipulating public opinion, persuading legislators, developing relations with administrators, participating in litigation, and building up alliances with other groups.[67] Again movements, except certain wholly revolutionary ones, are likely to participate in all these endeavors. The important difference between pressure groups, as usually visualized, and movements is that the change mission of the latter precludes the routinization of their relationships with governmental institutions. The innovations required by movements provoke negative reactions,

---

[65] The collective nature of a movement distinguishes it from innovating individuals (e.g. Peter the Great; the Gaullist government in France).

[66] Frank J. Sorauf, *Political Parties in the American System* (Boston: Little, Brown, 1964), pp. 2–4.

[67] V. O. Key, *Politics, Parties, and Pressure Groups*, 5th ed. (New York: Thomas Y. Crowell, 1964), pp. 130–41.

subverting the mutual accommodation that underlies regularized lobbying. When pressure groups seek far-reaching change, they are, ipso facto, movement organizations.

activities

There are three principal interrelated activities through which a movement carries out its functions. First, the movement identifies grievances and points out remedies so as to attract and maintain a membership. It is the medium through which members of the collectivity communicate with each other and find their common identity. In other words, the movement acts as an *agent of political socialization* for individuals within the collectivity from which it emerges.

According to Lukács, "[the] reform of consciousness is the revolutionary process itself." [68] The development of a movement contributes to political resocialization, that is, to the reform of consciousness, in a number of ways. The most obvious is through explicit propagandizing—exhorting potential followers to join; showing how the collectivity suffers deprivation; capitalizing on events to demonstrate systematic ill treatment; and devising and advertising alternatives to the status quo. Movement organizations often devote most of their time and energy to the communication process: publicizing grievances, activities, and aims; creating internal communications networks; and conducting meetings in which members address sympathizers and each other. The growth of the movement makes its message more persuasive as it offers to potential recruits the model of numerous other adherents. For those already convinced of its message, it constitutes a reference group supportive of ideas and activity considered deviant within the larger society.

The movement develops membership solidarity and consciousness not only by transmitting ideas but also by facilitating the development of personal relationships among individuals with common interests. It may also provide material services to its members. The movement, as an entity, takes on a symbolic aspect for its members, causing them to identify its successes or failures as their own. Thus, as well as creating attachments on the basis of generalized beliefs, it generates emotional identification and gratitude.

Interest articulation constitutes the second principal activity of a movement. Almond and Powell define this as "the process by which individuals and groups make demands upon the political decision makers. . . ." [69] We would prefer to redefine it as *the process by which groups make demands and justify themselves to the rest of society,* since Almond and Powell's formulation tends to assume a regularized system for the expression of political demands, from which movements would be excluded.

In its role as socializing agent the movement communicates with its

[68] Lukács, "Legality and Illegality," p. 259.
[69] Almond and Powell, *Comparative Politics,* p. 73.

adherents and potential members. As an interest articulator it communicates with publics outside the collectivity from which it emerges. These publics include both potential allies and targets which have been identified as the source of grievance. By articulating the interests of a collectivity which is demanding changes in the mode of distributing benefits, the movement explicitly confronts the extant political formula. In this way it challenges the prevalent definition of which issues are legitimately topics of political debate:

The definition of the alternatives is the supreme instrument of power; the antagonists can rarely agree on what the issues are because power is involved in the definition. He who determines what politics is about runs the country, because the definition of the alternatives is the choice of conflicts, and the choice of conflicts allocates power.[70]

An example of the confrontation with the political formula and its effects is presented in Chapter One where we discuss the machine, Progressivism, and community control. Until recently the machine and Progressive reform were the only alternatives presented in the debate over the governance of American cities. Neighborhood groups demanding power have now changed the definition of institutional conflict in cities by articulating the third choice of community control. They have tried to change the nature of the debate, because neither of the old competing alternatives could place them in improved power positions.

The mere articulation or voicing of interests, when those interests are commonly ignored or given short shrift in the normal political process, is inadequate to bring about a change in the distribution of benefits. Thus, the third critical activity of a political movement is *the creation and utilization of power.* Movements create power through the expenditure of power resources provided by their members.[71] Among the resources which may be converted into power are money and credit; control over jobs; control over information; political office; social standing; knowledge and expertise; popularity, esteem, charisma; moral appeal; authority; group solidarity; votes; time; and energy.[72] Some of the resources available to movements are a simple addition of those accruing to individual members; for example, the cumulation of monetary contributions creating sufficient funds for the movement to pay staff or buy publicity. Others, such as credibility, visibility and retribution at the polls are emergent properties which derive from collective solidarity and may increase as much with cohesiveness as with numbers.

Etzioni names three types of power or ways of enforcing obedience:

Coercive power rests on the application, or the threat of application, of physical sanctions. . . .

---

[70] E. E. Schattschneider, *The Semisovereign People* (New York: Holt, Rinehart & Winston, 1960), p. 68. Ital. in original.

[71] See Chapter Seven.

[72] This list is a modified version of the one presented in Nelson Polsby, *Community Power and Political Theory* (New Haven: Yale University Press, 1963), pp. 119–20.

Remunerative power is based on control over material resources and rewards. . . . *Normative* power rests on the allocation and manipulation of symbolic rewards and deprivations through employment of leaders, manipulation of mass media, allocation of esteem and prestige symbols, administration of ritual, and influence over the distribution of "acceptance" and "positive response." [73]

Violence, boycott, and picketing are common ways in which movements have exercised each of the three forms of power respectively.

Different kinds of movements are likely to rely more heavily on different forms of power. The Nazis, operating in a social situation where governmental authority was disintegrating, used coercive power heavily. The Progressives, who were upper and middle class, completely eschewed coercive power but, while resorting mainly to normative power, were also able to employ remunerative power. The civil rights movement, which had limited resources besides moral appeal and solidarity, was restricted primarily to the use of normative power. Similarly, urban political movements, although they have attempted on occasion to use other forms of power, have had to rely heavily on the manipulation of symbolic rewards and deprivations.

The ways in which a political movement carries on the three major activities of political socialization, interest articulation, and power conversion determines its character. Each of these activities is, of course, integrally related to the others, and critical events or decisions affecting one activity become magnified through interaction. So, for example, because the movement's most important resource is a highly mobilized membership, success in acquiring power resources depends upon its capability as a socializing agent. Similarly, the more powerful a movement becomes, the more easily it can gain followers, maintain cohesiveness, and act with credibility as an interest articulator. This strong feedback or interactive relationship explains why movements can snowball, suddenly reaching a critical mass and making a major impact, or conversely, why they may disintegrate even more quickly and easily.

Political movements are thus characterized by a high degree of instability, as the very word "movement" implies. It is this continually changing nature which differentiates them from other structures with similar activities. Our choice of terms in this book has arisen largely from our identification of the emergent qualities of the groups we examine—their most significant behavioral characteristic is their strong susceptibility to the interactive effects described here. Accordingly, despite their lack of a large, active mass base we have stuck to the term "urban political movements" and seen them as phenomena within the conceptual framework analyzed in this appendix.

[73] Amitai Etzioni, *A Comparative Analysis of Complex Organizations* (New York: Free Press, 1961), p. 5. Ital. in original.

index of names

Addams, Jane, 15
Alinsky, Saul, 32, 136, 201–2, 252
Almond, A., 253, 258
Altbach, Phillip G., 176
Altshuler, Alan A., 8, 245
Apter, David, 207
Arendt, Hannah, 250
Arnstein, Sherry R., 201
Austin, David M., 172

Babchuck, Nicholza, 177
Balbus, Isaac, 239
Banfield, Edward C., 14, 15, 16, 17, 18, 21
Baraka, Imanu (Le Roi Jones), 138
Baron, Samuel H., 244
Bay, Christian, 256
Bell, Daniel, 13, 242
Bendix, Reinhard, 185
Berube, Maurice R., 9, 37, 225
Bittner, Egon, 255
Blackmun, Justice, 13
Blau, Peter M., 186
Blauner, Robert, 6
Bloomberg, Walter, Jr., 191
Blumer, Herbert, 250
Bonjean, Charles M., 32, 55, 173, 175, 186
Bowen, Don R., 172, 175, 177, 178, 245
Bowen, Elinor, 245
Brager, George, 37, 193
Bramgart, Richard G., 176
Breasted, Mary, 248

Brill, Harry, 33, 46, 174
Brinton, Crane, 123, 228
Brown, Roger, 250
Bryce, James, 16
Burnham, Walter Dean, 21, 207, 216, 217

Cameron, W. Bruce, 238
Campbell, Angus, 4
Carmichael, Stokely, 6, 7, 244
Chambers, William N., 207, 216, 217
Chambers, Clarke, 21
Chard, Jim, 252
Christie, Richard, 256
Clark, Kenneth, 32, 33, 173
Cloward, Richard A., 231, 232
Cochran, Thomas C., 19
Cohen, David K., 56
Cohen, Nathan, 172, 204
Cohen, Richard, 37
Cohen, Sol, 21, 249
Cole, G.D.H., 242
Coleman, James S., 5, 228
Colon, José, 51, 52
Connery, Robert H., 253
Costner, Herbert, 55, 175, 177
Craise, Judith L., 256
Crow, Wayman J., 173, 175, 177
Crozier, Michael, 96, 210, 211
Curie, Elliott, 255

Dahl, Robert A., 87, 176, 186, 190

261

subject index